Animation Craft

For 3D and 2D Animators

This book is for those who want to learn the craft or mechanics of animation, how to actually animate a scene from start to finish, or take their animation to the next level. Using over 600 examples, this book answers the questions about the craft of animation that are often not taught in schools or books.

Each chapter contains step-by-step examples explaining the principles of animation and how to avoid common problems that occur when animating. This book also teaches you how to critique an animated scene objectively, rather than subjectively — then fix what's wrong with it.

Animation Craft for 3D and 2D Animators will be a great resource for any beginner looking to learn the fundamentals of animation, or more experienced animators looking to hone their craft.

Jonathan Annand has been animating since he was very little, when he would make flip books from the overrun cardstock his father would bring home from work.

He began his career in animation as a messenger for The Ink Tank in NYC and has since worked for J.J. Sedelmaier Productions, Walt Disney Feature Animation (where he was an animator on characters including Stitch from Lilo and Stitch and Kenai Bear from Brother Bear), Electronic Arts (where as a senior animator, he created the non-gameplay cut scenes for Madden Football) and Iron Galaxy Studios where he was a principal animator animating on Rumbleverse and Killer Instinct, among others. Jonathan is an adjunct instructor at the University of Central Florida's graduate gaming school, Florida Interactive Entertainment Academy (FIEA).

Animation Craft

For 3D and 2D Animators

Jonathan Annand

CRC Press
Taylor & Francis Group
Boca Raton London New York

CRC Press is an imprint of the
Taylor & Francis Group, an **informa** business

Designed cover image: Jonathan Annand

First edition published 2025
by CRC Press
2385 Executive Center Drive, Suite 320, Boca Raton, FL 33431, U.S.A.

and by CRC Press
4 Park Square, Milton Park, Abingdon, Oxon, OX14 4RN

CRC Press is an imprint of Taylor & Francis Group, LLC

ISBN: 9781032422404 (hbk)
ISBN: 9781032422398 (pbk)
ISBN: 9781003361893 (ebk)
ISBN: 9781003597223 (eBook+)

DOI: 10.1201/9781003361893

Typeset in Futura PT
by KnowledgeWorks Global Ltd.

Publisher's note: This book has been prepared from camera-ready copy provided by the authors.

Access the Support Material: www.routledge.com/9781032422398

For my three best teachers,

John Canemaker, Tissa David, and my Pop

Photograph courtesy of Joe Kennedy

Animation Craft

For 3D and 2D Animators

Jonathan Annand

Acknowledgments

I would like to thank John Canemaker for his encouragement to write this book and especially for his help with chapter 2.

Lenore Annand for her tireless work designing and laying out this book.

Ricardo Medina Fernández for his wonderful character rigs. Daniel Driussi for modeling the characters. Jeff Panek for the environments. And props to Matthew Young for his props.

A big thank you to Ryan Fisher and Kellie Driscoll for their technical help. I would have been lost without them.

Many thanks to Ron Weaver, Stephanie de Sousa, Rich Grula, Cheryl Griggs, and Ben Noel at The University of Central Florida's graduate school, Florida Interactive Entertainment Academy (FIEA), for their help and generosity.

Thank you to Iron Galaxy Studios, especially Chad Newhouse and Cedric Busse, for your support.

Special thanks to the ever so kind and generous Byron Howard.

Thank you to David Annand for the detailed indexing.

I don't know how one you could be an animator without animation historians such as John Canemaker, Donald Crafton, Amid Amidi, Didier Getz, Devon Baxter, Jerry Beck, Michael Barrier, Michael Sporn, Mark Mayerson, Charles Solomon, Leonard Maltin, Juke S. Friedman, Joe Adamson, John Culhane, Mark Kausler, Greg Ford, Don Hahn, Pete Docter, Eric Goldberg, Frank Thomas and Ollie Johnston, Richard Williams, and the best boss I ever had, J.J. Sedelmaier.

Read anything by them and listen to anything they have to say.

Thank you to Will Bateman, my editor, for his help and patience.

Finally, thank you to Jamie Robertson. This book begins and ends with her and I could not have done it without her.

Contents

Foreword by J. J. Sedelmaier   xii

Introduction   1

Chapter 1 — The Basics   3

Chapter 2 — A Brief History of Character Animation   7

Chapter 3 — Squash and Stretch   47

Chapter 4 — Posing   59

Chapter 5 — Rhythm   73

Chapter 6 — Exaggeration   83

Chapter 7 — Weight and Balance   93

Chapter 8 — Foot Plant   111

Chapter 9 — Arcs   119

Chapter 10 — Walk and Run Cycles   127

Chapter 11 — Timing and Spacing   145

Chapter 12 — Slow-In & Slow-Out   161

Chapter 13 — Overlap and Follow-Through   169

Chapter 14 — Successive Breaking of Joints   181

Chapter 15 — Anticipation   189

Chapter 16 — Breakdowns and Inbetweens   199

Chapter 17 — Accents   213

Chapter 18 — Secondary Action   221

Chapter 19 — Expressions   229

Chapter 20 — Dialogue   247

Chapter 21 — Staging   259

Chapter 22 — Putting It All Together   275

Chapter 23 — Critiquing a Scene   283

Chapter 24 — Scene Checklist   293

Footnotes   297

Selected Bibliography   316

Index   318

Credits   331

Foreword

Congratulations!

You've chosen to add "Animation Craft" by Jonathan Annand to your animator's toolbox of essentials. This terrific volume not only combines helpful and inspiring instruction for animators of all ages, but is also a marvelous background history of the animation industry and its key players through the years. It's chock full of reference of all kinds and gives the reader a solid foundation of what animation is all about as art and filmmaking.

I met Jonathan about 30 years ago. My wife Patrice and I had been running our own animation studio (J.J. Sedelmaier Productions, Inc.) in White Plains NY, and my friend (and Master Animator) Tissa David, unsolicitedly mentioned that we "MUST hire Jonathan Annand!" I respected her word and opinion, and we immediately looked for a place in the studio for him. We all soon found out why Tissa recommended Jonathan so strongly. He was not only a talent beyond his young years, but dedicated, enthusiastic (in his unique manner), and deeply dedicated to being the best he could be. It was our loss when he made the decision to leave our shop to work at the Walt Disney Feature Animation unit down in Orlando, Florida. He later segued into gaming production, but throughout his professional and personal journey he's evolved and grown into a stellar talent.

The reader of "Animation Craft" benefits from Jonathan's life voyage because he's included not only what he's learned, but HOW he learned it. The people and films that influenced him are there for all of us to see and learn from, but also to interpret with the baggage we all personally bring to the drawing board/tablet. So it's not just the fundamentals that he's chosen to teach us, but WHY they're fundamental.

Finally, what I find of infinite use, is the fact that Jonathan has worked in so many different areas and phases of the animation process. Not only has he taught his craft at the university level, but the guy can draw, and he's applied his talent in both classical/traditional realms of animation, and also spent years in the digital domain. He speaks a modern dialect and the visuals reflect that. I LOVE the fact that the book also comes with links to show actual animation footage, that can also be downloaded and added to one's library!

This is a manual for the 21st Century!

Once again, congratulations! Now, get to work!!

J.J. Sedelmaier – Animation Film Director/Producer/Designer

Introduction

"Animation is not simply making things move," animator Tissa David would tell me. Animators Ollie Johnston and Glen Keane would say to "animate from the heart." But how do you animate from the heart if you're having trouble simply making things move properly?

Just as a musician needs to learn chords and scales, a painter needs to learn composition and color, or a writer needs to learn grammar and punctuation — having a solid understanding of the craft of animation will give you the freedom to animate from the heart and to put on the screen what you actually intended.

You may feel you understand the principles of animation, but then why doesn't your scene have Milt Kahl's snappy timing or Frank Thomas' subtle movement? You may have great ideas for scenes but not know where to begin. Perhaps your scene works, but it may have been a struggle to do or is not what you originally intended.

What are you doing wrong?

The acting teacher Stella Adler once said, "You'll begin to act when you can forget your technique — when it is so securely inside you that you need not call upon it consciously."[1]

Unfortunately, many books on animation assume you already know how to animate. They can be like "how-to-draw" or "how-to-sculpt" books where on the first page there's an oval, on the second page is the oval with a center and eye line, and then on the third page a fully rendered face. What happened between pages two and three? How did I go from an oval with a few lines through it to a fully rendered portrait?

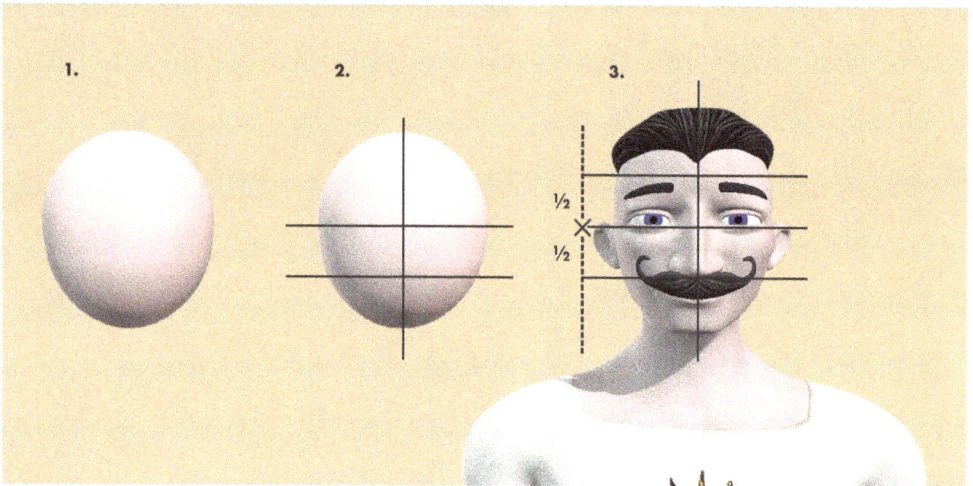

Figure 0.1

In Animation Craft, we'll learn how to create entertaining, believable animation from start to finish, how to apply the principles of animation as we animate, what to check for, and what to avoid. Using hundreds of examples we'll learn, among other things, not only how to make a strong pose, but how to link poses together, how to add breakdowns and inbetweens practically and, finally, how to look at your scene objectively and fix what doesn't work. We'll even learn that complex scenes are easier to achieve than you think — if you truly understand the craft of animation.

DOI: 10.1201/9781003361893-1

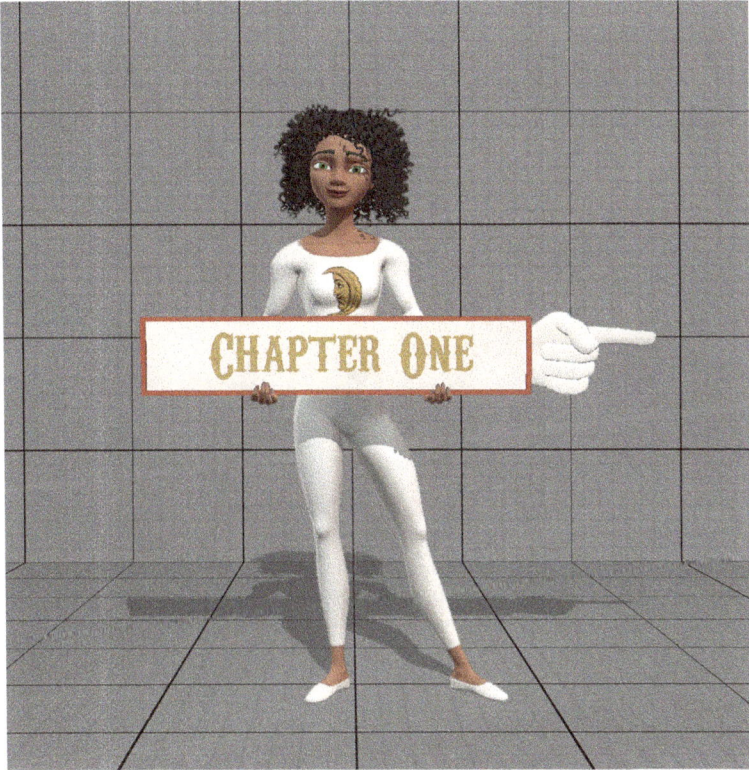
CHAPTER ONE

Chapter 1. The Basics

Why the Basics?

Sometimes beginner animators are too eager to impress and forget the fundamentals. They may add inbetweens before perfecting key poses — leading to bland or watery animation. Or, they don't trust weight and balance and their animation looks floaty. More experienced animators may waste valuable time animating completely on instinct or they animate themselves into a corner by not taking the time to plan.

Animators who understand the basics, and are not afraid to start simply, will be able to work quicker and animate more complex and sophisticated scenes with less stress.

Milt Kahl animated Medusa's swaggering double-bounce walk in **The Rescuers** (1977) by building upon the standard walk formula — the same walk formula used for Mr. Magoo in **Magoo's Canine Mutiny** (1956).

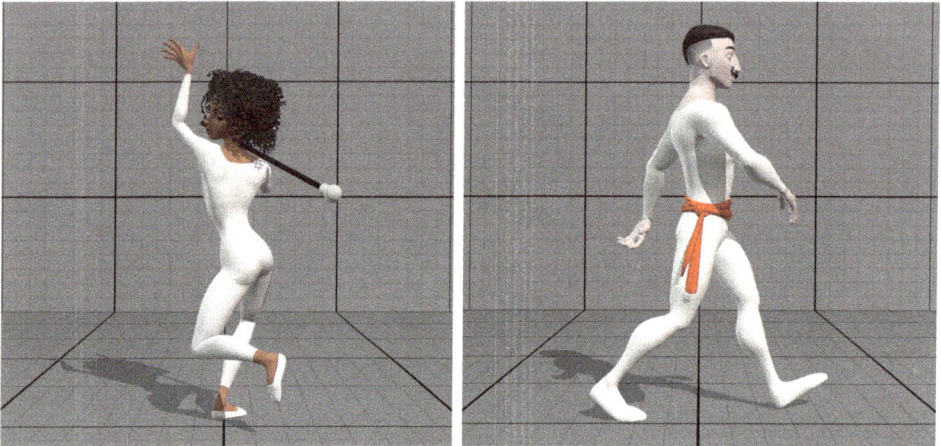

Figure 1.1

First things first — Animation is difficult! Even for accomplished animators, animation is not easy to do. "It's a very difficult medium," said Kahl. "You have to understand movement, which in itself is quite a study. You have to be an actor. You have to put on a performance, to be a showman, to be able to evaluate how good the entertainment is. You have to know the best way of doing it and have an appreciation of where it belongs in the picture. You have to be a pretty good story man. To be really good at animation, then, you have to be a jack-of-all-trades. I don't mean to say that I'm all these things, but I try hard."[1]

Kahl understood the basics so thoroughly that he could animate the performance he imagined.

But it takes work.

Even the great Freddy Moore would sometimes forget the basics. "He had a set of values that he had learned," said animator Frank Thomas. "Very objective points, and he used to say, every time he got back a test that was not right, it was because he had forgotten something he had learned earlier. They were real basic things."[2]

Don't be afraid to start with the basics. Don't think they're beneath you. And don't be afraid to admit that you don't completely understand the basics. The basics are what make you a stronger animator and allow you to animate complex actions more easily.

Mocap is easier to clean up if you have a solid understanding of the basics of animation. What if you don't have the animation clips you need, or your actor didn't give you everything you wanted? You'll have to adjust it with keyframing or by "Frankensteining" clips — splicing together bits and pieces of animation to form a scene. But if you understand the basics, you'll know where the weight is, how to overlap action and create a rhythm between clips, etc.

Understanding the basics will also help you determine what's wrong with your animation and fix it more quickly — like Freddy Moore.

DOI: 10.1201/9781003361893-2

The ~~Twelve~~, Thirteen Principles of Animation

The original "Twelve Principles of Animation" are animation techniques that were developed by Disney animators in the 1930s. By 1940, when the animators were working on **Pinocchio**, the twelve principles became a shorthand vernacular to obtain more predictable results. "Get more stretch on him," they'd say. "Wow! Look at the squash on that drawing!"[3] In 1981 Frank Thomas and Ollie Johnston made the "Twelve Principles of Animation" famous with the release of their "Bible" of **Disney Animation, The Illusion of Life**.

So, why thirteen and who am I to add to the commandments it took animators over fifty years to figure out?

The original "Twelve Principles of Animation" are:

1. Squash and Stretch

2. Anticipation

3. Staging

4. Straight Ahead Action and Pose to Pose

5. Follow Through and Overlapping Action

6. Slow In and Slow Out

7. Arcs

8. Secondary Action

9. Timing

10. Exaggeration

11. Solid Poses (Drawing)

12. Appeal

But let's add another:

13. Weight and Balance

One of the most common problems with poor 3D animation is a lack of weight and balance, so I'm making it a thirteenth principle.

Learn to trust the basics and then build upon them. Don't try to show off out of the gate. Understand the principles so thoroughly that you can see what you're doing wrong as you animate.

Another thing — don't be lazy! Don't settle on a pose or an action when you know in your heart that it's not good enough.

Try to make it better.

Each of us can tell when something lacks quality — a movie with poor acting or cheesy special effects, a video game with bad gameplay or too many bugs. If you care about your craft, always try to improve and continue to learn.

"There's a vocabulary of two thousand things — just as if they were two thousand separate words — that you have to learn about animation," said Grim Natwick, creator of Betty Boop and lead animator of Snow White. "If you've got that vocabulary, you're a great animator. If you have two hundred of them, you could get by today. A lot of animators are getting by with a very small vocabulary. What do you know about animation today and what will you know ten years from now? You'll find in ten years you'll be able to do in one hour what you take a day to do now. That's because you keep piling knowledge upon knowledge till pretty soon you have five hundred words in that vocabulary that will make it a lot easier."[4]

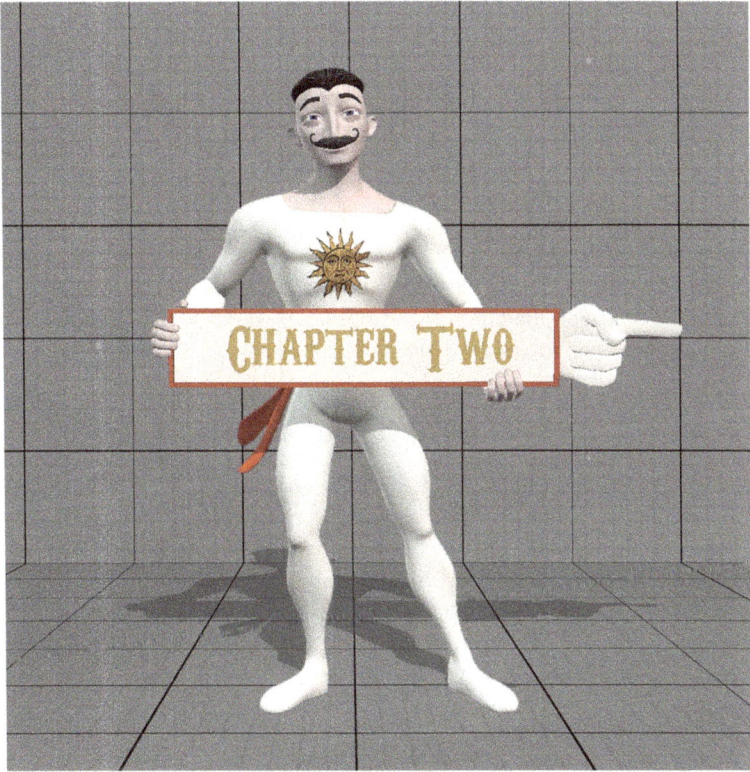

CHAPTER TWO

Chapter 2. A Brief History of Character Animation

Introduction

Why should an animator know the history of character animation?

Every artist, musician, filmmaker etc. has an influence — a person or genre that shaped their style. The lasting artists so thoroughly love their craft that they want to learn everything about it: the artists who influenced them, their techniques, and the history of their craft. Knowing the history and styles of animation and animators gives you a greater vocabulary to work with. And a greater vocabulary helps you push your craft forward. The people who are best at their profession are always learning.

Winsor McCay

In 1914, Zenas Winsor McCay, a legendary newspaper cartoonist best known for his comic strip *Little Nemo in Slumberland*, released his third animated film, *Gertie the Dinosaur*. It was a revelation that took the rest of the animation industry another twenty years to catch up to.

Until Gertie came along, animation was primarily trick-films "concerned with making objects appear to move with a mysterious life of their own."[1] There were also novelty films of "lightning-sketches," a popular vaudeville act in which an artist stood before an easel, and performed a monologue, while rapidly drawing a picture. The artist, or perhaps just his hand, would draw a caricature at an accelerated speed "by intentionally slow cranking of the camera."[2]

Substitution splices – an edit over one frame that made it appear as if a facial expression had changed in a pop – were later perfected by the "father of special effects" Georges Méliès.

Eventually, audiences grew tired of trick-films. The discovery of shooting sequential drawings on film frame-by-frame led to animation. J. Stuart Blackton created the illusion of movement through a metamorphosis of chalk drawings on a blackboard and cut-outs in *Humorous Phases of Funny Faces* (1906) and stop-motion puppets in *The Haunted Hotel* (1907). But it was Emile Cohl, the first person to choose "animator" as a full-time career, who created what is considered "arguably the first true animated cartoon"[3] *Fantasmagorie* (1908). *Fantasmagorie* is a charming film — a stream of conscience flipbook drawn in black ink on white paper, then printed in negative to look like chalk on a chalkboard.

Around 1911 Winsor McCay, most likely influenced by Blackton and Cohl, began his animated film career. What McCay did differently with *Gertie the Dinosaur* was to create a character with a personality. "The personality traits McCay invested in his cartoon character make Gertie truly unique," wrote McCay's biographer John Canemaker. "They give her a soul and a familiar temperament, not unlike that of a child."[4]

McCay's approach to mechanics was groundbreaking. As Gertie rocks from side to side, there's a slight overlap between her feet and her neck. When she shifts her weight over her left foot, she sticks out her right foot for counterbalance. And as she raises herself after laying on her side, her legs uncross naturally; she then lifts first the front half of her body and then the back half — showing successive breaking of joints.

McCay was also a pioneer in the technical approach to animation. He timed out Gertie's breathing with a "large clock with a big second dial"[5] "to judge how long she was inhaling and how long it took her to exhale."[6] He repeated cycles of drawings. "I only drew her breathing once," he said,

DOI: 10.1201/9781003361893-3

"But I photographed that set of drawings over fifteen times."[7] And he developed what was perhaps his proudest achievement, the "McCay Split System," which was basically animating pose-to-pose, then adding breakdowns and inbetweens.

Gertie the Dinosaur would inspire countless future animators, including Otto Messmer, Vladimir (Bill) Tytla, Paul Terry, and Chuck Jones. Even live-action film legend Buster Keaton! "Buster had seen Winsor McCay's animated dinosaur short *Gertie the Dinosaur* and wanted something like that for *Three Ages* [1923]."[8] He asked the Fleischer studio, future animators of the Popeye cartoons, to create a stop-motion sequence of Keaton riding a dinosaur for the film.

"Winsor McCay was the first to recognize animation as an art form,"[9] wrote Disney master animators Frank Thomas and Ollie Johnston.

Rubber Hose

Because of Cohl, Blackton and McCay, animated films became more popular and animation studios, such as Hearst International, Raoul Barré and J. R. Bray, began popping up. Bray would be called the "Henry Ford of Animation"[10] because of the assembly-line production techniques he patented (including the use of cels), which allowed his studio workers to turn out an extraordinary number of films — "some five-hundred-and-forty animated films of the cartoon and educational genres were produced by Bray between 1913 and 1927."[11] The artists hired to create these films came mostly from newspapers. They knew how to draw cartoons, but not necessarily how to move them. "There was no place to learn animation except the studios where the men learned by trial and error,"[12] wrote Charles Solomon. There weren't many, if any, draftsmen the caliber of a Winsor McCay, so characters tended to be animals. Animals "could be expressed with a very simple formula," said Grim Natwick, designer and lead animator of Betty Boop. "It takes years to learn to draw a good human being. Animals were [easier], almost any child will try to draw a picture of a cat, or a dog, and if they're very skillful they may draw rabbits or horses — which take a little more skill. And they found that they could do that and that they animated freely. They had formulas that kept them very simple."[13]

Because the early animated characters were designed by newspaper cartoonists, they were more angular, and the animation tended to flicker. Bill Nolan, one of the fastest animators in the country, and the person who came up with the pan background, redesigned Otto Messmer's version of Felix the Cat to be more circular, and he devised what became known as "rubber-hose" animation. "Instead of bending a cartoon character's arms, wrists, and knees at the joints (a series of successive breaks, as in nature)," wrote Canemaker, "Nolan eliminated the angularity (and realism) of that action by substituting smooth hose-like connections for the limbs. Arms and legs that resembled macaroni looked and moved funny and were easy to draw and animate."[14]

Rubber-hose animation relied on formulas rather than observation — what historian Donald Crafton calls 'figurative performance'. Instead of looking inward for character, figurative performance or cartoon "acting" relied on stock formulas. Characters tended to move the same way, using "instantly identifiable facial and body expressions."[15] A character may bounce up and down to show excitement, put their hands on their hips and tap their foot to show frustration, or turn to the camera breaking the fourth wall to acknowledge a joke with the audience. "Another popular routine was to have a cartoon figure come up toward the camera, usually until his mouth filled the screen, and then retreat to his original position, using the same drawings shot in reverse,"[16] wrote Frank and Ollie. "The audience was fascinated with animation that repeated the same action over and over."[17]

Budget-saving animation cycles were used heavily. Repeat actions were similar to the way blueprints work in game animation in that they allowed cycles to flow in and out of each other. Cross-overs, cycles duplicated on the same cell to make it appear as if there were multiple characters in one shot doing the same thing, were used to great effect when characters danced, such as the skeletons in *The Skeleton Dance* (1929).

In spite of repetitious animation, and not always in the best taste, rubber-hose animation could be wonderfully creative, such as *Betty Boop in Snow White* (1933), *The Cuckoo Murder Case* (1930) and *Mickey's Fire Brigade* (1935). The Fleischer Brothers were paid homage in Miyazaki's *Porco Roso* (1992). The video game *Cuphead* (2017) and Disney's short *Get a Horse* (2013) beautifully capture the best of the rubber hose and circle genre.

Clear personalities emerged when stand-out animators like Grim Natwick, Ub Iwerks and Otto Messmer began adding recognizable human traits to their performances. Messmer's Felix the Cat was resourceful. He would pace back and forth to solve a problem – a walk that cartoon lover Buster Keaton paid homage to in *Go West* (1925) – then come up with an innovative solution, usually through metamorphosis. "It is important to remember that Felix was a thinking character," wrote Canemaker, "not a mindless action figure like cartoons from other studios of the period."[18] Canemaker summed up Messmer's animation style as "simple, direct pantomimic acting; dry wit expressed through visual puns."[19]

Grim Natwick, creator of Betty Boop and mentor to animators Chuck Jones, Marc Davis and Tissa David, could draw thanks to his fine art studies in Europe. "I think — because of Betty Boop," Natwick told Michael Barrier in 1976. "Walt had an idea all the time that maybe I would be able to draw Snow White."[20] "Animation historians, as well as Natwick's colleagues, agree that only he would have the ability and the confidence to devise a female character with an even remotely realistic body,"[21] wrote Leonard Maltin. Natwick would be a springboard into a new, more realistic style of animation.

Ub Iwerks could also draw. He was the first person hired by Walt Disney for his Laugh-O-Gram Studio and quickly became known as one of the best and fastest animators in the country. When he heard that Bill Nolan had done five-hundred drawings in a day, Iwerks topped him with seven hundred. "At that time just making a character move was an accomplishment," said animator and director, Friz Freleng of Iwerks. "He could make characters walk and move; he could move a house in perspective. I thought he was a genius when it came to the mechanics of animation."[22] Iwerk's animation of Oswald in *Oh What a Knight* (1928) for instance, is musical in its movement, hitting every accent and full of flowing s-curves — whereas the Walter Lantz version of Oswald in *Hells Heels* (1930), done after Disney was dropped by his distributor Charles Mintz, is clunky and tends to morph from pose to pose. "The animation he did was so superior to the Eastern animators,"[23] said Chuck Jones of Iwerks.

After the success with Mickey Mouse, Iwerks, "feeling overworked and somewhat unappreciated by Walt at the time, went out on his own."[24] The cartoons Iwerks made in his new studio could be great to look at, but his characters tended to lack appeal and the stories were generally weak. "Anticipating Bob Clampett,"[25] Iwerks' cartoons could also be surreal as in *Balloon Land* (1935), and a little strange as in *Stratos Fear* (1933). Ten years after going out on his own, Iwerks would lose his distribution deal with MGM and return to Disney "not as an artist or director — but as a technical problem solver."[26]

In the ten years without Iwerks, Walt Disney would hire top animators and trained artists who would help him pursue another path; a path away from the figurative rubber-hose animation toward realism.

A path of knees and elbows, so to speak.

Be Like Les

"I was born in 1912. Two years before Winsor McCay did **Gertie the Dinosaur**," said Chuck Jones in a 1999 interview. "There was a long dead period after that when animation was just moving comic strips, you might call them, until **Steamboat Willie** (1928). And then it came to life again."[27]

Steamboat Willie wasn't a break from rubber-hose animation by any means. In fact, Frank and Ollie, describing a scene Ub Iwerks animated in **Steamboat Willie** said, "the animator had no knowledge — or concern — about bones and muscles; his job was to create sprightly movement that put over the gag."[28]

What made **Steamboat Willie** special was that it was "truly a musical cartoon rather than a cartoon with music."[29] Wilfred Jackson, an assistant to Walt at the time, later to become a director, "figured out a way to synchronize animation with music using a metronome, which was then converted into a music track. It was an innovation that debuted in **Steamboat Willie** and left other studios in Disney's dust for more than a year."[30] The popularity of the film led to Mickey Mouse Clubs and merchandising, and money started rolling in.

Les Clark, just out of high school, "met Walt Disney for the first time while serving ice cream in a confectionary."[31] He asked Walt for a job and eventually apprenticed under Iwerks.

Though Clark was not classically trained in drawing, he made every effort to improve. "He's the only guy I know at the studio who continued going to art school the whole time he worked there," said Frank Thomas. "Other guys could say, well. I'm too good to go to art school. I don't need to sit in on life drawing classes with a bunch of beginners. Les wouldn't care. He needed to keep working to learn more and he studied what the other guys were doing. He'd talk to you about it."[32] Ken Peterson, one of Clark's assistants, said, "He would do a thing over and over again. [I] always respected Les because he would get you quality. He would get you all the quality that was within him to get you."[33] Clark took over animating Mickey when Iwerks left and gradually adjusted Mickey's design, giving "Mickey more appeal by rounding and shortening his limbs thereby making his body slightly more compact. His shoulders were narrow like a child's would be," wrote Clark's daughter, Miriam. "Les found that if he were more than three heads high, his body would appear gangly and less appealing."[34]

The animation of Mickey also changed. Where Iwerks was a master of rubber-hose animation, Les was sympatico with Walt's beliefs that animation should be based on reality. "Our study of the actual is not so that we may be able to accomplish the actual," Walt wrote the Disney studio's art instructor, Donald Graham, in a memo from 1935. "But so that we may have a basis upon which to go into the fantastic, the unreal, the imaginative."[35] Compare Iwerks' last Mickey short **The Cactus Kid** (1930) to Clark's **Mickey in The Band Concert** (1935). The opening shot in **The Cactus Kid** has Mickey on a rubber-hose horse performing various figurative gag movements over a repeating pan background. When Mickey arrives at the café at the end of the background, he slides off his horse without showing weight. Just five years later in *The Band Concert*, the first Mickey cartoon in color, Mickey tries to conduct during a tornado. Wearing an oversized band coat, a costume that requires much better draftsmanship, his actions are more realistic. Clark's animation of Mickey comes from observations of human action, not from canned formulas. Mickey's acting had improved — he began to develop a recognizable persona, and his movement became more believable. This was just what Walt was looking for.

"Three years later," wrote Canemaker. "Clark's animation of Mickey Mouse as *The Sorcerer's Apprentice* (1940) showed how masterly he had become."[36]

Be like Les.

Walt's School

As Walt prepared for *Snow White and the Seven Dwarfs* (1937), he made *The Flying Mouse* (1934), *The Band Concert* (1935) and *The Old Mill* (1937), to push the craft of animation. "He knew he had to get in better artists, and he had to educate them to do what he wanted done," said Marc Davis, one of the Nine Old Men. "This is where Walt deserves enormous credit, and he probably was making absolutely nothing."[37]

Walt encouraged his animators to share what they learned and to help develop the newer animators. "If possible," Walt wrote Donald Graham, an instructor in life-drawing at Chouinard Art Institute, "Have some of the animators over to talk to them about problems they were confronted with in the picture, and what the animator himself would do if he had a chance to do the animation over."[38]

The studio had "become more like an art school than a business."[39] No doubt Walt was influenced by his meetings with Nelbert Chouinard, founder of Chouinard, and Graham. "When I couldn't afford the school in the very early days," said Walt. "I made a deal with Mrs. Chouinard to take some of my boys, some of these youngsters and put'em in the night classes."[40]

Dailies, or sweatboxes, were used to critique animations. "Every foot of rough animation was projected on the screen for analysis, and every foot was drawn and redrawn until we could say, "This is the best we can do," Walt wrote in 1941. "We had become perfectionists, and as nothing is ever perfect in this business, we were continually dissatisfied."[41]

"One thing he kept asking for was refinement, refinement, refinement,"[42] said Frank Thomas.

The hard work paid off. *Snow White* was predicted to be "Walt's Folly." Instead, it became a sensation and made just what Walt's undemonstrative financier at the bank told him after a screening: "a pot full of money."[43]

"Walt found such a great angle on *Snow White* and the warmth of the characters, and I guess maybe the naiveté of the times, too, had something to do with it," said Marc Davis. "I think it's the best that Disney ever did, and I think it's one of the best of all time, too."[44]

Snow White herself is beautifully animated, though her acting is histrionic and vaudevillian at times — from the "Dora Standpipe" school of acting. Each of the seven dwarfs had a unique, defined personality. "When *The Three Little Pigs* [1932] had presented a trio of similar characters with distinctly different personalities," wrote Leonard Maltin, "It had been hailed as a major step forward. Now Disney topped himself by creating seven wholly individual personalities, each with physical characteristics all his own and a point of view to match."[45]

"I was sitting behind Carole Lombard and Clark Gable and they were laughing like kids," said animator Ward Kimball. "And when the dwarfs came to the bier when Snow White was dead, I began to hear people crying and blowing their noses. We had achieved something so believable that people had a great sorrow when Snow White was poisoned."[46]

The Disney Studios posted this in the 1939 Chouinard Art School catalogue:

> "Much of the future of the animated pictures depends upon obtaining artists who have not only creative talent, but who are well-grounded in the fundamentals of art. The days when a mere "cartoonist" could get along are gone forever."[47]

The Fleischer Studio

The Fleischer Studio was Disney's chief competitor, but where Walt had a "general abhorrence of everything ugly,"[48] the Fleischer's relished the urban, gruff, and gritty. "They're absolutely distinctive," said Maltin. "They reflect the New York ethos of the animators of that time, just as Disney's reflected that of the midwestern animators of that studio."[49]

Max Fleischer began his career as a cartoonist for the *Brooklyn Daily Eagle*, where he worked with and befriended J.R. Bray. Eventually, he became an art editor at *Popular Science Monthly* — a job that suited him perfectly. "I realized I was not only artistically inclined," Max wrote in his unpublished autobiography. "But had a very keen and instinctive sense for mechanics."[50]

In love with the movies, Max opened an outdoor movie theatre in the Brownsville section of Brooklyn. Not foreseeing mosquitos or rain, the theatre struggled and finally closed when "a hardtop Loews movie theatre opened across the street."[51]

It was Max's boss at *Popular Science Monthly*, Waldemar Kaempffert, irritated by one of J.R. Bray's cartoons, who told Max he could do better. Animation had always been in the back of Max's mind, and "with the gentle push from Kaempffert,"[52] the mechanically inclined Max repurposed the movie projector from his failed theatre, the only thing he had kept, into what would be his first invention — the Rotoscope.

The Rotoscope uses a camera projector to project live-action film, one frame at a time, onto a light-table, enabling an artist to trace the action onto animation paper.

After spending close to a year rotoscoping a two-minute and thirty-second section of a Charlie Chaplin film, Max found interest from distributors but was told he needed to "reference" (rotoscope) something other than Chaplin for legal reasons. He would also need to work more quickly. So, with Max directing, his brother Dave donning a clown costume he had worn working as a professional clown at Steeplechase Park in Coney Island, and their brother Joe behind the camera, they shot the live-action reference for the first Koko the Clown short — though the clown wouldn't officially be called "Koko" for another four years.

All three brothers helped out rotoscoping this time and six months later Max brought the film to Paramount President Adolph Zukor. Outside Zukor's office Max ran into his old friend, J.R. Bray. Bray, who had a contract with Paramount and the staff Max would need to produce the shorts, hired Max to create the Koko shorts.

Koko the Clown would make the Fleischer's reputation, but it would also foretell Max's disinterest in perfecting the craft of animation. Max would always be more interested in the technical side of production, and rotoscoping was an easier, though still labor intensive, way to produce smooth "animation" quickly. Whereas Disney ran, or practically galloped, from figurative animation toward "embodied animation," which is more akin to "The Method" style of acting or "animating from the heart," Fleischer made an art form out rubber-hose animation.

After Koko, Fleischer's next "stars" were Betty Boop, Popeye, Gulliver, and Superman.

Of all the Fleischer characters, E.C. (Elzie Crisler) Segar's comic strip Popeye fit the Fleischer Studio best. Each Popeye short of the 1930s, the Fleischer Golden Age, was a "black comedy"[53] set in Brooklyn — even *King of the Mardi Gras* (1935) takes place on Coney Island. "It was a new type of storytelling for animation," said Harvey Deneroff. "Increasing levels of violence. It was this sort of thing, which was a staple of silent comedy, that the Fleischer's for the Popeye cartoons pick up [on]. It is then copied by the Looney Tunes, Merrie Melodies, MGM, Tom and Jerry cartoons, and so forth and so on."[54]

Dave Fleischer, often credited as a director though actually more of a producer – "He never directed an animated cartoon in his life!"[55] wrote animator Shamus Culhane – had some theories about animation, among them that every scene should have a gag. Dave would "pick up your scene and flip it," said animator Dave Tendlar. "And he'd say, "Where's the gag in this?"[56]

The gags in the Popeye cartoons were often clever and inventive. In *Fowl Play* (1937) Popeye punches Bluto so hard he knocks the paint out of him leaving only his inked outline; Bluto boos Olive Oyl's singing in *Morning, Noon and Night Club* (1937), then turns a radiator valve on and off to "hiss" her; Popeye beats up a giant bird and serves it up as a roasted turkey "with gravy!" in *Popeye the Sailor Meets Sinbad the Sailor* (1936); and in the classic short *A Dream Walking* (1934) Olive Oyl sleepwalks on the steel girders of a high-rise building under construction — a lesson in comic timing and mechanical animation. The gags could also be a little disturbing, especially in the earlier shorts, as in *Can You Take It* (1934) when Popeye blows smoke out of his good eye!

Instead of animators having the final say in the timing of their animation, the timing would be handled by Fleischer's "Timing and Checking Department". The Timing and Checking Department "decided that we should never animate a drawing that did not overlap the preceding figure, which of course is utter nonsense,"[57] wrote Culhane. Any wide spacing between drawings needed "extra" drawings to fill in the gaps. This reduced the impact of fast actions by making the timing unvarying and is the reason "for much of the plodding movement that characterizes the Fleischer pictures of the thirties."[58] (see Ch. 11)

Dave Fleischer also liked idling characters to bounce up and down to the beat of the music. This is more common in cartoons with dominant background music, such as *Axe Me Another* (1934) or *Seasin's Greetinks* (1933). "That up-and-down bit, with that bouncing," said animator Myron Waldman. "Drove us crazy."[59]

Lip sync in the early Popeye cartoons is kept to a minimum. This is because Popeye's muttering dialogue was ad-libbed in post-production by Jack Mercer. Mercer, an inbetweener, replaced Billy Costello (aka Red Pepper Sam), the original voice actor, in 1935 when Costello was fired for becoming too difficult. When there was an attempt at lip sync, mouth shapes pretty much stuck to the Fleischer Studios "Mouth Action Chart" formula rather than forming mouth shapes that resembled the sound being made. For instance, in *I Yam What I Yam* (1933) Wimpy says the line, "You bring the ducks." Wimpy's lips stretch out like a Coke bottle to pronounce the "OO" sound in "yOU" using mouth action number 6 or 16, depending on which chart you're following.

"There were various theories, some absolutely absurd now that we can look back," wrote Culhane. "One, a Fleischer idea, was that the mouth closed after every word! Imagine the mess that made of the dialogue! Another more prevalent theory was that when there was a loud voice, the character's mouth should be opened so wide it looked as if the jaw dislocated."[60]

Eventually Culhane "was unhappily aware that much of the animation around me was very poor."[61] One day on an elevator ride Culhane debated Max about the quality of animation at the studio. The debate went nowhere and Culhane soon left the studio. Years later Culhane received a letter from Fleischer:

> "In my opinion, the industry must pull back. Pull away from the tendencies toward realism. It must stay in its own backyard of "The Cartoonist's Cartoon". The cartoon must be a portrayal of the expression of the true cartoonist, in simple, unhampered cartoon style. The true cartoon is a great art in its own right. It does not need the assistance or support of "Artiness." In fact, it is actually hampered by it."[62]

Indeed, Max's fascination with all things technical took precedence over animation — but it's what made the early Popeye cartoons so special. To counter Disney's monopoly on Technicolor (Fleischer's was relegated to two-strip color because of Disney's exclusive two-year[63] contract for the use of 3-color Technicolor), Max developed a three-dimensional background effect, or setbacks — little miniature sets that gave the Popeye cartoons a View-Master feeling of depth. These can be seen to great effect in *For Better or Worser* (1935), *Little Swee' Pea* (1936), *I-Ski Love-Ski You-Ski* (1936) and *I Never Changes My Altitude* (1937).

With the success of *Snow White* for Disney, Paramount gave the greenlight for the Fleischer's first feature, *Gulliver's Travels* (1939). Made in a fraction of the time Walt spent on *Snow White*, Gulliver's Travels "was in effect a crash course"[64] in realistic animation for the Fleischer animators. The Fleischer's were given a new contract from Paramount, along with the okay to relocate the studio to Miami Florida — a move that would turn out to be a "monumental, tragic mistake."[65]

The character Gulliver would be fully rotoscoped using "Sam Parker, announcer for the Miami CBS radio station WIOD"[66] as the actor. "Although the Disney animators tried to conceal the live-action origins of their animation of Snow White," wrote historian Michael Barrier. "The Fleischers' Gulliver is unmistakably, even flagrantly, a tracing."[67]

"I remember meeting Walt," said director Frank Tashlin. "And he said, we can do better than that with our second-string animators."[68]

The last great Fleischer series were the Superman cartoons. Beautifully produced with sophisticated composition, low, and Dutch angles, the Superman cartoons showed Max's love for expressionist film, special effects, and all things mechanical. But as with Gulliver, the Superman cartoons "show so little aptitude for – or interest in – realistic animation styles," wrote film critic Janet Maslin. Maslin pointed out that the best character animation of the first Superman cartoon *Superman* (1941) is the raven. The "raven is wildly alive, like any real Fleischer creation, and the film sneaks in as many raven's-eye glimpses as possible. Heroic human figures have little to do with the grim, witty hallmarks of the Fleischer's imagination."[69]

Only nine Superman cartoons would be made by the Fleischer Studios. Max and Dave had stopped talking to each other after the move to Miami and could no longer work together. "Paramount called their loan, which effectively bankrupted the Fleischer Studios."[70] Production of Superman and Popeye moved back to New York to Paramount's new animation division, Famous Studios.

"I think as Famous Studios took over, the Popeye cartoons, they started to become blander," said animator Eric Goldberg. "They already had started to become more streamlined in the war years. And then the post-war years they started to become suburban. Olive Oyl's living in a suburban house. They're not in the city anymore. The animation's very smooth, but it's not very exciting a lot of the time. Even though it's many of the same artists, just somehow the edge was taken off of it and so the stuff just became a little smoother and a little less interesting."[71] "Perhaps part of the reason that the Fleischer cartoons changed was the impact of "Disneyfication," wrote Mark Langer. "Many of the Fleischer staff of the Forties had worked for Disney or Iwerks in the Thirties."[72] They didn't understand that the charm of the 1930s Popeye cartoons was their perfected imperfection.

Ironically, Shamus Culhane came back to run Famous Studios in the 1960s. Talking with Nick Tafuri one day, one of the original Fleischer animators, Tafuri told Culhane, "At least Max and Dave wanted to make the pictures funny. I know you never thought much of Dave's' gags, but at least for Crissake he tried."[73]

Art Babbitt

By the end of the 1930s, Art Babbitt was one of Disney's highest-salaried animators. Babbitt had come to Disney from Terrytoons, followed eventually by his co-worker and friend Bill Tytla.

Babbitt's talent as an animator was quickly recognized. While watching one of Babbitt's scenes in *The Mad Doctor* (1933), animation supervisor Ben Sharpsteen "leaned over to Walt. "We're going to have to hold this guy down," he said. "No," Walt replied, "we'll bring the other guys up!"[74]

Babbitt shared Walt's ambitions to elevate animation as an art form. For a while he held life-drawing classes at his home until Walt moved the classes to the studio. His use of a movie camera to analyze movement "helped turn Goofy from a minor character into a star."[75] These led to classes in action analysis taught by Donald Graham. But it was Babbitt's 'ability to put into words the processes most animators only knew by instinct'[76] that most helped the animators and led to what are now known as the principles of animation.

In addition to developing and animating Goofy, Babbitt also animated: Abner, a mouse in the Oscar-winning short *The Country Cousin* (1936); the Wicked Queen in *Snow White and the Seven Dwarfs*; Geppetto in *Pinocchio* (1940); the dancing mushrooms in *Fantasia* (1940) for which Babbitt referenced The Three Stooges for "certain movements of the knees of Hop Low, the smallest"[77]mushroom. "I was studying it once, and I suddenly noticed the large mushrooms are changing size dramatically," said animator Richard Williams. "They're shrinking, they're going down, they're coming at you and they're getting smaller, and then they're getting bigger. I mean, it's absolutely violating all laws of perspective and size, and you completely accept it. He said he was doing it in order to save work, the other day, which disillusioned me!"[78]

In 1941 Disney was the last non-union major studio and Babbitt was chairman of the Screen Cartoonists Guild's Disney unit. The Screen Cartoonists Guild's demands were pretty straightforward: higher pay for low-level workers, a five-day work week, two-weeks notice before layoffs, etc. Walt refused, but it was a little more complicated — the studio was losing money because of the war in Europe. Not knowing about the studio's dire financial situation, Babbitt lead the Disney employees to strike on May 28, 1941. When the strike ended nine weeks later, 263 employees were either let go or had moved on. Babbitt, not surprisingly, was persona non grata at the studio.

It could be said that the Disney strike, in effect, was animation's "Big Bang". Many talented people left to work at different animation studios or other professions. Though animation, arguably, would never achieve "the delicate artistry and expressive storytelling of the Golden Era"[79] again, new studios and styles of animation would emerge. Disney animator Steve Bosustow would co-found United Productions of America, better known as UPA — joined by colleagues art director John Hubley and colorist Jules Engel; animator Kenneth Muse would go to MGM to work on the Tom and Jerry shorts for Bill Hanna and Joe Barbera; animators Don and Ray Patterson would soon follow; animators Ed Love and Preston Blair would work for Tex Avery at MGM; animator Bill Melendez went to Warner Brothers, then to UPA, and eventually he produced and directed the Peanuts television cartoons. Production designer Maurice Noble left to design backgrounds for Chuck Jones at Warner Brothers; storymen P.D. Eastman, Virgil Partch, and Aurelius Battaglia moved on to careers as print cartoonists and children's book illustrators.

After a long legal battle with Walt, Babbitt, feeling "he was treated like a "leper,"[80] accepted "a large cash settlement"[81] to resign. Ironically, the animator who helped Walt achieve his goal of realism in animation would find work at UPA, innovators of a modern graphic style of animation. At UPA Babbitt "animated on the first Mr. Magoo short, and it is rumored that the character's irascibility was at least partially based on Babbitt," wrote historian Jake Friedman. "He went on to work on commercials and co-ran a small studio called Quartet Films, winning a slew of awards for his commercials and industrial films."[82] His commercials for Western Airlines and Faygo Black Cherry Soda are beautifully animated and show how Babbitt was a master at combining classic full animation techniques with modern design. A foreshadowing of Babbitt's later style is seen in *Snow White* [Scene 38] when the dwarfs push Dopey upstairs to check the bedroom for ghosts. Doc hands Dopey a candle and then squirms oddly into the group as they ascend the stairs.

Perhaps Babbitt's greatest influence would be as a teacher. The classes Babbitt gave at Richard Williams' studio in London during the 1970s can be found in Williams' seminal book, *The Animator's Survival Kit*.

"I know that when Cal Arts got into animation — Disney-type of animation classes, I actually suggested Art Babbitt," said animator Milt Kahl. "I don't think he's the greatest animator in the world, but he was more highly qualified to handle that than anybody else who was available."[83]

Bill Tytla

Perhaps the saddest casualty from the strike was animator Bill Tytla.

Born in Yonkers, New York of Ukrainian immigrant parents, Vladimir William Tytla was the first animator hired at the Disney Studios to have a studio art education. He attended The Art Students League of New York studying under Boardman Robinson, an illustrator influenced by Daumier; then he went to Paris to study painting, and briefly sculpture with Rodin's assistant, Charles Despiau. "It has often been noted that Tytla's animation has the solidity, weight, and dynamism of sculpture,"[84] wrote John Canemaker.

But the richness of Tytla's animation was primarily derived from his empathy and emotional connection with the characters he animated. "The range of Bill's characters was phenomenal," wrote Frank Thomas and Ollie Johnston. "His ability to get inside the innermost reaches of their personalities enabled him to develop great scope in his work. He seemed to understand the problems that his characters faced as well as their feelings about what was happening to them."[85]

Influenced by Richard Boleslavsky, a student of Konstantin Stanislavski, the originator of method acting, Tytla was, perhaps, the first "method" animator. "Yet, as there are no two oak leaves alike, there are no two human beings alike," wrote Boleslavsky in *Acting: The First Six Lessons*. "And when an actor creates a human soul in the form of a character, he must follow the same wise rule of Nature and make that soul unique and individual."[86]

In a lecture on animating the dwarfs during the making of *Snow White and the Seven Dwarfs*, Tytla borrowed from Boleslavsky in his own Tytlanian way by stressing the importance of making each character different. "It is so easy to have one merge into another. That's the point I cannot stress hard enough," he said. "We developed a distinct walk for each of the characters in the group — no two will walk alike. Otherwise, geesus [Disney spelling], they all merge as one — you can't tell one from the other."[87]

Two of the greatest examples of personality animation animated by Tytla attest to his remarkable range — the devil Chernobog ("Black God" in Slavic mythology) in the *Night on Bald Mountain* segment of *Fantasia*, and the eponymous baby elephant in *Dumbo* (1941). "Tytla captured the feral quality of Chernobog — his immensity and his awesome power," wrote Canemaker. "In a nuanced performance, the god of evil believably displays an emotional range from unabashed glee to profound despair, expressing physical pain at the sound of church bells at dawn. Chernobog is Vladimir Tytla's supreme achievement in personality animation and marks a zenith of his career."[88] "It's one of the greatest things I've ever seen in my life,"[89] said animator Marc Davis.

No doubt drawing on Boleslavsky's lesson to become the character you're playing, Tytla described his process for animating Chernobog: "I imagined that I was as big as a mountain and made of rock and yet I was feeling and moving."[90]

"When I am all made up and dressed, I feel like the person I am supposed to represent," wrote Boleslavsky. "I'm not myself then."[91] Boleslavsky underscored the importance of posture to create more interesting poses. "Analyze now in detail the posture of your head, go to the galleries, or look into books. Look at Van Dyck, look at Reynolds ... Study the hands of Botticelli, of Leonardo, of Raphael."[92]

"Get personality and character in the hands," said Tytla. "A good definite outline and a proper break will give you all the character and personality you want without a lot of cross-hatching to go with it."[93]

And then there's Dumbo. "Dumbo was gentle, all truth," wrote animator Michael Sporn. "The honest performance meant keeping everything above board and on the table. That is undoubtedly the performance Tytla drew. In my opinion, it has to be one of the greatest animation performances ever drawn for a film. It's quite extraordinary and cannot be undercut in any possible way."[94] Inspired by his infant son Peter, Tytla created a believable, innocent character. "I gave him everything I thought he should have," said Tytla. "It just happened. I don't know a damn thing about elephants. It wasn't that I was thinking in terms of humans, and I saw a chance to do a character without using any cheap theatrics. Most of the expressions and mannerisms I got from my own kid."[95] The "Baby Mine" sequence, when Dumbo visits his mother who is locked in a circus wagon, could have easily been corny or schmaltzy, but instead it is heartbreaking.

Other characters Tytla animated show why he is one of the greatest character animators. For example, Grumpy in **Snow White**, a character more complex than his name implies. "Could anyone's thoughts be portrayed in a better way than Grumpy's after Snow White kissed him?"[96] wrote Frank and Ollie. Or Stromboli in **Pinocchio**, with his unpredictable mood swings. "What is probably the very best piece of dialogue animation was done by Bill Tytla for Pinocchio," noted Shamus Culhane. "Stromboli's struggle to pronounce English words when he is talking to Pinocchio in his caravan is a fabulous interpretation."[97] There is also Yen Sid (Disney backward), the Sorcerer in **The Sorcerer's Apprentice** segment of **Fantasia**. Tytla "gave the Sorcerer Walt's raised eyebrow of disapproval when he takes his magic hat back,"[98] then revealed Walt's sense of humor when the Sorcerer tries to conceal a smile from a remorseful Mickey. Also noteworthy are the four gossipy elephant ladies in **Dumbo**. "Bill Tytla is justifiably celebrated for certain scenes in this film, particularly Dumbo's bath and the "Baby Mine" section," wrote animator Mark Mayerson. But he "doesn't receive enough attention for the other elephants. Within this film, he shows enormous range of acting, portraying both heroes and villains, innocence, and repulsiveness. The four antagonist elephants are self-righteous, insensitive, and cruel. Tytla works both sides of the street, so to speak, stressing Dumbo's appeal while also showing how repellent the other elephants are. It's this combination that creates the film's emotional impact."[99] "Every scene he animated was a painful, intense, emotional experience,"[100] wrote Culhane.

"I was for the company union, and I went on strike because my friends were on strike," Tytla said. "I was sympathetic with their views, but I never wanted to do anything against Walt."[101] Tytla resigned from the Disney studios on February 35, 1943, almost two years after the strike was settled."[102] "Will felt unhappy there after the strike," said his wife, Adrienne. "He felt discriminated against for his 'disloyal opinions' against the studio."[103]

Tytla returned to the East Coast to Terrytoons, then moved on to Paramount and 20th Century-Fox, finally opening his own short-lived commercial studio in New York City. Though Tytla would create the Post cereal Sugar Crisp Bear and was an animation director for the feature **The Incredible Mr. Limpet** (1964), the artistic challenges he relished at Disney were never there and his health declined.

"Bill was not a businessman," said his friend animator George Bakes. "He was an artist."[104]

"He died a thousand deaths after he left the [Disney] studio," said Marc Davis. "He never really belonged in any other place."[105]

"He was able to get more power in animation than anyone else," said Frank Thomas. "I've studied his drawings and studied his film and I can't see what it is that he did, just this "Pow," this strength that no one else has ever been able to get."[106]

Fred Moore

There was "a certain aura about Fred Moore," said Ollie Johnston. "He was such a nice guy. Actually, not a complex guy, but he had this ability to draw with so much appeal, and he also had so much facility in his drawing."[107]

In 1930, Robert Fred "Freddie" Moore, 19 years old and fresh out of high school, went to an interview at the Disney studios in place of a friend and was hired as Les Clark's assistant. Though his art training was only a few night classes in exchange for janitorial work at Chouinard,[108] three years later the naturally gifted Moore was a key animator on Disney's Silly Symphony *Three Little Pigs*. "Animation came too easily for him," Clark once observed, perhaps with a bit of envy. "He didn't have to exert any real effort."[109] "After Pigs, Moore became such a dominant influence at the studio that even Walt would drop by Moore's animation table just to watch him."[110]

"Fred was just right for the time," said Ward Kimball. "He was the first one to escape from the rubber-hose school. He began getting counter movement, counter thrusts, in the way he drew. More drawing. He decided to make Mickey's cheeks move with his mouth, which had never been done before when you drew everything inside that circle. He squashed and stretched him more."[111]

Moore's drawing style would become the look of Disney animation until the rise of Milt Kahl. "I credit Fred as the one that really created the Disney style," said Marc Davis. "The drawing that people think of when they think of Disney was inspired by Fred Moore."[112]

"Probably the biggest thing Fred had going for him," said Frank and Ollie. "He had the ability to tell when something was better one way than another."[113] This is the reason Moore's animation is so fun to watch — his acting choices are unique, simple, and wonderfully entertaining.

A great example of Fred Moore's animation is a scene from *Fun and Fancy Free* (1947). Bongo the bear peddles his unicycle into the woods and experiences the wild for the first time. The description in the animation draft has eight parts for a 39-second scene:

1. Bongo riding downhill

2. Hits rock & lands in flowers

3. Jumps in air

4. Runs around in a circle

5. Trips over log

6. Sniffs

7. Tries to growl

8. Squirrel runs thru the scene in front of Bongo

A lot to do in just 39 seconds, but the animation never feels rushed. It's a wonderful scene, animated clearly and full of snap. Moore contrasts his poses in order to lead from one action into the next — thinking ahead to what Bongo will do next and starting that action early. This gives him time to add personality bits, such as Bongo adjusting his cap.

"Don't clutter up your scene with a lot of extra bits of action. Do one thing at a time," Moore told Frank Thomas. "Don't move too much while you're doing it. Hit a pose and get the expression you want, and then move on."[114]

"One of the basic things that Freddy taught us was rhythm in drawing, the motion, the movement," said Eric Larson. "He never made a drawing that didn't have a flow to it and this is basic in animation, this is what you have to look for in new talent."[115]

"Freddie could bring such an appealing quality to a character just by the tilting of a head or an innocent and boyish stance as in the case of Mickey or Pinocchio,"[116] said Les Clark.

Clark's "innocent and boyish" observation could also apply to Moore himself. While the new animators at the studio had a hunger to learn and take their animation to a new level, Moore stubbornly refused to grow. Passing by animator Morris Gollub's desk, Moore noticed a book on horse anatomy and prints by horse painter George Stubbe. "We're a cartoon studio. We don't do stuff like that," he said.[117] Moore, "had deep inner conflicts that he would have difficulty in resolving,"[118] wrote Miriam Leslie Clark, Les Clark's daughter.

In 1946 Walt reluctantly fired Moore. "Walt fired him because he couldn't straighten him out," said Ollie Johnston. "He figured it would shock him."[119] Moore worked at Walter Lantz's studio, where he redesigned Woody Woodpecker. Then, in 1948 Walt gave him a second chance.

Moore would die tragically in 1952 from "injuries received in an automobile accident"[120] at the age of 41.

In addition to Mickey Mouse and Bongo, other notable characters Moore animated include *The Three Pigs* (1933), Dopey in *Snow White* ("Freddy Moore was the one that made (the seven dwarfs) cute," said animator Bill Justice.);[121] Lampwick in *Pinocchio*; Timothy Mouse in *Dumbo*; the mice in *Cinderella* (1950); the Boy and Sir Giles in *The Reluctant Dragon* (1941); and various characters in "All the Cats Join In" from *Make Mine Music* (1946) – all are a showcase of the Freddy Moore style.

"There wasn't one of us here that came here as a genius, except Freddy Moore,"[122] said Eric Larson.

The Nine Old Men

With the war ending in late 1945, the Disney Studio was at full-steam again and Walt found himself overstretched. "Forced to delegate responsibilities,"[123] he created an "Animation Board" composed of nine top animators: Les Clark, Marc Davis, Ollie Johnston, Milt Kahl, Ward Kimball, Eric Larson, John Lounsbery, Woolie Reitherman, and Frank Thomas. Christened by Walt "The Nine Old Men" after "President Roosevelt's description of his hostile Supreme Court,"[124] they were basically "the in-house animation review board."[125]

"They did not invent the basic principles. Or even the basic Disney style, [which] came from Freddy Moore," Glen Keane told John Canemaker. "They were doing something that was beyond what their teachers had given them. To me it was a complexity of acting. There was a subtlety in the drawing that their acting required, and it was something that they were able to dig down deeper into themselves and it was something they got to by study."[126]

And despite working together and sharing all the same information for thirty or forty years, each of the Nine Old Men developed their own style.

Marc Davis

Walt referred to Marc Davis, one of the best draftsmen at the studio, as his "'Renaissance Man' because he could do anything."[127] Davis, who also taught at Chouinard's, animated many of the classic female characters. "Being able to draw a little better than any of the other men, I sometimes got sidetracked on the more difficult-to-draw characters, which are not always the most fun,"[128] said Davis. Alice, in *Alice in Wonderland* (1951), Tinker Bell in *Peter Pan* (1953), both Aurora and Maleficent in *Sleeping Beauty* (1959), and his tour de force — Cruella de Vil in *One Hundred and One Dalmatians* (1961). In 1962, Walt moved Davis over to WED (Imagineering) where he would have another career designing attractions for Disneyland. Davis created thousands of concept drawings for theme park attractions such as the Pirates of the Caribbean, the Haunted Mansion, and the Country Bear Jamboree. "[Davis] was wonderful," Milt Kahl told Richard Williams. "He was awfully gawdamn good, but Disney took him away from us to design on Disneyland. That was very upsetting."[129]

Ollie Johnston

Ollie Johnston had "a very personal approach toward animation," wrote Andreas Deja. "One where the animator analyzes and eventually identifies with the character's emotions."[130]

Turn off the sound when watching a scene Ollie animated and you can see how skillfully he captured the inner emotions of the character with the subtlest of expressions. The slight smile the mouse Bernard gives when his girlfriend Bianca rests her head on his shoulder as he tries to read the rescue manual in *The Rescuers* (1977). The dog Perdita cowering under the stove as her mate Pongo tries to comfort her in *One Hundred and One Dalmatians*. And the classic scene (also from *The Rescuers*) of Ollie's doppelgänger, Rufus, an elderly cat, consoling the orphan Penny when she wasn't adopted from an orphanage. Ollie's brilliant animation of Smee from *Peter Pan* deserves a chapter of his own. It's a terrific example of secondary action (see Ch. 19). Also worth studying is Ollie's wonderful staging of the female characters in the highly active, though chauvinistic, scene from *Reason and Emotion* (1943). It's as if he took Freddy Moore to another level.

Ollie "is very intuitive and has to feel it from the inside," said Frank Thomas. "He has a sign up on his desk that says, 'what is the character thinking, and why does he feel that way?' Very perceptive. You know if you can answer those two questions, you're way down the road toward getting a scene out of it."[131]

Woolie Reitherman

Wolfgang "Woolie" Reitherman was best known for his action scenes — both comedic and dramatic. His animation of Goofy and "the Wave" in *Hawaiian Holiday* (1937) could explain why he was typecast as an action animator. Reitherman continued honing his broad animation style on numerous Jack Kinney-directed Goofy shorts including *El Gaucho Goofy* (1943) and *How to Ride a Horse* (1950).

Reitherman's talent for dramatic action can be seen in the sequence he animated of Monstro the whale chasing Pinocchio and Geppetto in *Pinocchio*; the battle between 'Rex' and 'Steg' (the tyrannosaurus and stegosaurus, respectively) in *Fantasia*, and the fight between the dog Tramp and a rat in *Lady and the Tramp*. In the *Sleepy Hollow* segment of *The Adventures of Ichabod and Mr. Toad* (1949), Reitherman animated both comedic and dramatic action in a wild chase between the Headless Horseman and Ichabod Crane.

Ward Kimball had animated a version of the duel between Peter Pan and Captain Hook at Skull Rock but Walt found it too cartoony, so he gave the scene to Reitherman. "Kimball's Hook was real shortsy," said Frank Thomas, referring to Kimball's over-the-top Warner Bros. version. "And the timing was bing-bing-bing — things that had no sincerity or believability to. Woolie, even though he was in the shorts philosophy, still had believability; when the guy hit that rock, he hit a solid rock."[132]

Reitherman shone with his rare chance to do a calmer personality animation in *Donald's Cousin Gus* (1939). Gus the goose's opening sequence has excellent weight, timing, and tasteful exaggeration — as when Gus, after double-checking Donald's address on the mailbox, swings himself around using his foot as momentum, then heads up the walk to visit his cousin. (A similar motion is seen in *Captain Underpants: The First Epic Movie* (2018) when 'Cap' enters a building after saving a cat in a tree.)

Reitherman became a sequence director on *Sleeping Beauty*, supervising the fight between the Dragon and Prince Philip. He transitioned into directing full-time with the 1960 short *Goliath II*. "I became a director because Walt said, 'Be a director!'"[133] said Reitherman. "Thank God for Woolie," said Milt Kahl. "Because he's the best director we've ever had in this place. He's an awfully nice guy. He was a pretty darned good animator too."[134]

John Lounsbery

"John Lounsbery was the quietest of the Nine Old Men and yet the characters that he animated were anything but,"[135] wrote Bob Thomas. Ben Ali Gator in the *Dance of the Hours* sequence in *Fantasia*; George Darling, the father in *Peter Pan*; and two scenes from *Lady and the Tramp* (1955), Tony and Joe the dog-loving cooks serving a romantic dinner, and the wonderfully staged tussle between a 'Cop' and a 'Professor' outside the zoo, demonstrate how an introverted animator can be an extroverted actor. George Darling and The Colonel, the old English sheepdog in *One Hundred and One Dalmatians,* show Lounsbery's mastery of squash and stretch. "Very much like Freddy Moore," said story artist Burny Mattinson. "John was one of the best. An animator's animator."[136]

Lounsbery "had a reputation for being an animator who could turn his assistants into animators," said animator John Ewing. "It was his training, I presume; his methods seemed to lead an artist more smoothly into animation."[137] Lounsbery "turned out to be a good one. He was so self-effacing. He didn't know he was so good," said Ward Kimball. "There again, I always thought he apologized too much. He was good."[138]

Eric Larson

Though Eric Larson wonderfully animated some human characters such as Alice in *Alice in Wonderland*, and Joe and Jenny in the *Once Upon a Wintertime* segment in *Melody Time* (1948), he was most adept at animating anthropomorphic characters. His animation of the kitten Figaro in *Pinocchio* "is one of the finest examples of pure pantomime ever done at the studio," wrote Frank and Ollie. "The acting, texture in timing, and inner feeling for the character were remarkable things to achieve without the benefit of dialogue."[139] According to Milt Kahl, the best animation in *Lady and the Tramp* is "Eric Larson's dog, the one with the Veronica Lake hairdo"[140] Peg, "the faded star of the Dog and Pony Show."[141] Larson, who was skilled at animating flying creatures, "became known as a bird-man."[142] Friend Owl in *Bambi*; Sasha, the Russian sparrow from the *Peter and the Wolf* segment of *Make Mine Music* (1946); the birds who help Cinderella; and the vultures in *Jungle Book* (1967) are among the avian critters he animated. In *Fantasia*, Larson animated the Pegasus family of winged horses and centaurs, though he felt his animation of the latter fell short. Instead of studying horses, Larson focused on the human half, using himself and two co-workers as references. "We didn't do proper research," he lamented. "It was my job and I did it animating the centaurs and centaurettes the easy way, like humans do it, consequently they were not humans or animals."[143]

Larson was fond of timing each body part separately, so he would have a different timing chart for each part of the body (see Ch. 11). Key assistant animator Dale Oliver called it his 'Atomic charting'. "There would be a chart over there, and then here would be another chart; the tail here would be another chart and watch this leg and here would be about three or four timing charts on this drawing. So, he'd cover his bases right there. You just kind of knew what the timing should be."[144]

In 1970 Larson, "was placed in charge of finding and training new animation talent."[145] Many of the animators he mentored would go on to be part of the Disney animation renaissance of the late 1980s and 1990s. "Eric was more comfortable with handing on the baton than any other of the Nine Old Men," former Larson trainee John Pomeroy recalled. "While the remainder of the giants here still were furthering their careers, Eric saw a need to pass on this language and this knowledge."[146]

Ward Kimball

"Walt would stick his head into Milt [Kahl's] door and say, "Where's the genius?"[147] He wasn't looking for Milt, he was looking for Ward Kimball — and also giving Milt a ribbing.

Ward Kimball was one of the most versatile of the Nine Old Men. An artist of many styles, and extroverted clothing, Kimball excelled at breaking the rules of animation while still maintaining Disney realism. His animation of Tweetle Dee and Tweetle Dum in *Alice in Wonderland* is broad and cartoony, with lots of squash and stretch, but maintains enough solidity and 'breaking of joints' (see Ch. 14) to be grounded in reality and work eclectically with Alice.

The title song from **The Three Caballeros** is the animation Kimball was most proud of. "I was given no story business or action instructions by the director," said Kimball. "I had this long singing sequence — five minutes, or so it seemed — with little idea on how to stage it."[148]

"I sat around for a week feeling sorry for myself,"[149] he said. Eventually, Kimball went over to Griffith Park to the merry-go-round, a favorite thing to do, and got the idea to make the animation a literal interpretation of the song. The final sequence is a masterclass in cartoon animation. In a section of scene 19, Donald, Panchito, and Jose are stuck together moving as one character, another favorite Kimball thing to do, when Panchito sings, "...The one, two, and three goes, we're always together..." They split apart, run frantically around the stage pistols poppin', doing a backflip, arm pulling, swinging hats, etc. and none of the animation is cheated. Every footstep is clearly planted and there is no help from smears, wipes, or dry brush (see Ch. 23).

Kimball wanted to quit during the making of **Snow White**. The "Grim Reaper,"[150] said Kimball, referring to Walt, cut two of his sequences: the seven dwarfs building Snow White's bed, and a soup-eating sequence also with the dwarfs. "I actually went into Walt's office to quit," he said. Walt, probably knowing why Kimball was there, "softened the blow by telling him: "We have this picture, **Pinocchio**, coming up next, and we've added a little character that's right up your alley, Jiminy Cricket."[151]

"I hated the cricket,"[152] said Kimball who designed and animated Jiminy. "It's not a cricket," he said. "It is a blob. It is a little man creature with no ears, and he wears little English outfits."[153] "Still," wrote John Canemaker, "Jiminy Cricket is arguably the warmest, most sincere, and psychologically three-dimensional personality that Kimball ever animated."[154]

Other standout Kimball characters are the crows from **Dumbo**; Lucifer the Cat from **Cinderella** who would sneak up the stairs "so low that the contour of his body fits the zigzag staircase"[155]; the Cheshire Cat and Mad Tea Party from **Alice in Wonderland**; and Pecos Bill from **Melody Time**.

Kimball won an Academy Award for directing **Toot, Whistle, Plunk and Boom** (1953), the first cartoon in CinemaScope. Made in a modernist style it's "a clean steal from the Bosustow [UPA co-founder, Stephen Bosustow] cartoons (which, in turn, borrowed tricks from such modern artists as Paul Klee)," wrote Time magazine. "Toot takes Disney in one jump from the nursery to the intellectual cocktail party."[156] For **Toot**, Kimball used a hybrid of limited and full animation. The Owl teacher in the opening and closing of the short is full animation, while the middle of the film is limited with a Disney touch — the bodies of the characters are still, but the appendages and mouths move in a beautifully fluid and full manner. Kimball said the use of limited animation, "was to give it a different look, like you were looking through a book."[157]

Kimball, "a UFO fan,"[158] was proud of the space exploration trilogy he directed for television: **Man in Space** (1955), **Man and the Moon** (1955), and the at times hysterical **Mars and Beyond** (1957). Kimball would win another Academy Award for directing **It's Tough to be a Bird** (1969) but would retire in 1973. "It just wasn't fun anymore,"[159] he said.

Les Clark

Les Clark, as mentioned, became an expert animator of Mickey Mouse. His animation of Mickey bringing the brooms alive in **The Sorcerer's Apprentice** and conducting an orchestra in **The Symphony Hour** (1942) is often mistaken for Freddie Moore. A quiet man, Clark often lost out on meatier roles snatched up by the other eight Old Men. Clark would take what was given to him but would always come through with a solid performance. He animated many great scenes from **Pinocchio** including the classic scene of Pinocchio holding an apple and turning around as his head stays in place; in **Mr. Duck Steps Out** (1940) he animated Donald Duck's double-bounce "trucking" dance; in the **Nutcracker Suite** segment of **Fantasia** Clark animated the Sugar Plum Fairies in scenes Walt was fond of. The darting and hovering of the Fairies "was taken from a hummingbird action because that's how I visualized it,"[160] said Clark. One of his most charming scenes is the anthropomorphic "Train to Baia" in **The Three Caballeros**. It shows how he took what he learned from Ub Iwerks to another level.

Art Babbitt said that Clark "never received the recognition the others did. And he should have because he was marvelous! Terrific animator, very inventive. But taken for granted!"[161]

Just as Les Clark was shut out of plum rolls so were other fine animators. John Sibley, Eric Cleworth, Hal Ambro, Hal King, Riley Thomson, and Blaine Gibson — to name a few. Director Pete Docter called Sibley the "Tenth Old Man" and said his animation of Goofy in **How to Be a Sailor** (1944) "was simultaneously fluid, graceful, caricatured, and extreme, yet it felt completely believable; it was also hilarious." [162]

Eric Cleworth's scene in **Jungle Book** of the elephant Colonel Hathi bragging about receiving the Victoria Cross is brilliant and stands up to anything John Lounsbery did in the film.

"Walt should have had thirty "Nine Old Men, not nine,"[163] said Disney modeler Bob Jones.

"Naturally, the Nine Old Men were the reason that none of the artists in my age group reached the top level of animation direction at Disney," said Blaine Gibson. "Because the Nine Old Men didn't get any worse, they got better as they got older, and they were not even that old."[164]

Tissa David once mentioned to me that she felt the Nine Old Men were at their most confident when they made **One Hundred and One Dalmatians**, saying they weren't afraid to hold drawings or to animate on two's (one drawing for every two frames of film) and make it look as if it were animated on one's (one drawing for every single frame of film) — as when Roger, in **Dalmatians**, descends the stairs singing the Cruella De ville song.

"I think their influence is overwhelming, "said Richard Williams. "They did it! They're the ones who set the standard for everybody, for the medium. And to build on."[165]

Frank or Milt?

If you asked someone who their favorite of the Nine Old Men is, it's usually either Frank Thomas or Milt Kahl. Some may choose Ward Kimball, or maybe even Marc Davis, but usually it's Frank or Milt.

What made Frank special was his acting ability. "Some liken him to Laurence Olivier because of the variety of roles he has played and the depth of emotion he has wrung from them,"[166] wrote Canemaker. What made Milt special was his phenomenal draftsmanship — even Frank Thomas would tell you that there was no one who drew better than Milt: "I saw Milt doing very realistic drawings of Alice [from **Alice in Wonderland**] with very subtle features, the nose in particular, and I went to see Ollie and I asked, "How do you draw that stuff?"[167]

Winsor McCay

Max Fleischer   **Dave Fleischer**

Ub Iwerks

Les Clark

Art Babbitt

Donald Graham

Bill Tytla

Freddy Moore

John Hubley

Figure 2.1

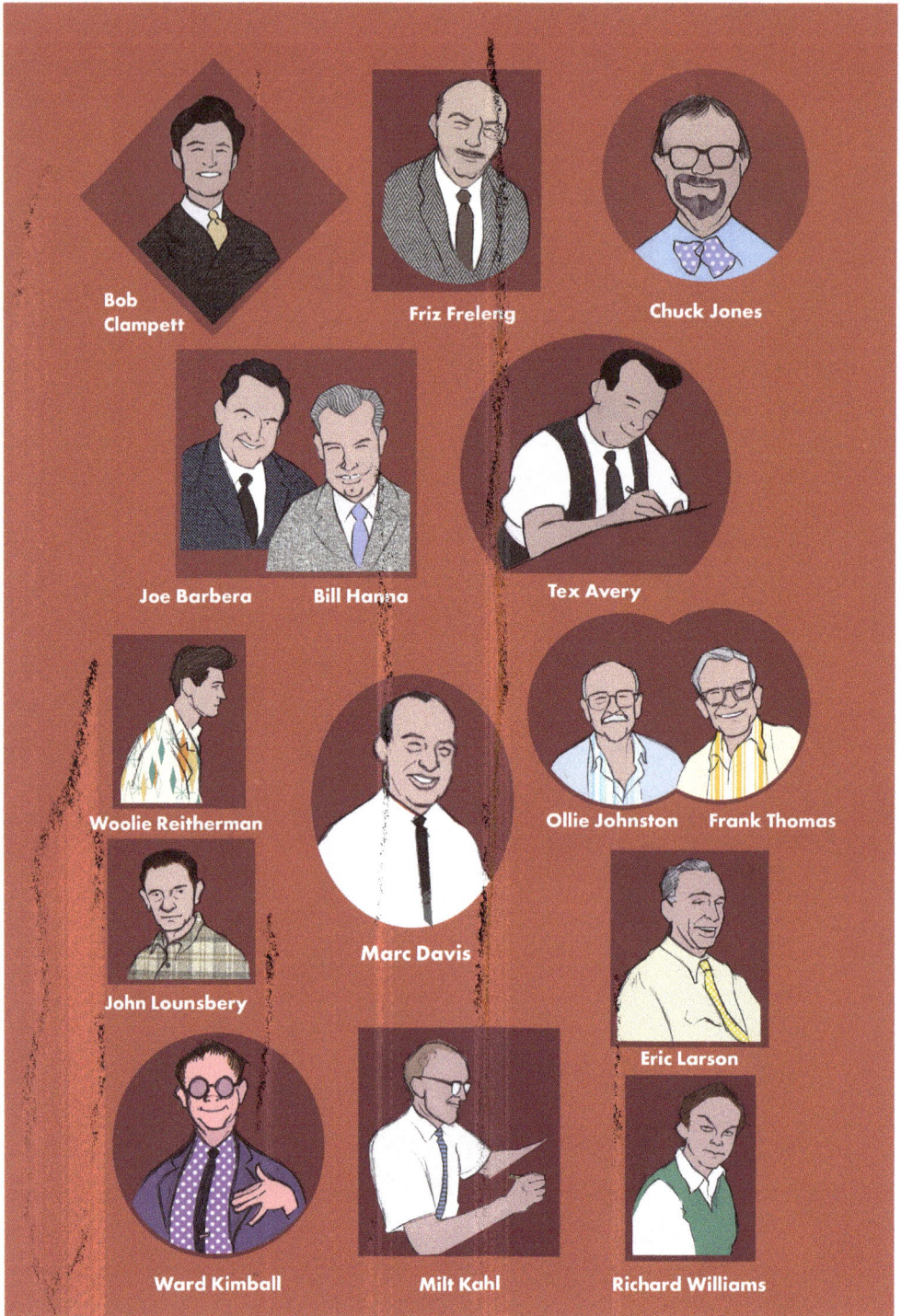

Bob Clampett

Friz Freleng

Chuck Jones

Joe Barbera   Bill Hanna

Tex Avery

Woolie Reitherman

Ollie Johnston   Frank Thomas

John Lounsbery

Marc Davis

Eric Larson

Ward Kimball

Milt Kahl

Richard Williams

Figure 2.2

What Frank and Milt had in common was a total mastery of the craft of animation. They understood the fundamentals of animation so completely they could focus on the nuances of performance.

You can see how special Frank's animation is as far back as **Mickey's Elephant** (1936). His animation of Pluto moves with purpose — the poses linking together more gracefully than even Pluto's master animator Norm Ferguson.

Milt, on the other hand, animated mostly crowd shots until **Ferdinand the Bull** (1938) — for which he also provided Ferdinand's falsetto voice. Milt didn't really start to become Milt until **Snow White** when he animated the turtle and some of the prince.

Both Frank and Milt had a knack for creating classic scenes. Frank's animation of the dwarfs crying over Snow White's bier; Minnie kissing Mickey after a miscommunication about killing seven flies and not seven giants with one blow in **The Brave Little Tailor** (1938); Pinocchio singing "I got no strings to hold me d — " then tripping and falling down the stairs; the exasperating doorknob in **Alice in Wonderland** saying, "One good turn deserves another!"; Thumper teaching Bambi how to ice skate; and Lady and Tramp chewing the same strand of spaghetti and meeting in a kiss.

Both the **Bambi** skating sequence and the **Lady and the Tramp** spaghetti sequence were going to be cut — the Bambi sequence because Walt was losing interest in it, and the spaghetti sequence because "Walt thought it was kind of distasteful or something or other,"[168] said Frank. Both scenes were saved by Frank's persistence and talent.

Some of Milt's classic scenes are Pinocchio skipping to school, the skip that will forever be the reference for how to animate a skip; Tramp waking up in a train station and showering under a dripping drain pipe; Roger singing Anita the Cruella de Vil song in **One Hundred and One Dalmatians**; Wart, (the future King Arthur), pulling Excalibur from the stone in **Sword in the Stone** (1963); and the "bouncy, trouncy, flouncy, pouncy" Tigger in **Winnie the Pooh and the Blustery Day** (1968).

"Frank would analyze things to death," said animator Art Stevens. "And the studio — the accounting department — was up in arms a bit because he spent five thousand dollars on analyzing knitting for the wicked stepmother in **Cinderella**."[169]

Milt also believed animators should study their subject so thoroughly "you don't have to use the reference anymore."[170] "You've got a lot of lazy people in the business," he said. "You shoot live action and they'll follow it blindly because it's easier than thinking."[171] Even with similar approaches to action analysis, Frank and Milt's animation styles are distinctly different. Frank's animation is subtly complex; the little bounce when Lady and Tramp's muzzles meet while eating the same strand of spaghetti; the circular arm movement Merryweather makes at the end of the waltz with the mop and bucket in **Sleeping Beauty**; and the double-take Perdita does in the park when she's caught looking at Pongo in O**ne Hundred and One Dalmatians**.

Milt's animation doesn't shy away from showing his virtuosity; Jiminy Cricket getting dressed as he chases after Pinocchio; the closeup of Roger's startled hand fumbling with his pipe when Pongo licks his hand in Dalmatians; Georges Hautecourt the eccentric lawyer in **The Aristocats** (1970) dancing the tango, then sitting down and preparing his fountain pen to change Adelaide's will.

"The difference was that Frank was always thinking character first. "He'd throw out a 'good' drawing if it didn't support his overall goal for the scene," said Frank's son, director Ted Thomas. "In contrast, Milt argued with him that you can always use a "good" drawing, and when you're lucky enough to get one, that should be the tent pole for the rest of the scene, even if it meant retooling the scene to build in and out of that pose."[172]

Because Milt's poses are so strong, his scenes are sometimes easier to break down than Frank's. Milt's poses have clear highs and lows and he tends to accent dialogue hard with the head or an index finger. Frank, on the other hand, didn't depend upon "golden poses" (see Ch. 4). As Ted Thomas mentioned, with Frank it was always character first. When Pinocchio starts singing, "I've got no strings, to hold me down," Frank animated his gestures off the beat of the song to show how uncomfortable he is. "I felt pretty strongly that it ought to be very amateurish," he said. "I was talking to Milt one day and said, "He's never rehearsed this, he doesn't know what he's going to do, he's making it up as he goes along. I'm going to have him be late on his sync on some of the words." Milt looked at me and said, "Are you crazy?!? God! That's the lousiest idea I've ever heard anywhere!" I was looking at it just the other day, and when Pinocchio says, "I've got no strings, to hold me down," the gesture comes after he says, "Down." That was just what I wanted it to do, and no one has objected, although I can still hear Milt scream, "Oh for Christ's sake!"[173]

Other memorable characters Frank animated: The Queen of Hearts in **Alice in Wonderland**; Captain Hook in **Peter Pan**; Pongo and Perdita in **Dalmatians**; Madam Mim and, one of the more touching personality scenes ever animated and a favorite of Tissa David's, the two squirrels in **The Sword in the Stone**. "I probably had the most fun animating the squirrels in **Sword in the Stone**,"[174] said Frank.

Other memorable characters Milt animated: The reluctant jitterbugging llama from **Saludos Amigos** (1942) one of "the funniest piece of animation I think I've ever seen," said Marc Davis. "Just wonderful."[175]; Madam Mim in **The Sword in the Stone**; Pecos Bill and Slue-Foot Sue from **Melody Time**; Shere Kahn the tiger in **Jungle Book**. "I'm a beginner!" cried Richard Williams in awe and admiration when he first saw Milt's virtuoso animation of Shere Kahn. "I don't know anything!"[176]; and arguably the pinnacle of his career, Madam Medusa from **The Rescuers** (1977). Geraldine Page provides the voice, "You are too soff-teh!" "She's a magnificent actress," said Milt. "She forces you to 'plus' things."[177]

Frank and Milt worked hard at their craft and expected everyone to work just as hard. "[When] I got away from Frank and I wasn't working under him anymore," Frank's assistant Blaine Gibson told his successor Dale Oliver, "It was like taking off lead boots."[178] Iwao Takamoto, Milt's longtime assistant, said that animators would show Milt a scene they were working on and sometimes he would lose his patience. But, he adds, "Milt had to work hard to achieve exactly what he wanted."[179]

"I just tried to be a real good craftsman and be an all-around master of the craft,"[180] said Milt.

UPA

In 1943, three newly unemployed Disney strikers, art director Zack Schwartz, layout artist David Hilberman, and animator Stephen Bosustow founded Industrial Film and Poster Service in "a single room in the Otto K. Olesen building in Hollywood."[181] The company initially produced film strips (a slide show accompanied by a record) for the war effort. Their first production was **Sparks and Chips Get the Blitz** (1943), a film strip on factory safety. To supplement their income, they also created posters — hence "and Poster Service" in their name. Meanwhile, former Disney art director John Hubley, a soldier in the First Motion Picture Unit was hired by The United Automobile Workers (UAW) to create storyboards for a cartoon supporting Roosevelt's 1944 reelection. When the boards for *Hell-Bent for Election* (1944) were completed, Chuck Jones of Warner Bros., "a Roosevelt man,"[182] agreed to moonlight as director, but they still needed a production facility. *Hell-Bent for Election* was turned down by every studio as being "too political,"[183] so, the "left-leaning, pro-union, and pro-Roosevelt Industrial Film and Poster Service got the job."[184]

Hell-Bent for Election was a success and Industrial Film and Poster Service decided to change their name to attract more clients, first to "United Film Productions" and then, in December of 1945, to "United Productions of America". "In my opinion an equally ridiculous and even more bombastic moniker." said Zack Schwartz. "Which mercifully, in a very short time, became UPA."[185]

New contract work included four cartoons for the U.S. War Department and what is now considered the first true UPA cartoon, *The Brotherhood of Man* (1944), a film made for the UAW about race relations in auto factories. Although the film had a modernist production design by Hubley and former Warner Bros. background artist Paul Julian, and Saul Steinberg influenced the character designs, the animation by Robert "Bobe" Cannon, Ken Harris, and Ben Washam of Warner Bros. resorted to realism – characters turn in space with dimensionality.

Flat Hatting (1946), a short about reckless flying made for the U.S. Navy, and the first film Hubley directed after joining UPA full-time, unlocked the UPA "style." Except for a few characters that move dimensionally in space (a butterfly and a bee), the animation in Flat Hatting remains flat to match the backgrounds. "Hubley conceived the film as "an animated lithograph."[186] "The Disney concept was always volume," Hubley explained. "You had a character was on a round volume. Think of it as a ball. The mouth was there and the nose was there and the result [was] you would be able to turn it." UPA "was an attempt to work with flat shapes," he said. "You know, screw the volume, just move it as a shape."[187]

Any fast actions or head-turns jump from one pose to another without in-betweens, anticipating Tex Avery's *Symphony in Slang* (1951). There is also "a highly evolved use of match cuts," wrote Amid Amidi. "In which eight scenes are linked together by a constantly metamorphosing animation element — a plane morphs into an axe, then a book, a mouse, and so on."[188] No doubt anticipating the morphing musical instruments in Disney's *Toot, Whistle, Plunk and Boom*.

The UPA style "came out of Matisse, Picasso, modern painters," according to Hubley. "Just flatten it up."[189]

Despite UPA's possibilities, in 1946 Hilberman and Schwartz sold their shares of UPA to Bosustow. The studio struggled through 1947 trying to get contracts they had to downsize their office and reduce their staff. But early in 1948, 'Bosustow negotiated a deal to produce theatrical shorts for Columbia Pictures, which had recently shuttered its in-house cartoon division.'[190]

Columbia insisted UPA use their own characters, Fox and Crow, for the first two cartoons. *Robin Hoodlum* (1948) has moments of interesting animation with the Fox as Robin Hood, but it's the backgrounds, by Bill Hurtz, and color design by Herb Klynn and Jules Engel that dominate. The animation in *The Magic Fluke* (1949) is much stronger and the comedy more interesting than the premise — perhaps inspiring Tex Avery's *Magical Maestro* (1952).

"After *The Magic Fluke* we kept hitting Columbia with, 'We want to do original shorts and we're stuck with tired animals,'" said Hubley. "Our strength and our vision is to do human characters."[191]

Ragtime Bear (1949) did have a bear, but the star was UPA's first original character, Mr. Magoo. Art Babbitt was one of the animators on the first Magoo cartoon and his scenes noticeably use live-action references. Magoo also looks more like W.C. Fields than Magoo in Babbitt's scenes, but that's because the character's design had not been nailed down. Eventually, Magoo's design became simplified and consistent and his animation more refined — especially when animated by animators like Rudy Larriva, who would also animate the opening titles UPA created for the original *Twilight Zone* (1959-60) TV show.

The Magoo shorts were a hit. ***When Magoo Flew*** (1954) and ***Magoo's Puddle Jumper*** (1956) both won Academy Awards. "What are the reasons for the popularity of Mr. Magoo?" wrote David Fisher. "Mr. Magoo represents for us the man who would be responsible and serious in a world that seems insane; he is a creation of the 1950s, the age of anxiety; his situation reflects our own."[192]

In 1951, ***Gerald McBoing Boing***, a cartoon short that would cement UPA's reputation as innovators of modern animation, was released. "The UPA cartoons up to that point had leaned toward the reductive," wrote Amid Amidi. "But none had been as confidently minimalist as Gerald." From an original story by Ted Geisel (Dr. Seuss), ***Gerald McBoing Boing*** "is the story of a small boy who speaks in noises rather than words, and who is in consequence rejected by his playmates and even by his own father."[193] The animation is gentle and succinct. There are unique walk cycles for each character such as a mid-stride hop for Gerald's walk — a walk that would be familiar to Popeye fans who have seen Popeye pushing a stroller in ***Little Swee' Pea*** (1936). There's even "rubber-hose" animation suitably used for Gerald's "spineless" parents. ***Gerald McBoing Boing*** won the Academy Award that year.

The better UPA animators, such as Rudy Larriva, Bill Melendez, Phil Monroe, Frank Smith, Art Babbitt, and Grim Natwick, fully understood the craft of animation. They were able to stylize it to fit UPA character designs while keeping the characters believable. Rudy Larriva got his start at Disney, then moved on to Warner Bros. and UPA. Though Bill Melendez started at Disney he said, "within four years I had rejected that idea [of realism] completely."[194] But he first learned the craft of animation in Don Graham's classes at Disney and then rejected it. "I wish now I could apologize [to Walt] for not thanking him for having the school there,"[195] he said. Phil Monroe was one of Chuck Jones's favorite animators at Warner Bros. Frank Smith paid his dues at Fleischer and MGM before working in Bobe Cannon's unit at UPA. Smith, along with Melendez, was also one of the animators of the Saul Bass-designed credits for ***It's a Mad, Mad, Mad, Mad World*** (1963).

UPA's influence has been lasting. Tex Avery's 1950s cartoons have a UPA look. So does Disney, in not just Ward Kimball-directed films, but also anything the brilliant Tom Oreb had a hand in designing, such as ***Sleeping Beauty*** (1959). Hanna-Barbera used UPA-style backgrounds in their early cartoons, such as ***Postman Panic and Lullabye-Bear*** (1959). Jay Ward Productions, creators of ***Fractured Fairy Tales*** and ***Rocky and Bullwinkle***, couldn't help but be influenced by UPA because many of their artists and animators were, according to production designer Bill Hurtz, UPA "refugees."[196] "***Powerpuff Girls*** and other animated series hatched on cable TV's Cartoon Network wouldn't have existed without the example set by UPA,"[197] wrote Gene Seymour. Even the credits in ***Monster's Inc.*** (2001) and the three ***Jerry's in Soul*** (2020) show UPA's influence.

In 1952, John Hubley was forced to resign from UPA for refusing to name names to the House Un-American Activities Committee. In 1959 Columbia Pictures dropped UPA for Hanna-Barbera. In 1960 Stephen Bosustow sold UPA.

Hanna-Barbera at MGM

Bill Hanna and Joe Barbera are two of the more familiar names in animation, mainly because of the incredible amount of television animation they produced — "138 series in 30 years."[198] There was a time, however, before the 1970s when Hanna-Barbera cartoons were not predominantly 'illustrated radio', as Chuck Jones would say. "The Flintstones move exactly the way Yogi Bear moves, and Yogi Bear moves exactly the same way something at Filmation moves, and so on,"[199] said Jones. Ouch.

Bill Hanna began his animation career at Hugh Harman and Rudolf Ising's studio Harman-Ising (Harmonizing, get it?), mainly carrying out "custodial tasks and running for coffee."[200] Harman-Ising produced the early "Looney Tunes" and "Merrie Melodies" for Warner Brothers. When Warner Bros. decided to set up their own animation studio, they canceled Harman-Ising's contract. Harman-Ising then signed with MGM, but they were "slow in delivering the required quota of cartoons,"[201] so MGM also "decided that it was time to develop its own cartoon studio instead of relying on outside contracts."[202] By this time Hanna had moved up from custodian to director. MGM named Fred Quimby as head of the new animation department; impressed with a short Hanna had directed called *To Spring* (1936), Quimby asked Hanna to stay on.

Joe Barbera began his career at the Fleischer Studios in New York. On his third day there, he was promoted to the inking department. Inkers, as they were called, traced the animators' drawings onto cels in ink. He asked one of his new colleagues how long he had been in the inking department. "Three years," he replied. Barbera quit the next day.

On the strength of his portfolio of gag cartoons, Barbera got a job as an in-betweener at the Van Beuren animation studio. It was serendipity that he was seated next to animator Carlo Vinci. Realizing Barbera knew nothing about in-betweening, Vinci showed him what to do. Vinci would later become one of Hanna-Barbera's top animators, animating "the first Flintstone cartoon single-handedly."[203]

When Disney signed with RKO, Van Beuren lost its distribution contract and went out of business. Barbera got a job at the Paul Terry studio in New Rochelle, New York where found his true calling — story.

In 1937 Fred Quimby, in need of talent for his new animation department at MGM, poached a number of artists from the Terry studios and Joe Barbera found himself sitting next to Bill Hanna in the MGM animation story department.

Jerry Mayer, MGM's business manager, would frequently stop by the animation department "threatening to turn it into a wardrobe building."[204] With the ongoing threat of unemployment, Hanna and Barbera decided to come up with their own characters. "I settled on a cat and a mouse," said Barbera. "Which everyone thought was about the most unoriginal, stupid idea."[205]

With Hanna's "keen sense of timing"[206] and Barbera's gag writing and drawing ability, the partners put together a more elaborate version of a story or pose reel. "Joe and I decided to elaborate on the pose reel concept," said Hanna. "We expanded the test film to include more drawings to get a better feel for refining the finished product."[207] "The technique used far fewer individual drawings than a fully finished cartoon — fewer than 1,800,"[208] said Barbera.

The limited animation demo would be vital to their second act on television.

Hanna and Barbera's first short, **Puss Gets the Boot** (1940), would be nominated for an Academy Award and they would make Tom and Jerry for the remainder of their time at MGM.

Bill Hanna was "absolutely mesmerized by the faultless grace"[209] of **Snow White and the Seven Dwarfs**. For the Tom and Jerry cartoons Hanna said he, "derived a special satisfaction from the challenge of trying to impart our cartoons with their own hallmark of animation excellence."[210]

Initially, the Tom and Jerry cartoons were slower-paced and Disney-like, influenced by Rudolf Ising. But in 1941 Tex Avery came to MGM and his innovative approach to animation was inescapable. Hanna honed his timing skills by studying the shorts Avery's unit produced, running them "on the moviola, frame by frame."[211]

The Tom and Jerry cartoons not only became faster-paced; they became more violent — helped by the strong posing in Barbera's storyboards. Barbera's storyboards "looked like animators' extremes," said animator Bill Littlejohn. "It moved for you right there."[212]

To keep pace with accelerated timing, animators came up with go-to actions for Tom and Jerry: Characters run in place as an anticipation to running; they back-peddle or slide to stop quickly as in Jerry's entrance to **Tennis Chumps** (1949); they move in big arcs on turns; run in place to get traction; perform big anticipations on get-ups; use takes and double-takes on expression changes, etc. All things to keep the action continuously moving.

The main Tom and Jerry animators were Kenneth Muse, Ray Patterson, Irven Spence, and Ed Barge. Muse and Patterson, both former Disney animators, animated with more naturalism, so they handled more of the personality scenes.

Ken Muse, who had been Freddy Moore's assistant, "always had a sense of the extra grace note," said Eric Goldberg. "It's not just that a character arrives at a pose, but it will recoil a little bit and the hair will catch up, you'll see the tail flow. It's all those kinds of little touches that are very Disneyesque."[213] Muse's animation flowed. He seemed mindful of creating a nice pattern to his motions, as when he animated Tom laying on the couch and using Jerry as a paddleball in the opening to **Triplet Trouble** (1952); or Tom playing the piano — which he did several times, first in **The Zoot Cat** (1944), then to perfection in the Academy Award winning cartoon **The Cat Concerto** (1947), and also in **Saturday Evening Puss** (1950). Other notable Muse scenes are Tom catching 17 lightbulbs that Jerry throws off a fireplace, then rocking Butch to sleep in **Quiet Please!** (1945); or Tom singing "Is You Is or Is You Ain't My Baby" in **Solid Serenade** (1946); and the battle on the golf course in **Tee for Two** (1945).

At Disney, Ray Patterson animated the marvelous clown firemen in the "Save My Baby!" sequence in **Dumbo**. He also animated several Pluto cartoons, including the best scene in **Bone Trouble** (1940) — Pluto encountering a hall of mirrors. Perhaps his experience with Pluto was why he was given so many scenes of Spike the bulldog at MGM. A strong personality animator and great at dialogue, Patterson, along with Irv Spence, "did a lot in setting the tone for the personality animation of Tom and Jerry," said Hanna. "Give the character a mind and the personality comes out," said Patterson. "It's like Pluto — he'd stop and think."[214] In **Mouse Cleaning** (1948), Patterson shows his mastery of personality animation in a marvelous sequence of a pouty-faced Tom making a muddy mess of a newly cleaned kitchen. Other notable Patterson scenes include Tom discovering he can swim underwater in **The Cat and the Mermouse** (1949); Tom lip-syncing to "If You're Ever Down in Texas, Look Me Up" in **Texas Tom** (1950); and Jerry's eccentric, singing Uncle Pecos in **Pecos Pest** (1955).

Irv Spence, who was the most cartoony of the Tom and Jerry animators, first worked for Charles Mintz, then Ub Iwerks, and then for Tex Avery at Leon Schlesinger Productions. "I like action," he said. "That's what they wanted on Tom. He had a lot of gusto."[215] More Tex Avery than Disney, Spence chose funny over realism. In *Quiet Please!* (1945), Spence animated Spike blown up by a giant firecracker, landing in an exaggerated squash, then immediately popping up into an anticipation pose and rolling up his sleeve. He charges after Tom, his legs a single spinning rubber tire, using a dry brush effect rather than actual steps. There is none of the naturalism Muse or Patterson would have put into it, but it's funny. Spence takes the same liberties in *Zoot Cat* (1944) where he animated the Jive dance between Tom and his girlfriend Toots. Instead of accurately capturing the Jive dance movement with shifting weight and breaking joints, Spence animates a moving funny pose, alternating each foot kicking out with three drawings — left foot kicking out, right foot kicking out, and an inbetween with both feet favoring the foot on the ground to help indicate switching legs. In *Polka-Dot Puss* (1949) Spence animates Tom laying on the couch, using Jerry as a yo-yo. It's the same gag Muse would animate in *Triplet Trouble* (1952) but without Muse's finesse. Spence's animation seems to smooth out more in the 1950s but is still funny. In *Little Runaway* (1952), Spence's Jerry leaves his house wearing his swim trunks, takes a deep breath, runs, and dives into the backyard pond only to crash into a seal that has run away from the circus. Later, Spence animates Jerry tap-dancing with a dead fish.

Ed Barge was another animator who came from Harman-Ising. "He was a very quiet guy, almost bashful," said Hanna. "But a good animator. Eddie was probably a little better at animating Tom than Jerry, but he did a good job on either one."[216] In a way Barge was like Les Clark, a very good animator who, for the most part, animated the less glamorous scenes. But when he did get a gag scene, he handled it masterfully. "It was Barge's hallmark to give weight and solidity to the characters," said Mark Kausler. "One gets an extraordinary sensation of volume and a three-dimensional quality to his animation."[217]

Tom and Jerry starred in 114 theatrical cartoons.[218]

In 1957, MGM abruptly shut down their animation department. TV was cutting into profits and the higher-ups at MGM decided that, instead of making new cartoons, they would just re-release the old ones. Hanna and Barbera decided to go into television. "Instead of the 25,000 to 40,000 drawings we used in a 'Tom and Jerry' short, we were able to make a cartoon with 1,200 to 1,800 drawings," Barbera said in 1988. "But you had to be an animator to understand where to use those drawings and how to use camera moves to give them more life. We learned you can cover a lot of ground with dialogue."[219]

"In order to be a good HB animator, you first should be a good Disney animator, because if you learn how to animate full then the other is very easy, much easier," said animator Mike Lah. "The fellas that never worked at Disney and never learned how to become good animators are still having a miserable time doing a lot of it and don't make much money at it."[220]

Tex Avery at MGM

Frederick Bean "Tex" Avery was a modest man for an animation genius — and a distant relative "of Daniel Boone and the notorious Judge Roy Bean."[221] Praise embarrassed Avery. "He'd rather back off than step forward and take justifiable bows,"[222] said Mike Maltese, Chuck Jones' top story man. Heck Allen, Avery's writer at MGM, said Avery worked alone because "he just doesn't want to argue with people."[223]

Avery began his animation career inking cels on the Oswald cartoons at the Winkler studio. "From there he went to Universal, again as an inker," wrote Michael Barrier. "He moved up rapidly, becoming an animator by 1930."[224] From Universal, Avery went to Warner Bros. and introduced himself to animation head Leon Schlesinger as a director. "Hey, I'm a director," Avery recalled. "Hell! I was no more a director than nothing, but with my loud mouth, I talked him into it."[225] "Leon never checked," said Chuck Jones. "So, he hired him as a director."[226]

At Warner Bros. Avery is credited with inventing Bugs Bunny in **A Wild Hare** (1940) and Elmer Fudd in **Little Red Walking Hood** (1937). "There were a few Bugs Bunny's made before Tex," said Chuck Jones. "But Tex was the first to have him say, "What's up, doc?" and give him what you might call controlled insanity, as opposed to wild insanity. Originally, Bugs was very much like Daffy."[227]

Avery left Warner Bros. in 1941 after being suspended by Schlesinger for refusing to cut a gag from the Bugs Bunny cartoon **Heckling Hare**. "When Tex Avery came to MGM in the early 40s from Warner Brothers, he really hit his stride,"[228] wrote Leonard Maltin. With bigger budgets, Avery "could perfect things more," said Eric Goldberg. "He could hone more. So, he could make fewer cartoons more perfectly."[229]

"Tex Avery came over and started this fast timing," said animator Michael Lah. "It was so fun, his pictures began overwhelming everybody,"[230]

As Bill Hanna could attest, Avery's timing set the bar. The bullied white kitten blowing a whistle whenever he's in trouble in **Bad Luck Blacky** (1949); George and Junior, the dimwitted dog-hunters in a high-speed motorboat, chasing a duckling onto land and slamming into a rock wall in **Lucky Ducky** (1948); Droopy coming home to his junkyard home and putting on a record at the start of **Dixie Land Droopy** (1954); and all of **The First Bad Man** (1955) a prehistoric history of Texas outlaws, are just a few examples of Avery's masterful timing.

What many animators don't always recognize is that there are a lot of quiet moments in Avery cartoons. "A lot of the stuff that was funny was because of the way it was timed," said Lah. "Not just the speed, but comparative timing between pieces of action."[231]

"If you look at any of Tex's pictures, with the wild movement and the wild animation," said Chuck Jones, "He'd always start his pictures in a very quiet way. You know these characters were going to do something wild, but you didn't know when, and that was the whole point. So much in today's television, people start out crazy and go crazy. Even Roger Rabbit, which is very well done, the guy never came to a rest."[232]

Humor in Avery's cartoons also comes from the strong poses, especially the later shorts, and the economic way the characters move from pose to pose. "We wanted to get more gags in," said Avery. "We'll time this as fast as we can because we've got so much more to come!"[233]

In **Rock-a-Bye Bear** (1952) the "warden" of the city dog pound asks the dogs behind bars, "Any of you slobs want a job?" A little dog "volunteers" Spike by sticking him with a hat pin. Listening to the warden telling Spike what the job offers (free room and board, private bath, all the steaks you can eat, plus two-hundred bucks a week), the little dog goes through a series of emotions, from schadenfreude to jealousy to devious scheming. The sequence is easy to follow because the poses are so strong and the transitions between poses are so quick. "The timing was so fast that you didn't have time to put in inbetweens," said Lah. "You'd lose the meaning of the poses."[234]

Avery would take this further in Droopy's **Double Trouble** (1951) when Droopy looks around the kitchen for Spike — his head darting from pose to pose without any inbetweens. And further still in **Symphony in Slang** (1951), a hysterical minimalist cartoon where "Avery alternates fully animated characters in certain scenes with absolutely still drawings in others."[235]

Avery began using UPA-style backgrounds to further clarify gags. "UPA started the new trend in backgrounds," said Avery. "I liked them; they were so simple, and your characters read better."[236] The wild "Tex Avery take" is a genre of its own. There still is no one better at takes than Avery. A few examples: **Little Rural Riding Hood** (1949), **Ventriloquist Cat** (1950), and **Northwest Hounded Police** (1946), which is basically a short about takes. Again, Avery's takes wouldn't be as funny if he hadn't set-up the take with quieter contrasting moments.

Contrast can be seen in the Avery classic **Magical Maestro** (1952) when the Great Poochini, his body a held drawing, watches in boredom as Mysto the Magician wildly demonstrates his surefire magic act. "If you've got two people working in a scene," said Avery. "Slow one of them down until he's static if you want to build up to a laugh with the other one."[237]

"Avery's sense of the absurd," wrote Leonard Maltin. "Flourished in a world of self-contained logic. Even his craziest gags made sense — on their own terms."[238] Characters literally broke apart as in **The Chump Champ** (1950); turned themselves inside-out in **Slap Happy Lion** (1947); ran off the film frame in **Dumb-Hounded** (1943), and then again in **Northwest Hounded Police**; or ran past a sign that read "Technicolor Ends Here" entering a world of black and white in **Lucky Ducky**.

With all his wildness, Avery's cartoons still adhere to the principles of animation. In **Deputy Droopy** (1955) the lead villain Slim repeatedly slaps his accomplice Shorty for something dumb he did. Slim shows successive breaking of joints, squash and stretch, and overlap throughout the action. In Droopy's **Double Trouble**, Droopy and Drippy exit the kitchen and step down onto the patio — their ears showing overlap as they drop. It's a subtle detail handled with enough naturalism to make even taking a step funny.

"I couldn't compete with Disney, and I didn't attempt to," said Avery. "I attempted to do things that Disney wouldn't dare to do."[239]

"Tex never knew how good he was,"[240] said Chuck Jones.

The Auteurs of Termite Terrace

"Under the Warner system I had nearly complete creative control over my own films, within severe money and time limitations,"[241] said Bob Clampett.

Bob Clampett, Chuck Jones, and Friz Freleng were the core directors at Warner Bros. during the Golden Age of Animation, and each director was, in a sense, an independent filmmaker making their own personal shorts with their own recognizable style. Auteurs.

Bob Clampett

Of all the directors at Warner Bros., it was perhaps Bob Clampett who pushed the limits of animation, and taste, the furthest. "The word that really comes to mind is energy," said Leonard Maltin, talking about Clampett. "Energy is the thing above all that separates his cartoons and kind of comic anarchy in that energetic presentation."[242]

There's almost constant motion in a Clampett cartoon. Characters' heads change size based on the emotion of the scene. Their eyes stretch, they gesture in forced perspective, and often break the fourth wall to talk to the audience. In *Bugs Bunny Gets the Boid* (1942) Bugs Bunny, thinking he's been horribly mangled, turns to the audience and says, "Gruesome, isn't it?" Exaggeration is pushed past 10 up to 11 as in *The Old Grey Hare* (1944) when an elderly Bugs Bunny chokes an elderly Elmer Fudd — looking very much like Ollie Johnston. "He was a frantic director,"[243] said animator Phil Monroe.

Clampett wasn't afraid to use jump cuts, as when Porky asks Daffy to sit on an egg to hatch it in *Baby Bottleneck* (1946). He'd also switch animators in the middle of a scene as in *Book Revue* (1946) when Bob Mckimson starts a scene and Bill Melendez finishes it, or Bill Melendez starts a scene and Manny Gould finishes it. Anything was possible in a Clampett cartoon.

Though he started out as an animator, Clampett didn't think much of his drawing ability. He would have layout artist and animator, Tom McKimson, Bob's brother, draw the animation layout sketches for him. Clampett would then act out the scenes for his animators while drawing on a piece of paper over the layout sketches "indicating how he wanted the action in a scene to flow."[244] "I would sketch with a big, soft grease pencil. The scribbles and the dynamics of it," he told Barrier. "The paths of actions, and the anticipations and squashes and stretches, the changes in perspective and size, like a hand swinging up and past the camera."[245]

"I had very good animators at Warner's [who] always tried to do each scene exactly in the manner that I had originally conceived it,"[246] said Clampett. Izzy Ellis' hysterical scene of Daffy Duck pacing restlessly waiting for the mailman to bring him his comic book in *The Great Piggy Bank Robbery* (1946); Bill Melendez's unforgettable scene of Daffy running on a conveyor belt with an impossibly long left leg in *Baby Bottleneck*; and numerous Manny Gould scenes, including two gruesome cats in a horse costume in *A Gruesome Twosome* (1945) and Daffy Duck trying to get ahold of himself after the draft board calls him in *Draftee Daffy* (1945).

It's impossible to talk about the Clampett style without talking about animator Rod Scribner.

Scribner's animation was probably the most in tune with Clampett's manic style. Influenced by comic strip artist George Lichty, Scribner had a loose, fluid way of animating. He aggressively pushed overlap and foreshortening, showing a lot of gnashing teeth as *in Falling Hare* (1943), when an angry Bugs Bunny chases after the Gremlin with a wrench, or in *Tortoise Wins by a Hare* (1943), when Bugs paces furiously trying to figure out how the Tortoise always wins. Scribner was "obsessed with wrinkles," said animator Mark Kausler. "He loved drawing them."[247] Scribner's tour de force wrinkle scene is probably from *A Corny Concerto* (1943) when Bugs faints and wrinkles up after being shot by a squirrel.

"Rod Scribner learned under Bob McKimson, to a certain degree," said Phil Monroe. "However, Rod went on, over and above that, after he knew the basics, and he turned out to be an excellent animator."[248]

Bob McKimson was the Yin to Scribner's Yang. McKimson "really balanced out the insanity with his beautiful, beautiful animation,"[249] said Jerry Beck. McKimson "was one of the first animators outside of the Disney studio whose animation had some of the same refinement and precision that the best Disney animators brought to their work,"[250] said Michael Barrier.

"My mother, being an artist, taught each of us [Bob and his brothers, animator Chuck and layout artist Tom] everything she knew about drawing from the time we could hold a pencil," said McKimson. McKimson pursued 'additional fine art training at local art schools'[251] and studied with individual instructors, like Donald Graham. "I went for one semester to Don Graham's class. He spent most of his time talking to me," said McKimson. "He was fascinated with the fact that we could talk anatomy... I learned quite a bit from Don."[252]

Because McKimson was such a great animator and draftsman, he was made head of animation at Warner Bros. He refined the design of Bugs Bunny 'from the oval-faced rabbit of the [Tex] Avery cartoon [*A Wild Hare* (1940)] to the softer-muzzled, longer toothed, and more expressive Bugs of the early 1940s. Soon, the McKimson Bugs was adopted by all the directors at Warner Bros. cartoons.'[253] "Bob would check the other animators to make sure they were keeping the characters consistent with the model sheets,"[254] wrote Martha Sigall, inker and painter at Warner Bros. McKimson "taught his animators the mechanics, the basic mechanics of animation, and then what they did on their own, over and above that, was really good,"[255] said Phil Monroe. Monroe, along with Ken Harris and Ben Washam were some of the animators McKimson trained. "I always thank McKimson for making me an animator,"[256] said Monroe.

McKimson 'animated for both Avery and Clampett and he finished his animation career with Clampett in 1944.'[257] Some of the wonderful scenes McKimson animated for Avery and Clampett are: Bugs Bunny sitting on a bomb reading 'Victory Thru Hare Power' in *A Falling Hare*; Bugs faking his death in Elmer's arms in *A Wild Hare* and again in *The Old Grey Hare*; Daffy Duck channeling Danny Kaye in the extended song number in *Book Review* (1946); and the beautiful character animation of Bugs Bunny pretending to be an Italian waiter in *Hare Ribbin* (1944).

Bob McKimson would become a director when Clampett abruptly left Warner Bros. in 1945 after Eddie Selzer replaced Leon Schlesinger as the head of animation. Though he directed some classic cartoons such as *Daffy Doodles*, *Acrobatty Bunny* and *Walky Talky Hawky* from 1946, *Easter Yeggs* (1947) with its obnoxious little kid ("I wanna Easter egg! I wanna Easter egg!") and his creepy William Faulkner Southern Gothic family, and *Gorilla My Dreams* (1948), McKimson was arguably a better animator and part of team that brought Bob Clampett's bizarre vision to life.

"'The illusion of life' applied to certain kinds of animation," said Michael Barrier. "But what you have in Bob Clampett's animation is not the illusion of life — but life itself."[258]

Chuck Jones

"In Chuck's cartoons there's an awareness of the camera that a lot of directors don't have,"[259] said Eric Goldberg. *Bully for Bugs* (1953) has many Orson Wellesian low-angle shots of Bugs and Toro the bull. *My Favorite Duck* (1942) features a terrific cross-cutting sequence of Porky Pig rubbing two sticks of dynamite together as Daffy Duck covers his ears. After the inevitable explosion, we see Daffy in closeup, his pupils are Porky's silhouette falling to the ground.

Jones' loved long forced-perspective background pans. An example of a forced perspective pan is the long pan down the 'Umpire' State Building in *Much Ado About Nutting* (1953). There are more in *Mouse Wreckers* (1949) and *Conrad the Sailor* (1942).

Editing played a big part in Jones' cartoons. He said that Conrad the Sailor was influenced by Russian filmmaker Sergei Eisenstein.[260] The ending of *Drip-Along Daffy* (1951) features a terrific Eisenstein-like montage for the 'Western-type' gunfight. *Duck Dodgers in the 24½th Century* (1953) "had 95 different cuts in it, different shots," said Jones. "*What's Opera Doc?* (1957) had 104."[261]

"Part of Chuck's coming of age at Warner Brother's, as a director, was experimenting with the look of the films," said Leonard Maltin. "The actual design of the films."[262] *The Aristo-Cat* (1943) features a production design by John McGrew. "The dynamic design of wallpaper decoration combined with outrageous pans and camera work took me by force," wrote Michael Sporn. "The violently repeating patterns reach to the forefront of this short. All of this exuberant design completely acted to support the character's state of mind. Anxiety, fear, and terror jumped from the backgrounds."[263]

In Jones' later cartoons, his backgrounds became more abstract — more like UPA, the studio Jones helped start. Working with top production designers Maurice Noble on *Duck Dodgers in the 24½th Century* and *What's Opera, Doc?* and Robert Gribbroek on *Barbary-Coast Bunny* (1956) and *One Froggy Evening* (1955), Jones created some of the most visually stunning cartoons ever.

"At the beginning I kind of tried to imitate the Disney style to find out what the heck it was all about,"[264] said Jones. "There was only one guy that tried cute stuff," said Jones' writer Michael Maltese. "Chuck, at the time—and he'll admit it. Had the Disney Syndrome: the urge to try to make the most beautiful cartoons going."[265] Once Jones got the painfully cute Sniffles the Mouse cartoons out of his system, the Chuck Jones style emerged.

Jones' layout poses "were of a more understated quality with very subtle emotional shadings,"[266] said John Canemaker. Jones "would go through every scene and make a drawing, several poses in each scene, of attitude and expressions and size and composition, just of the characters,"[267] said animator Phil Roman. Animators then took Jones' layout poses and began animation.

There's a misconception that Jones' animators just inbetweened his layout poses. "Chuck could always draw well, but he couldn't animate,"[268] said Phil Monroe. "You could either do it his way, exactly... or you could start using your imagination a little bit and changing his stuff as you went along... His "A" animators did that."[269]

A couple of examples of how Jones' best animators went beyond the layout poses are Phil Monroe's hysterical animation of Charlie Dog begging for his life in *The Awful Orphan* (1949) and Ken Harris' remarkably weighty scene of Henery Hawk struggling to carry Daffy in *You Were Never Duckier* (1948).

Monroe was an adept personality animator. Bugs Bunny rescuing Scotsman Angus MacRory from his own bagpipes in *My Bunny Lies over the Sea* (1948), the great opening scenes of Daffy Duck in *You Were Never Duckier*, "You mean I came all the way from Dubuque for a measly five bucks?"

and Bugs Bunny shaving Elmer Fudd in **Rabbit of Seville** (1950) are a few good examples of how Monroe didn't just move his characters but expressed their intrinsic personality.

"Ken Harris was a great action animator," said Michael Barrier. "Particularly good at animating action that was physically plausible but ridiculous at the same time."[270] Harris "loved to dance"[271] and animated most of the dance sequences for Jones: the classic scene of Bugs Bunny tap dancing in **Mississippi Hare** (1949); the ballet sequence in **What's Opera Doc?** (1957); Bugs waltzing with Elmer Fudd in **Rabbit of Seville** (1950); and the unforgettable high-stepping Michigan J. Frog dance in **One Froggy Evening**. "Harris's animation of Mama Bear's stage performance for her fuming husband in **A Bear for Punishment** [1951] is a masterpiece,"[272] said Jones. "Ken had this way of working where he's drawing but it looks like he's just writing a letter,"[273] said Phil Roman.

Ben Washam "was brilliant with dialogue,"[274] said Jones. "More often than not Chuck had him animate the last scene in a Bugs cartoon."[275] Two examples are Bugs Bunny saying, "ain't I a stinker!" at the end of **Duck Amuck** (1953), and "Remember, mud spelled backwards is dum(b)!" at the end of **Operation: Rabbit** (1952). During **Duck Amuck**, Washam was ready to quit after showing Jones a long pencil test, without the dialogue track, of Daffy talking. Adding dialogue to a pencil test was too costly at the budget conscious Warner Bros. "I had a terrible row with Chuck, I thought I was gonna pack my bags about that time. I had a long, long scene of Daffy just talking," said Washam. "I timed it with very positive hesitates. Sometimes holds...And he declared that it didn't work and had to be done over."[276] After screening the scene with the soundtrack, Jones admitted it worked. "He became a truly great animator," said Jones. "One of the most sensitive, one of the most subtle — able to extract laughter by the quirk of a ducky eyebrow, the flick of a rabbit's eye."[277]

In **The Dover Boys at Pimento University or the Rivals of Roquefort Hall** (1942), Jones and animator Bobe Cannon used smears (quick, elongated inbetweens — see Ch. 23) to dart quickly from pose to pose, parodying melodramatic 19th Century theatrical acting. Ben Washam and Lloyd Vaughan would make animated smears into an art form. Though Clampett employed smears in **A Tale of Two Kitties** from that same year, "the effect is completely different," wrote Michael Barrier. "Clampett calls attention to the distortions — whereas Jones calls attention to the poses."[278] Vaughan's smears in **Long-Haired Hare** (1949) where Bugs Bunny pretends to be the conductor Leopold Stokowski, and Washam's smears of Wile E. Coyote in **Zipping Along** (1953) are masterful.

Lloyd Vaughan's dream was to work for Disney, but he was turned down because he "didn't quite come up to their standards and also that he was too old to start — he was 26."[279] Vaughan animated the classic scene of Bugs and Daffy arguing about whether it's duck season or wabbit season in **Rabbit Fire** (1951); Daffy as polka-dotted flower-headed platypus in **Duck Amuck**; and Bugs' introduction to Toro the bull, "Of course, you know, this means war?" in **Bully for Bugs** (1953) — a line taken from the Marx Brothers, one of Jones' comedic influences. (**Hair-Raising Hare** (1946) is littered with Groucho references.)

Jones experimented with animation, mise-en-scène, and subject matter — some of his films are incredibly dark, such as his Three Bears shorts featuring the dysfunctional Bear family.

"If you really start to study his films, you'll see a great filmmaking director at work," said Canemaker. "He was an extraordinarily intelligent man, a very gifted man and sensitive man, and all of that went into his work. And I think he extended the emotional parameters of animation."[280]

Friz Freleng

Isadore "Friz" Freleng's cartoons may not have had Clampett's surrealism, or Jones' elegance, but they were funny. Freleng was a master of timing. "I don't think I've ever worked with an artist, an animation director, a layout person, an animator that had the sense of timing that Friz Freleng did,"[281] said David DePatie, producer of Freleng's Pink Panther series.

Unlike other directors, Freleng first timed out his storyboards using bar sheets. In a nutshell, bar sheets allow the director to break down the timing of the whole film into musical beats. "Some guys," said Freleng. "Worked only on exposure sheets and just wrote down the action, and the musician had to make it work. . . But I made it easy for Carl [composer Carl Stalling], by using bar sheets to start with... I worked with four or eight-bar phrases; if a guy ran for two bars and in the next bar he fell down or something, I'd put a mark there for a bang so it'd go da...da... da... bang — in rhythm."[282] A good example of what Freleng is talking about is in a scene from *Baseball Bugs* (1946). As a batter for the Gas-House Gorillas rounds the bases the animation is evenly timed, da...da...da..., until Bugs Bunny tags him out at home plate — bang.

Another wonderfully timed Freleng scene is the end of *Slick Hare* (1947). Virgil Ross animated Bugs posing as a waiter ordering pies from Elmer, "One coconut custard pie with whip cream!," picking up the pies ("Pick up pie!"), leaving the kitchen and immediately returning to throw them at Elmer ("Your pie, sir!") all while keeping a quick vaudevillian pace. "I was really proud of that thing for the timing where it came in and out with the pies — it worked perfectly," said Freleng. "I look at it now, and it's amazing how it timed out. I don't know how I did it. I couldn't do it again."[283]

"Everything Friz does threatens to become a musical at any time," said director Greg Ford. "It could become a musical at the drop of a hat."[284] "Freleng set the tempo of any given character movement like a musical."[285] For instance, characters in Freleng cartoons often ascend or descend stairs in 4/4 time as in Little *Red Riding Rabbit* (1944), *Back Alley Oproar* (1948), *Buccaneer Bunny* (1948), and *Putty Tat Trouble* (1951).

Unlike Jones, Freleng would have layout artist Hawley Pratt draw the layout poses. Animators would then be assigned scenes. Unfortunately, Freleng didn't always know what he wanted from the animation until he saw it. There was "a reluctance on Freleng's part to commit himself," wrote Michael Barrier. "Freleng's animators at Warner Bros. had to bear in mind while animating every scene that he might have to redo their animation — with no extra time allowed — if Freleng decided when he saw it that he wanted something else."[286]

"Friz would bring us in and decide what needed to be changed," said Virgil Ross, one of Freleng's top animators. "We were assigned just individual scenes with no idea what had happened before or what was happening after. It was pretty hard to judge them that way because in order to analyze them properly, you really should know what it's going to be hooked up with. If they had run the scenes connected with all of the others, I doubt we would have had to make so many changes."[287]

"Every guy had his own technique," said Freleng. "Gerry Chiniquy would always do dance stuff because he could analyze it mechanically; he's the only one I could do that with. Virgil Ross was a great animator for personality, and Art Davis was great on action — the wild stuff."[288]

Gerry Chiniquy (shin-a-KEE), a former child actor who bore a "striking resemblance to Gene Kelly"[289]was "a personality animator who was best at drawing cantankerous characters like Granny and Yosemite Sam."[290] As Freleng mentioned, Chiniquy animated just about every Freleng dance scene: Bugs and Yosemite Sam soft shoeing in *Bugs Bunny Rides Again* (1948); Bugs dancing as Carmen Miranda in *Slick Hare* (1947); and Bugs dancing down the street, "Look I'm dancin'!" in *A Hare Grows in Manhattan* (1947) — to name a few. Some other scenes Chiniquy animated are the terrific opening to *Rhapsody Rabbit* (1946) of Bugs walking onstage and preparing to play the piano only to be interrupted by a person in the audience who can't stop coughing; the hysterical scene of Daffy in the shooting gallery in *His Bitter Half* (1950); the badminton scene in *Bad Ol' Putty Tat* (1949); Bug's classic pitching, "Eh, I think I'll perplex him with my slowball," in *Baseball Bugs* (1946); and the majority of *I Taw a Putty Tat* (1948). Chiniquy liked to draw Bugs thin-headed and cross-eyed, notes Don Yowp.[291] Chiniquy "was always so meticulous," said Phil Monroe. "He studied hard, and he just made himself into a good animator."[292]

Virgil Ross' animation was smoother and subtler, so he handled a lot of acting scenes in Freleng cartoons. "I always had a feeling for flowing motion, and I don't like to see anything jerky," said Ross. "What pleases me is watching something like ice-skaters, or Fred Astaire. That's the type of thing I always liked to put into my animation, something with a flowing quality."[293]

Among the scenes Ross animated are Bugs Bunny's interview with "Lolly" in *A Hare Grows in Manhattan*; the scene of Yosemite Sam wooing Granny to take her $50 million, and Bugs Bunny masquerading as a Frenchman slapping Sam with a brick in a glove in *Hare Trimmed* (1953). Ross was proud of the cocky, Curly-Howard-Three-Stooges walk Bugs does at the end of the scene; Sylvester trying on hats in a department store in *A Bird in a Guilty Cage* (1952), a scene taken from Buster Keaton in *Steamboat Bill Jr.* (1928); Bugs helping Rocky get dressed in *Racketeer Rabbit* (1946); and a chatty Bugs in the back seat of a bank robbers car being told to "Shaddup shadding up!" in *Bugs and Thugs* (1954), a remake of *Racketeer Rabbit*. An accomplished jazz piano player, Ross' masterpiece is perhaps Bugs' playing piano in *Rhapsody Rabbit* (1946). "If you've ever looked at Virgil's originals, they're very sculpted," said Mark Kausler.. "He really worked hard to get the construction of the heads right and where the shoulders are placed, the hats - all the stuff that's very difficult to draw."[294]

Art Davis, the 'first true in-betweener in American animation'[295] assisting Dick Huemer at Fleischer's, is better known as a director having taken over Clampett's unit when Clampett left Warner Bros. As an animator, "Davis worked "straight ahead," without first analyzing the scene frame-by-frame," wrote Chris Walsh, "He worked very roughly, then reviewed and revised the completed group of drawings, retiming the animation by dropping or adding drawings."[296] "He was very broad," said Freleng. "I'd have to tone him down."[297] An example of Davis' delightful animation for Freleng is the vacuum sequence from *Canned Feud* (1951). But it could be argued that Davis' best animation was for Robert McKimson's cartoons, such as the scene of Bugs dressed as Pagliacci the clown singing "laugh, clown, laugh" in *Acrobatty Bunny* (1946).

Ken Champin and Manuel "Manny" Perez, were wonderful animators who were given the less crucial scenes to animate. Champin's scene in *Kit for Cat* (1948) of Sylvester trying to frame a kitten by pouring milk on him, then when it backfires banging his head in frustration, and Perez's scene of Bugs trying to hide, as an annoying parrot keeps pointing out his hiding places "He's in there! He's in there!" from *Buccaneer Bunny* demonstrate what adept personality animators they were.

"I think Friz Freleng gets taken for granted sometimes because he isn't as flamboyant, let's say, as some of the other directors and he doesn't show off as much," said Leonard Maltin. "But then you look at the body of his work, and you look at some of the specific gems that he made over the years and realize just how many really wonderful cartoons he made and you realize that he takes a backseat to nobody."[298]

Richard Williams and Persistence of Vision

Richard Williams decided to become an animator when he first saw Disney's **Snow White and the Seven Dwarf**s at age five. Ten years later, at a Toronto art gallery he saw paintings by Rembrandt. "I didn't know anything about fine art, but I saw these Rembrandts and I went to pieces," said Williams. "It made such an impact on me that I immediately dropped anything to do with animation or cartoons."[299]

A gifted artist, Williams paid his way through the Ontario College of Art by drawing advertisements. "Those commercial art jobs also allowed him to take two years off to paint seriously in Ibiza."[300] On that Spanish island in the Mediterranean Sea, Williams got an idea for an animated film. "I decided to go to England because television was opening up."[301] Williams worked "freelance as an animation director, making television commercials for George Dunning,[302] head of UPA's London office and future director of **Yellow Submarine** (1968), to finance his short, **The Little Island**. The Little Island won the BAFTA award for Best Animated Film in 1959. "I never wanted a studio," said Williams. "But I was friends with George, and he let me down on a lot of stuff, and I just said, "Oh, I'm going into competition now.'"[303]

"I had a master plan," said Williams. "I decided to become the very best on the commercial side and then master the techniques of the art of personality animation. I wanted it all."[304] The Richard Williams Studio would eventually animate over 2,500[305] TV commercials and over a dozen film titles, earning over 175 international awards.

In the late 1960s, Williams started bringing in animation veterans he could learn from. A big fan of Chuck Jones' Roadrunner and Coyote cartoons, he first coaxed Ken Harris out of retirement. Harris "traveled to London from 4 to 6 months each year for the next twelve years."[306] When Harris saw the animated sequences the Williams studio made for **The Charge of the Light Brigade** (1968), with a mid-19th century crosshatch style and elaborate cross-dissolves, he said to Williams, "All that cross-hatching. All that work. But it don't move too good."[307]

"At 35 years old, already the head of a successful animation studio," wrote Williams' daughter Natasha, "Dick realized he would literally have to go back to the drawing board and develop his animation skills."[308] "When I first worked with Ken Harris," said Williams. "I was amazed at what he could do. I've since learned there are principles that he's using. A lot of it is knack. But a lot of it, as Milt Kahl says, is so simple. The basic things are simple, but nobody knows them. I think it takes two to five years to learn."[309]

Harris' animation of the Pink Panther in the credits for **The Return of The Pink Panther** (1975) is outstanding, and the dynamic camera moves foreshadow Williams' future work.

Through a producer of a commercial he was working on, Williams was introduced to Art Babbitt. "He had seen some of our work and he said, well, you don't know what you're doing, obviously, but you're doing an honest job." And I said, "Teach us, please."[310] Babbitt took a leave of absence from Hanna Barbera in Hollywood, where he was directing commercials, Williams shut down his London studio for a month, and Babbitt gave his now-famous masterclass. "Dick took copious notes," wrote

Tom Sito. "And they became one of the most copied, underground how-to books in film history."[311] These would be some of the same notes Tissa David would use for her animation classes in NYC. 'Babbitt ended up staying and working with Williams for the next ten years.'[312]

Chuck Jones had also seen the titles to the film *Charge of the Light Brigade* and wanted Williams to recreate the crosshatch style for a project he was producing for ABC television — *A Christmas Carol* (1971). Unlike *Light Brigade*, *Christmas Carol* would have Ken Harris who would sit on a stool behind Williams. "Dick would make a drawing," said Jones. "And then Ken would tell him how to change the drawing."[313]

With only nine months to animate the half-hour special, Williams and the staff "slept under our desks . . . it was a tremendous race against time."[314] When Williams called Jones to tell him he feared he wasn't going to meet the deadline, Jones sent over three of his top animators to help: Abe Levitow, George Nicholas, and Hal Ambro. "Abe Levitow taught and animated for the studio," said Michael Sporn. "His scenes for *The Christmas Carol* are among the most powerful."[315]

Though made for television, Jones submitted *A Christmas Carol* for an Oscar and Williams won the Academy Award for Best Animated Short Film the following year.

With the success of *A Christmas Carol*, Williams began bringing in more animation masters to speak at the studio, including Milt Kahl, Frank Thomas, John Hubley, Chuck Jones, and Ollie Johnston.[316]

"It was fantastic," said Williams. "To go back to school and find out how much you still had to learn."[317] "Disney's *The Old Mill* was a trial run for *Snow White*," said Williams. "*A Christmas Carol* was trial run for *Nasruddin*."[318] *The Amazing Nasruddin*, eventually retitled *The Thief and the Cobbler*, would be Williams' unfinished magnum opus. "The film seems to have been made to challenge animators," wrote Michael Sporn. "The animation for this film is beyond complicated and done so extraordinarily well."[319]

"Cuts are a visual drumbeat," said Williams. "I want it to just flow."[320]

The camera is almost constantly moving in *The Thief*, tracking the action. This meant "drawing every frame and drawing every frame in perspective."[321] The Cobbler sliding down an animated banister-like kinetic versions of John McGrew backgrounds; Ken Harris' spectacular animation of the Thief, his head surrounded by a swarm of flies, balancing on a tightrope while the camera zooms in and out; a polo match on an animated background reminiscent of Oskar Fischinger's hills in Fantasia's Toccata and Fugue sequence; floating bubbles reflecting a tiled floor; rendered flowers spinning in space; endless forced perspective pans of Errol le Cain's intricate paintings; culminating in a layout tour de force by the genius Roy Naisbitt of the War Machine sequence. All without the aid of computers.

"We were doing such complex things on *The Thief* with Roy and the Camera Department, it was unbelievable," said cameraman John Leatherbarrow. "We had backgrounds like rolls of wallpaper. We literally had to stick them to the walls and move them across."[322] *A Christmas Carol* brought in a new feature film project — *Raggedy Ann and Andy: A Musical Adventure* (1977). Williams "seemed the only person we could hit upon who was capable artistically of equaling the early Disney things,"[323] said producer Richard Horner.

"The thing to do, if I have to do commercial work, which I'm going to have to do," thought Williams, is "I'll do my own work in parallel. So, that's what I've done, I've just kept chewing — gnawing at the bone on my own — learning, learning, studying, studying, and constantly doing the commercial work at the same time."[324]

Notable animators were brought in to work on **Raggedy Ann and Andy**: Grim Natwick, Tissa David, Hal Ambro, Gerry Chiniquy, Corny Cole, Irv Spence — and Emery Hawkins, who animated **The Greedy**, the eternally hungry taffy-pit monster,[325] which is arguably the best sequence in the film. "It's masterful,"[326] said Art Babbitt.

Michael Sporn, who worked on **Raggedy Ann**, described Williams' working habits. "He would draw his drawings incredibly light going quickly through the entire scene. The pencil line of that first round was almost invisible. Then he'd go back and work over those lines just as lightly and just as quickly. Then he'd do it again, and again, and again. This gave him the opportunity of changing and adjusting as he went along. It also is a method somewhat similar to the one that Tytla and [Norm] Ferguson used in the 1930s. They'd go for the "forces" and then go back and build up from there."[327] In 1985 Williams met with Robert Watts, the vice-president of European Lucasfilm, and showed him a ten-minute clip from **Thief**, hoping to get backing from George Lucas. Lucas wasn't interested, but Watts showed it to Steven Spielberg who was "blown away".[328]

Spielberg was producing **Who Framed Roger Rabbit** (1988) with Robert Zemeckis directing. Williams' love of moving the camera would be a perfect fit for Zemeckis' style of filmmaking. "Bob wanted to shoot a modern movie," said Williams. "He said, 'all these animation directors I've talked to, they want a locked off camera, like **Mary Poppins** — Dick Van Dyke's dancing and the camera's steady.'"[329] "I said, 'Let's move the camera; let's move it all the time.' It was more work, but it made the illusion work,"[330] said Williams.

"Maybe I'm old-fashioned, but it moved too fast for me," said Virgil Ross of **Roger Rabbit**. "It was too much, and I couldn't follow it. What I saw was a lot of great animation going by in a flash and being wasted."[331]

Still, **Roger Rabbit** grossed over $238 million worldwide in its initial release[332] and ushered in the Disney Animation Renaissance. "Though he won an Academy Award for his work on **Rabbit**, Williams seemed indifferent to the critical and box-office success, feeling that the film was no longer the picture he'd envisioned,"[333] wrote James B. Stewart. Williams would never complete **The Thief and the Cobbler**. The script kept changing, and the animation was reworked or expanded. Tissa David, who worked for more than a year animating the twin sisters, Yum-Yum and Mee-Mee before they were cut, told me that Williams animated the bravura scene of ZigZag shuffling cards several times and it was perfect the first time. "If a scene worked out nicely," said lead animator Michael Schlingmann. "He would just make it longer."[334]

"Williams treated content as an excuse to create elaborate visuals," wrote Mark Mayerson. "But he didn't much care what the content was and may not have been able to tell the difference between good and bad content."[335] Perhaps Williams should have also brought in the great animation writers Mike Maltese or Bill Peet to lecture at his studio.

In 1992, Warner Bros., the distributor of **Thief**, dropped out when it learned that Williams had still not finished it. "The Completion Bond Company, a motion picture insurance company, paid Warner Bros. off and took over the film from Williams."[336] Songs were added, the two non-speaking pantomime title characters were given voices, and the film was released in 1995 by Disney's Miramax as

Arabian Knight, three years after the suspiciously similar *Aladdin* (1992), and twenty-seven years after Williams had begun his labor of love.

"I'd place the break in animation from Richard Williams onward," wrote Michael Sporn. "Dick had studied all the masters, imitated and reworked many of their best moves. He turned his thriving studio in the seventies and eighties into the pinnacle of the medium, teaching animation to many gifted artists and producing commercials, predominantly, had trained a small army to go out into the world and make good, strong theatrical style animation of the highest caliber. Rules were reworked and made to work to get the richest form of the medium. Animation was reborn in the style of Richard Williams and his influences such as Art Babbitt, Ken Harris. and Milt Kahl.[337]

"Persist. Keep going," said Williams. "Don't get stopped. You know because they're going to stop you if [they] can."[338] Richard Williams may not have developed the principles of animation, but he understood the importance of learning from those who did. "If it ain't broke, don't fix it," said Eric Goldberg. "It took those guys sixty years to develop it, it must be good for something!"[339]

Animators such as Williams or Hayao Miyazaki are able to do magical things because they understand the basics — just look at the spectacular crowd scene from *The Wind Rises* (2013) to see how the craft of animation can be art.

"It's like knitting. It's a craft, isn't it?" said Williams. "Proper craft. All this stuff. A craft which can be an art."[340]

"You're crazy if you don't learn from others,"[341] said Chuck Jones.

Chapter 3. Squash and Stretch

Introduction

Squash and Stretch is the most fundamental component in animation, and one of the more overused terms: "It needs more squash and stretch!" It's also one of the more difficult things to get right in 3D animation. Not enough squash and stretch can make your character look stiff. Too much can make your character look rubbery. And poor timing of squash and stretch can make your animation look floaty.

This is going to sound extremely rudimentary, but it's best to start here, at the very basic of basics — squash and stretch!

What's Squash and Stretch?

Squash and stretch is contrast, and contrast is a change of shape. Everything you do in animation will be based on a change of shape — it brings life to your character. As Eric Larson said, "squash and stretch might as well be called the visual needs of animation life. Close attention and application of them in all our work is our responsibility."[1]

Think of a bouncing ball. A ball is dropped from a certain height. The ball starts at its out-of-the-box neutral volume.

As the ball falls it picks up velocity and starts to stretch. The ball hits the ground – this is the squash. The ball bounces back up — this is the stretch again.

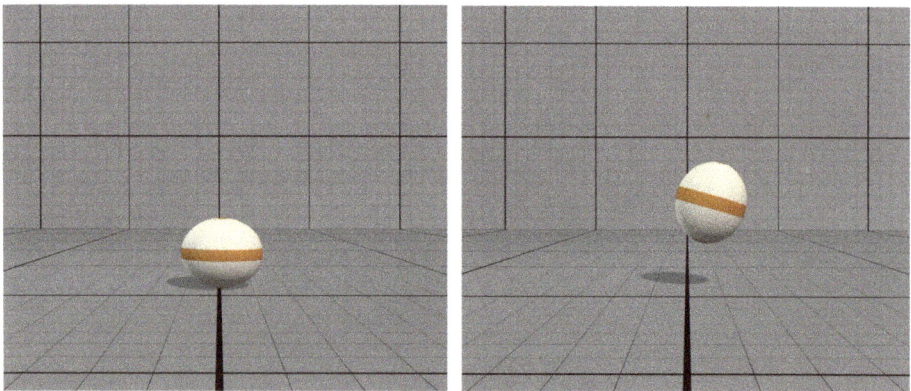

Figure 3.1

How much you squash and stretch will depend upon your character, the amount of naturalism you want, and your own good judgment.

Believability

How much your character squashes and stretches is up to you, but you need to set a range of squash and stretch for your character and pretty much stick to it. This is the most my character will squash, and this is the most my character will stretch. Refer back to the neutral pose if you get lost.

DOI: 10.1201/9781003361893-4

Figure 3.2

Even a 3D character can go off-model by squashing or stretching too much or for too long.

If your character has a stiff uniform like Buzz Lightyear from the *Toy Story* films or a rigid exoskeleton like Beetle in *Kubo and the Two Strings* (2016), you'll have to get squash and stretch by using successive breaking of joints (Ch. 14).

Good Judgment

Keep squash and stretch consistent within your scene to maintain your character's believability. Daffy Duck can be wildly broad, squashing and stretching to ridiculous extremes, as in Clampett's *Baby Bottleneck* (1946). Or he can be solid, with a more realistic anthropomorphic duck skeleton as in Jones' *Rabbit Seasoning* (1952). In both shorts Clampett and Jones established how much Daffy would squash and stretch in their world and stuck with it.

In *Super Rabbit* (1943), a spoof of Superman, Bugs Bunny falls to the ground landing with an incredibly exaggerated squash and stretch. The unexpected "squash and stretch" is the gag.

Figure 3.3

Don't overdo squash and stretch unless you want to draw attention to it. It's easy to go overboard because something looks funny. This only pulls the viewer out of the scene.

On the other hand, don't be afraid to push the squash and stretch on subtle characters. It's animation after all!

Squash and stretch doesn't mean your character needs to be always bouncing and distorting. It's any time you want to show contrast.

In a walk or run cycle, the body stretches on the passing or up pose, then bends or squashes on the down pose.

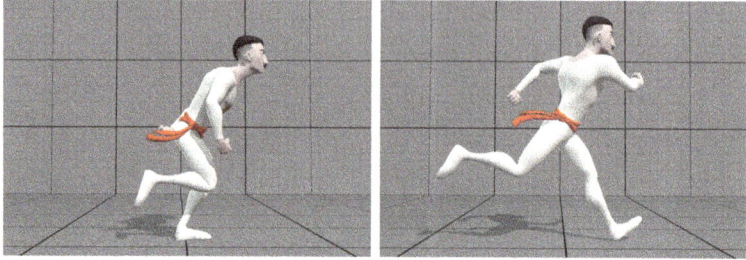

Figure 3.4

Any action that uses anticipation can show squash and stretch — such as a take.

Figure 3.5

Standing up shows squash and stretch.

Figure 3.6

Pointing.

Figure 3.7

We can get more detailed within the face with squash and stretch. Eyes and eyebrows can squash tightly in frustration or stretch in shock.

Figure 3.8

Cheeks can puff out or cave in.

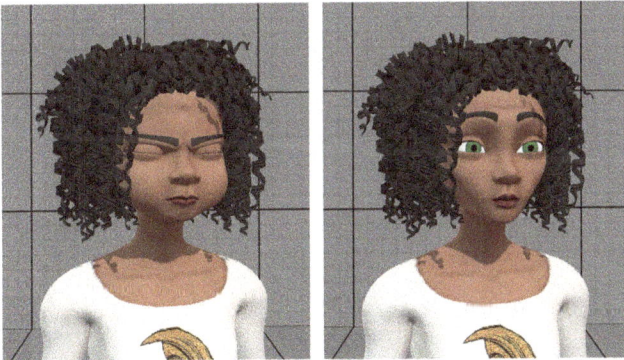

Figure 3.9

Lips can be tight or purse.

Figure 3.10

A hand placed down on a flat surface is first in a neutral pose, relaxed with slightly bent fingers. When it presses down on a flat surface, the palm squashes, and the fingers stretch. As the hand lifts off the table, the palm relaxes and the fingers stretch.

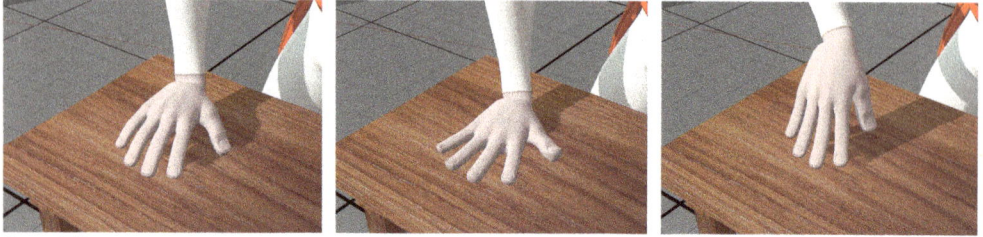

Figure 3.11

Making a fist is a squash. The hand starts in a neutral pose and then squashes.

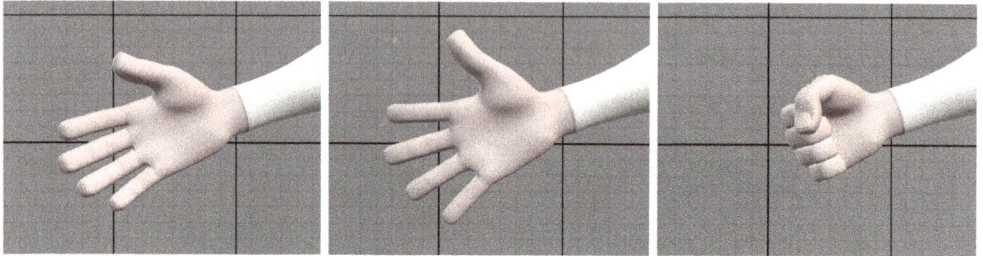

Figure 3.12

Squash and stretch is contrast or change. Any change in your character will add interest and believability.

Always go back to your neutral pose when deciding how far to push your squash and stretch. It's easy to get lost and add squash or stretch to an already squashed and stretched pose. Your character will not only start to drift off model, but they could also begin to look rubbery!

The Bouncing Ball

Just about everything you'll do in animation is contained in the bouncing ball exercise: squash and stretch, timing and spacing, arcs, weight, jumps, takes, changing direction, accents — you name it.

So, do the bouncing ball exercise. It's not beneath you. The bouncing ball exercise is like learning scales if you play an instrument. You'll be so glad you did it.

As Frank and Ollie said, it's "surprisingly rewarding in terms of what could be learned"[2] from the bouncing ball!

You could animate a bouncing ball straight ahead — that is, start with the ball in-air about to drop; then the first squash; then the next in-air pose bounce; then the second squash, etc.

However, if you'd like your bouncing ball to hit certain points in your environment, pose-to-pose may be easier to control — and quicker!

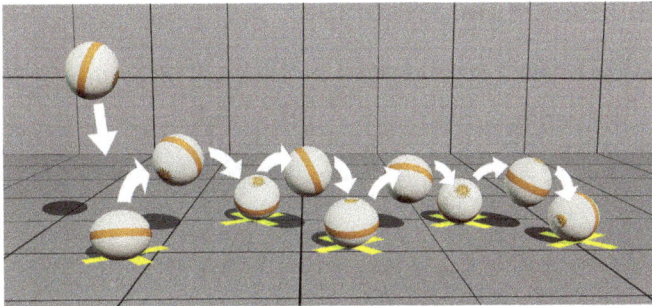

Figure 3.13

This may sound silly, but thumbnail your bouncing ball scene! Picture how many bounces you'd like — then thumbnail it. Drawing it out will help you feel the timing and spacing of each bounce.

For this example, the ball will bounce four times and then roll to a stop.

Figure 3.14

Start with the in-air start pose. Set the Y translation to the height you pictured. For this example, the Y translation is set to 10.

Do not animate the master controller! In fact, hide the master controller on another level and forget about it!

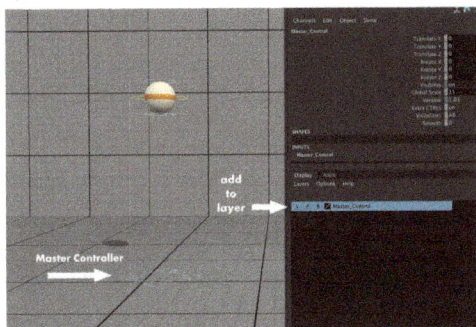

Figure 3.15

Next, set the position of all five of your squash poses. Space and time them however you'd like but don't squash them yet. For this example, the squash poses are on frames 7, 19, 25, 29 and 33. Also, add the end position of the ball when it rolls to a stop.

Remember that the farther you space them, the more time you'll need.

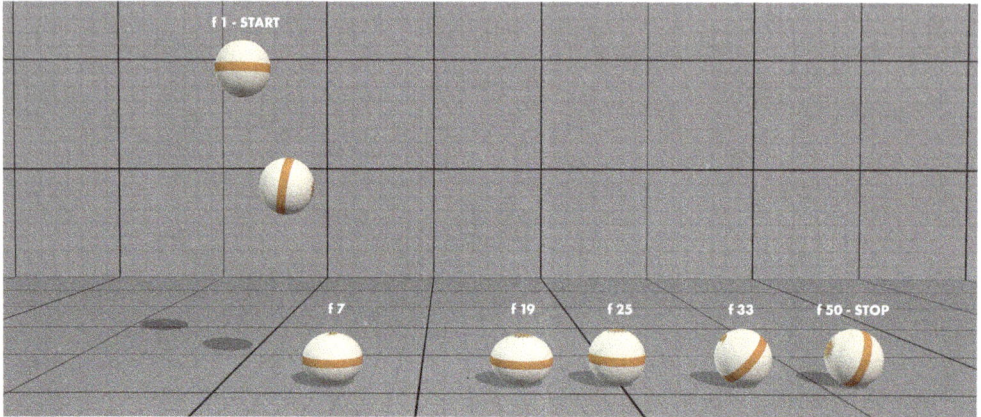

Figure 3.16

How about having the ball spin as it bounces? If your ball rig can squash, you'll want either the top or the bottom of the ball facing up so that your squashed ball is flat on the ground and not squashed at an angle.

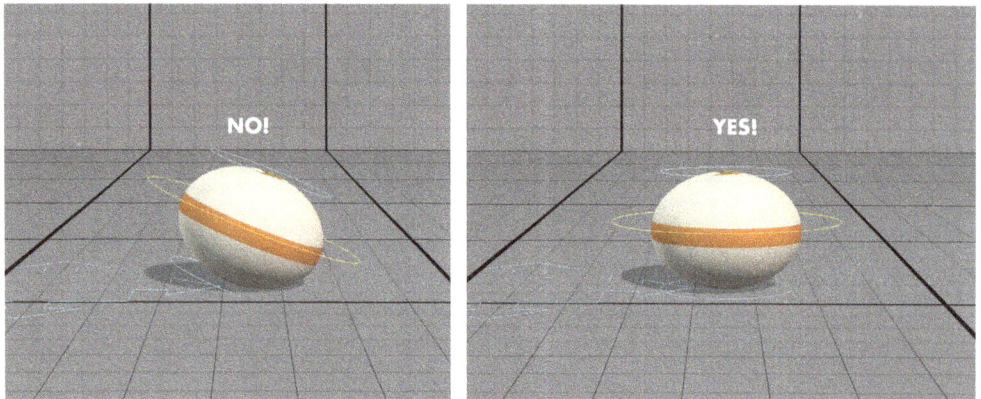

Figure 3.17

Set the rotation for the first squash on frame 7 to -180° then squash the ball down as much as feels right.

Next set the rotation for the second squash (frame 19) to -360° and the rotation for the third squash (frame 25) to -720°. (A full rotation looks better than a -180° flipping pancake!) The amount of squash should lessen as the ball bounces.

The ball wouldn't need to do a complete rotation for the fourth or fifth bounce. A partial rotation of around -745° is good for the fourth bounce on frame 33. Eyeball how much the ball rotates for the fifth bounce.

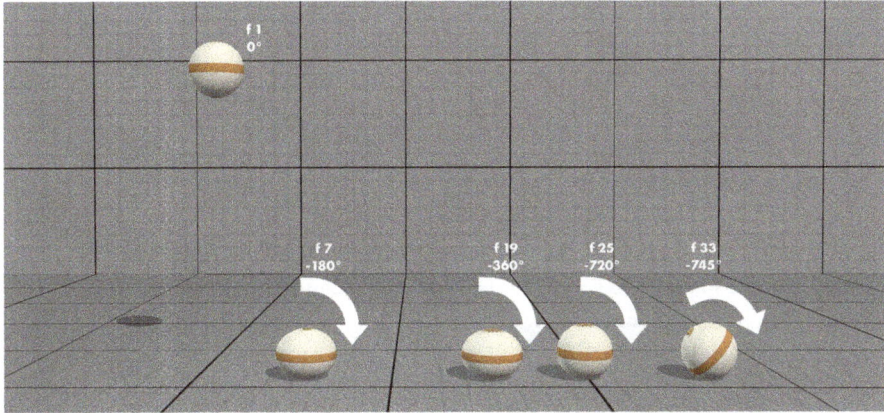

Figure 3.18

Make sure to key everything, all parts of the ball rig, on frames 7, 19, 25, 29 and 33.

Now translate the ball in Y for the bounce on frames 13, 22, 27 and 31. Again, the height can be whatever you'd like. For this example the Y translations are set to:

Frame 13 = 6.5

Frame 22 = 3.75

Frame 27 = 2.25

Frame 31 = 1.25

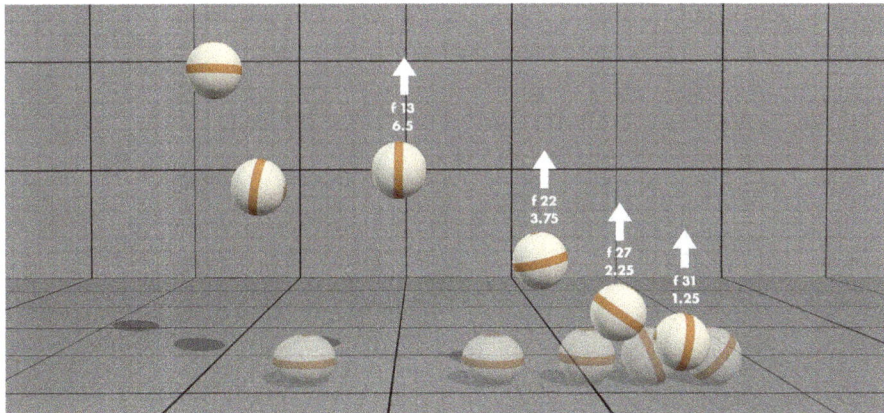

Figure 3.19

Zero out the squash and stretch of the ball rig on frames 13, 22, 27, and 31 so that the ball returns to its normal volume at the peak. It wouldn't bounce squashed.

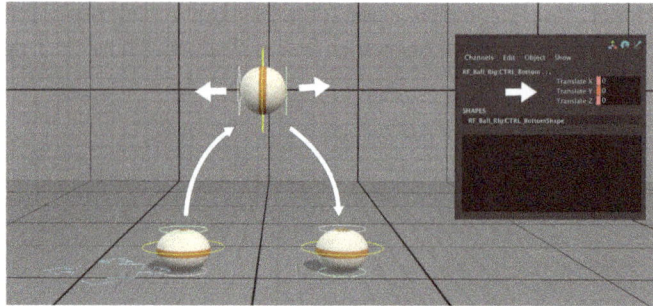

Figure 3.20

Now in your graph editor, select all the Y translation keys for the bounces on frames 7, 19, 25, 29, and 33 and set those tangents to linear. This will give you nice snappy bounce.

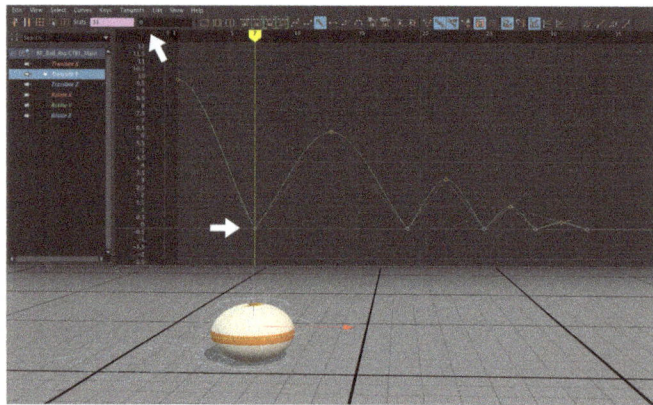

Figure 3.21

Add a breakdown pose before and after the squash poses to control the amount of squash and stretch your ball has. (We'll look at breakdowns in chapter 16.) The breakdown pose for a bouncing ball can be the first frame before the squash and the first frame after the squash.

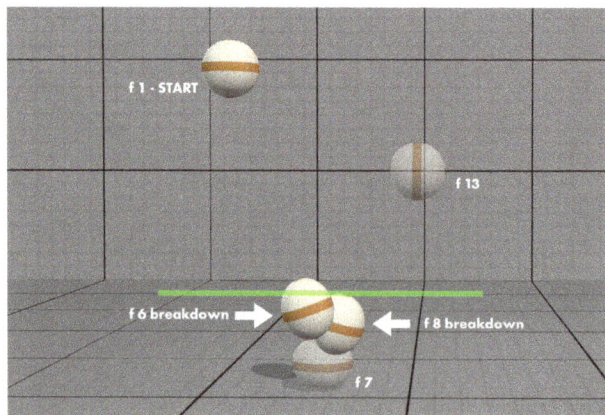

Figure 3.22

As your ball rolls to a stop, use landmarks on the ball as a guide to keep your ball from rolling in place. Roll over a stripe or marking. If the stripe is sliding back, your ball will be sliding in place.

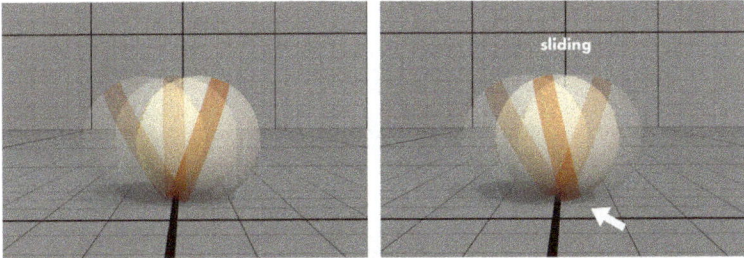

Figure 3.23

Slow-in to the stop. Use the spline tangent in the graph editor. This may take some noodling to get right!

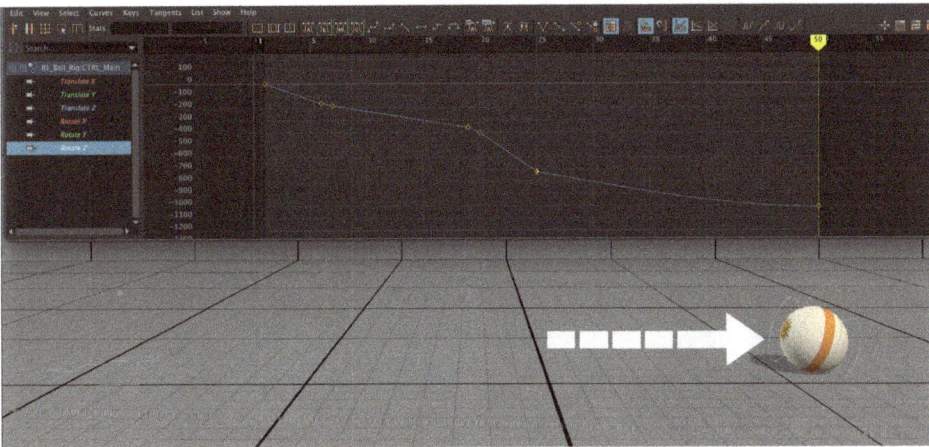

Figure 3.24

Common Bouncing Ball Problems

Squash poses will flash if they're too big. Tone down the squash until you feel it more than you see it.

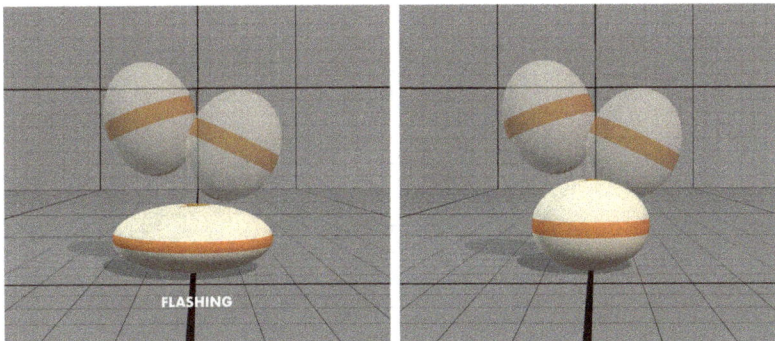

Figure 3.25

Unless there's a reason, the height of the bounce and the amount of squash should gradually diminish.

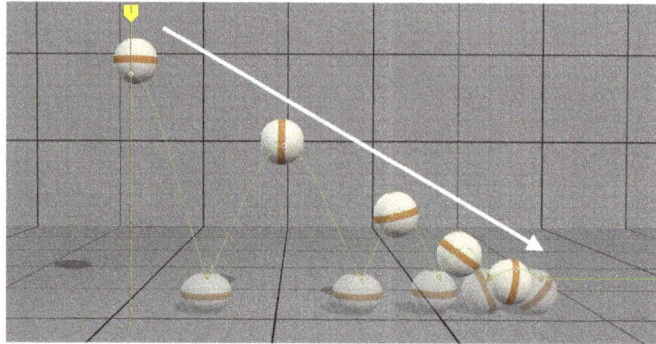

Figure 3.26

The ball would keep going if it didn't hit the ground, so keep it stretched until the squash pose. Similarly, the ball would stretch as it bounces up after a squash. Gauge the amount of stretch to feel right for the bounce.

Don't stretch the ball to look faster than it should be.

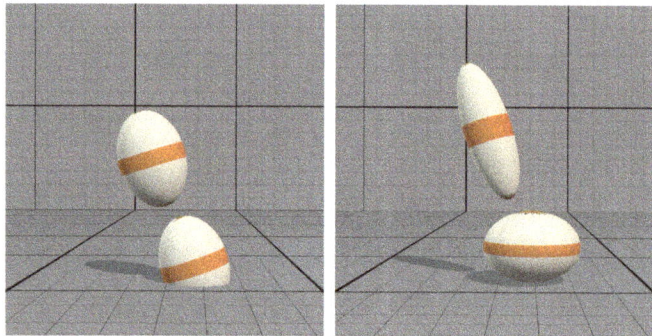

Figure 3.27

Don't have the breakdown poses before and after the squash at the same height. If they're set at the same height, they may overpower the squash because you'll see two poses at the same height. Offset them slightly.

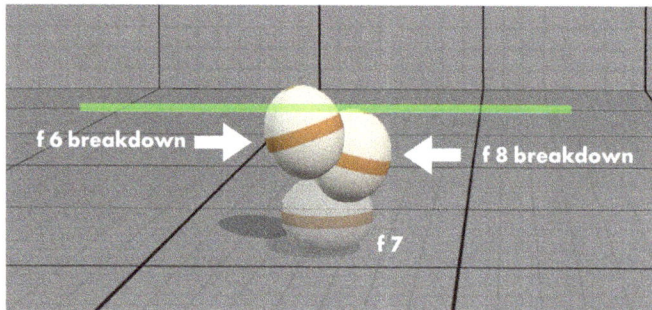

Figure 3.28

When filming your bouncing ball scene, on frame 1 the ball should be out of frame. On frame 2 the ball should be just slightly inside the frame.

Don't pose the ball too far inside the frame or it will appear to pop into the scene.

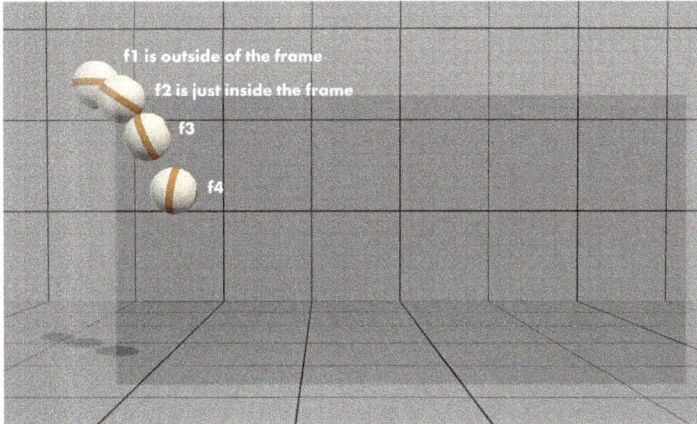

Figure 3.29

Learning the bouncing ball exercise will make it easier to solve problems because it's seen in all kinds of actions such as a jump!

Figure 3.30

Animation Exercise — Animate a bouncing ball!

Chapter 4. Posing

Introduction

Making a pose that sells the attitude of your character, while still being clear and dynamic, can be a challenge for even the most experienced animator. Are your poses strong enough? Are you pushing them enough? Do your poses clearly represent the emotion you're going for? Does your pose look good from every angle?

These are some of the things to think about when posing a character.

Attitude

What is your character thinking at that very moment? Show it!

Donald Graham said that an animator, "must have complete understanding and recognition of the fact that it is the emotion that comes first; the action comes second. The action is a secondary thing — it is a result of the thought or feeling."[1]

Before you begin posing a character, ask yourself what the core emotion is. What is your character feeling at that moment? Are they happy, sad, angry, afraid, disgusted? Show it in the posture.

Figure 4.1

Even a character idling in a game should be thinking something: "I'm a tough guy!" or "I'd like to go home now." This thought should be conveyed in their stance.

Facial expressions are important, but what if your character's back is turned to us or they're wearing a mask?

Figure 4.2

You should have a good idea of how a character is feeling from their posture.

DOI: 10.1201/9781003361893-5

Search for the Right Pose

"There's no one 'right' way to pose a character," wrote Walt Stanchfield, co-creator of the Disney training program with Eric Larson. "Fifteen artists may be drawing the same pose, so there would likely be fifteen versions of the pose. However, each version must contain that one much needed common factor — communication — the communication of the story idea."[2]

Don't be afraid to use reference for even the simplest pose! Off the top of your head, can you think of fifteen different and interesting variations of the same pose?

Figure 4.3

Don't settle for the first pose that comes along. The more you act out the pose you're making, the stronger it will get. This is why actors rehearse.

"Lift your arm. Lower it," said the acting teacher, Michael Chekhov. "What have you done? You have made a gesture. Now make the same gesture, but this time color it with a certain quality. Let this quality be caution. Do it again and again and then see what happens."[3]

The stronger your poses are, the better your scene will be when you start connecting a series of poses.

Line of Action

Can you express what your character is feeling with just a single line? A line of action is an imaginary line that runs through the body, through any object they're holding, and shows the attitude of your character. Starting with a line of action will help strengthen the pose. But remember that when working in 3D a line of action should be clear from all angles!

A hunched-over line of action could show sadness. A strong line of action could show pride.

Figure 4.4

A line of action thrusting forward may show aggression. A curved line of action may be a character sleeping.

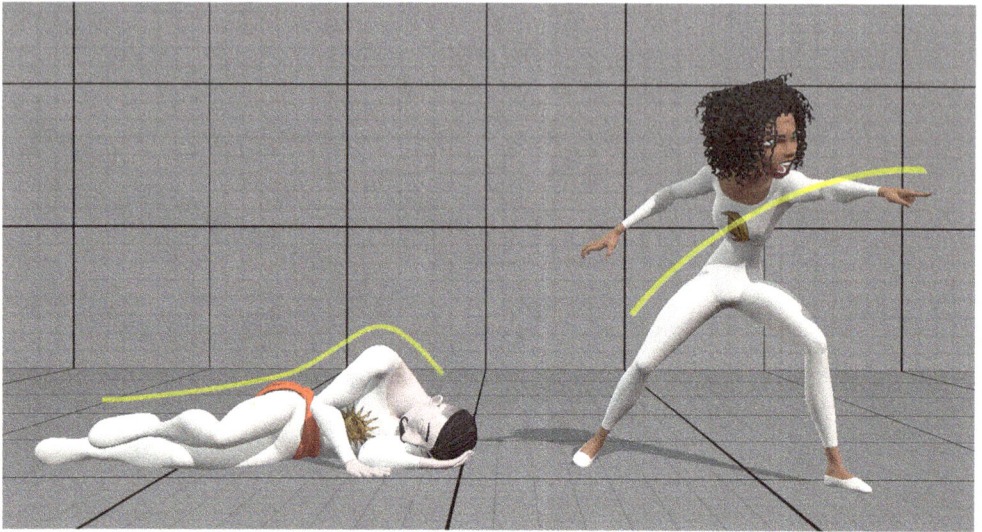

Figure 4.5

The line of action should help refine your poses to their simplest and clearest essence.

When two characters share the screen, a clear line of action should run through them both.

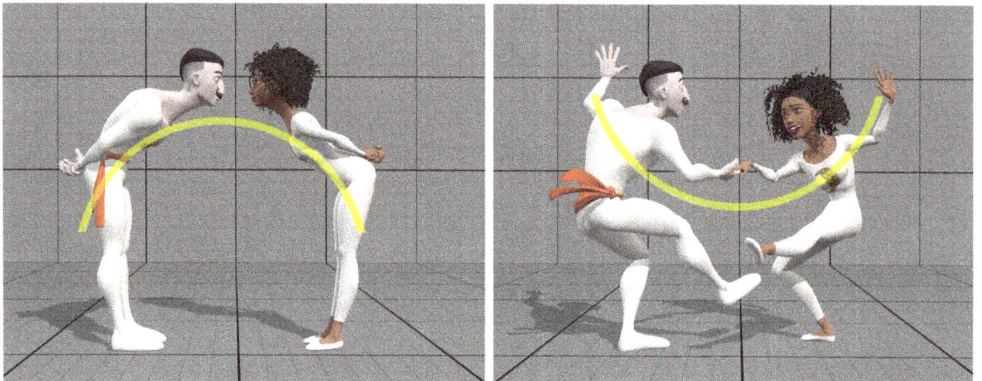

Figure 4.6

Gesture

Gesture is the body posed along the line of action. It's organic. "Gesture's greatest gift is to show, on a fundamental level, how to move gracefully and dynamically from the head to the neck, from the rib cage to the hips, all the way through the body," said artist and teacher Steve Huston. "Gesture is what makes the separate parts one whole. In other words, gesture composes."[4]

When we apply gesture to posing in 3D, we're roughing in the character over the line of action. Don't worry about details. Don't try to get the fingers perfect, or the expression just right — try to get the body moving gracefully along the line of action as a shape.

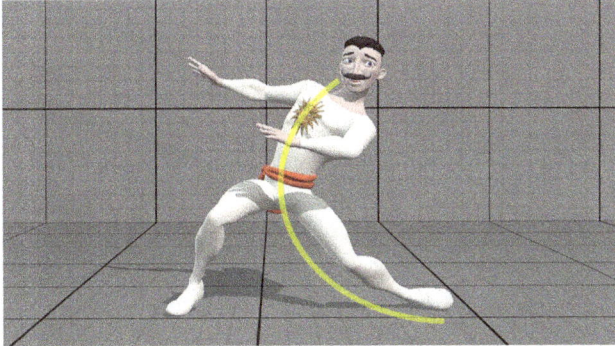

Figure 4.7

Stick to the line of action when blocking in the gesture! Is your character landing from a jump? A common mistake is to pose an arm or foot that looks nice but doesn't follow the line of action.

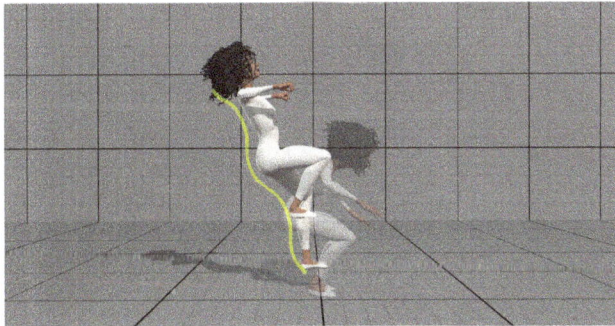

Figure 4.8

All parts of the gesture should follow the line of action. Raise the height of your landing pose to make room for a stretch.

Figure 4.9

Once you're happy with your gesture, fill in the details. Pose the anatomy over the line of action. Don't break up the line of action with an oddly turned hand or foot. Stay true to your line of action.

Grouping

Grouping is what the old masters did when they thought of the figure as boxes, balls, and tubes so that they could quickly lay in a gesture, and then add the details.

Figure 4.10

Group fingers so that they don't break the line of action. Don't pose the hand in an awkward way just because you want to show how nicely you can pose fingers!

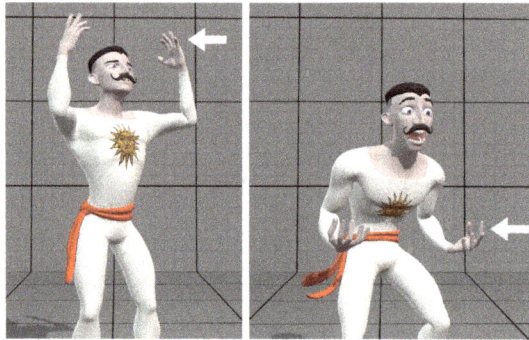

Figure 4.11

Think of the whole form.

Figure 4.12

Individual parts stuck together and not grouped can make your character look "Frankensteined."

Another way to think of grouping is when drawing a tree full of leaves. You wouldn't start by drawing each individual leaf. Besides taking forever to draw, it would give you a drawing of a bunch of leaves and not a tree. Group sections of leaves on the tree to get the overall mass, then fill in the details.

Figure 4.13

Contrapposto

Contrapposto in art means a relaxed standing pose with the weight on one leg and the hips and shoulders angled in opposite directions. But it can also be thought of as any pose with opposing positions of the shoulders and hips. Sculptures before contrapposto, such as the Kouros (530 B.C.), though beautiful, were stiff and vertical. Sculptures with contrapposto, such as the Venus (1st Century A.D.), show a more relaxed and natural pose.

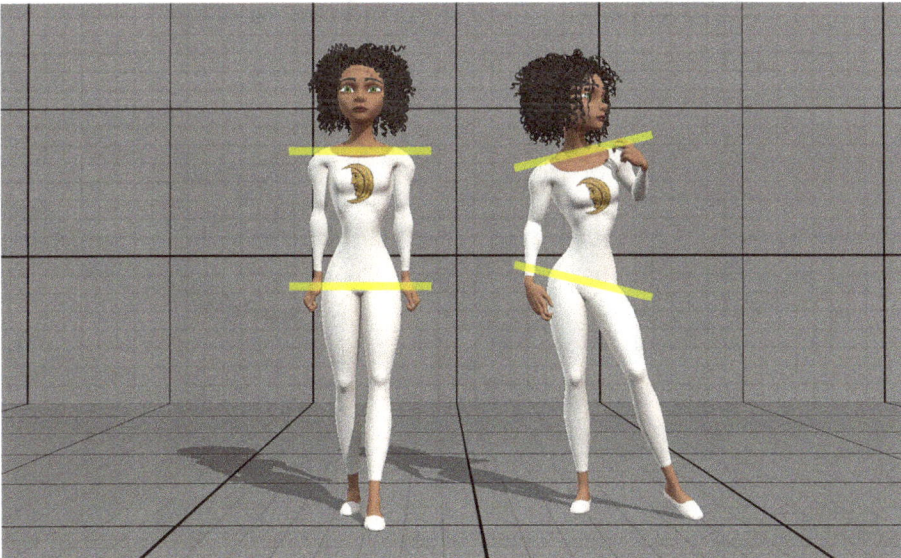

Figure 4.14

Even in the most subtle pose, a slight weight shift looks and feels more natural. It takes more effort to stand like the Kouros, with your weight evenly distributed, than it does to slightly shift your weight.

Figure 4.15

Contrapposto isn't limited to standing poses. When laying down, your character can look really boring, or dead if it's stiff and straight.

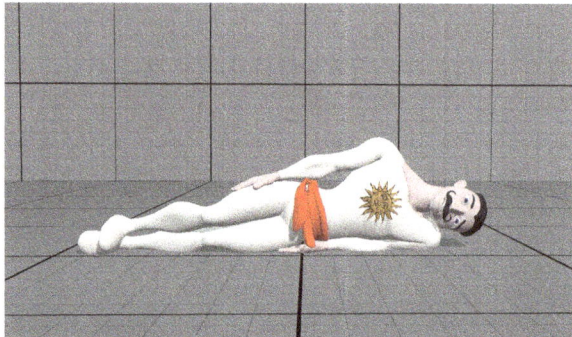

Figure 4.16

Contrapposto brings life to your pose!

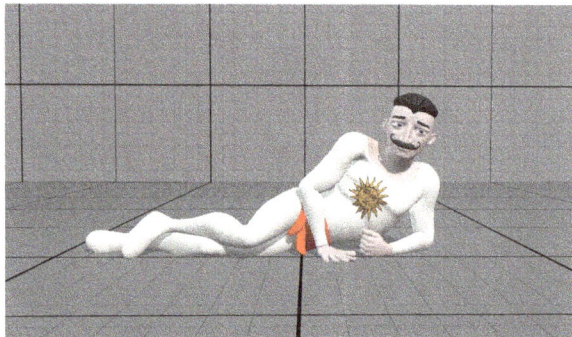

Figure 4.17

You're already off to a good start when you add contrapposto, or asymmetry, to your pose. Asymmetry is contrast and contrast adds life to your animation.

A good way to figure out weight shift is to think of a vertical line through your character. The hips will favor one side of the line over the other.

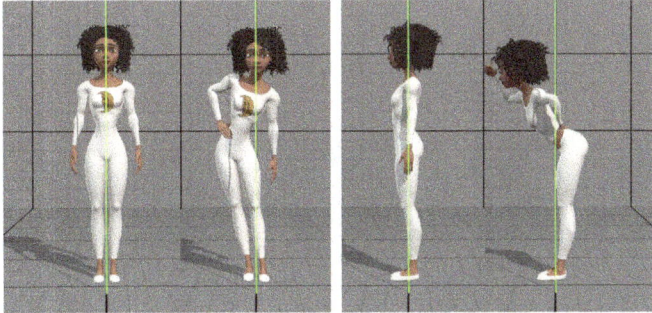

Figure 4.18

Twinning

Twinning is another thing you'll hear a lot when being critiqued, "Your animation is twinning!" or "Don't twin!" Twinning is when both sides of the body are posed pretty much the same. A twinning pose can be boring or wooden because you're "using a straight line of action".[5]

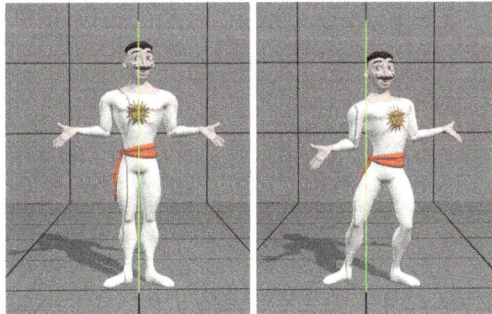

Figure 4.19

When it comes to twinning in animation, I'm more in the Richard Williams camp and believe that twinning isn't all that terrible — as long as you enter or exit a section that's "twinning" with asymmetrical posing.

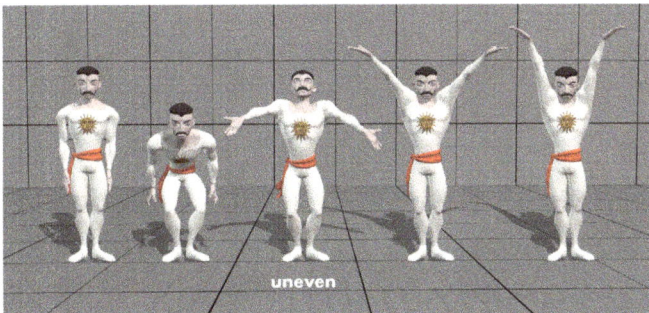

Figure 4.20

Negative Space

Negative space is the space around and between an object.

Rubin's Vase, developed by Danish psychologist Edgar Rubin, is the most common example of negative space. Lighting just the vase, or positive space, and you see a vase. Light the negative space around the vase and you see two faces.

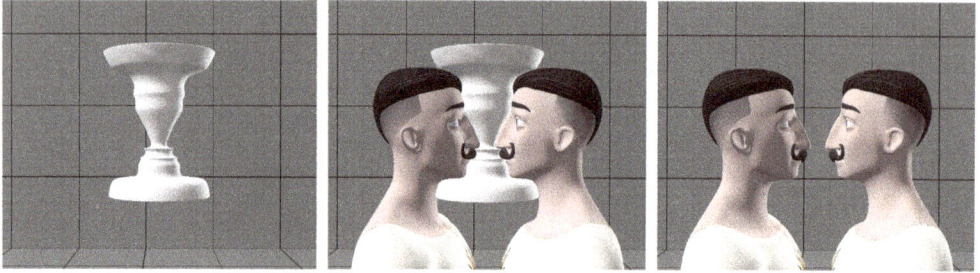

Figure 4.21

Always look for the negative spaces surrounding your character. Good use of negative space helps balance your pose and makes it read better. Adjust the arms so the negative is more even. Balance your character.

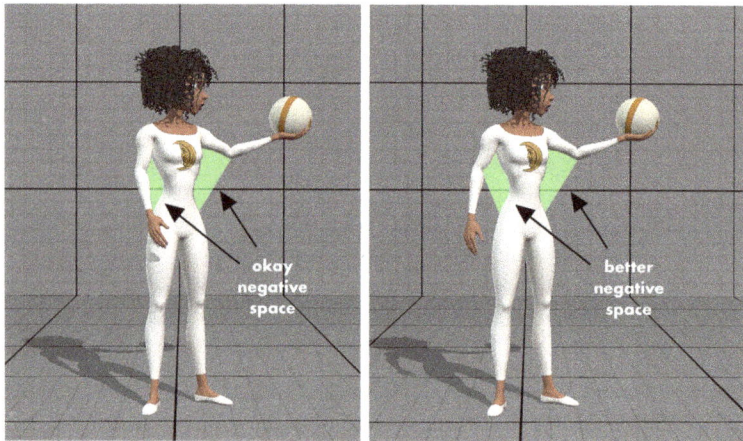

Figure 4.22

This doesn't mean the arms are always at the same angles! Just look for equilibrium between the shape of the character and the space around them. If you don't have equilibrium, one part of the character will dominate and your pose will look awkward.

Make sure the negative space looks right from all angles.

Silhouette

A clear silhouette in posing became important with black and white characters like Mickey Mouse and Felix the Cat. Body parts would disappear if the silhouette wasn't clear. Animating black and white characters helped animators later on because they learned that a clear silhouette made a scene read better.

"Chaplin maintained that if an actor knew his emotion thoroughly, he could show it in silhouette," wrote Frank and Ollie. "Walt was more direct. Work in silhouette so that everything can be seen clearly. Don't have a hand come over a face so that you can't see what's happening. Put it away from the face sand make it clear."[6]

"Turn you pose constantly," said sculptor Tony Cipriano. "Your pose should have a clear silhouette from every angle. If an arm or leg disappears in silhouette, you need to move something. What the figure is doing should be clear from every angle!"[7]

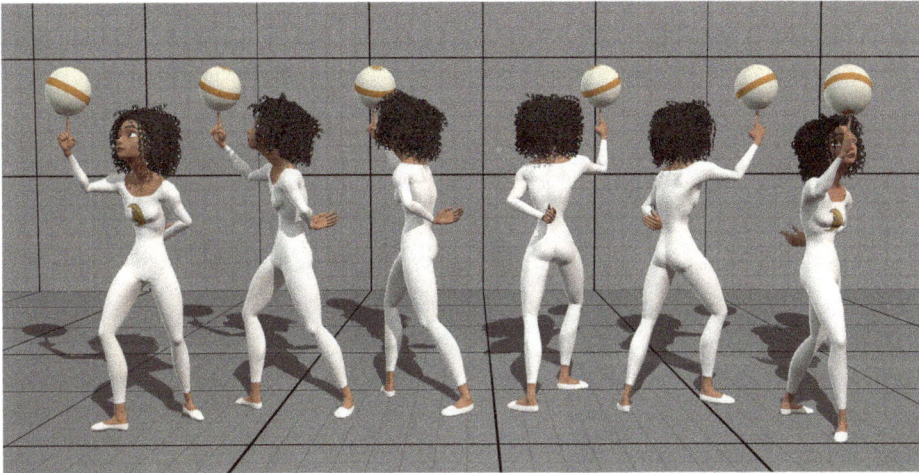

Figure 4.23

In video games you may have to pose your character to play to the gameplay camera. Adjust your poses so that the action reads clearly. Don't block the action.

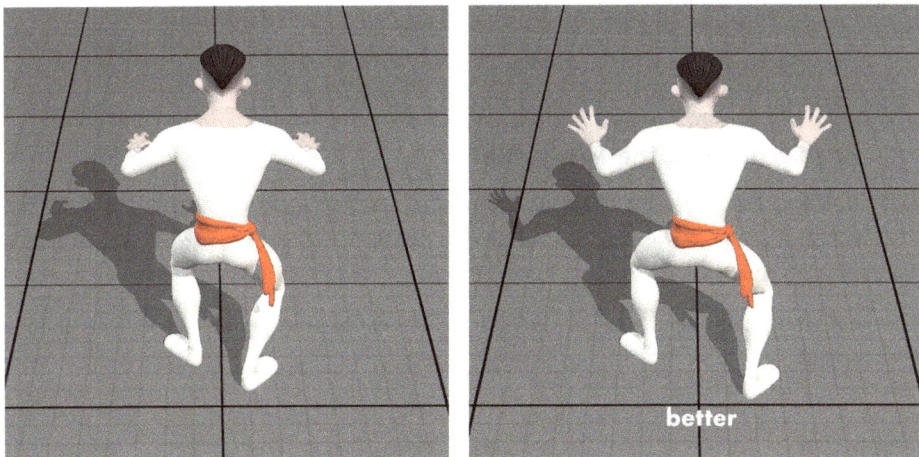

better

Figure 4.24

IK and FK

IK means "Inverse Kinematic" and FK means "Forward Kinematic". An easy way to remember what IK and FK are, is to think of the hand on your rig. When the hand is set to IK, it's sticky and you can only move the hand from the handle on the hand.

When the hand is in FK, you can move the hand by rotating the shoulder. Unless your character's hand is in contact with something, it may be best to keep the hands in FK. FK hands inbetween better in space. Keep the feet in IK unless your character is flipping in the air, spinning, or doing anything that needs smoother inbetweens.

Test the silhouette in Maya by hitting F7 on your keyboard. Use the angle of your final camera position of your scene. If your pose doesn't look strong enough in silhouette — push it!

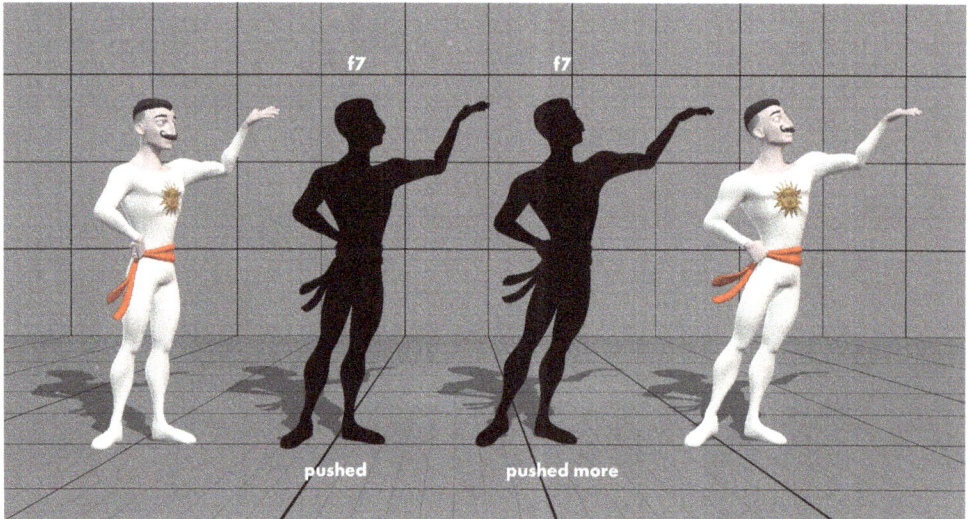

Figure 4.25

Don't Pose from Just the Waist Up!

Even if your scene will only be shot from the waist up, pose the whole body! By leaving out the lower half of the body, you're leaving out the weight shift. Not only will your animation be stiff and less believable — it's cheating!

Don't cheat your action because it will be noticed. Poses are stronger when you think about the overall posture.

You can also push the pose more because you know where the weight is.

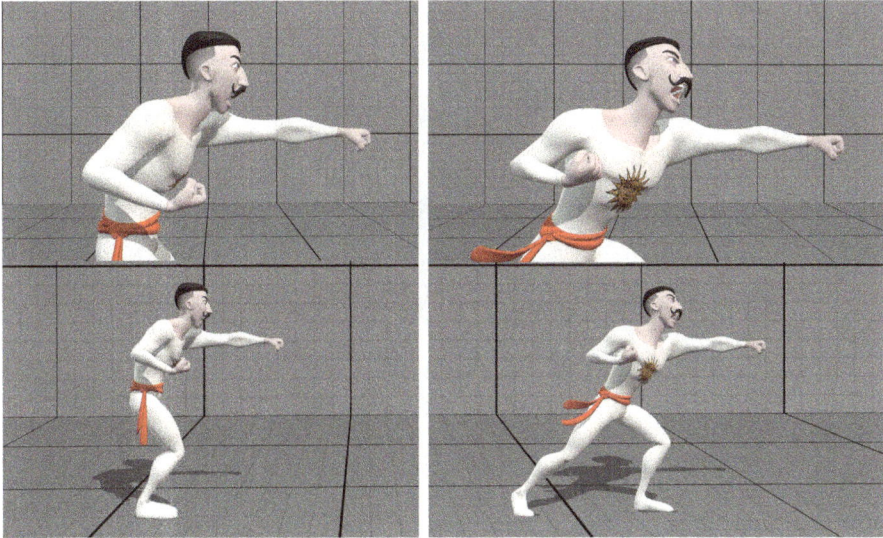

Figure 4.26

Tips

World Space and Object Space

A quick way to get the pose you'd like is to switch between world space and object space.

Use world space when you're translating or rotating your character in relation to their world. Use object space when translating or rotating your character from your character's point of view.

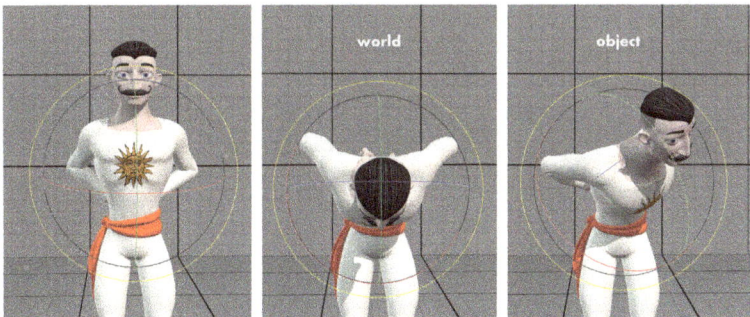

Figure 4.27

Maintaining a Line of Action in the Back

It's easy in 2D to get a nice line of action between the neck, spine, and hips — you simply draw it.

A painless way to get a nice curve throughout the neck, spine, and hips in a 3D rig is to rotate the hips backward, then rotate the spine forward.

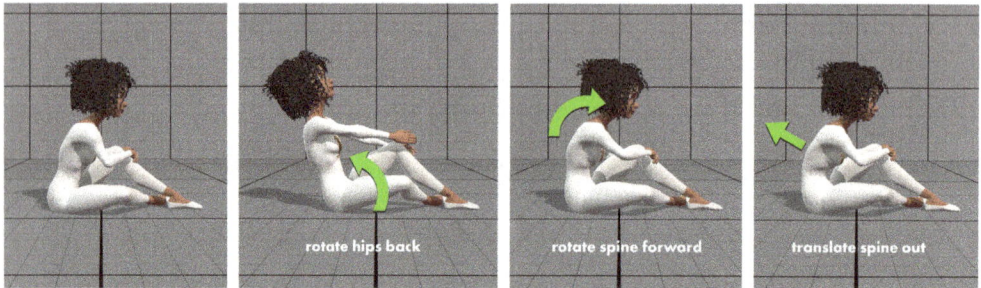

Figure 4.28

Use IK to push the pose

If your rig allows, use IK to push a pose.

Your character is standing like a superhero. Pull the IK in the hands and hips to stretch the rig as far as you can without breaking it. Then rotate the chest out and pull the hips forward.

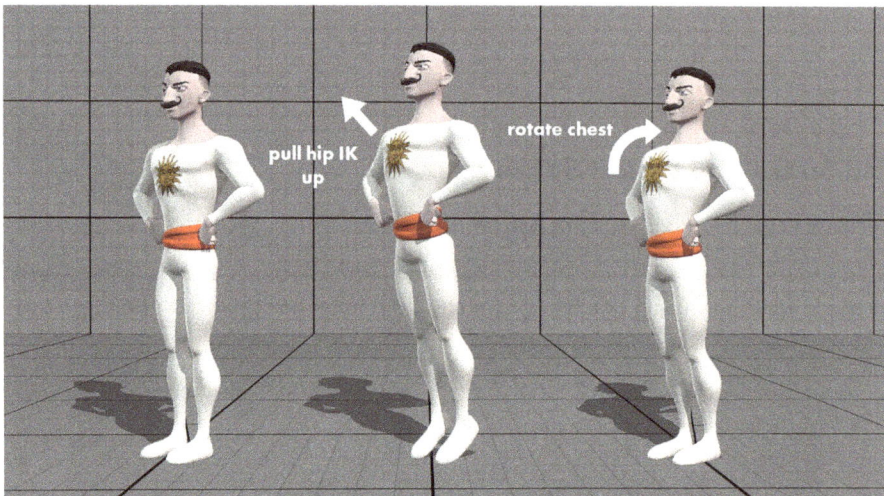

Figure 4.29

Animation Exercise — Create poses that show emotion. Can someone look at your pose in silhouette and know exactly what your intentions were? Is your pose readable from every angle? Does anything fight the line of action? Is the pose pushed enough?

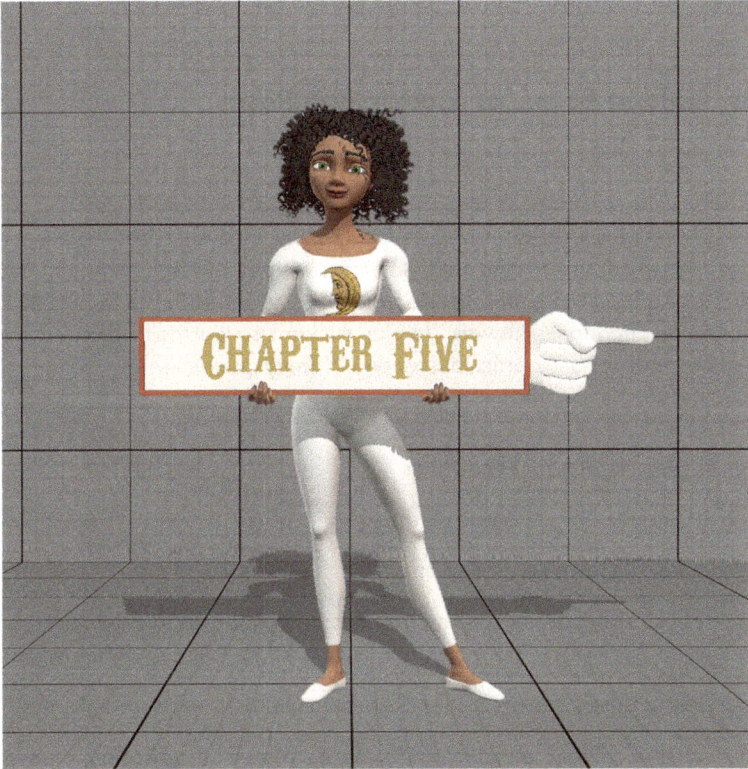
CHAPTER FIVE

Chapter 5. Rhythm

Introduction

Rhythm in animation, as in music, can refer to timing — but it can also be like melody, the flow of a sequence of poses. Eric Larson said that one of the things Freddy Moore taught the new animators was, "rhythm in drawing, the motion, the movement." He said that Moore, "never made a drawing that didn't have a flow to it and this is basic in animation."[1]

An animated scene without a pleasing pattern from one pose to the next can become monotonous. In this chapter we'll learn how to create a rhythm in your scene — from blocking in your scene to staging your poses for contrast.

Key Poses, Golden Poses, or Storytelling Poses

How many extreme poses do you need for a scene?

In 1920, E.G. Lutz wrote the first book on animation technique, "Animated Cartoons: How They are Made Their Origin and Development," the book Walt Disney took out of a local library and devoured. Lutz wrote that in a typical seven-minute cartoon there were about eight thousand drawings. "An appalling job to make that number of separate drawings," he wrote. But he went on to say that one of an animator's most important skills was, "to plan the work so that the lowest possible number of drawings need be made for any particular scenario."[2] Pretty insightful!

Glen Keane was more specific about the number of extremes needed:

- Enough to describe arcs and head turns

- Enough to describe any changes in shape

- Enough to indicate to you a desired effect[3]

Key poses, also called extremes, storytelling poses, or golden poses, are the main poses needed to describe an action. They tell the story of your scene. We'll go with storytelling poses for now.

How many storytelling poses would it take to describe a character waving "hello"?

You'll probably want about four: a neutral start pose, a pose of the wave start, a pose for the end of the wave, and the neutral pose again.

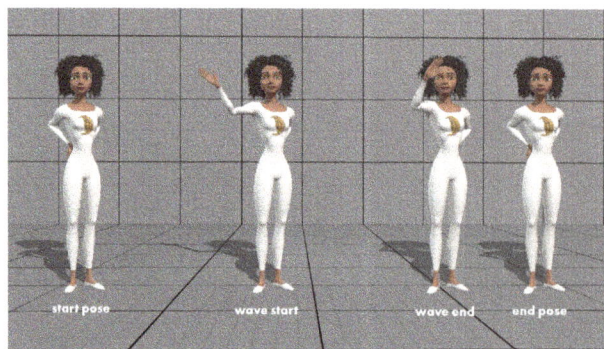

Figure 5.1

DOI: 10.1201/9781003361893-6

A supervisor, director, designer, or producer might think your character is just raising their hand if you block-in just one pose of the hand waving. Two poses describe a clearer "path of action" of the hand wave.

You could add a third wave pose, or breakdown, to further describe the arc of the wave, but that's not really a storytelling pose. Breakdowns describe how one storytelling pose transitions to the next storytelling pose.

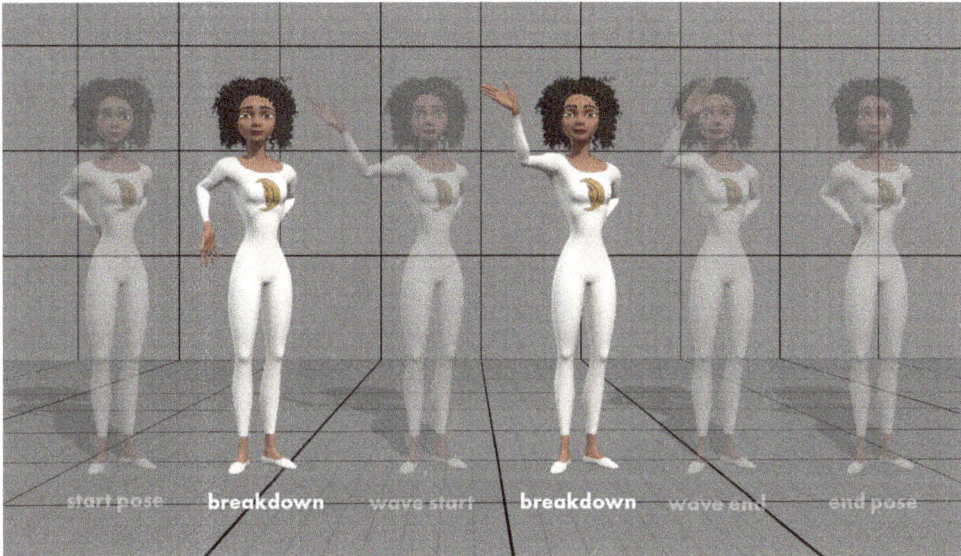

Figure 5.2

Restraint!

A common mistake for beginner animators is to add inbetweens to flesh out their animation before refining the storytelling poses.

For now, stick with only the storytelling poses. Add breakdowns and inbetweens later!

Don't fall in love with unnecessary poses just because they look good! If a pose doesn't fit the action — cut it.

Path of Action

What's a path of action? We know that a line of action is an imaginary line that represents the overall posture of your character. A path of action is an imaginary line that describes the flow of motion from one pose to another.

A Word About Stepped Tangents

A good way for a beginner, or the undisciplined animator, to pose their scenes is to use stepped tangents in Maya.

Rather than translating smoothly between keys, stepped tangents will keep one key the same until the next key.

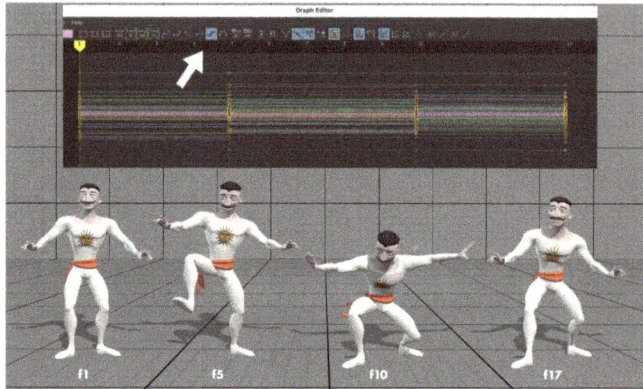

Figure 5.3

It's more of a pose-to-pose, traditional animation way to work; but it keeps the focus on making solid storytelling poses without getting sidetracked by adding inbetweens too soon.

It also makes it easier to add breakdowns and inbetweens later on.

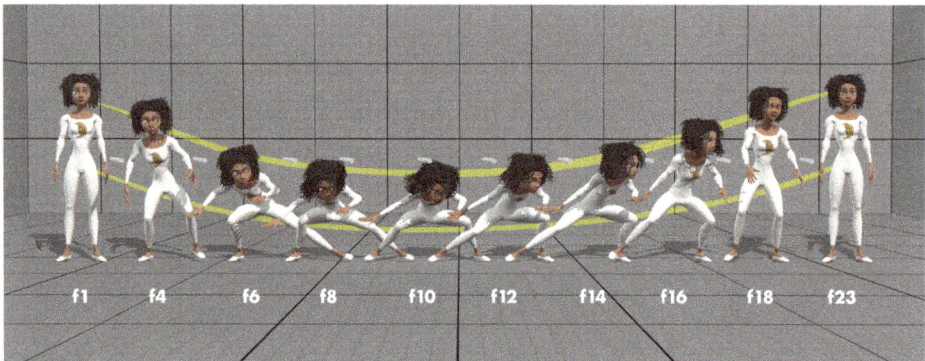

Figure 5.4

When posing out your storytelling poses, be mindful of the path of action. Everything in your scene will follow its own path of action: the head, the nose, the shoulders, the arms, the hands, the fingers, the hips, the thighs, the knees, the ankles, the feet, and the toes. If you don't know where to place an inbetween, follow the path of action.

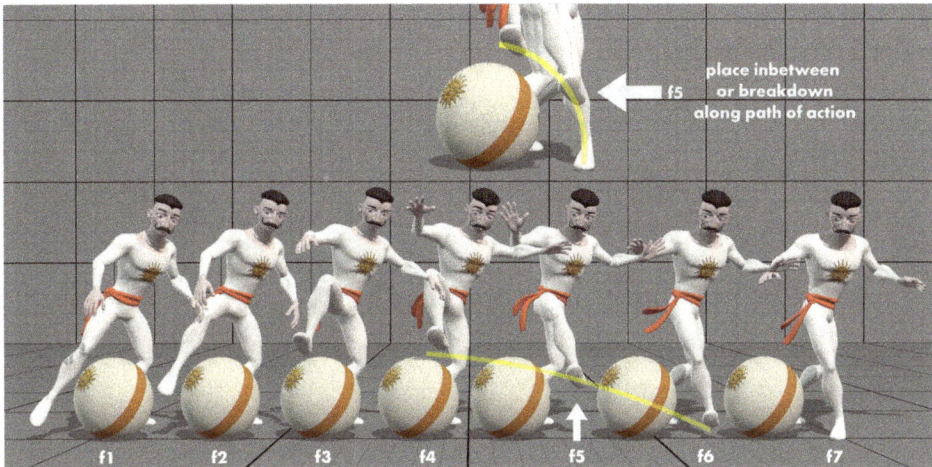

Figure 5.5

Animators like James Baxter, Ken Harris, or Frank Thomas, look for ways to make their paths of action more interesting.

A character uses their finger to follow the path a hummingbird is flying. The path the finger takes should be fun to watch. When posing out a pattern for the finger to trace, think of something like a paraph after a fancy signature.

Figure 5.6

Think Ahead

As you're posing your storytelling poses, think ahead about how they will flow together. Plan ahead, picturing how one pose will lead into the next. There should be a flow to your poses, a "rhythm of action,"[4] as Les Clark called it.

James Baxter said Milt Kahl, "would do these major key drawings, and then he would go in and fill in all the details, all the flamboyant little parts on every single drawing... He was so far ahead in the process, thinking two or three steps ahead, that he could figure out where things were going to be in space."[5]

A character throwing a ball is familiar, so it's easy to think ahead to what poses you'll need and how they'll flow together.

Figure 5.7

Animation by Ryan Fisher

Contrasting Poses

Animation is contrast. Always look for an opportunity to show contrast, or a reversal, in your poses.

A good way to check how your animation is flowing from one pose to the next is to toggle them. Toggle back and forth between key frames using the comma key "," and the period key "." to see the change between poses.

Toggling poses this way is much like flipping drawings in 2D animation! Traditional animators flip their drawings by holding up to five drawings at a time between their fingers and rolling them back and forth to see the change in movement.

If you lift your head, your hips may move back slightly. Show the contrast no matter how subtle!

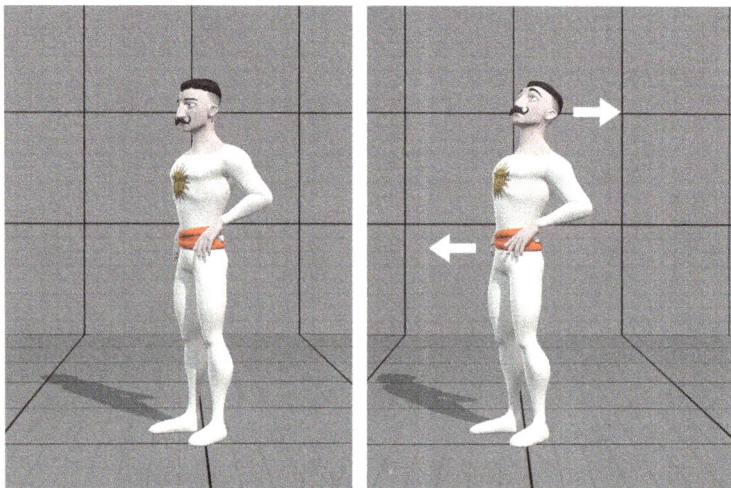

Figure 5.8

A character jumps into the frame and does a "Ta-da!" gesture. This action gives several opportunities for reversals.

Block in Facial Expressions!

Block in facial expressions as you pose your scene. Even if the expression changes, adding a temporary expression will help push the pose because you'll feel the emotion more. A blank expression won't help feel an angry pose as much as an "Aaargh!" expression would.

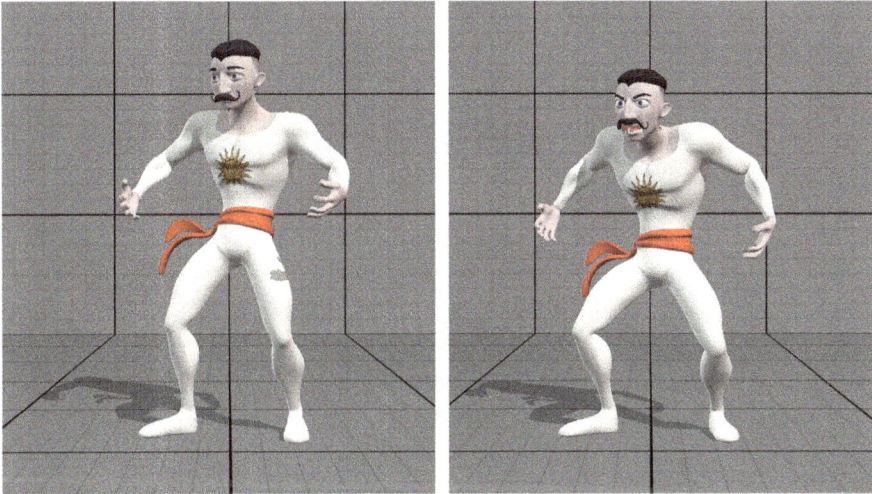

Figure 5.9

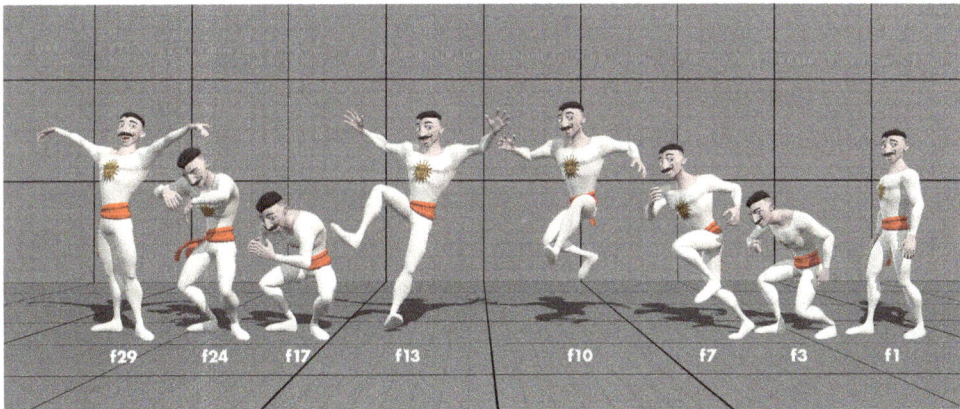

Figure 5.10

Everyone has a different way of working, but for this example we can start with an idle pose before the jump.

Next, pose out the "Ta-da!" pose. Flip back and forth, comma and period key, to make sure there's a clear change between the idle pose, and the enthusiastic "Ta-da!" pose.

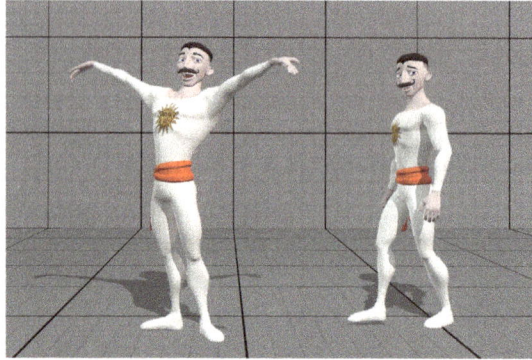

Figure 5.11

The jump is part of the story, so we should block out the jump. Picture the path of action for the jump.

You wouldn't want to make a jump that overpowers the "Ta-da!," so keep the jump more contained.

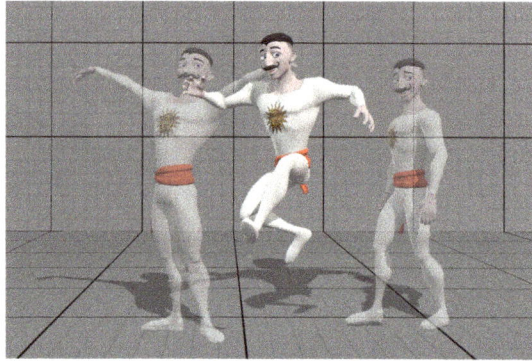

Figure 5.12

Add as many poses as necessary to describe the mechanics of the jump.

Show the anticipation, the leap, the in-air pose, the landing, the squash and the "ta-da!" pose.

Create a flow and rhythm through contrast. Adjust the poses as necessary so that they flow better. Streamline your action.

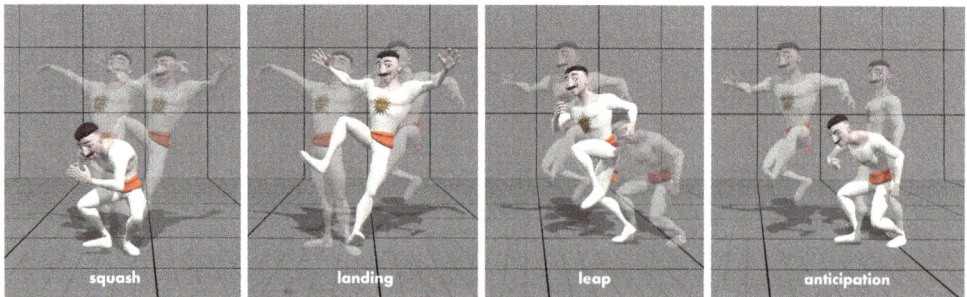

Figure 5.13

Is there part of the body not changing enough? Is there part of the body moving too much?

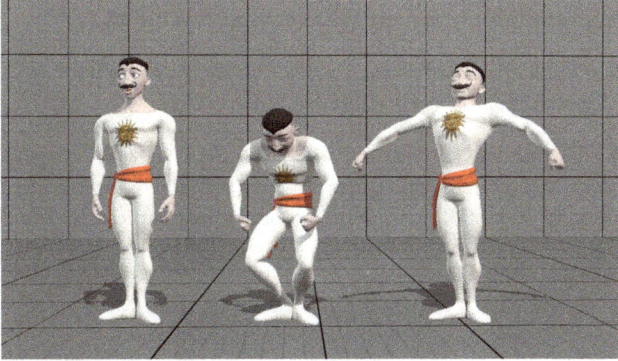

Figure 5.14

Push poses to create a better rhythm.

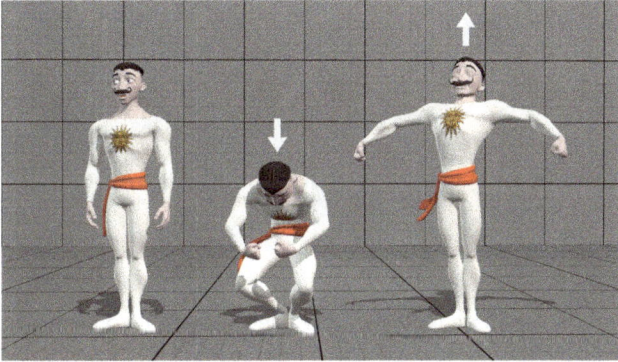

Figure 5.15

Remember to toggle your poses from every angle! In 3D your animation will look better if you can see clear contrast and flow from pose to pose from any angle.

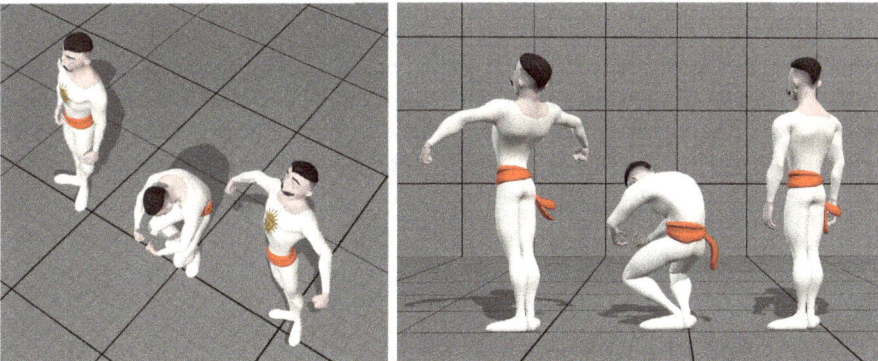

Figure 5.16

Analyze Reference!

To animate something believably, you need to understand how it works.

How do you animate dunking a basketball if you've never done it before or don't plan to? How does a giraffe run? How do you do a handstand?

The improv teachers Del Close and Charna Halpern talked about making "connections". Connections occur in improv when actors play off each other using information they've stored in the back of their mind. The more information an actor has stored, the better their improvisation will be.

"Honest discovery, observation, and reaction is better than contrived invention,"[6] they wrote.

Figure 5.17

"Everything that works is based on real life," said Glen Keane. "If you learn it because you have observed it, you can animate with conviction and it's a spark of life in your drawings."[7]

Animation Exercise - Create a sequence of storytelling poses — just enough poses to clearly describe the action. Do not add any breakdowns or inbetweens. Toggle back and forth checking the poses from every angle. Do you have nice reverses? How's the path of action? Does any part of your character stick from one pose to the next? Look for change — no matter how subtle the action is.

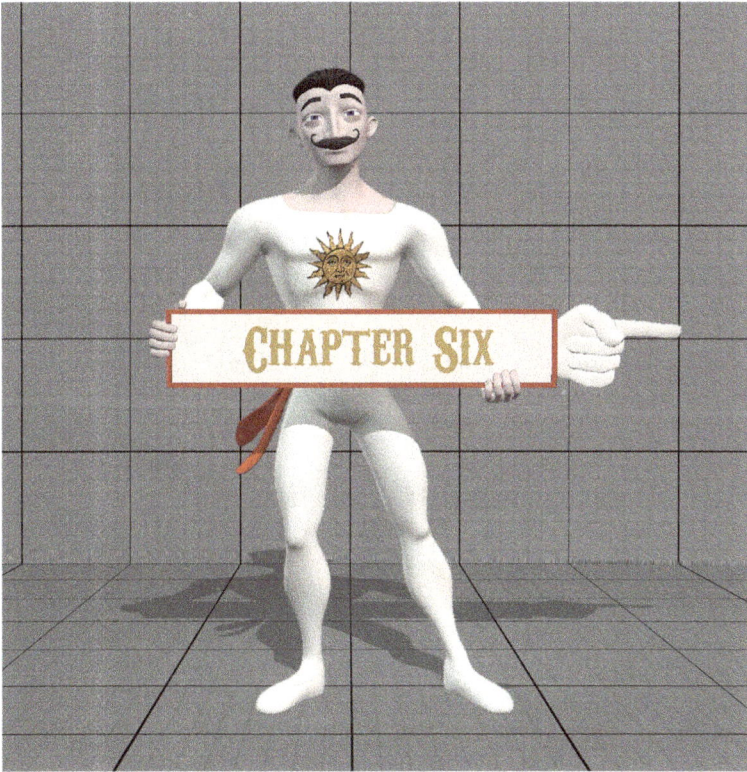

CHAPTER SIX

Chapter 6. Exaggeration

Introduction

Sometimes a scene doesn't read as well as you thought it did because you're not pushing your poses enough.

"Live action actors can get away with an amazingly minimal amount of movement," said Walt Stanchfield. However, "a slight bit of caricature is absolutely necessary in animation to keep movements from looking stilted."[1]

In this chapter we'll learn about pushing action to get the most out of your scene, and when exaggeration is going too far.

Caricature

Caricaturist Al Hirschfeld said, "you try to pick out what is salient and you make it important."[2] Caricature that is just grotesque or is pushed too much, he said, "has no wit. It's like looking at yourself in a spoon."[3]

The same is true for animation. Clarify the pose and make it more important. Analyze an action and then push it farther.

"If a character was to be sad," wrote Frank and Ollie. "Make him sadder; bright, make him brighter; worried, more worried; wild, make him wilder."[4]

Figure 6.1

"When you study the photographs he used for each painting," wrote Norman Rockwell's granddaughter, Abigail. "You can see how he went past what they depicted and revealed his own truth beyond the photo."[5]

Rockwell exaggerated arcs in backs, straightened arms, tilted heads more, turned in feet, etc. All to tell a better story.

DOI: 10.1201/9781003361893-7

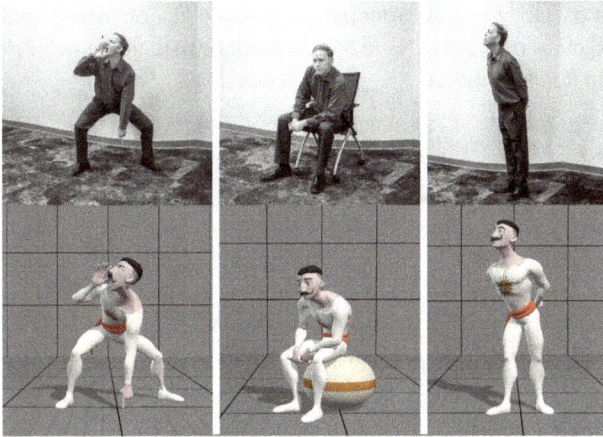

Figure 6.2   Poses by Ryan Fisher

As an animator you're creating a performance meant for entertainment; so your character should be larger than life, not ordinary. The great actors are fun to watch because they're not ordinary.

As Alfred Hitchcock said, "What is drama, after all, but life with the dull bits cut out."[6]

Analyze Mechanics

Analyzing the mechanics of our reference makes it easier to push poses and to make actions more interesting.

A good way to analyze reference is to look for the highs, lows, and tilts. Place grid lines on the top of the head and the top and side of the hips. Play through the reference frame by frame looking for the extreme high and low positions. Determine where the weight is at each moment.

If the body shifts to your character's left, the weight is over the left foot. If it shifts to the right, it's over the right foot. It's that simple!

Even if your reference appears to be standing still, with a grid line or overlay you'll most likely notice a subtle shift or drift.

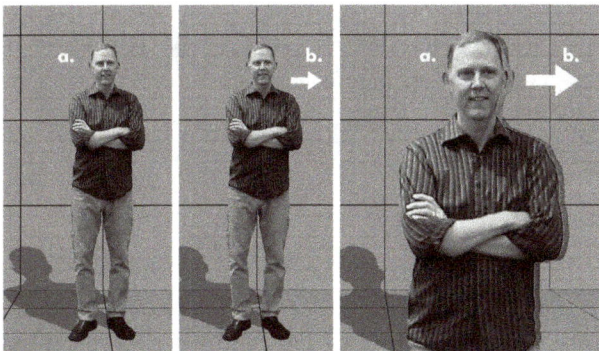

Figure 6.3

Exaggerate the shift as subtly as you want but exaggerate it! Contrast will make your animation more interesting and more believable. Grid lines make it easy to figure out weight shift when your reference is shot from just the waist up.

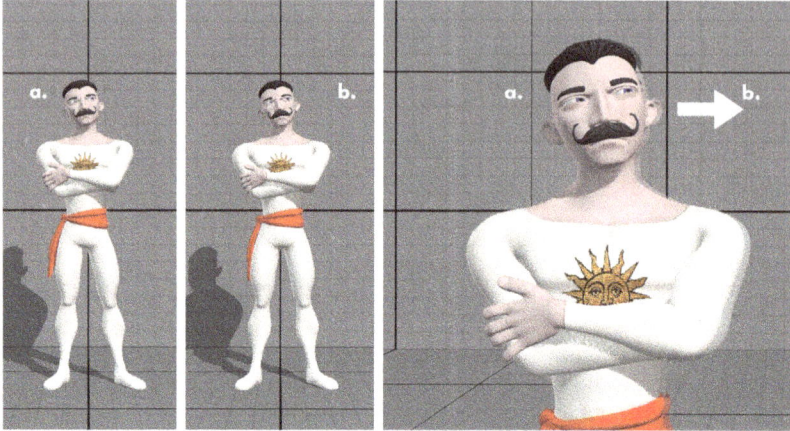

Figure 6.4

Check for tilts or arcs in the head by placing a line across the eyeline.

Figure 6.5

Push the tilts or arcs a little more so that they read better!

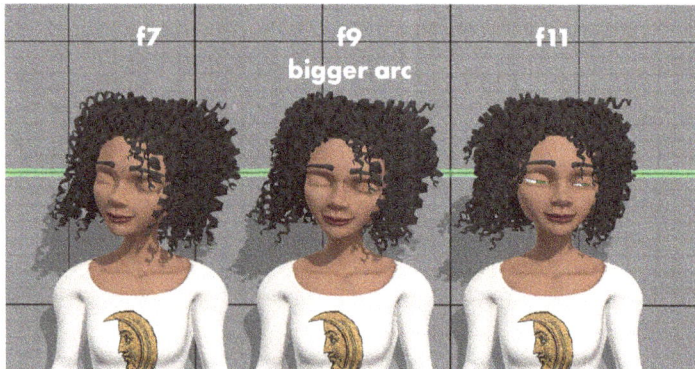

Figure 6.6

Identifying the highs and lows, side-to-side movement also makes it easier to break down a walk or run cycle shot from the waist up — especially when you know the formula (see Ch. 10).

When the head is at its lowest point in a walk cycle, your character is probably in a down position. When the head is at its highest point in a walk cycle, your character is probably in a passing or up position.

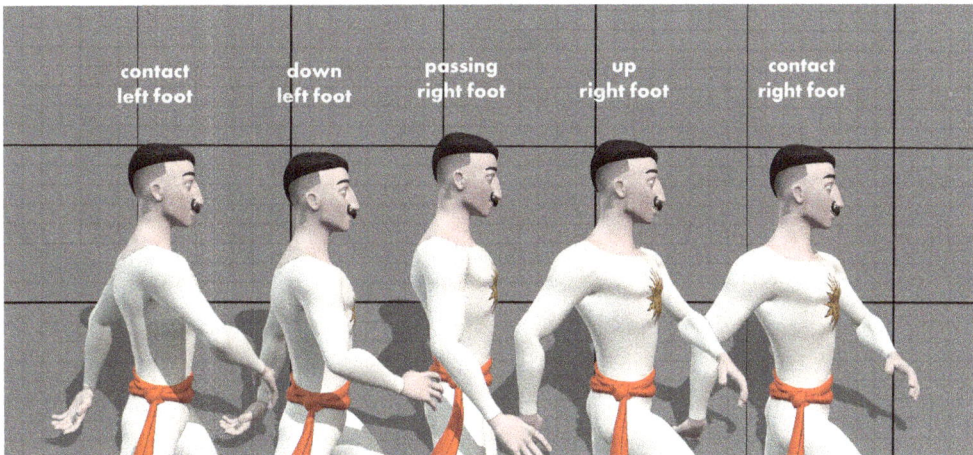

Figure 6.7

Study your reference. Look for the high and low and side-to-side movements — then push it.

It will get to where you don't need to depend upon it as much. "I've worked awfully hard and have studied how people move and you don't have to use reference then,"[7] said Milt Kahl.

Exaggerating Reference

"We strive to "overload" — to exaggerate the body shape, poses, attitudes, and movement of our character,"[8] said Eric Larson. "Do not allow any action you put on the screen to be routine — every action, every thought, every personality trait needs showmanship, a little ham acting, a little "overloading," some flare."[9]

A reference picks up a heavy ball and throws it from their chest.

Figure 6.8

Pick out the keys from your reference and block them in. What can be done to push the poses?

Start with the neutral pose and the character squatting to pick up the ball. Get a nice contrast.

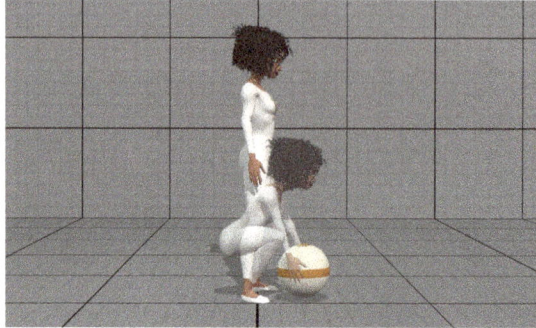

Figure 6.9

Then the character picks up the ball. It's heavier than the prop the reference used, so we can exaggerate how far they lean back with the ball against their chest. Blocking in the strain on the face will help push the pose.

Figure 6.10

The next storytelling pose is the throw from the chest. Push the contrast to make it larger than life! Reference should only be a guide.

Push the reference. Showmanship!

Figure 6.11

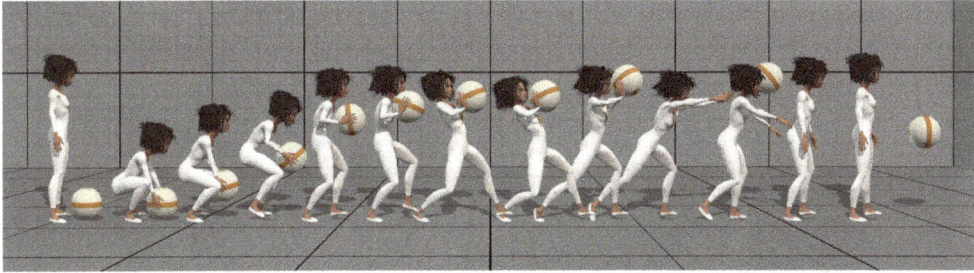

Figure 6.12

Did you ever trace a photograph? A traced drawing looks stiff because you're connecting lines rather than drawing an overall gesture. No matter how poorly you draw, a drawing is more appealing when you draw it freehand.

Rotoscoped animation can look a little strange because it's too on the nose. Compare the animation of Jerry, of Tom and Jerry, dancing with Gene Kelly in **Anchors Aweigh** (1945) with the penguins dancing with Dick Van Dyke in **Mary Poppins**. For most of the sequence, Jerry has no weight because the highs and lows of his steps aren't pushed. The successful moments, as when Jerry slips and falls, are when the animator animated free from the photostats.

For the four penguins dancing with Van Dyke, however, Frank Thomas interpreted the reference. Each penguin goes beyond the photostats — more squash and stretch, bigger arcs, and offset timing. The result is livelier and snappier animation.

A character reaches for something. Use your line of action to push the pose. Picture a line of action from the finger tips down to the toes and stretch your character along that line.

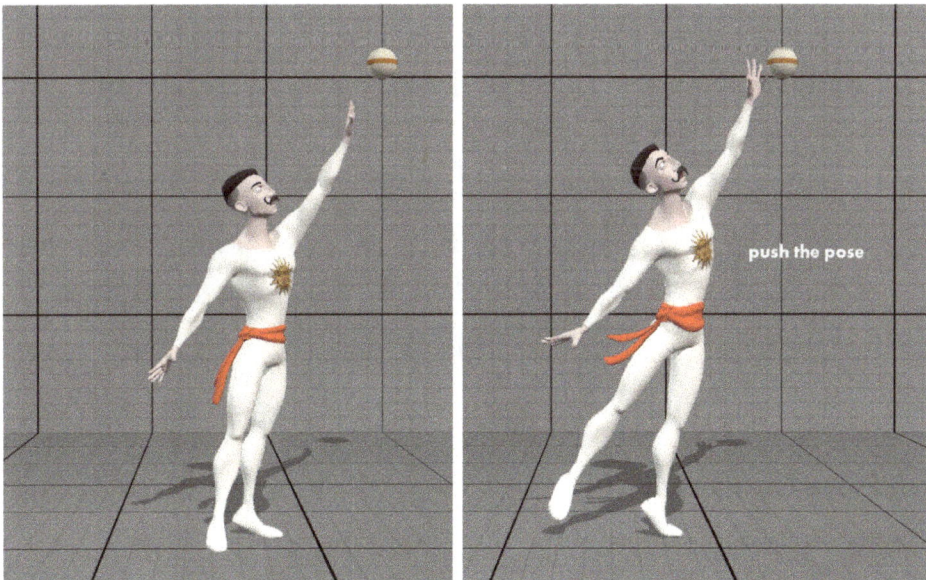

Figure 6.13

Fit the body along that line of action. Gesture!

Raise the heels so that the character is up on their toes. But don't cheat! Keep the toes on the ground. Turn the hips up on the side that is reaching. Raise the shoulder higher on the arm that is reaching.

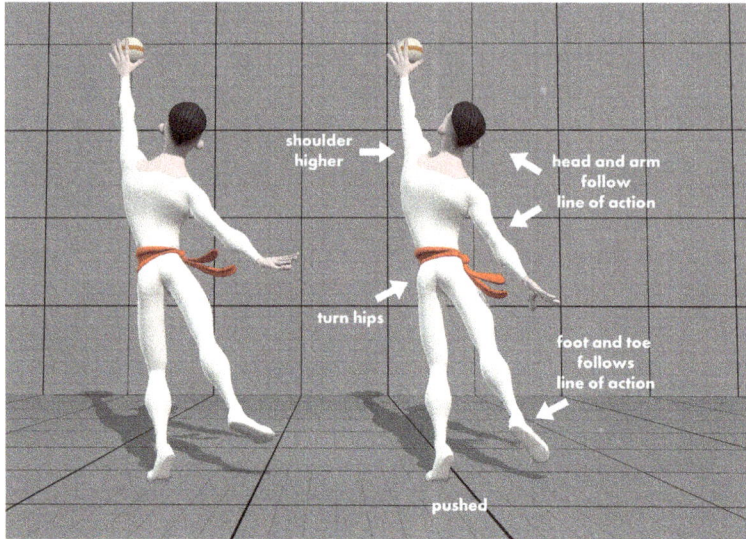

Figure 6.14

To make the stretch pose even stronger, contrast it with a big anticipation and an accent.

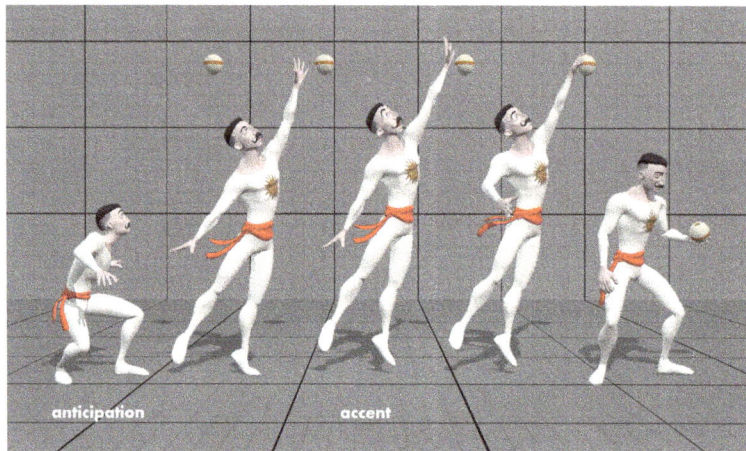

Figure 6.15

Push Poses Farther Still

Sometimes you may not always see what's happening on screen — but you can feel it.

"You must learn to respect that golden atom, that single frame of action, that 1/24 of a second," wrote Chuck Jones. "Because the difference between lightning and the lightning bug may hinge on that single frame."[10]

Step through a Rod Scribner or Lloyd Vaughn scene and you'll see drawings you had only felt when played at full speed.

Step through Milt Kahl's scene of Medusa pulling off her false eyelashes in **The Rescuers**. Look how far her eyelid stretches before the false eyelash snaps off and her eyelid wiggles back to normal.

"In action, you have to go a little farther," said Kahl. "If you don't go a little farther your eye won't pick it up."[11]

Go even further with your poses so that your scene has oomph!

When one hand claps down on another hand, the hands don't freeze in space; they continue to move and then recoil. This is called a hard accent (see Ch. 17). Hard accents go farther, then come back, so that your action reads better and has more impact.

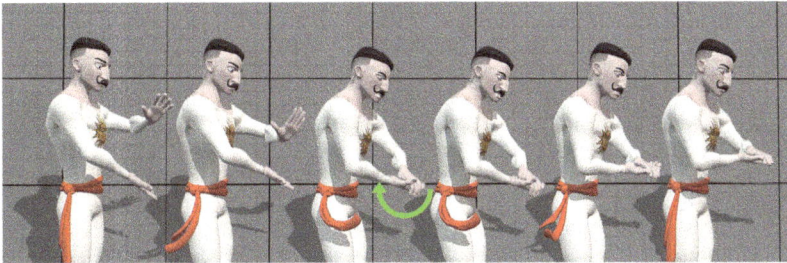

Figure 6.16

Believability

"Exaggerate but not arbitrarily," said Iwao Takamoto, the great Hanna-Barbera character designer and Milt Kahl's former assistant. There needs to be "a certain sound anatomical logic underneath it."[12]

Don't stray too far from the defined boundaries of your character, even if your animation is broad. The Crusher in **Bunny Hugged** (1951) is a wildly exaggerated character that stays within the limits Chuck Jones set — and that makes him more believable.

Unless your intention is to draw attention to the stretch, don't have a character that has been acting realistically throughout your film or scene, suddenly stretch in a cartoony manner. It takes you out of the scene and makes your animation less believable. Tone it down.

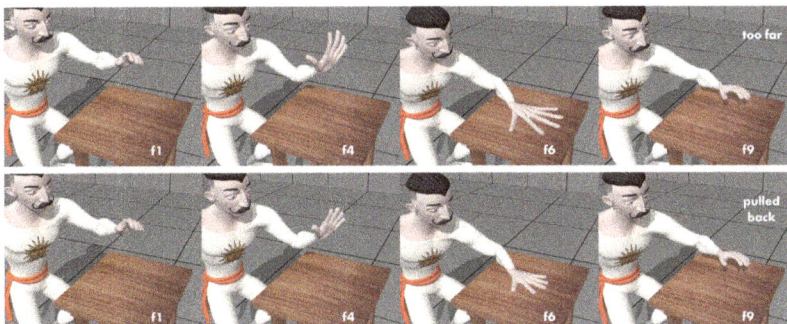

Figure 6.17

Good Judgment

Overly stretched poses can make your characters look like rubber-hose animation.

Figure 6.18

Exaggerate for a reason. Don't exaggerate something just because stretching your character is fun. Use good judgment.

Disney layout artist Ken O'Connor said Freddy Moore, "knew just when to exaggerate something and how much, and when to quit exaggerating."[13]

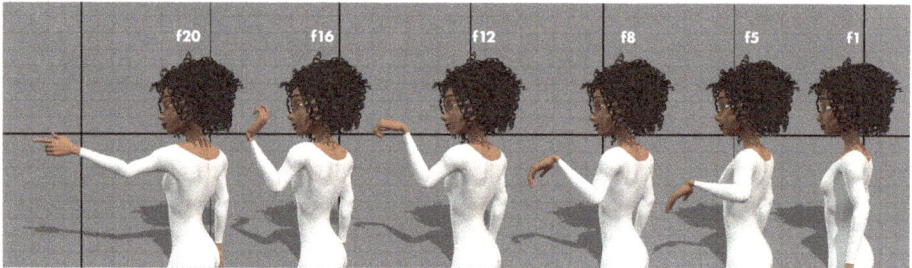

Figure 6.19

Animation Exercise – Copy some poses from reference and exaggerate them to make them look more interesting. See how far you can push them!

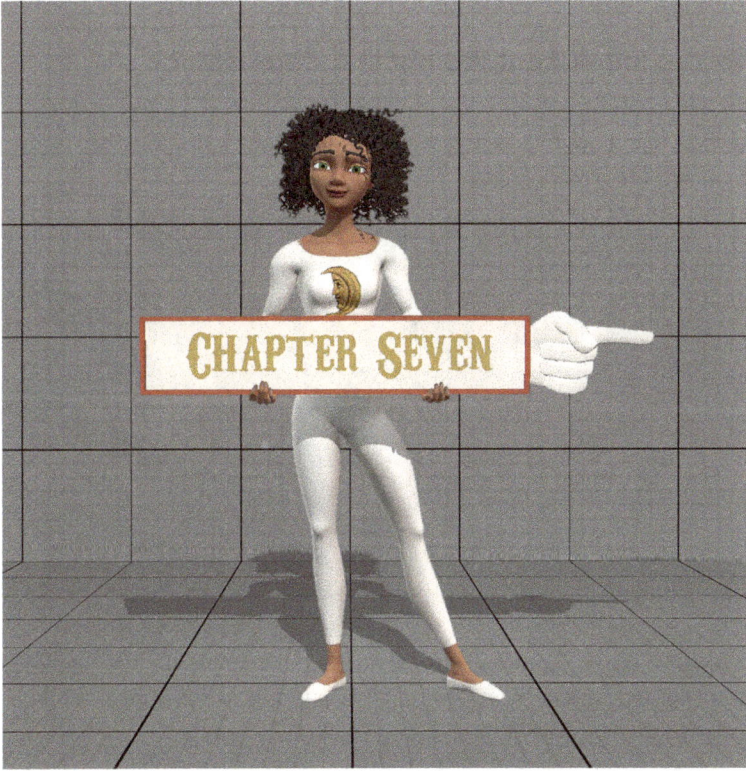

Chapter 7. Weight and Balance

Introduction

Why does Grumpy stomping off in Snow White show more weight than many characters in 3D films and games made today? Why do large, heavy characters in some animated films or games move as if they weigh the same as much smaller characters?

Cheating weight and balance makes your animation look less believable. In this chapter we'll learn how to make even the most unbelievable movement look and feel convincing with proper weight and balance.

How Do You Show Real Weight in a Character?

Showing weight in 2D animation is difficult enough, but in 3D animation it's especially challenging. How often have you seen a character in a 3D animated film or game running as if they're being held up by strings like a marionette?

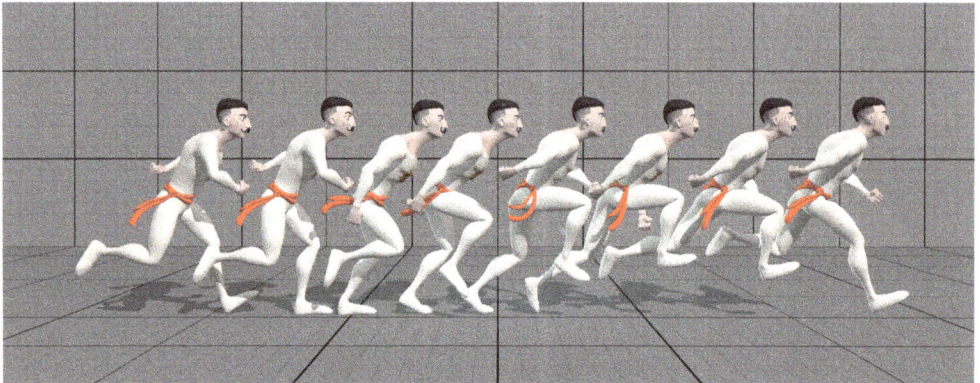

Figure 7.1

Or perhaps you've seen a character in a waist-up shot turn around like a roly-poly toy? The character simulates turning by doing an anticipation, then swings around with a lot of overlap. That's cheating!

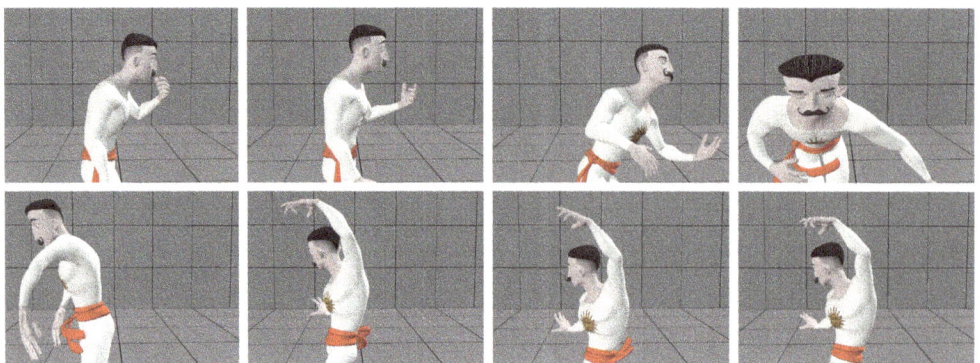

Figure 7.2

DOI: 10.1201/9781003361893-8

Who knows what's going on with the feet?

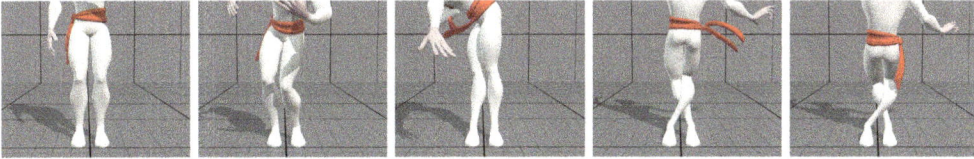

Figure 7.3

Or maybe you've seen a character jump up onto something without any effort, as if they weighed twenty pounds?

Figure 7.4

Too often animators don't trust the principles of weight and balance — or disregard them. It takes trust, and some elbow grease, to properly apply weight and balance.

There's the well-known story Richard Williams tells of when he asked Milt Kahl how he animated Shere Kahn the tiger in *Jungle Book* with such convincing weight. Kahl told him, "Well, I know where the weight is on every drawing, I know where the weight is at every given moment on the character; where the weight is, and where it's coming from, and where it's just traveling over and where the weight is transferring to."[1]

That, in a nutshell, is one of the big secrets of animation.

Balance and Center of Gravity

An easy way to understand weight shift is to think of your center of gravity. Center of gravity is an imaginary point in a body where the weight is concentrated. Standing straight with both feet under your shoulders, your weight is evenly distributed.

Your center of gravity is right in the middle.

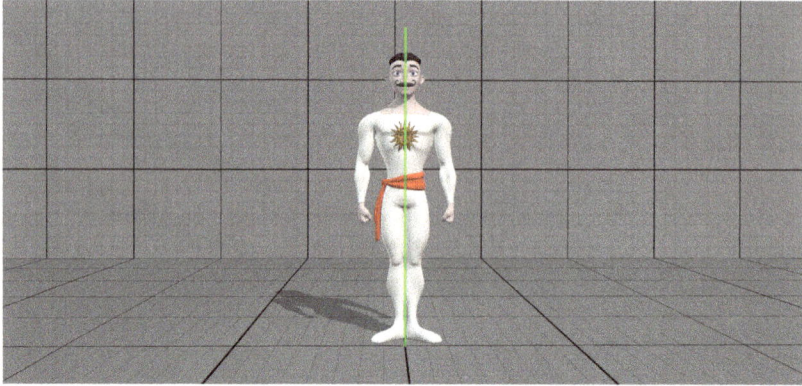

Figure 7.5

If you shift your weight to one side, your center of gravity is now over your supporting foot.

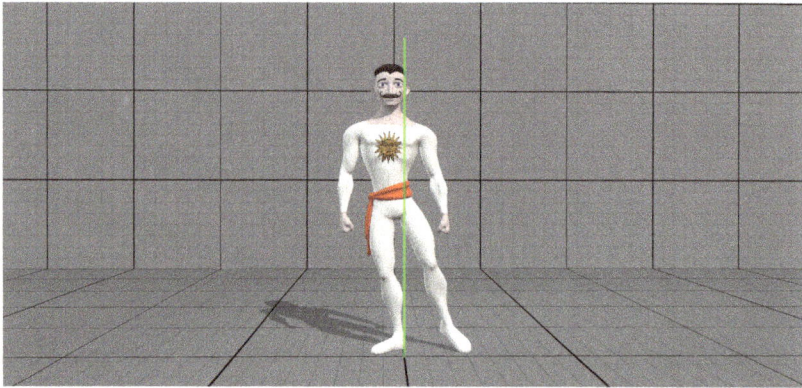

Figure 7.6

If your center of gravity moves past your supporting foot, you're off balance and you'll fall over.

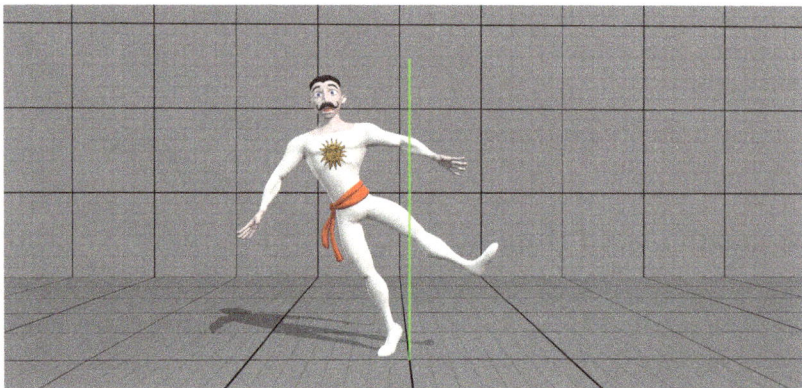

Figure 7.7

The center of gravity needs to be over some kind of support — a foot, a hand, a knee, etc.

Figure 7.8

Otherwise, your character is falling over!

Figure 7.9

Or, doing any other motion such as running, dancing, pitching, pushing something, etc. — any movement where the body is momentarily off-balance and then either regains its balance or falls.

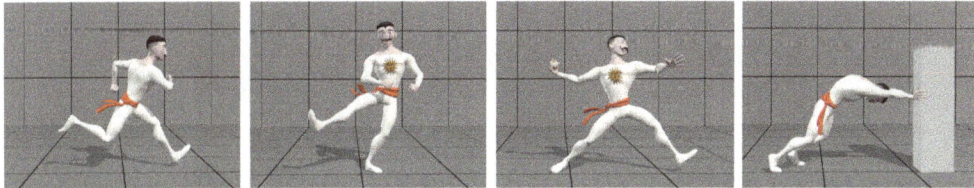

Figure 7.10

Kinematics or Action Analysis

Kinematics is the science of motion. In human movement, it is the study of the positions, angles, velocities, and accelerations of body segments and joints during motion.[2] In other words, kinematics describes the movement and timing of body movement. Action analysis classes started by Don Graham at Disney were basically the same thing; they analyzed and broke down motion.

The different anatomical planes of the body are the transverse, sagittal, and coronal planes. Don't worry, there won't be a quiz! All you need to remember is that dividing the body up into the top and bottom half (transverse), left and right side (sagittal), and the front and back halves of the body (coronal), makes it much easier to break down actions and understand weight shift.

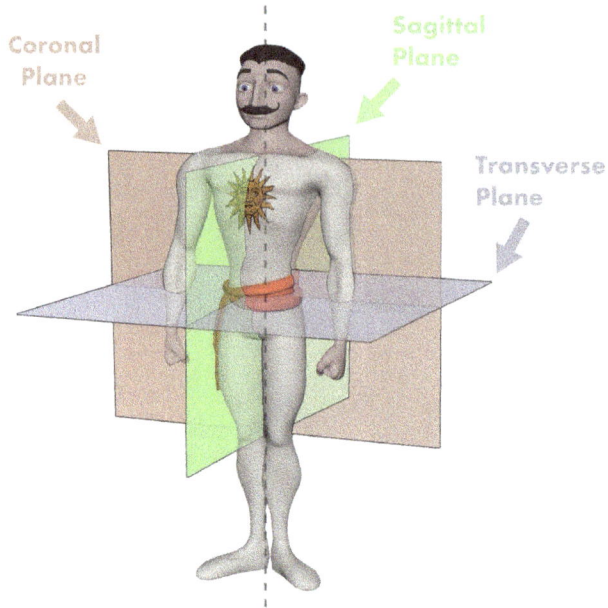

Figure 7.11

How far your character is leaning forward past their center axis will explain how fast they're moving. The farther a character leans past their center axis, the faster they're moving.

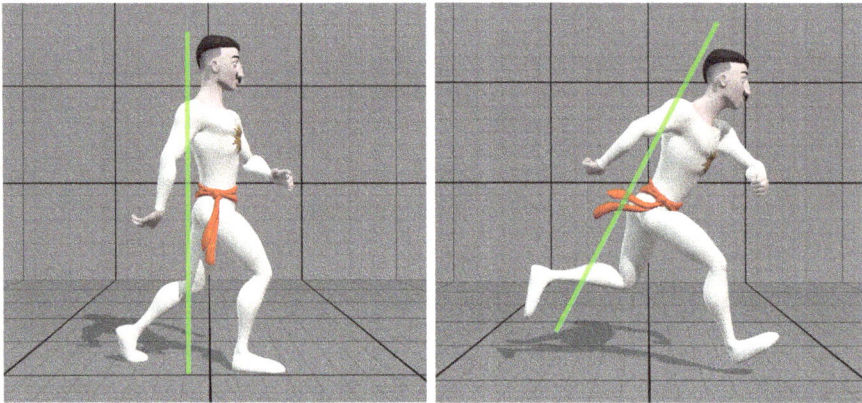

Figure 7.12

Counterbalance

Any time a character's hips shift forward or backward, or side-to-side, you need to add counterbalance or your character will look like they're falling over.

A character bends over and touches their toes. The weight should be evenly divided over their center axis (coronal plane). If not, they'll fall over.

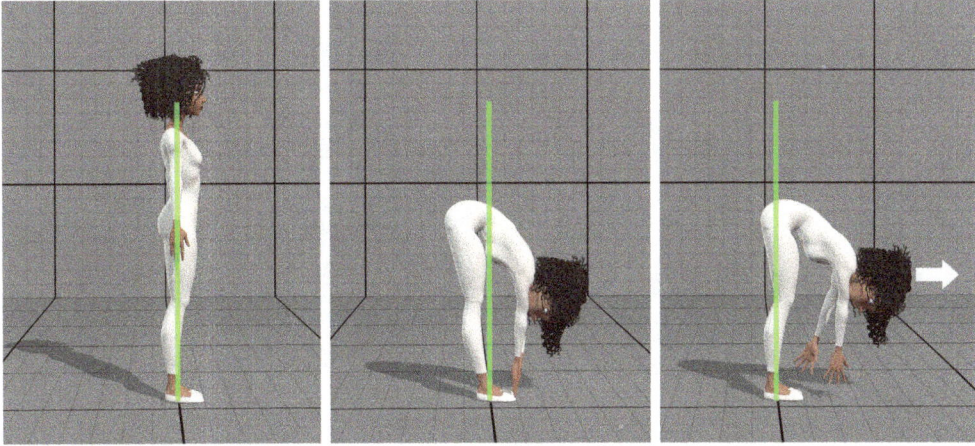

Figure 7.13

Remember, if your character is shifting their weight to the side, past the vertical axis (sagittal plane), counterbalance the shift or they'll look stiff or be falling over. Add counterbalance by curving the spine back over the axis.

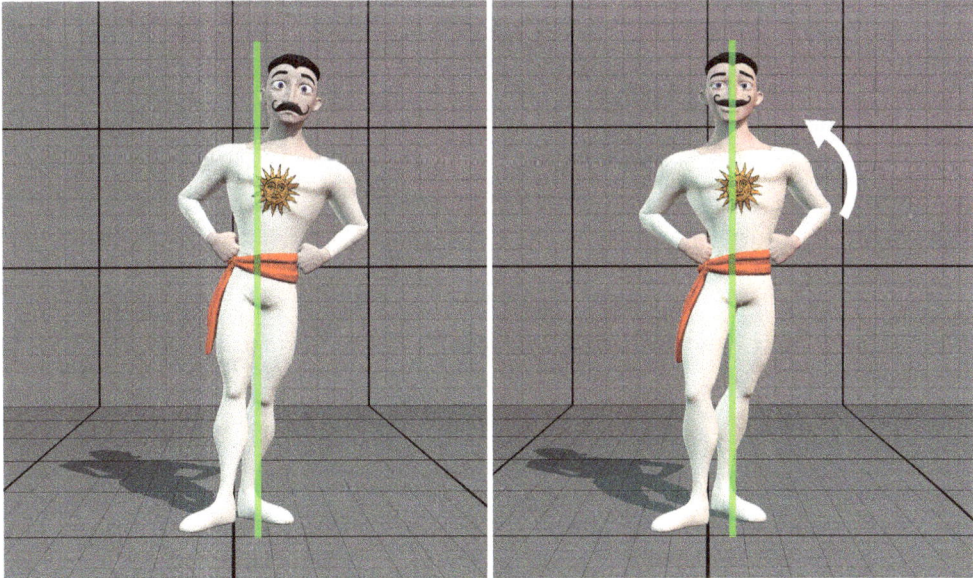

Figure 7.14

How many times have you had to put a hand down when squatting for too long? Squatting down requires balance.

In a squat the weight has to be evenly distributed both laterally and front and back.

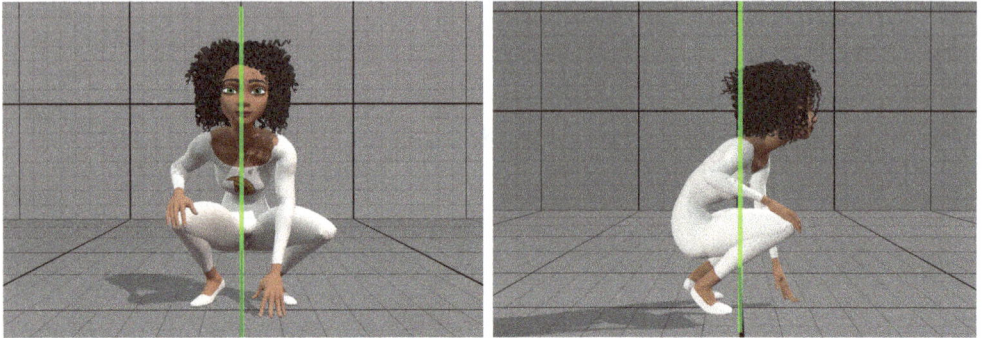

Figure 7.15

If not, you'll fall forward, backward, or to the side.

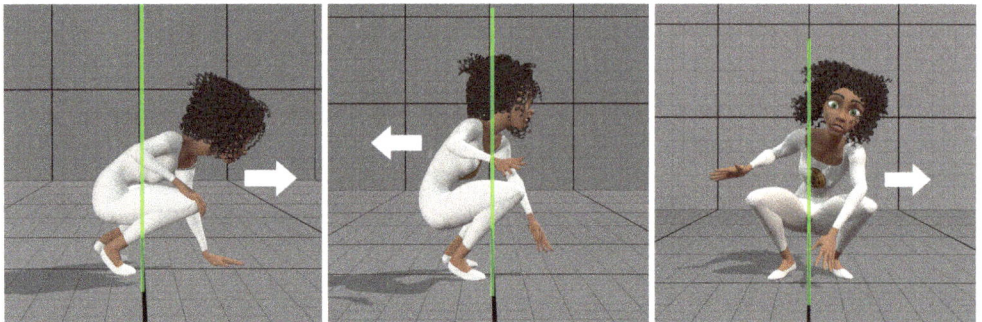

Figure 7.16

Where's the Weight?

How do we turn them around 180° without cheating?

Here are two poses of a character: a standing pose facing the camera and a standing pose with their back to us.

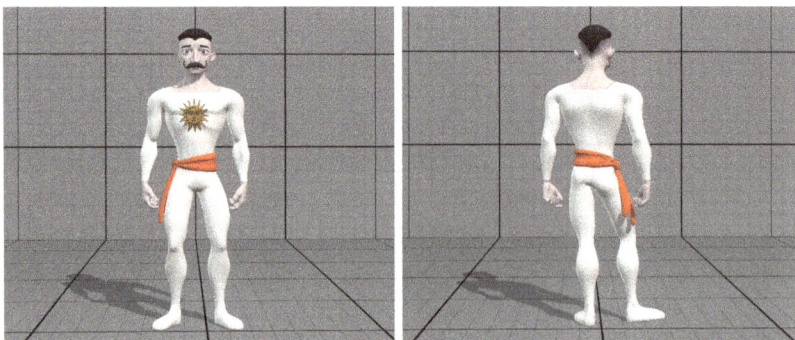

Figure 7.17

Start with your character in a neutral position with their back to us. Act it out. What part of your body do you turn first?

If your character turns to their right, they could look to the right first. Their weight will shift over their left foot.

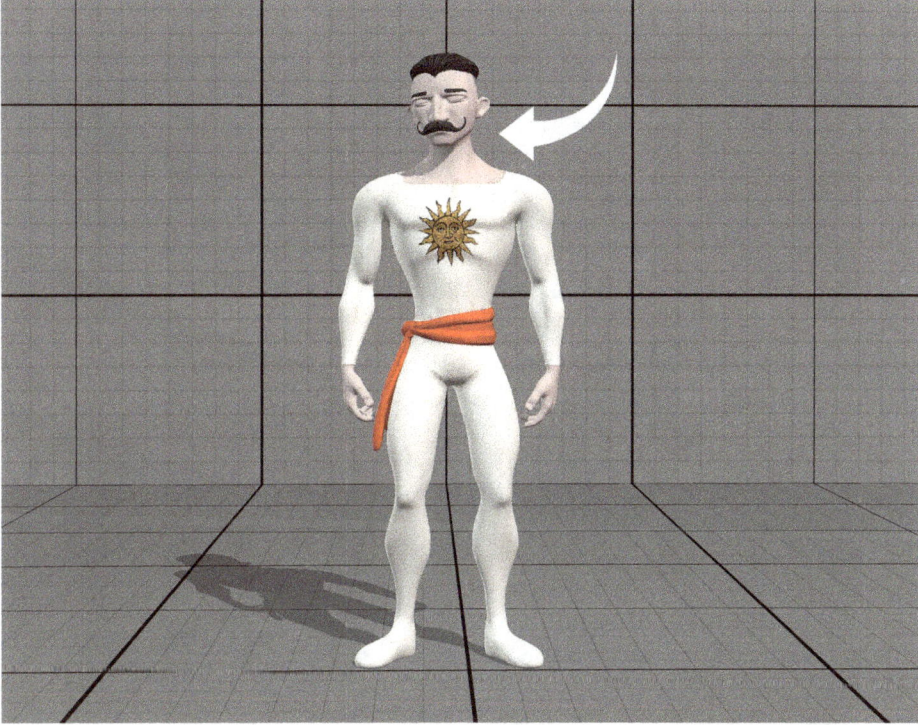

Figure 7.18

Transfer the weight! The weight must shift over the supporting foot for the opposite foot to lift!

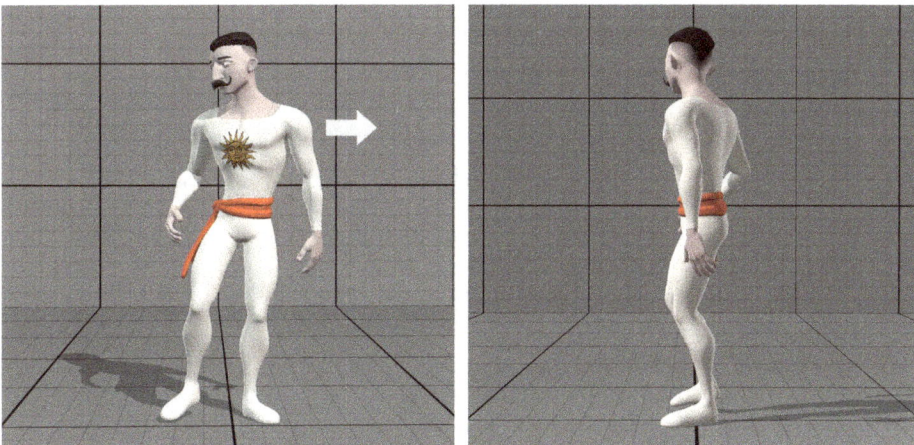

Figure 7.19

The 180° turn will probably take three steps: two with the right foot and one with the left foot. So, let's put the right foot down at about a 90° angle, or halfway.

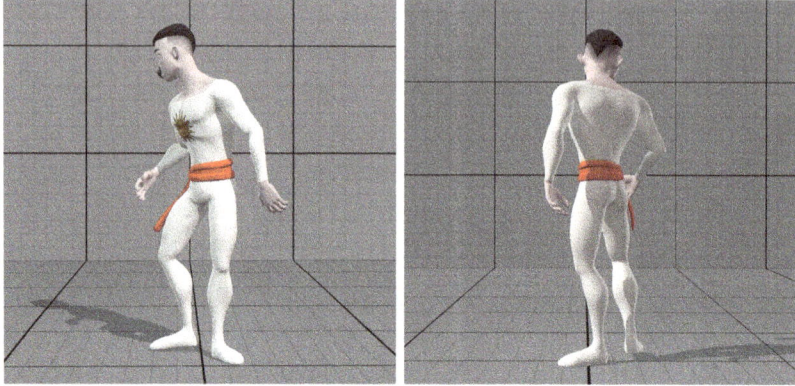

Figure 7.20

Their weight will now shift over the right foot so that they can lift their left foot.

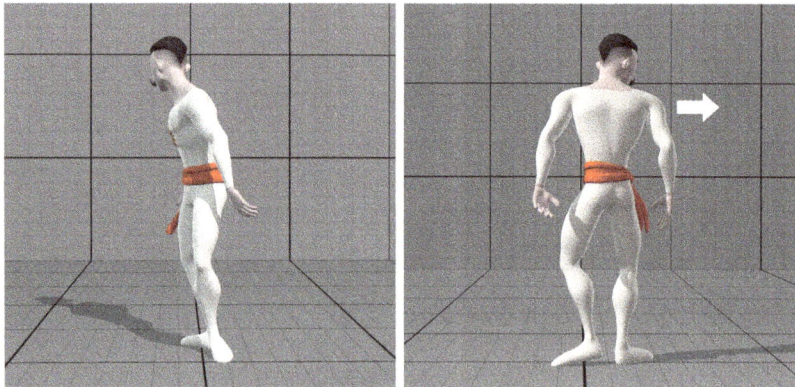

Figure 7.21

As they lift their left foot, their weight will shift a little more over the right foot.

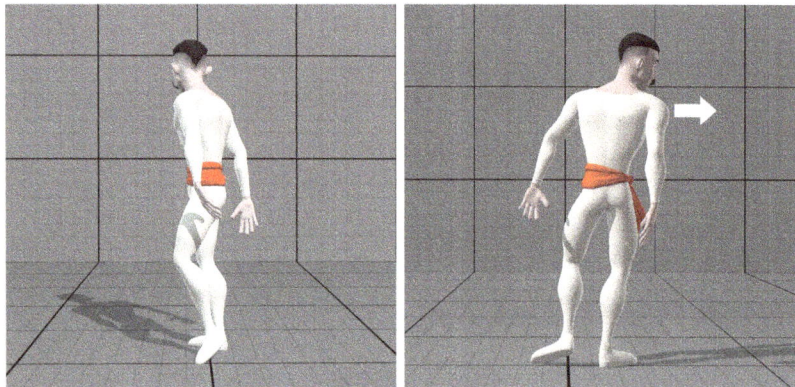

Figure 7.22

The left foot can now step into the final position.

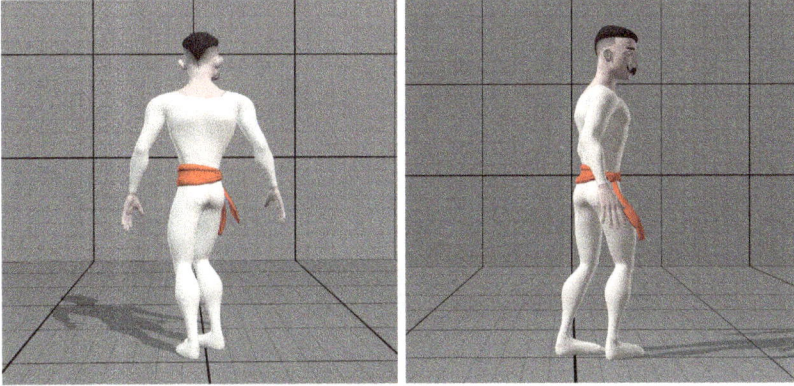

Figure 7.23

The weight shifts a little further over the left foot as the right foot lifts.

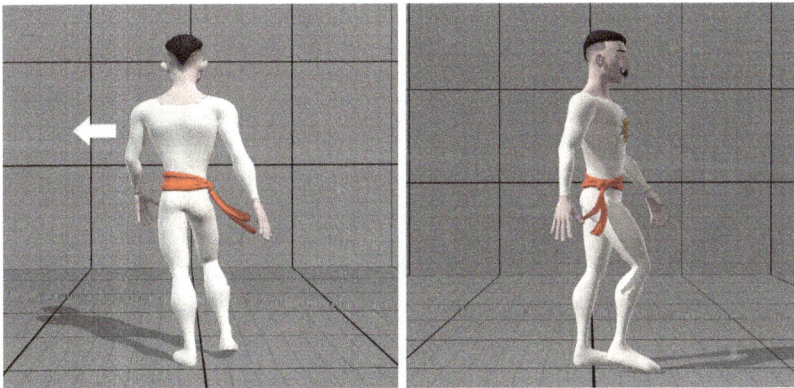

Figure 7.24

Then the right foot steps into its final position.

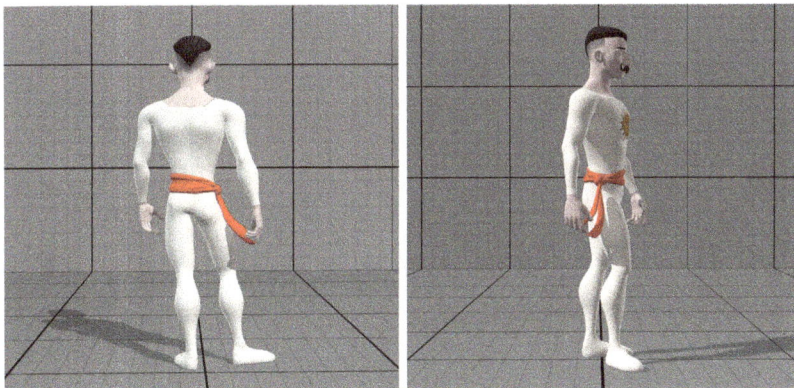

Figure 7.25

The weight can shift one last time, as your character returns back to a 180° neutral position.

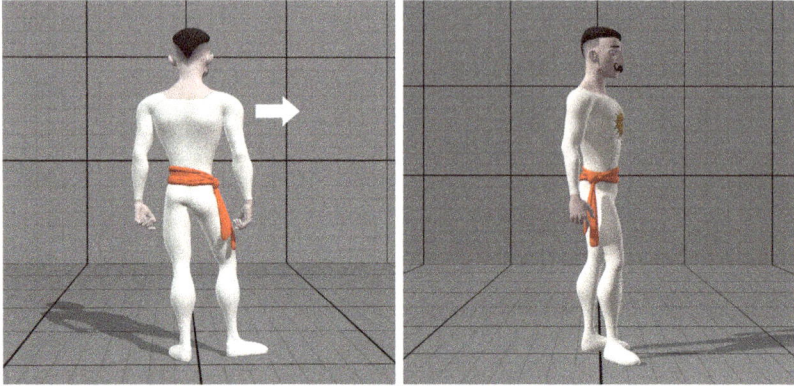

Figure 7.26

Obviously, there are endless ways to turn a character around.

If you wanted to turn your character around quicker, you could take out the step at 90° and rotate the right foot 180°. They would just end up a body width further to their right.

The faster the turn the more your character may lean because of the momentum. If that's the case, make sure you're still maintaining balance!

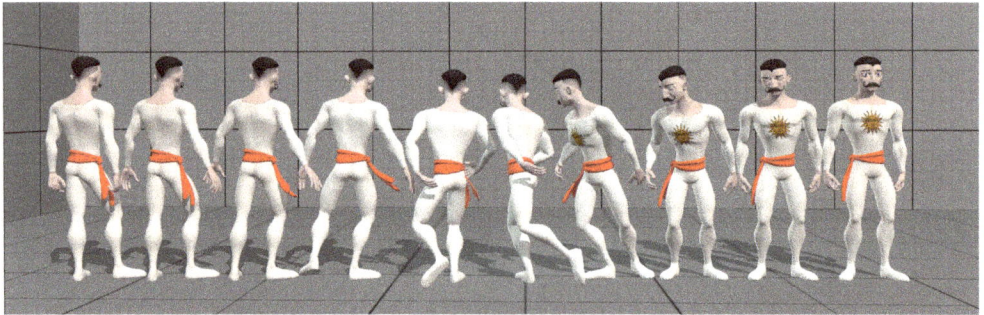

Figure 7.27

They could even hop up and turn around in the air.

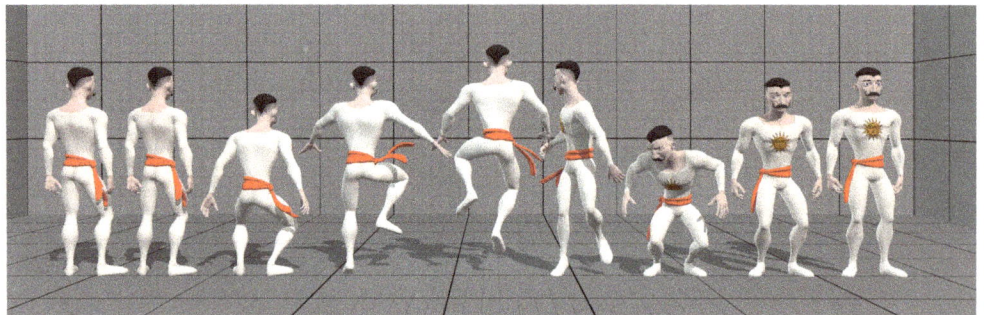

Figure 7.28

Maintain balance throughout the jump — even in the air. A balanced in-air pose makes it easier to land and show weight when landing.

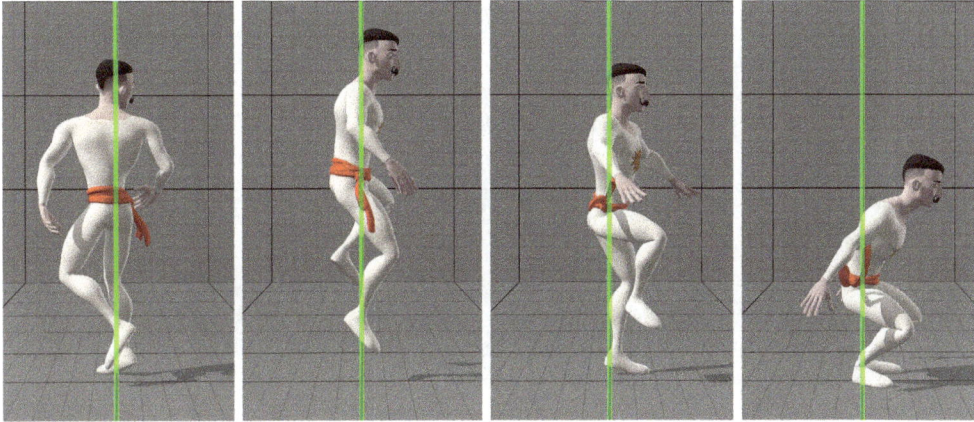

Figure 7.29

Showing Weight with Timing and Spacing

Scaling animation doesn't add weight to your character, it only creates slow motion. If you scale a fifty-frame ball bounce to one hundred frames, you're not adding weight, you're only adding more inbetweens.

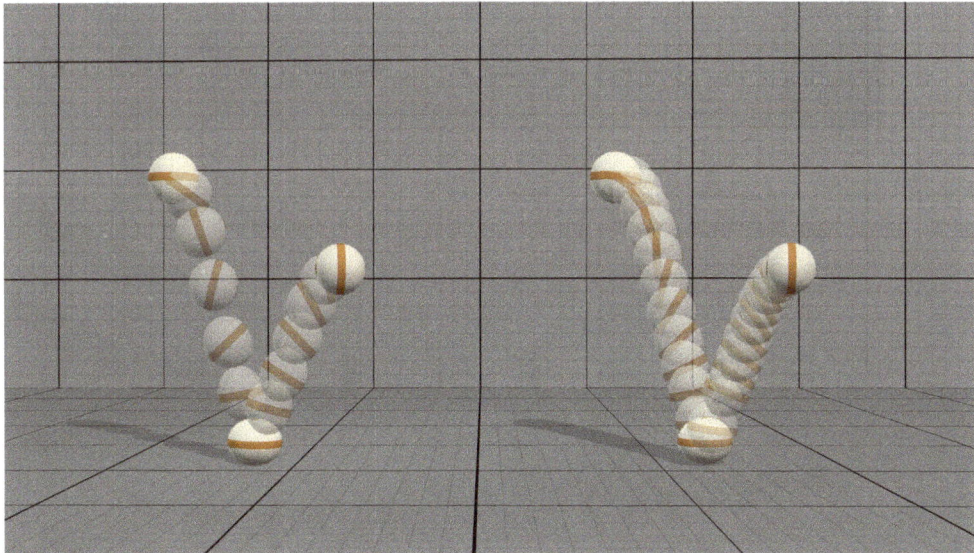

Figure 7.30

If you want the bouncing ball to have more weight, you can have the ball drop faster by spacing out the frames as the ball drops and reduce the height and distance of each bounce.

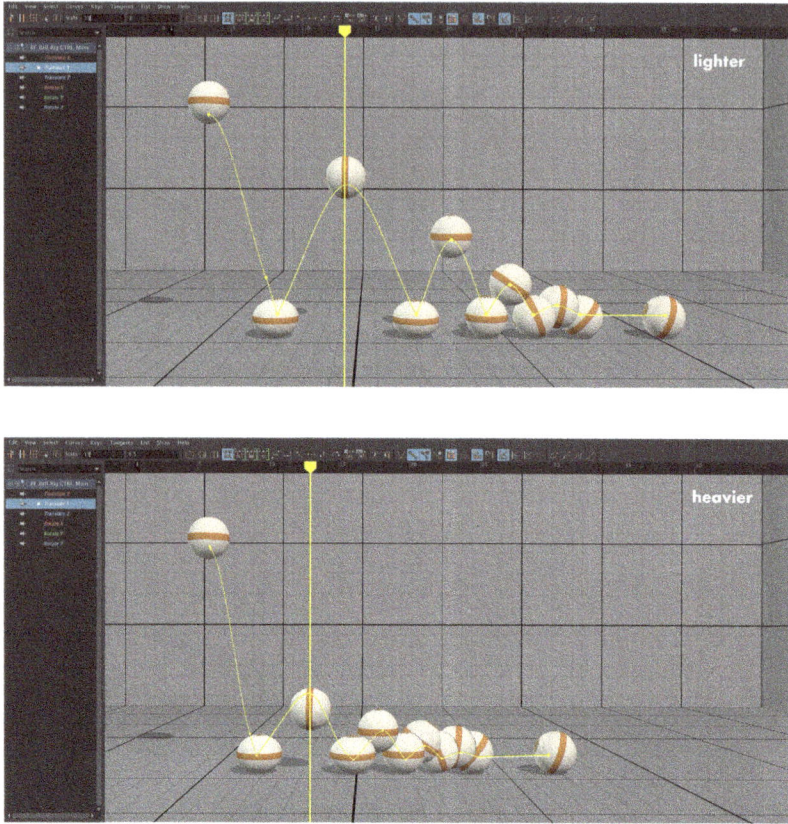

Figure 7.31

A heavy dinosaur takes longer to raise its body and to lift its dinosaur foot. Spending more time on the down poses with the feet on the ground, and less time with the feet in the air, adds weight.

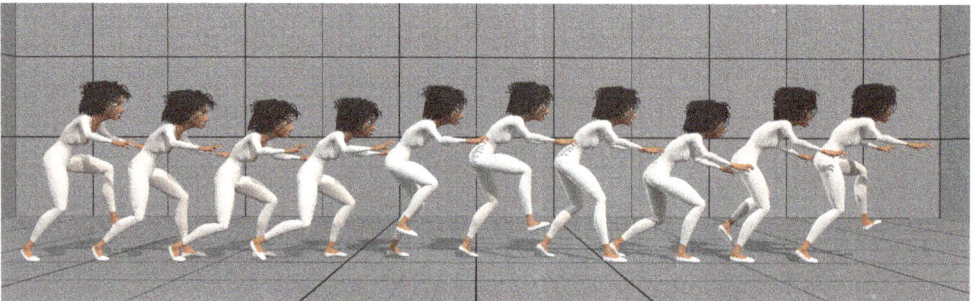

Figure 7.32

The same goes for wings flapping. If you want to give the impression of a bigger heavier wing, you'll need to show more effort in raising the wings, and then limit the height they raise.

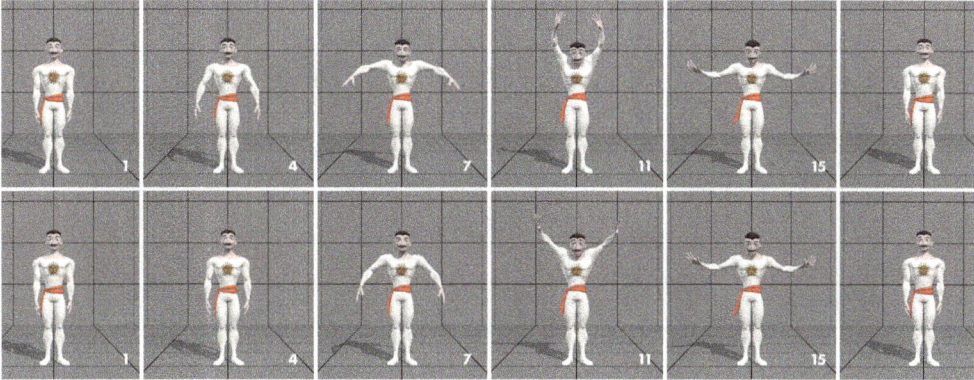

Figure 7.33

To show weight in timing and spacing: lower center of gravity, limited movement, and more time to change direction.

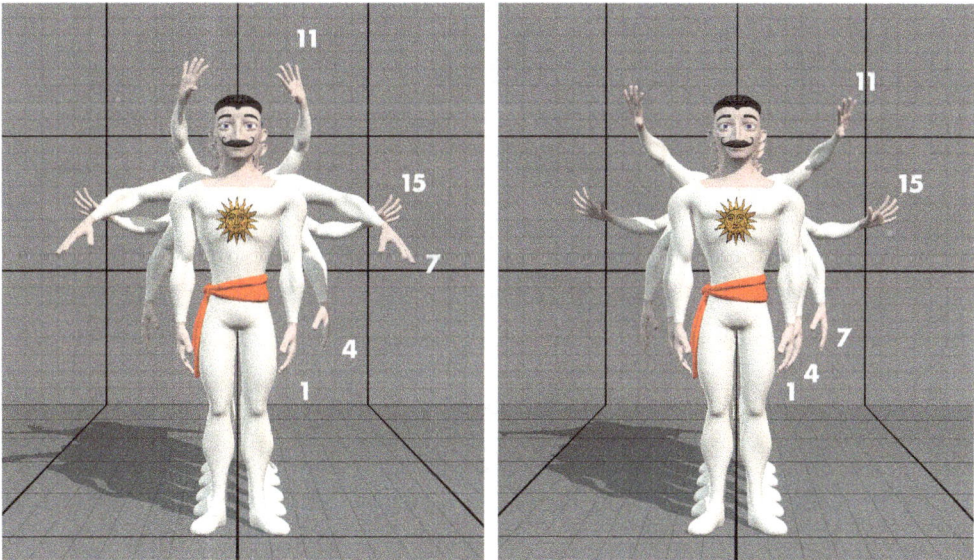

Figure 7.34

Counterbalance with a Weight

When your character lifts a heavy object, your character has a center of gravity, and so does the object they are going to lift.

As your character squats down to lift the object, keep your character balanced with the weight over the supporting foot.

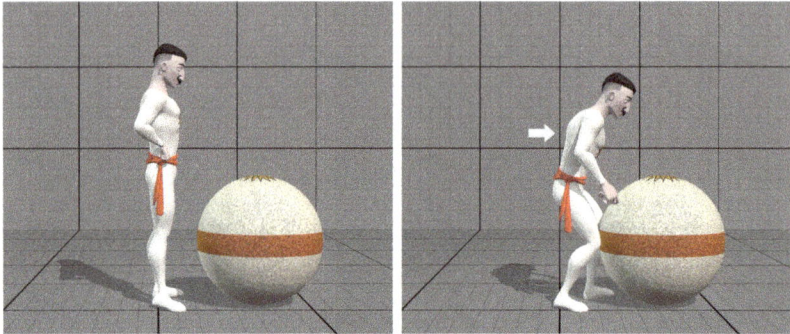

Figure 7.35

Your character's back could be either convex or concave when they are about to lift the object up. It's your choice. However, because we'll want our character to lean back (concave) when they have the weight in their arms, we'll make their back lean forward (convex) for the start pose. This will show contrast!

Figure 7.36

As your character lifts the heavy object, the center of gravity is still over the supporting legs.

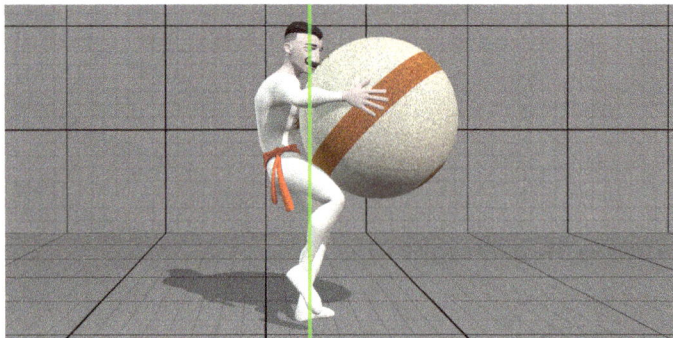

Figure 7.37

When they have the heavy object in their arms, the center of gravity shifts to include the weight they are carrying.

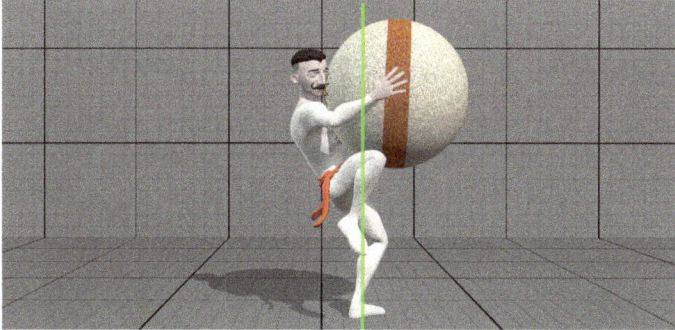

Figure 7.38

Whenever your character takes a step, the center of gravity is momentarily past the supporting leg, and they're basically falling.

Figure 7.39

So, they'll have to quickly regain their center of gravity by planting the foot. Show the force by adding a squash when the weight is on the supporting foot. Exaggerate! Show the highs and lows!

Figure 7.40

Remember, the center of gravity is always over the supporting foot unless your character is falling!

When you walk quickly or run, you're leaning past your center of gravity, so you're basically falling. You catch yourself by planting your foot in front of you and regaining your center of gravity.

Weight with Objects

There are different ways to show weight when moving, or trying to move, a heavy object. When trying to move an almost impossibly heavy object, look for reverses in the line of action.

Figure 7.41

Get creative! How many variations can you think of?

Figure 7.42

How do you show weight in an object being held or carried? First decide how much the object weighs. Then show the effect the weight has on the body.

Is it light? Or is the object so heavy it affects your character's line of action?

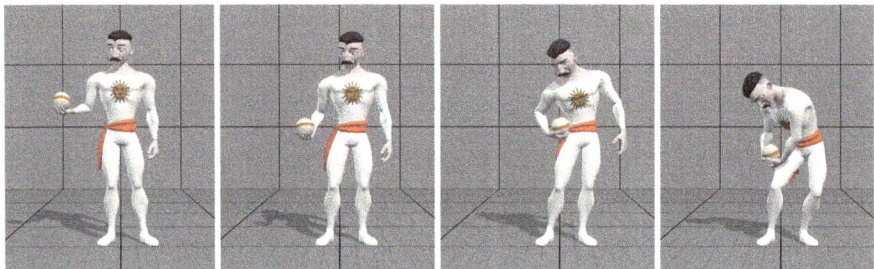

Figure 7.43

Getting a convincing feeling of weight in an object can be tricky. Use muscle memory!

"Practice opening a jar," said the acting teacher, Stella Adler. "Practice it over and over until your muscles remember just how much strength and energy are required in each case."[3]

Think about the weight of the object a character is holding. Try holding something with the same weight. Does it lower your forearm? Does it pull on your shoulder? Does it tilt you to one side?

Put that into your poses!

Believability

Don't treat different-sized characters as if they weigh the same. If they're different sizes, animate them differently.

Otherwise, your characters become boring and your animation is less believable.

Tissa David said that one of the secrets of character was to imagine the specific weight of each of her characters! "This character is 135 pounds."[4]

Bill Tytla said that the animation of each of the seven dwarves in **Snow White** was handled in different ways to make each of them unique. "The spacing on them is different, the way they handle their hands is different . . . and their timing in a certain situation."[5]

"I was dealing with realism first, but I realized that believability was much more important," said Chuck Jones. "I discovered that if you get a feeling of weight, you're all right."[6]

Show weight through posture, timing, and spacing, and squash and stretch. You'll be surprised how good your animation will look and feel when the weight and balance are correct!

Animation Exercise – Block in a scene of a character lifting a heavy weight. Use just a sphere as the weight. Start with an idle pose, then reach down and pick up the object. Show a change of weight in the posture. Do they walk with the heavy object? How does the weight affect their walk? Do they fall over?

Chapter 8. Foot Plant

Introduction

How many times have you seen a character's feet sliding from pose to pose? This isn't an issue unique to video games either. Many beginner animators don't consider foot plant when posing out a scene, and some seasoned animators may find some foot-sliding acceptable. Well, it shouldn't be acceptable. It's cheating, or just plain lazy, and produces unconvincing movement.

Because foot plant is so crucial in selling believable weight, it deserves to have its own chapter, even if brief — just to highlight its importance.

Showing Weight

Solid foot plant shows stability and stability helps sell weight. When a character's weight is shifted over their supporting foot, as in a contrapposto pose, the weight presses the foot down, so the foot isn't moving.

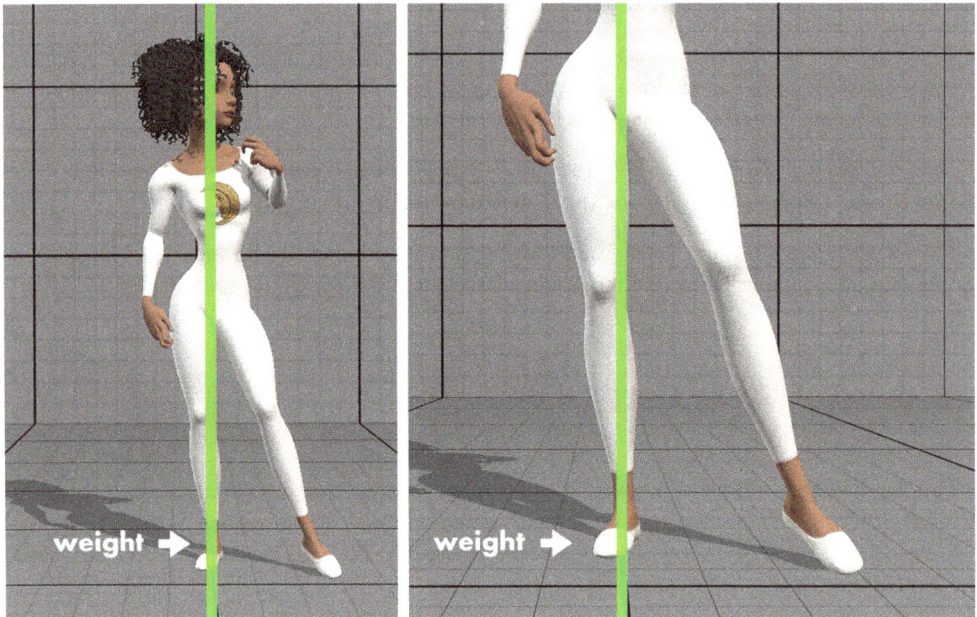

Figure 8.1

The more firmly planted your character's feet are before beginning an action, the more believable their weight will feel.

Chuck Jones would write "BAL" for "balance" on his exposure sheets. "And all my animators had to know what exactly [that] meant," he said. "BAL" might mean I'd want a particular character solid on his feet before he did something, so you'd know that there was a stability to the thing, before it moved into action."[1]

DOI: 10.1201/9781003361893-9

A character stomps their foot and then raises their heel. Keeping the feet solid as the knees bend, and aligning the toes helps sell the weight.

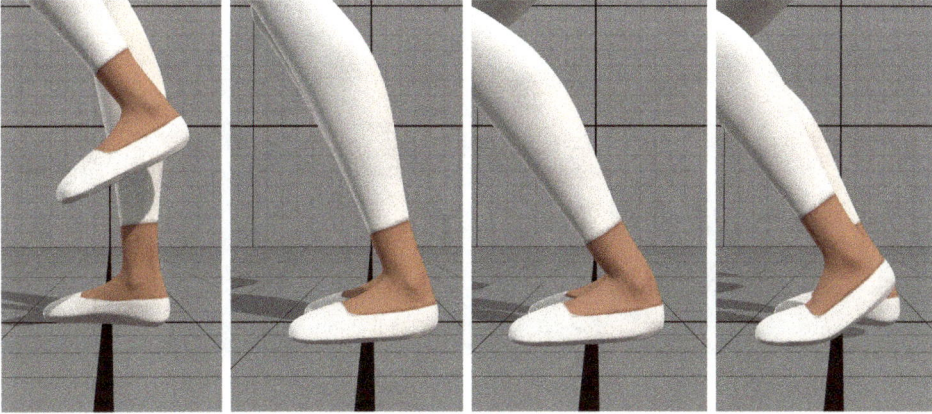

Figure 8.2

When a character jumps up, they push up off the balls of their feet, or maybe their toes.

Don't move the feet! Line up the big toes.

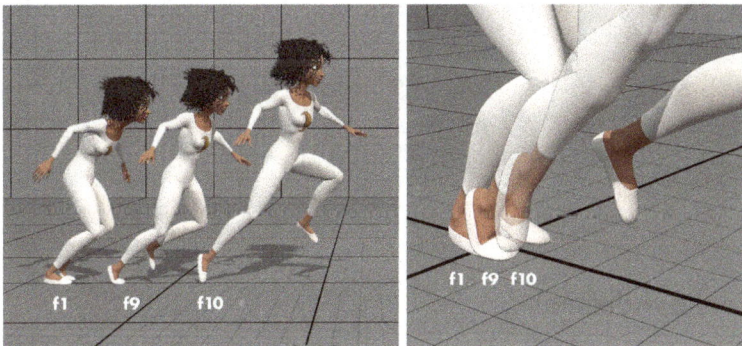

Figure 8.3

Look at the feet from multiple angles. Toggle back and forth between the neutral pose, the anticipation, and the pushing-off pose to make sure the feet aren't sliding.

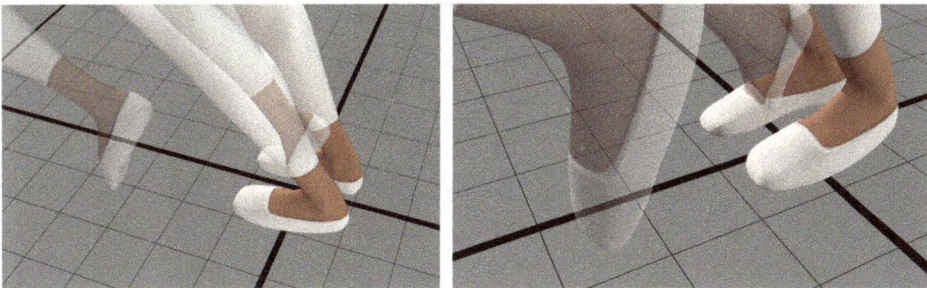

Figure 8.4

What if your character is rotating and needs to turn on their foot? Rotate on the ball of the foot using the big toe as the pivot point. Look at it from multiple angles, toggling back and forth to make sure that the big toe lines up — resting pose and rotated pose. Check the alignment from multiple angles.

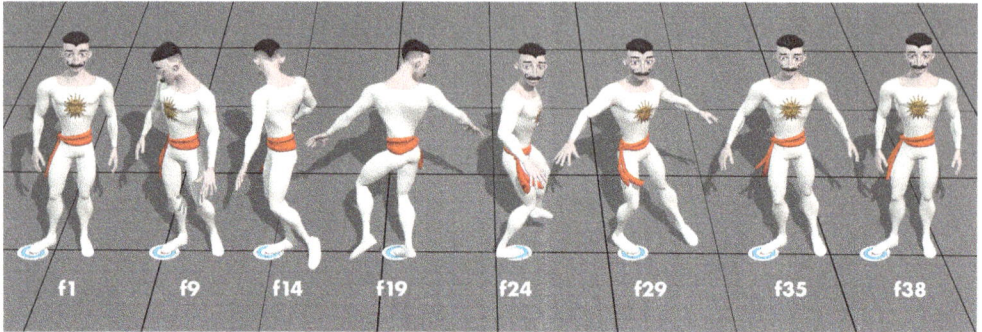

Figure 8.5

Rotating a foot can be tricky. You may need to go back and nudge your inbetweens so that the toes don't stray off the pivot point.

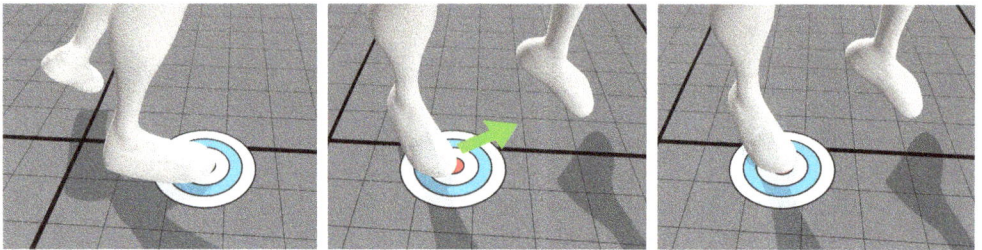

Figure 8.6

Moving Feet Syndrome!

Don't slide the feet from pose to pose. It was a pet peeve of animator Michael Sporn who called it "moving feet syndrome"[2] and it's a pet peeve of mine!

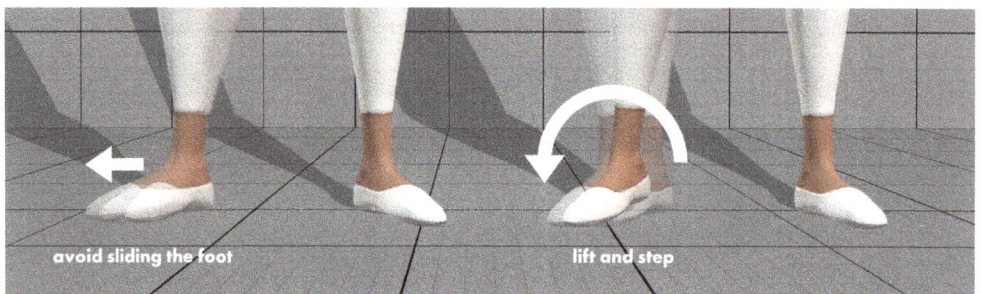

avoid sliding the foot

lift and step

Figure 8.7

Unless there's a reason for a foot slide, pick up each foot and step. Why ruin a nice scene with sloppy or lazy animation? It looks much better when a character shifts their weight and takes a step. Plus, you're also adding personality!

Figure 8.8

Taking a step is easy.

Start in a neutral position with the weight evenly distributed. Next pose out the contrapposto pose with the weight over the right foot. Remember to show contrast!

Figure 8.9

The subtler the change in poses, the less frames you'll need. The broader the step, the more frames you'll need.

Using frames 1 and 5 as the key poses, key frame 3, and raise the right foot to the desired height. We can get into more complicated spacing later, but for now keep it simple and use frame 3 as the breakdown. Tilt the toe down to show drag in the foot.

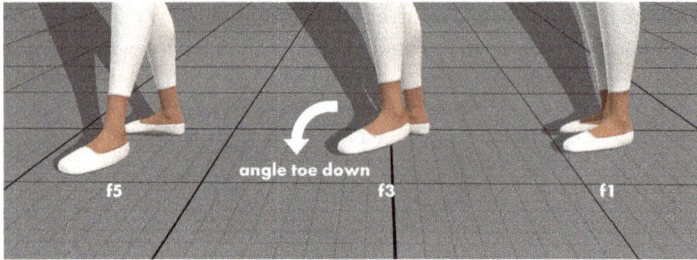

Figure 8.10

Now copy the foot on frame 1 and paste it down on frame 2. Raise the heel on the foot on frame 2 to show the push-off from the ball of the foot. Keep the ball of the foot aligned with the previous pose!

Figure 8.11

Frame 4 can inbetween by itself, or we can set a key.

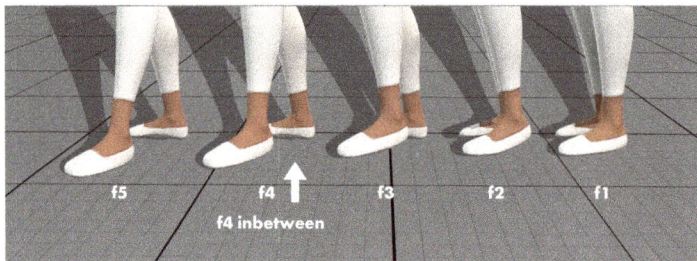

Figure 8.12

If we add a key, we can raise the toe for overlap on the inbetween stepping down — though it will probably look a little floppy with only a five-frame step.

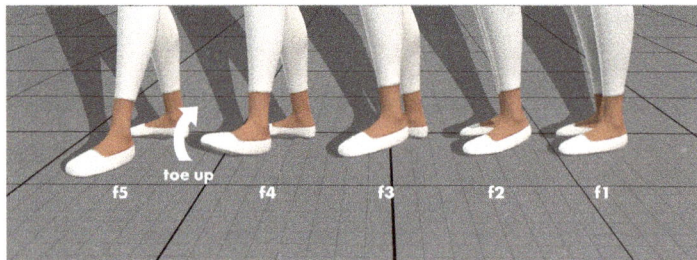

Figure 8.13

And that's as basic a step as there is!

Landing a Jump

When your character jumps or lands from a jump, aim the foot, heel, or toe at the planted foot position. Follow a path of action and align the landing or jumping with the foot pose on the ground.

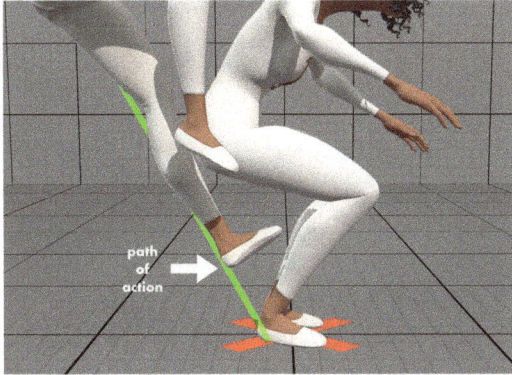

Figure 8.14

You don't want your foot to be off the path of action, and then suddenly jerk into place. That just looks odd.

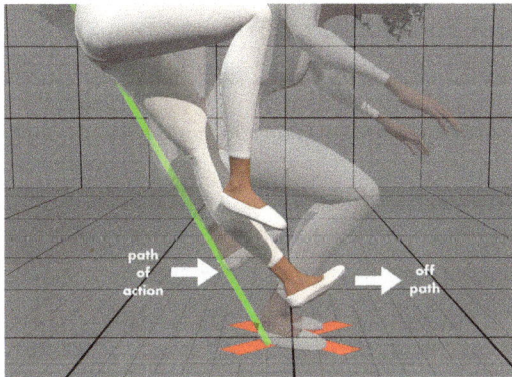

Figure 8.15

If you're going to land heel first, align the heel from the falling pose to the landing pose.

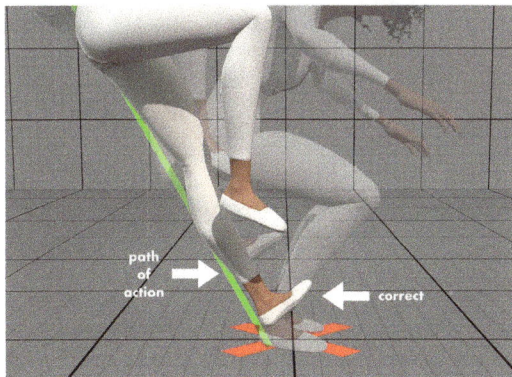

Figure 8.16

If you're going to land toe first, align the toe from the falling pose to the landing pose.

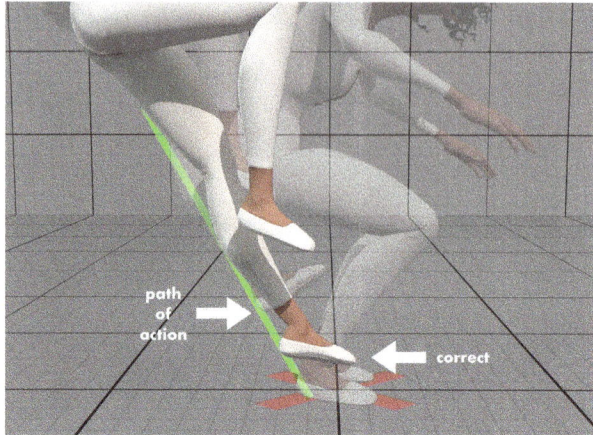

Figure 8.17

Aligning the foot on a jump or a landing with the planted foot may sound obvious but surprisingly, it's commonly missed.

A Quick Note About Foot Plant in Games

Feet in games can be tricky because you're blending clips — so, foot slide is sometimes unavoidable.

Come up with a neutral position for the feet in an idle that is easy to transition in and out of.

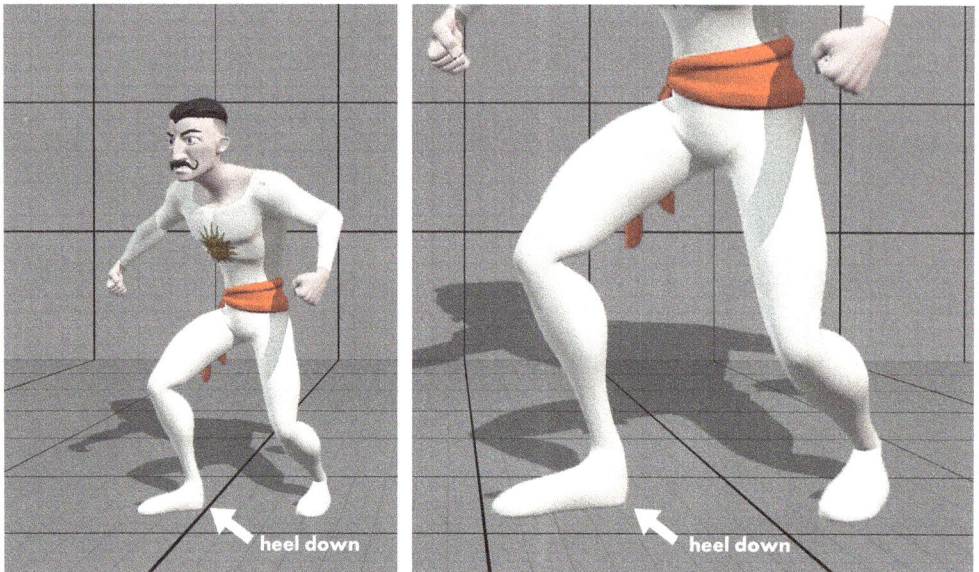

Figure 8.18

Avoid posing the feet in a way that draws attention to itself or makes for awkward transitions, such as a raised heel. Transitions in games are usually quick, so less time can be spent with the feet flat on the ground if the heel has to raise every time your character returns to idle.

The fewer foot-planted frames, the less weight your character will have.

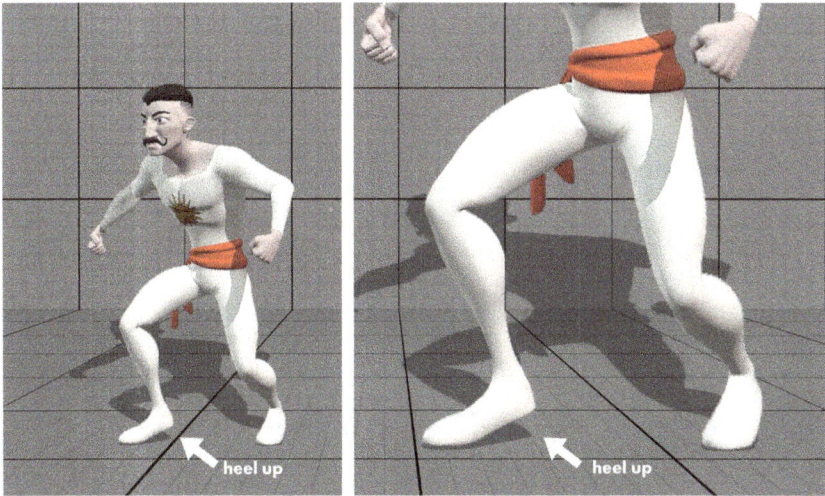

Figure 8.19

In games, if you know where the weight is in your character, it's much easier to blend clips. Match the foot supporting the weight in two clips, and you'll be on your way!

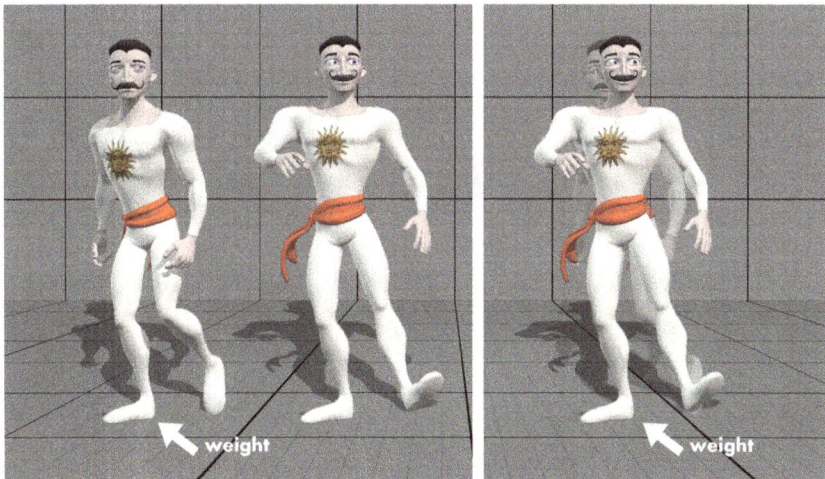

Figure 8.20

Animation Exercise — Animate a footstep! Start with a neutral pose, shift the weight over the supporting foot, lift the other foot, and step into a contrapposto pose.

Chapter 9. Arcs

Introduction

Unless you're animating a machine, even the subtlest of actions, will get an arc.

In this chapter we'll show how arcs are key to creating fluid animation, how to get arcs with a small number of frames, and how to double-check your arcs in the graph editor.

Everything Gets an Arc

"The movements of most living creatures will follow a slightly circular path,"[1] wrote Frank and Ollie. If you let the computer inbetween your animation, your inbetweens will be linear because that's what computers do.

A character looking to their right turns their head to look left. The computer inbetweens evenly.

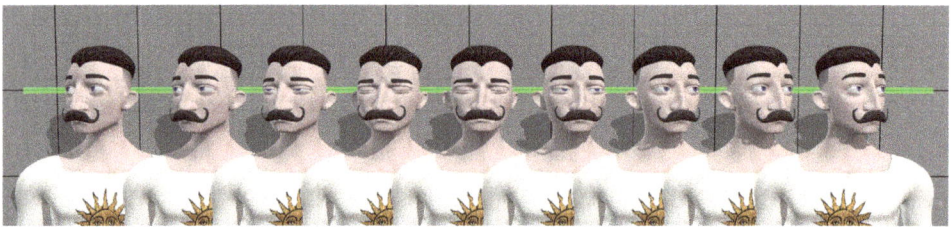

Figure 9.1

An arc to a head turn adds interest.

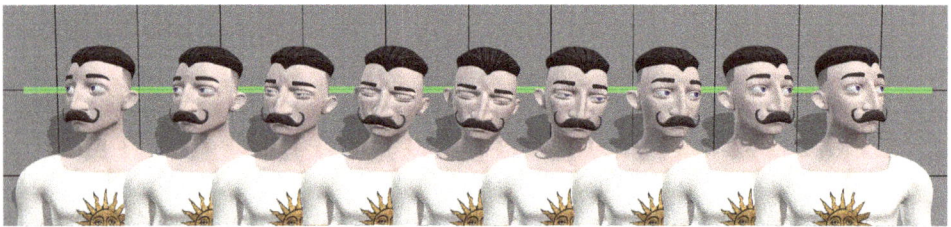

Figure 9.2

As we now know, everything in your scene follows its own path of action: the head, the nose, the shoulders, the arms, the hands, the fingers, the hips, the thighs, the knees, the ankles, the feet, and the toes. A path of action is made up mainly of arcs — but there could be some straight lines.

A ball rolling across the floor follows a straight path of action.

Figure 9.3

DOI: 10.1201/9781003361893-10

A character may drop from the sky or fly across the screen in a straight path of action.

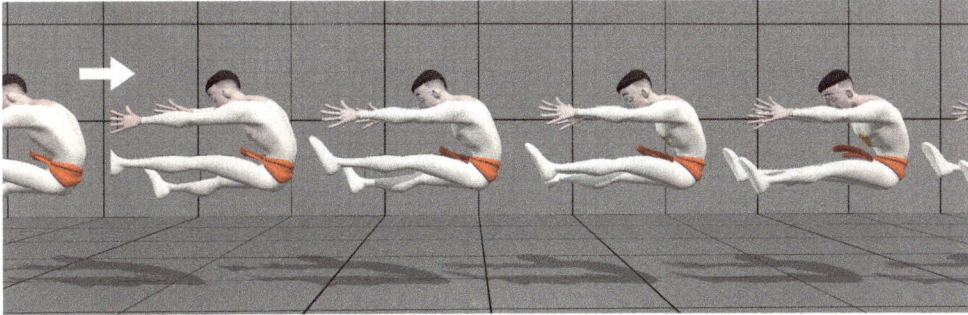

Figure 9.4

Whenever you have a straight path of action on a non-mechanical organic being, precede or end the straight path with an arc. A punch may follow a straight path of action...

Figure 9.5

... but it begins and ends with an arc. There's an arc when your character chambers or anticipates the punch.

Figure 9.6

And an arc at the end when the punch follows through.

Figure 9.7

Even when doing something as simple as pointing, your character may point in a straight line of action, but their finger needs to start or return in at least a subtle arc.

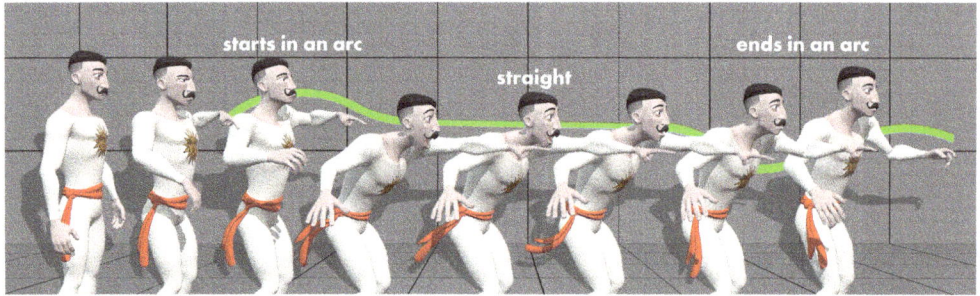

Figure 9.8

When animating a loop, don't arc back the same way. Find a different path. Add at least a small arc to the return otherwise your action will look mechanical, or as if you're playing your scene in reverse.

An arc is an arc, no matter how small!

Figure 9.9

Return in the same direction only if you're going for a comedic effect, such as a ball bouncing off a wall.

Or a mechanical effect — which, on a living creature, will most likely be another comedic effect.

Figure 9.10

For complicated actions, such as a sneak, be aware of every part of your character. Everything gets an arc: the head, nose, ears, pupils, shoulders, elbows, hands, fingers, hips, knees, and toes. Everything!

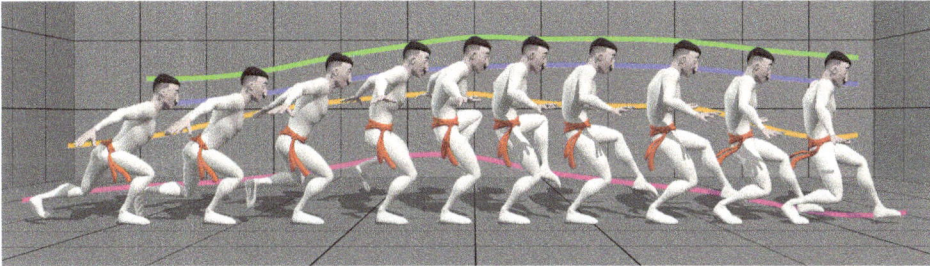

Figure 9.11

Arc Up or Down?

A character turns 90°. You may want to arc the hips slightly as the character turns, otherwise your action will look mechanical. Do you arc the hips up or down as the character turns?

Figure 9.12

It depends on what your next action will be. If your character is going to reach up after turning 90°, then you may want the hips to arc down because on the next action, the hips will move up. Why arc the hips up, then down, then up again? Keep the path of action simple.

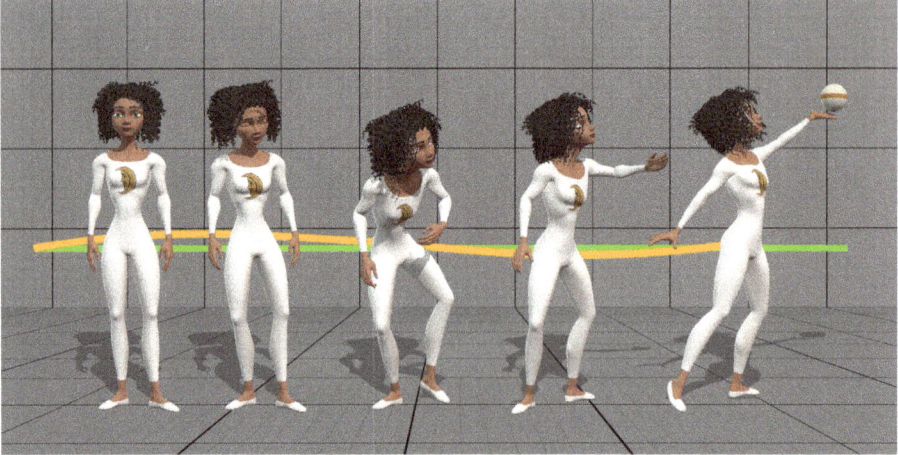

Figure 9.13

If the character is going to squat or kneel after turning 90° then you'll probably want to arc the hips up. This way the hips arc up as the character starts the 90° turn, then down into the kneel.

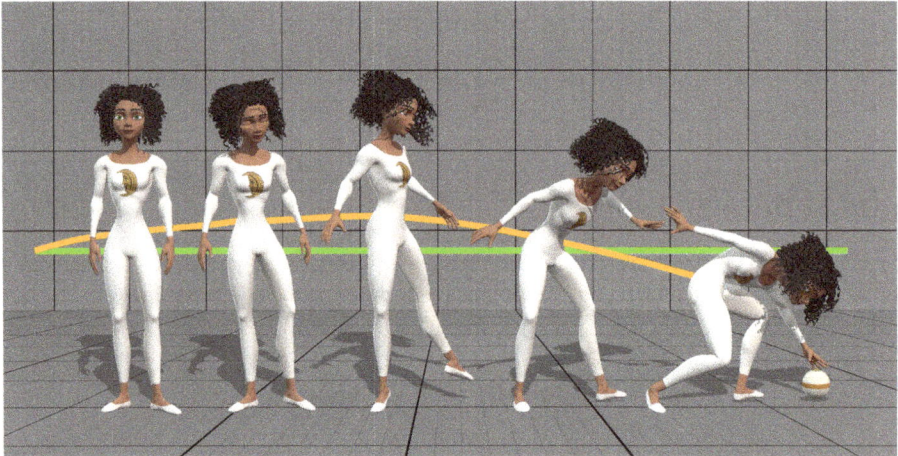

Figure 9.14

The simpler and more straightforward your arc is, the slower your action will appear. Refining arcs gives you more time!

Contrasting Arcs

Contrast could also determine the direction of your arc. To avoid two body parts moving in the same direction at the same time, contrast in the arcs.

A character passes a ball to the character next to them. You could arc the head over and the hand under, or the head under and the hand over.

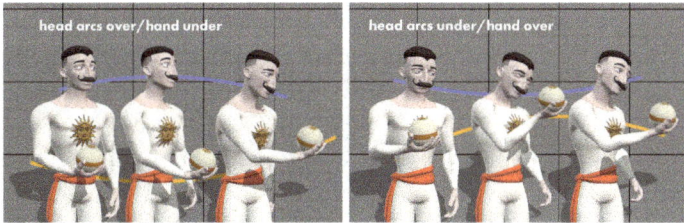

Figure 9.15

Contrasting arcs like this isn't a hard and fast rule — it's only something to consider. If you want two body parts arcing in the same direction, offset the timing by delaying one of them.

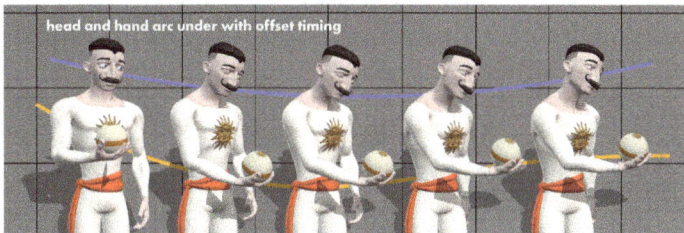

Figure 9.16

Check the Graph Editor

The better your arcs are, the smoother your animation will be. Don't have too many keys in your arcs. Keep them as simple as possible.

During a broad movement, such as an arm swing, you usually won't need as many keys. Two key poses and a breakdown or two to guide your arc should be enough.

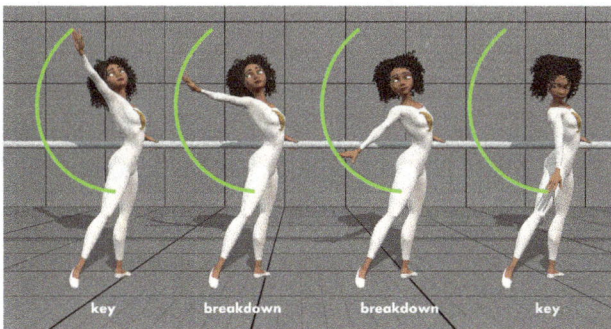

Figure 9.17

If your action is a little more complicated than that, see how many inbetweens you can delete without ruining the arc. If you have keys on the shoulder, elbow, and wrist, make sure that you key each of those joints for each key pose. You don't want to delete an inbetween and find that your key poses have been altered.

When deleting an inbetween, select the inbetween you'd like to delete in the graph editor, then look at your scene in the view pane.

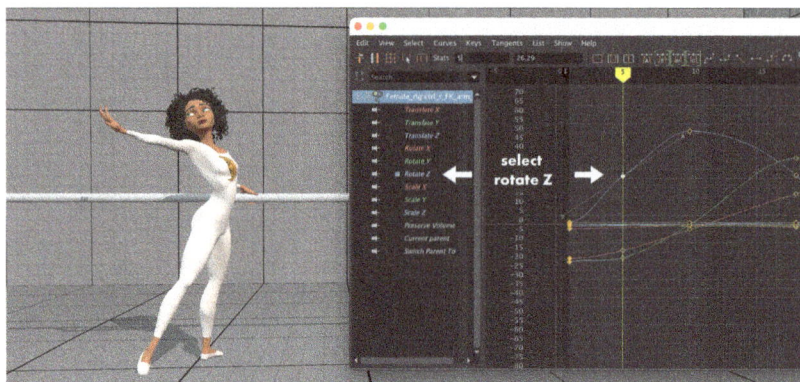

Figure 9.18

Keying Everything

This is a bit unorthodox, but I'll key everything on all my main poses.

For instance, if I have key poses on frames 1, 5, 10, and 18, I'll key everything that's keyable.

Figure 9.19

I like to animate in 3D in a more traditional animation way, thinking in charts (see Ch. 11).

Keeping it simple like this makes it easy to quickly change poses or timing without having to worry about ruining my key poses or breakdowns.

This is by no means the way to animate! It just works for me — and may not work for you! Use whatever method works best for you. If you prefer using a million layers, use a million layers!

While looking at your scene in the view pane, hit the delete button and watch for a change. If deleting the inbetween doesn't change the intent of your animation — you're good to go!

Figure 9.20

You can also smooth arcs in the graph editor by adjusting the tangents. Select each tangent one at a time to check your arcs. Start with the X translation and work down: X, Y, Z translation and then X, Y, Z rotation.

How does each one look in the graph editor?

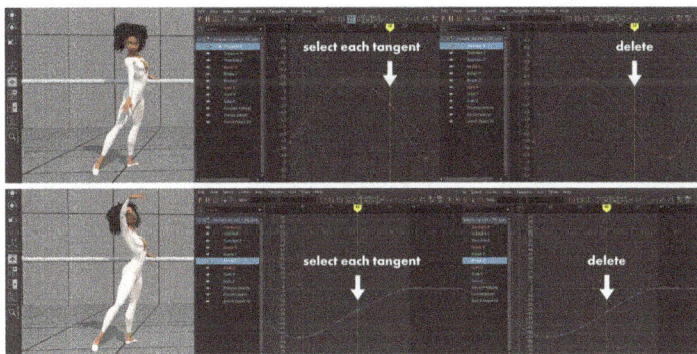

Figure 9.21

Fine-tuning tangents like this is where 3D animation can become like being a watchmaker or a miniature painter — it may seem tedious, but it will be worth it!

This attention to detail will make your scene look like butter. Or, as Bugs Bunny would say, "budder".

Animation Exercise – Animate a character gesturing with a nice arc. It could be throwing a ball or swatting away a gnat. Start with a neutral pose with the arms at the side. Then throw the ball or swat the gnat and return to a neutral pose.

Just worry about the arm that is throwing or swatting in this exercise! Try to get as smooth an action as possible.

Chapter 10. Walk and Run Cycles

Introduction

Walk cycles and run cycles can be unnecessarily difficult to do if you don't understand the basic formula. In this chapter we'll learn the formula for animating walk and run cycles, and how to build upon it to create complex and original walk cycles.

The Walk Cycle Formula

What do the walk cycles of Madame Medusa in *The Rescuers* and Mr. Magoo in *Magoo's Canine Mutiny* (1956) have in common? You guessed it, they're both based on the walk cycle formula. Magoo's walk cycle is as basic as you can get, while Medusa's walk cycle looks complicated — but it is based on the same formula.

Figure 10.1

There are eight poses for the walk formula: 3 contact poses, 2 down poses, 2 passing poses, and 2 up poses. The third contact pose is a repeat of frame 1.

At 24 frames per second, a standard walk cycle is 12 frames per step, or march time. March time is called "march time" because it refers to a piece of music that's easy to march to — usually 120 beats per minute, 2/4 time or, two steps per second. One, two, one, two, left, right, left, right.

"Everyone walks on 12s," said Milt Kahl. "Unless there's something wrong with them!"[1]

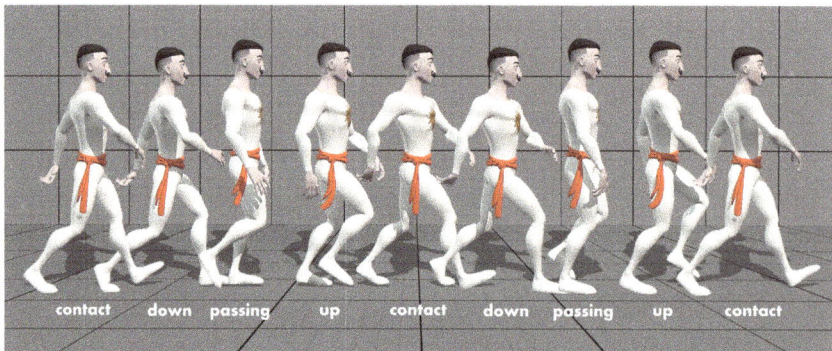

Figure 10.2

DOI: 10.1201/9781003361893-11

In games, and also in films, walk cycles are often animated in place — as on a treadmill. This is because you only need to animate a complete in-place cycle once. It can then be repeated endlessly and modified to fit the scene.

Contact Pose

Because we wouldn't want to disappoint Milt, we'll animate a formula walk on 12s, starting with the left foot. The left foot stride will be frames 1 to 12, and the right foot stride will be frames 13 to 24. Frames 1 and 25 would be the same pose.

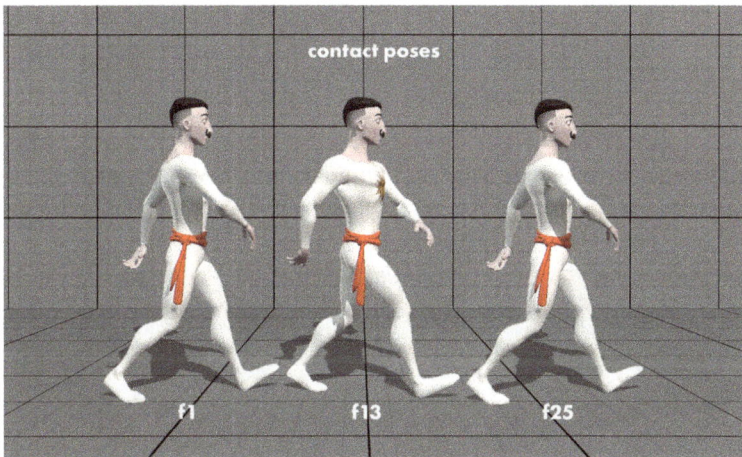

Figure 10.3

The contact pose is the stepping pose and establishes the length of the stride. The contact pose also helps describe how your character is feeling. For instance, a long stride could make your character appear more confident or determined, a shorter stride could make your character appear more relaxed or pensive.

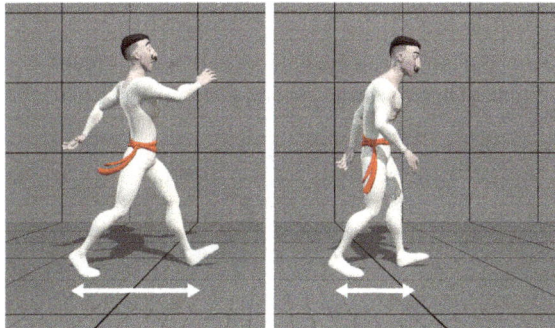

Figure 10.4

Richard Williams asked Milt Kahl what pose he did first in a walk cycle. "In a walk or a four-legged animal, two-legged person, whatever, I do the contact," said Kahl. "That way it's simple."[2]

Always listen to Milt.

The stride length could also show any limitations you may have with the rig. Too long a stride might hyperextend the legs. The hips being too high could also hyperextend the legs or pull the feet up off the ground.

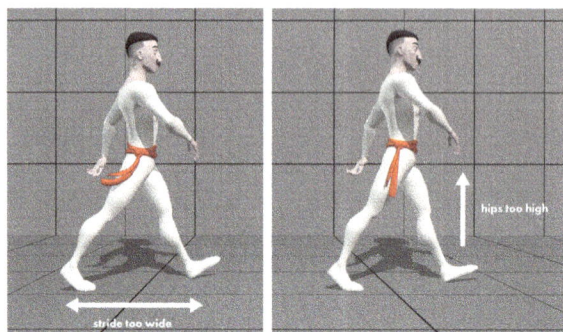

Figure 10.5

When you translate your walk, stride length will also determine how many steps you'll need to get to where you want to go. For instance, it may take three and 1/2 long strides or five and 1/4 short strides to reach your destination.

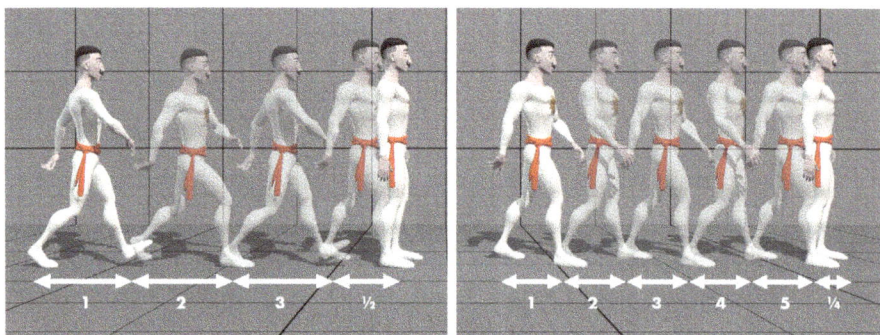

Figure 10.6

From a front or back view, the hips should be centered between the feet. Balance!

The arms swing opposite of the legs. So, if the left foot is forward, the left arm would be back. This may sound obvious, but getting the arm swing wrong is a rookie mistake!

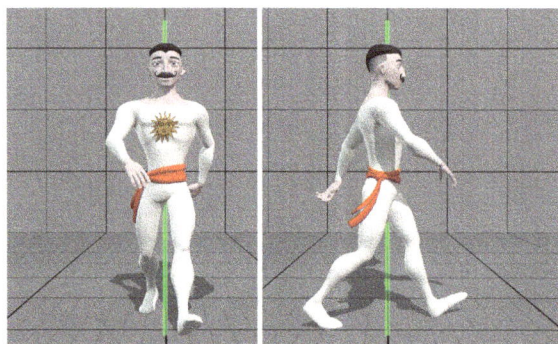

Figure 10.7

Frame 25 is a repeat of frame 1. Frame 13 will be a mirrored pose of frame 1 with the right foot forward.

It's good to start out from a side view, and toggle back and forth between pose 1 and pose 13, to get a mirrored version.

You may eyeball it or use the channel box to mirror your pose. Copy the values of the left foot forward to the right foot forward, the right foot back to the left foot back, etc.

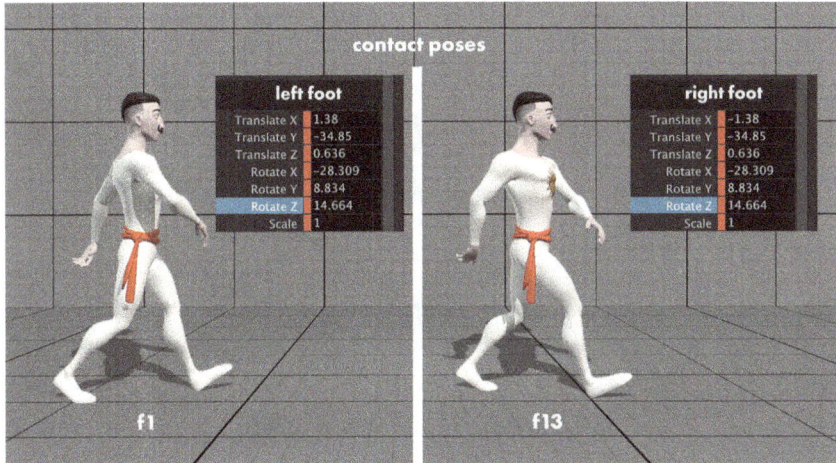

Figure 10.8

Passing Pose

Make the first passing pose on frame 7.

In a typical formula walk cycle the hips will be higher on the passing pose than they are on the contact pose. Toggle back and forth to make sure there is a nice change in the hip height. The arms are down at the sides on the passing pose because this is the middle of the arm swing. The weight should be over the supporting foot.

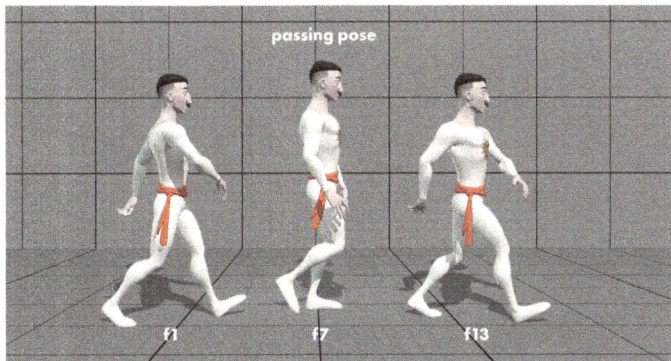

Figure 10.9

Once you get a passing pose that you're happy with, create a mirrored version on frame 19.

Here's a tip — copy the passing pose from frame 7 to either frame 18 or 20. This way, when you mirror the pose on frame 19, you can toggle back and forth between either frame 18 or 20. Copying the pose to the adjacent frame makes it easier to toggle back and forth.

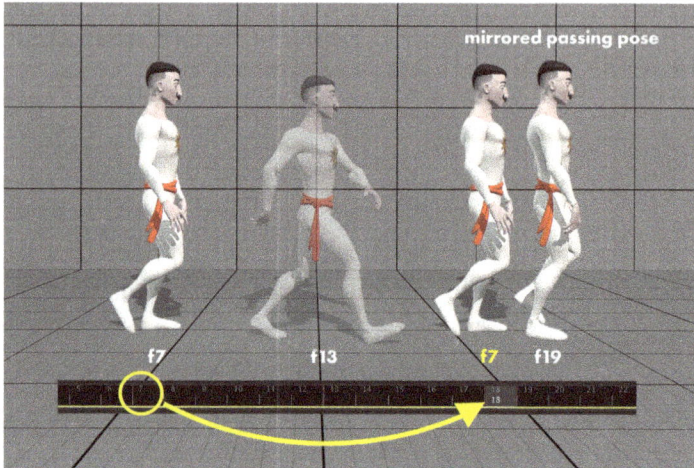

Figure 10.10

When you have the passing pose perfectly mirrored on frame 19, delete the extra pose on either 18 or 20. You now have three contact poses and two passing poses.

Down Pose

The down pose is where the body takes the most weight in the walk cycle.

The knees are bent and the weight is shifted over the supporting foot. The down pose is a squash, so there can be a bend in the spine or a twist in the shoulders toward the forward foot. How much bend and twist depends on what you're going for.

The more contrast the down pose has with the passing pose, the more dramatic your walk will be.

Add a down pose on frame 4.

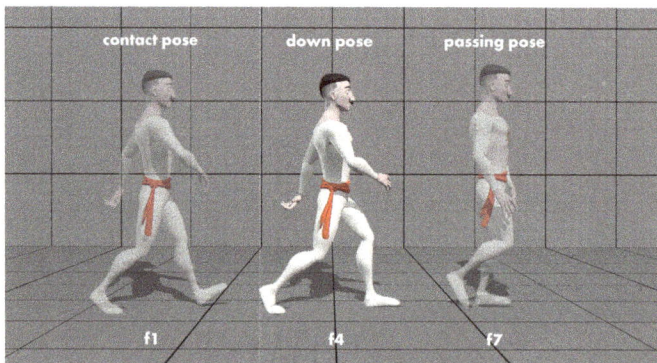

Figure 10.11

For now, let the arms inbetween themselves from the contact pose to the passing pose. When you get a down pose that you're happy with, mirror that pose to frame 16 — perfectly!

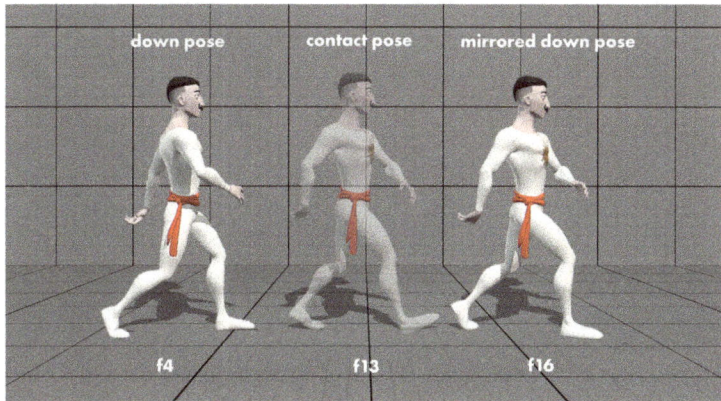

Figure 10.12

Up Pose

The up pose is the last pose to make. The up pose is the step, so the body will be off balance as the character falls, or steps, into the contact pose. For this example, the up pose could be on frame 10.

When you get an up pose that you're happy with, mirror it on frame 22 and, once again, mirror it — perfectly!

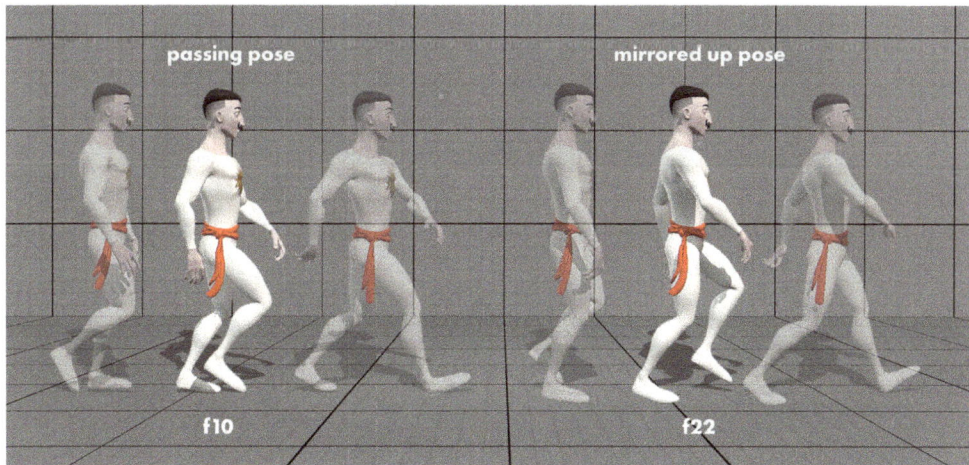

Figure 10.13

For a 12-frame walk cycle you don't need to have the foot float down over a number of frames from the contact pose to flat on the ground. Just have the contact pose, one inbetween, and then down flat.

Add a breakdown pose for the foot stepping flat by setting the X foot rotation for the forward foot to 0 in the channel box on frames 3 and 15 of the walk cycle.

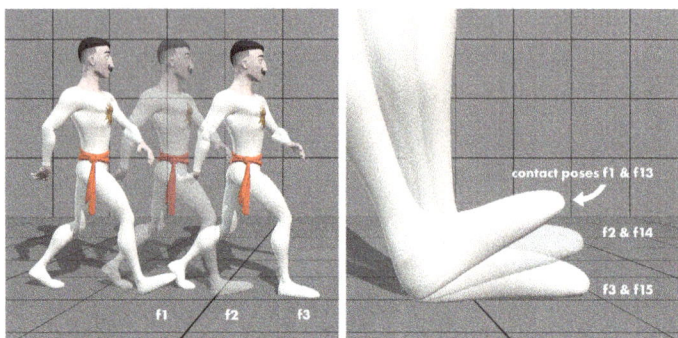

Figure 10.14

Keep the supporting foot flat on the ground as it slides back.

You'll only need two keys on the translation — one at the start of the sliding-back motion and one at the end. This will keep the foot moving back evenly.

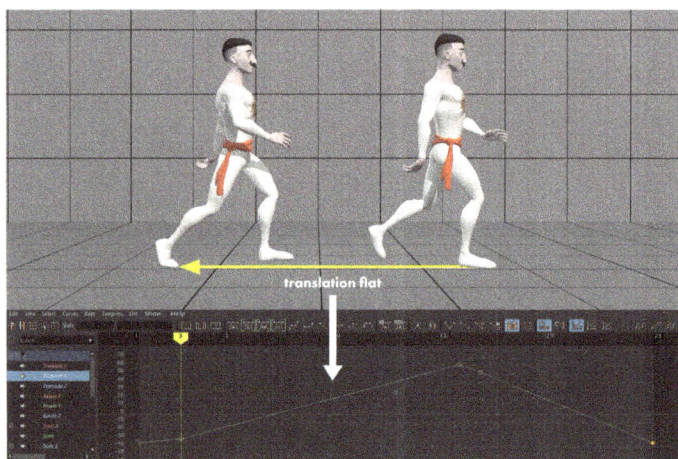

Figure 10.15

You should have a nice, basic, formula walk working now with only eight key poses and a couple of breakdowns for the foot plant!

Refrain from adding inbetweens too early. Get the formula working first!

Spreading the poses out, there should be a nice path of action for every part of the body.

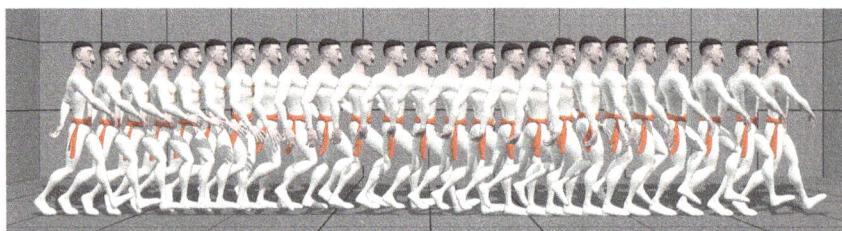

Figure 10.16

Refining Your Walk Cycle

Now that you have the formula walk working, we can refine it. The first thing we can do is to check for any noticeable imperfections.

The weight should be over the hips on the passing poses. Trying deleting the side-to-side X translations on the in-betweens. If the side-to-side movement looks better without inbetweens — great!

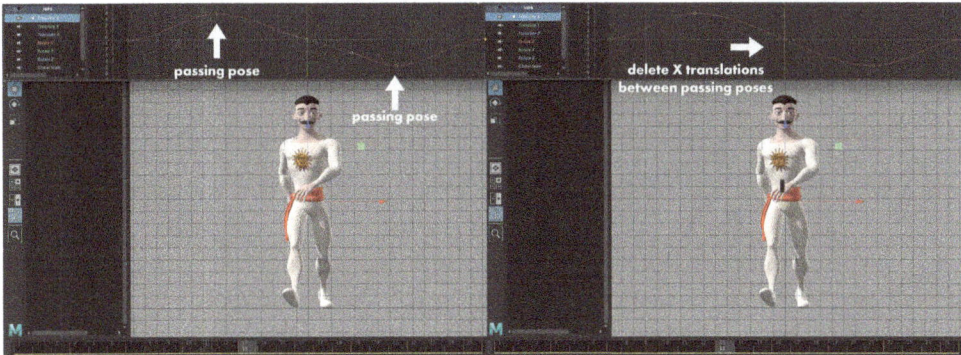

Figure 10.17

To make your contact poses more accurate, copy the down pose from frame 4 and paste it on frame 28.

The contact pose on frame 25 is a repeat of the contact pose on frame 1, so frame 28 would be where the next down position would be if the cycle repeated.

By extending the scene to frame 28, you're treating the contact pose on frame 25 as an inbetween.

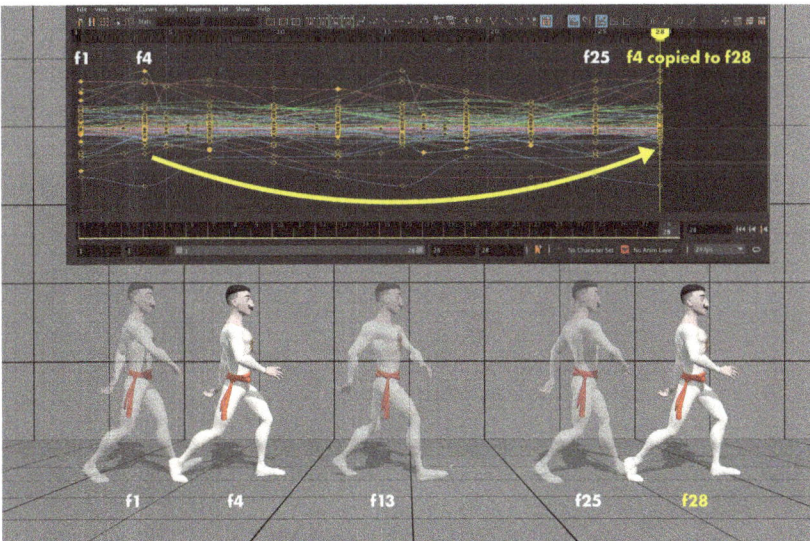

Figure 10.18

Now delete the hips on frame 25 and see how it looks playing through to frame 28. If it looks better, re-key the hips on frame 25 and copy that new key to frame 1.

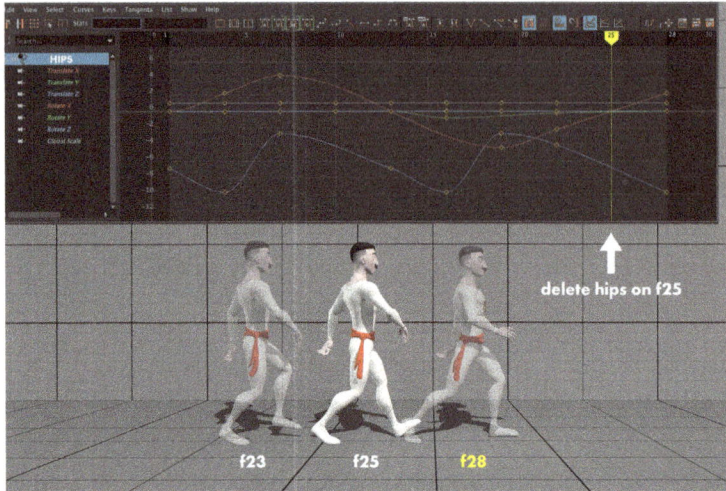

Figure 10.19

Extending the cycle to another down pose, deleting the repeating contact pose, and then re-keying it sometimes helps get a better arc in the cycle loop. Do the same for the spine, arms, or whatever else you think may need refining except for the feet — leave the feet alone.

Overlap

Next, you can add overlap to the head and arms.

There's a simple, but formulaic, method for adding overlap on the head. When the body is in the up position, tilt the chin down. When the body is in the down position, tilt the chin up.

This will give you a nice head bounce with only two keys. Remember to maintain a consistent eye line while the head is overlapping. Look straight ahead and not all over the place.

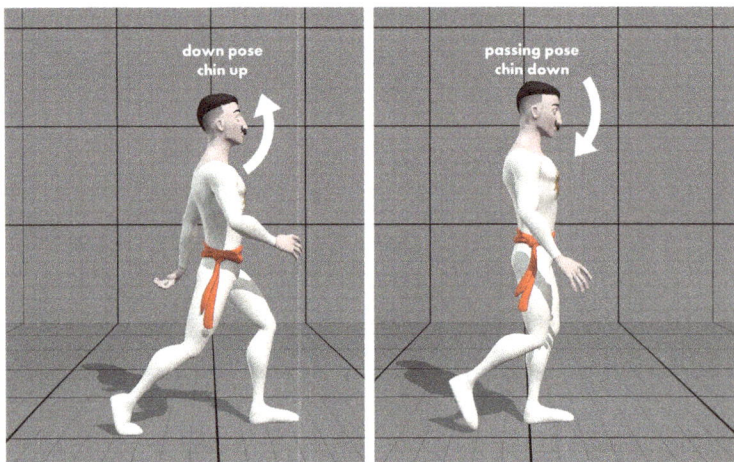

Figure 10.20

Adding overlap to the arms is a little trickier. Start with an overlap in the shoulders. It's easy in 3D to forget about the shoulders — especially in a walk cycle.

To add instant overlap to the shoulders, lower them on the passing poses and raise them on the contact poses. Try not to lower them too much so that your character loses its shape — just enough to notice a change in height from the passing position to the contact pose.

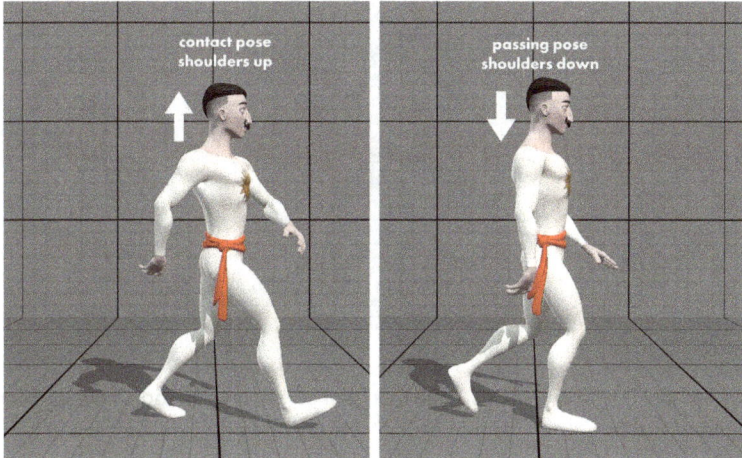

Figure 10.21

You can also rotate the shoulders forward when the arm swings forward, and back when the arm swings back. This adds a nice motion to the sometimes too-stiff shoulders on a walk cycle.

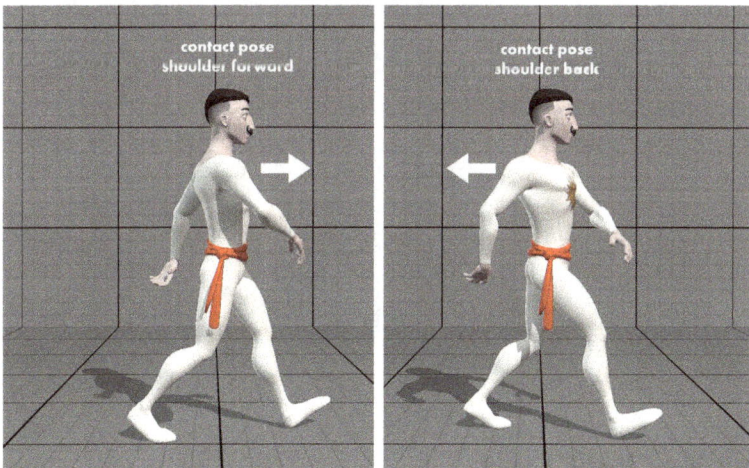

Figure 10.22

Here's the tricky part. Don't swing the arms back stiffly. Add drag to the forearms, wrists, and fingers as the arms swing forward and back. This is the successive breaking of joints — which we'll look at in Chapter 14.

Just after the contact pose, the front arm swings backward and the back arm swings forward.

Don't return the swing in the same direction.

Look at your walk cycle from the front (and the back and side views), and rotate the arms (shoulders, upper arms, and forearms) slightly to get a nice circular arc to the arms as they change direction.

Make sure the hands and fingers follow the path of action! Gesture first, then anatomy!

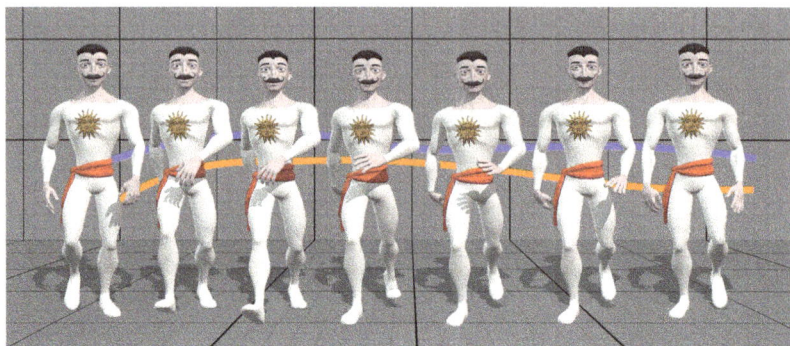

Figure 10.23

Don't forget to turn the hips. Turn the hips in the direction of the forward foot. If the left foot is forward, turn the left hip forward. Don't keep the hips straight and pull the back leg. Create a nice line of action.

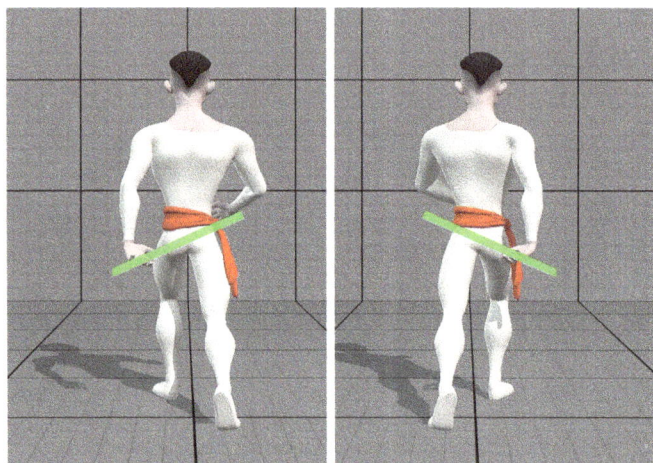

Figure 10.24

Translating Your Walk Cycle

Translating your in-place walk cycle is a good way to test the accuracy of your cycle. There are two ways to translate your walk:

1. Translating the master controller

2. Translating anything with IK (usually the feet and the hips)

If you just want to test the accuracy of your walk cycle, I'll allow translating the master controller — but just this once!

First, select your master control and add it to a new level in the channel box. Name the new level something original, such as "Master_Control".

Figure 10.25

From the side view, select the master controller and translate it forward so that the front heel of frame 2 matches where you feel the heel on the contact pose would step. Make sure you're keying on the new level!

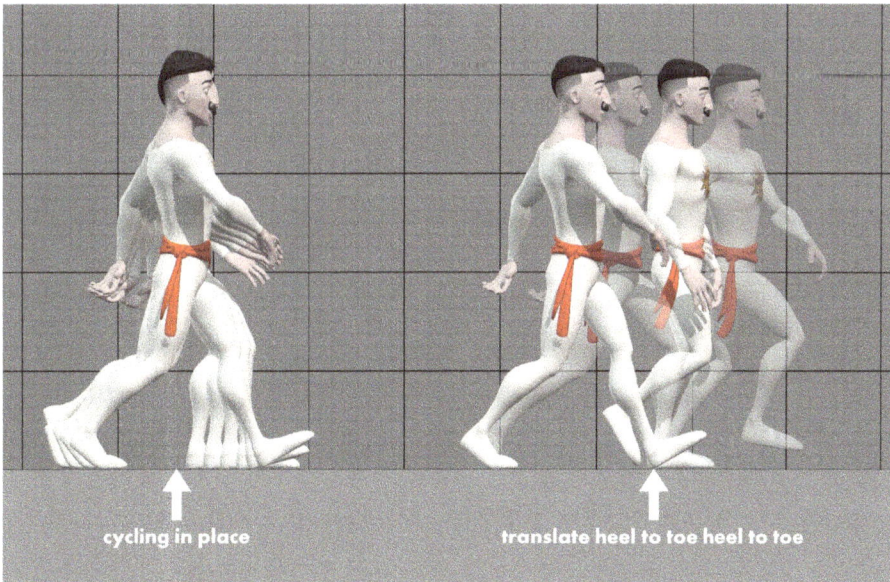

Figure 10.26

Keep matching heel toe, heel toe through frame 25.

If the walk cycle works perfectly when you're done translating the master controller — bully!

Usually though, the back foot lifting up from the down pose is a little off.

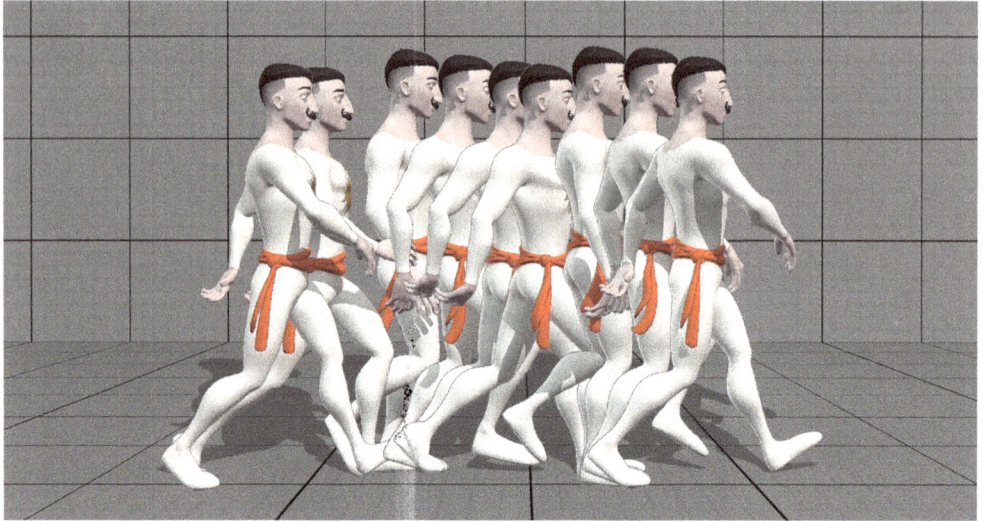

Figure 10.27

Fix anything else that may need adjusting, then turn off the master control layer in the channel box. Your walk cycle should look better now.

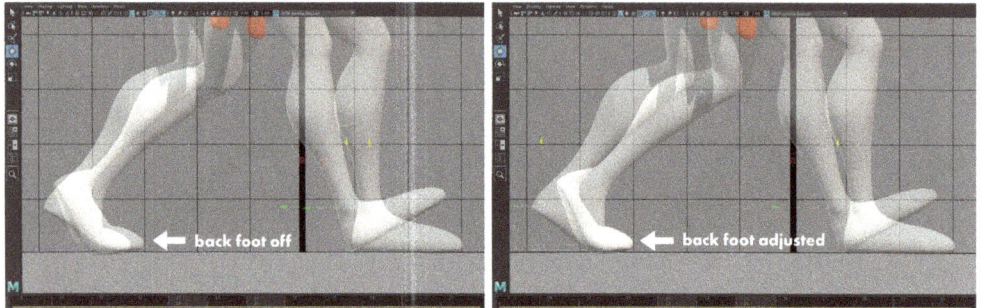

Figure 10.28

Translating anything with IK is the other way is to check your cycle's accuracy. Grab everything with IK, go to a side view, and translate your character forward — heel, toe, heel, toe. This way is better if you're actually translating your character in a scene.

Advanced Walk Cycles

Now that you know the basic walk formula, it's much easier to build upon the formula and go as eccentric as you like.

In the Bugs Bunny cartoon *Long Haired Hare* (1949), Phil Monroe animated a great angry walk by changing up the formula a little. To make the conductor, Giovanni Jones, appear angry as he walks, Monroe stomps flatfooted, instead of heel first, straight from the up pose to the contact pose with no inbetweens. Monroe also keeps Giovanni's arms at his side as he walks, ready to strangle Bugs.

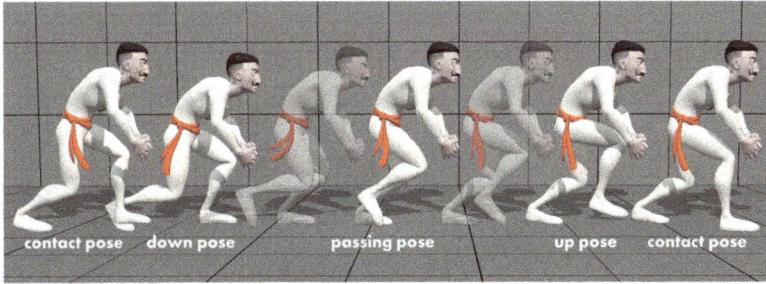

Figure 10.29

A double bounce walk is a lot of fun and very easy to do in 3D. Milt Kahl animates a classic double bounce for Robin Hood at the start of **Robin Hood** (1973).

For this example of a basic double bounce, the walk cycle is 32 frames long, or 16s instead of 12s — allowing more time for the exaggerated movement to read.

On the new layer, lower the translation for the hips in the up poses (frames 13 and 29) to the same height as they are on the down poses.

Simply copy the translation value for the hips from the down poses and paste it to the translation value for the hips in the passing poses.

Figure 10.30

The curves in the graph editor for this double bounce are perfectly even, but feel free to vary the height to give a less mechanical feel.

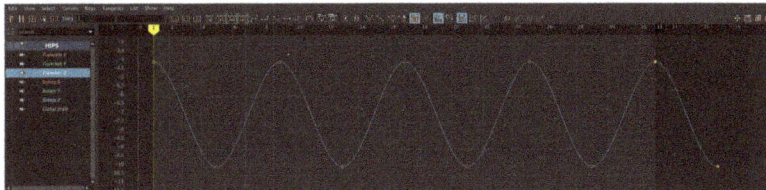

Figure 10.31

For one of Medusa's walk cycles in **The Rescuers**, Kahl added a hip swing to the double bounce. Medusa's hips swing out in an exaggerated manner over the supporting foot on the passing poses.

Add the hips to another layer and push the hip translation out on each passing pose. Rotate the hips higher on the side supporting the weight. Get a nice line of action curve in the back.

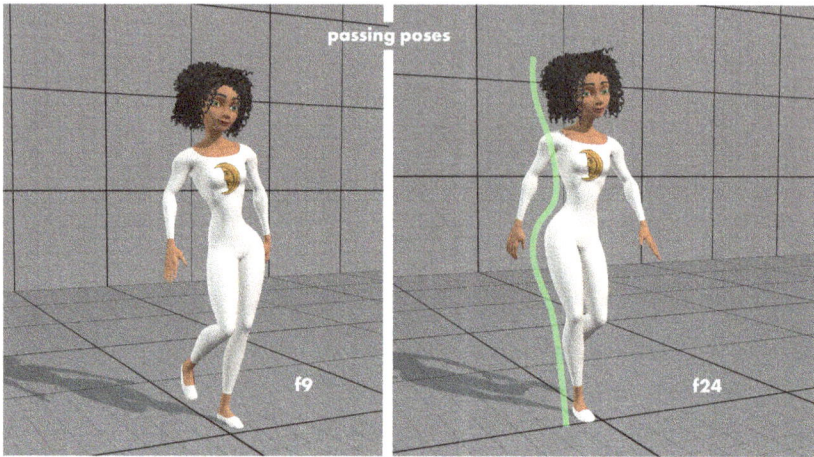

Figure 10.32

Sometimes you'll hear that you should lean the character forward more as they're walking. "A walk is a fall. You catch yourself before you fall by sticking your foot out."

I feel that how much your character leans depends upon their speed and or attitude.

I'll defer to Milt Kahl when it comes to walk cycles. "Sometimes you have a really slow walk," he said. "The slower it is, the more you're in balance."[3]

The Run Cycle Formula

Once you understand the walk cycle formula, the run cycle formula is that much easier.

The run cycle formula is similar to the walk cycle formula — the biggest difference being the up pose. In a run cycle-up pose, both feet are suspended off the ground.

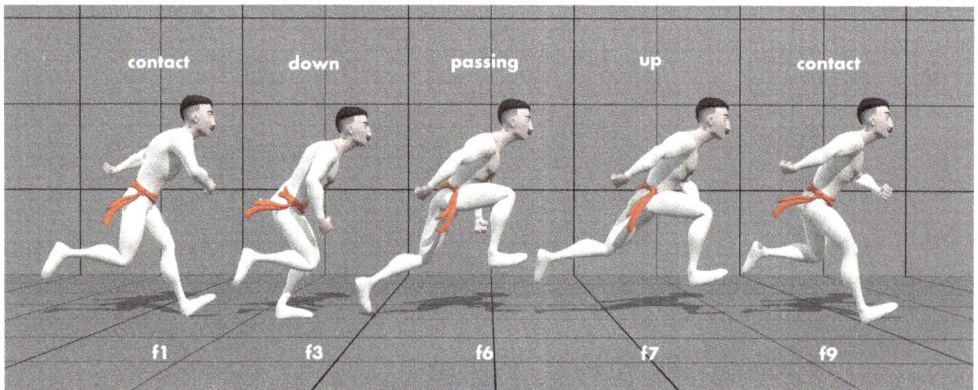

Figure 10.33

Because both feet are off the ground in the up pose, the contact pose is more or less a landing. The front foot contact pose is the same as the walk cycle contact pose, only the back foot drags.

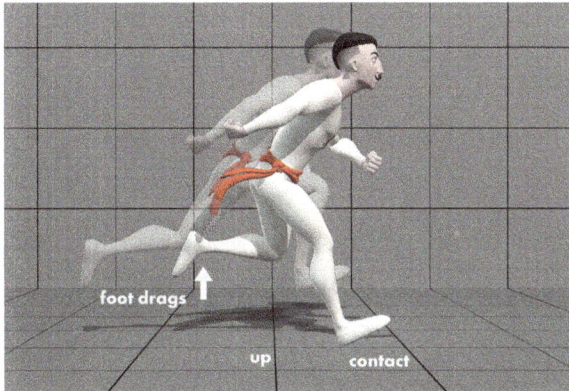

Figure 10.34

The down pose on a run cycle is similar to the passing pose of a walk cycle.

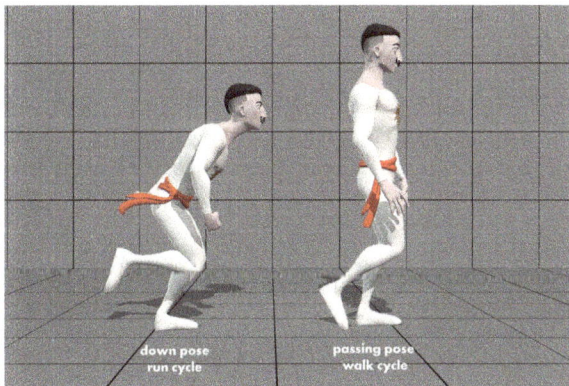

Figure 10.35

The passing pose on a run cycle is similar to the up pose on a walk cycle.

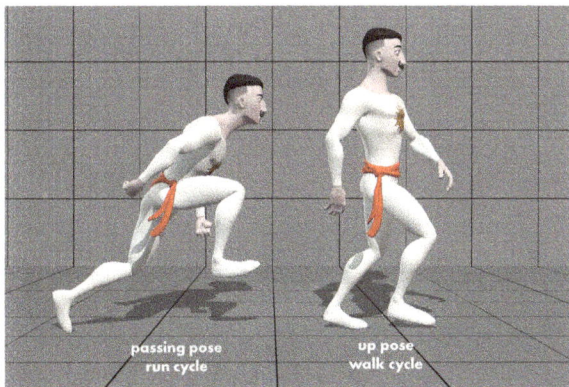

Figure 10.36

The greater the difference in hip height between the down pose and the up pose, the more weight you'll feel in the run cycle.

For a heavier feeling run, put more frames closer to the down pose. Keep the hips, the center of gravity, lower on the up pose. If you want a lighter feeling, raise them higher in the up pose and add more suspended poses.

Don't Fake It!

If your character is shot only in a waist-up medium shot, animate the entire body — then frame the scene from the waist-up. Faking a walk cycle by simulating the side-to-side or up-and-down movement looks, well, fake!

Take the time to animate a walk or run a cycle using the formula. It will save time in the long run, and your animation will be more believable.

Animation Exercise – Animate a walk cycle using the formula. Use stepped tangents and don't worry about adding inbetweens. Trust the formula! Get your poses in first, then put the tangents in spline. Make sure the weight is over the supporting foot. Check the poses from all sides. Then try a double-bounce or a run cycle!

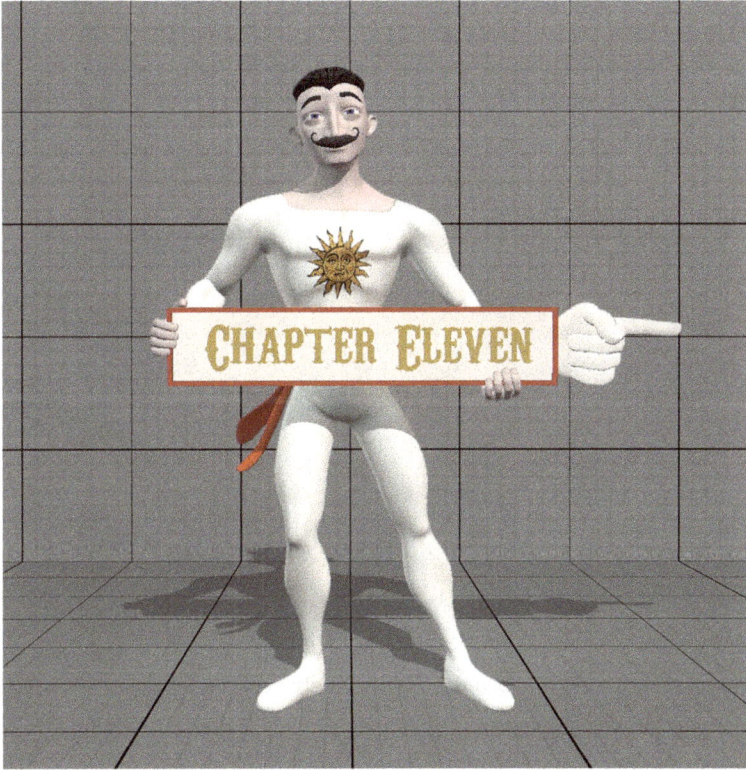

Chapter 11. Timing and Spacing

Introduction

The problem with a lot of 3D animation is that it tends to look floaty or watery. This is because the computer flattens arcs and creates evenly spaced inbetweens. An advantage 2D animators have is that they learn how to chart. Knowing how to chart animation, or think in charts, is key to getting snappy and complex 3D animation.

Timing and Spacing

What's the difference between timing and spacing? Timing is the overall length of the scene, or frame range, and the time from extreme to extreme. Spacing is how far apart your keys, breakdowns and inbetweens are.

Looking at the bouncing ball again, the timing is the overall frame range and the amount of time from bounce to bounce. The spacing is how high the ball bounces and how far apart the inbetweens are.

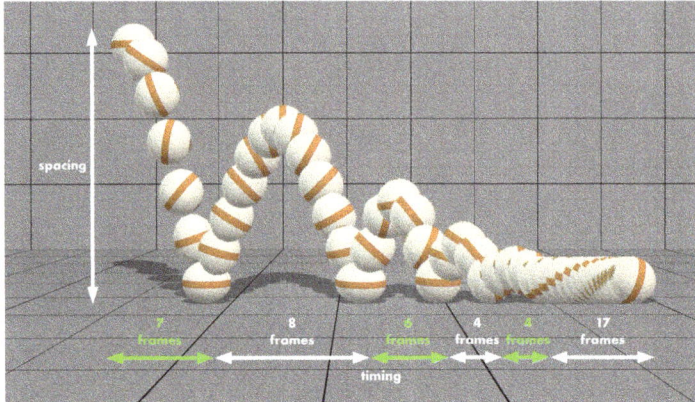

Figure 11.1

Fewer inbetweens means quicker movement. More inbetweens means slower movement.

A ball hitting a wall in 10 frames (a) will obviously move quicker than a ball taking 30 frames (b) to hit to the same wall. This is timing.

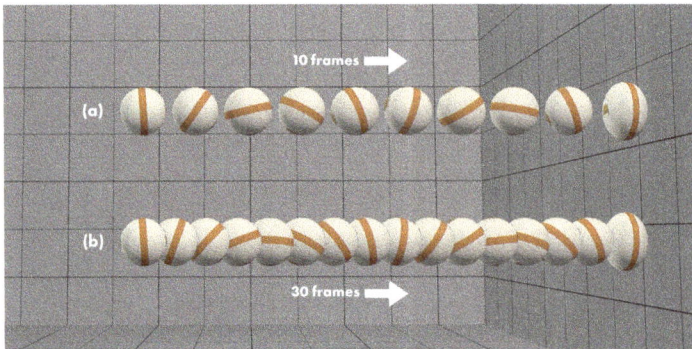

Figure 11.2

DOI: 10.1201/9781003361893-12

Move ball (b) farther back and it will appear to move faster than before because the wider spacing of the inbetweens means quicker movement. This is spacing.

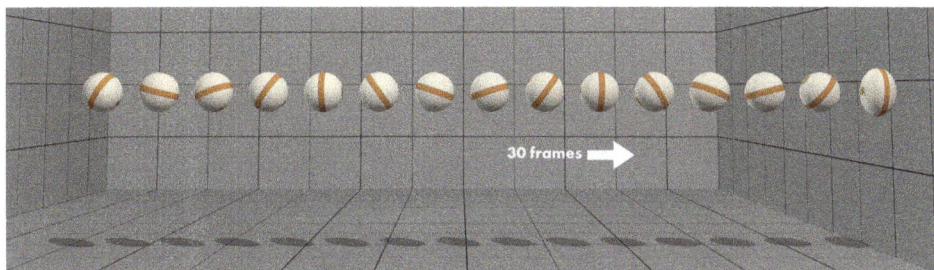

Figure 11.3

Animation Charts

Animator Dick Huemer more or less invented the timing chart. Huemer was working for the Fleischer's, who liked his work and wanted more of it. They suggested he take on an assistant, Art Davis.

"Being basically a very lazy fellow," said Huemer modestly. "I thought, 'Why not?'"[1]

So that Davis would know where to add inbetweens, Huemer drew a "curved line extended from one figure [extreme] to the other. This line [path of action] was carefully spaced with short lines indicating that other drawings would fill the empty space between the two key figures."[2]

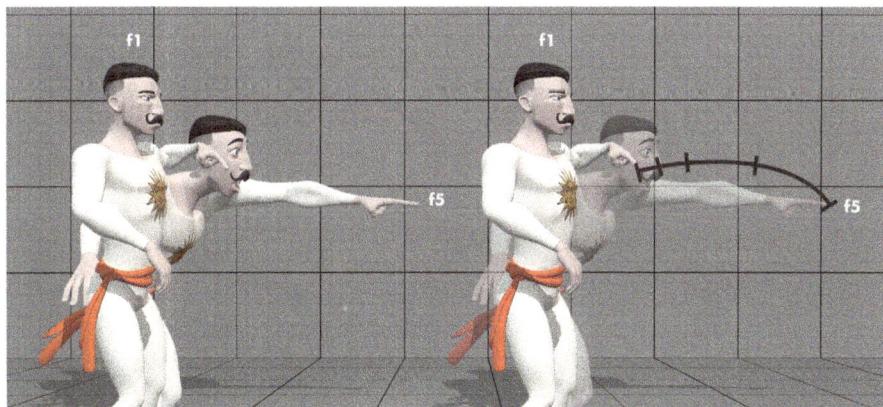

Figure 11.4

Grim Natwick started at Fleischer after Huemer left for Disney and expanded on Huemer's idea. He placed the line indicating inbetweens on the right side of the drawing and the animation chart was born.

In a 2D animation chart, extremes are the top and bottom numbers and are usually circled.

The bolder line with the underlined number is the breakdown. A breakdown is a pose between two extremes that describes how one extreme transitions to the next (Ch. 16).

The remaining lines are inbetweens.

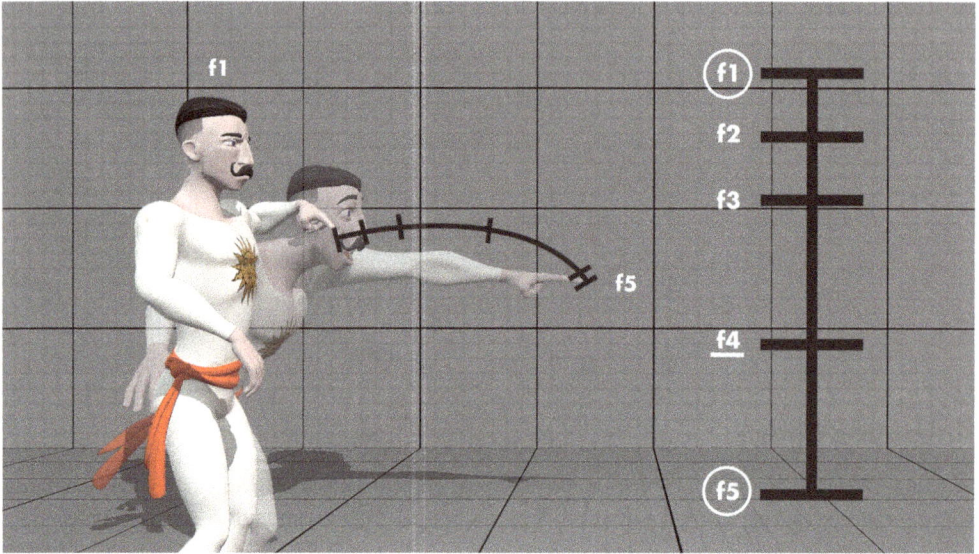

Figure 11.5

There are three basic types of charts: Halves, Thirds, and Favoring.

Halves is when the breakdown is exactly halfway between two extremes. So, if you have extremes on frame 1 and frame 5, frame 3 would be right in the middle.

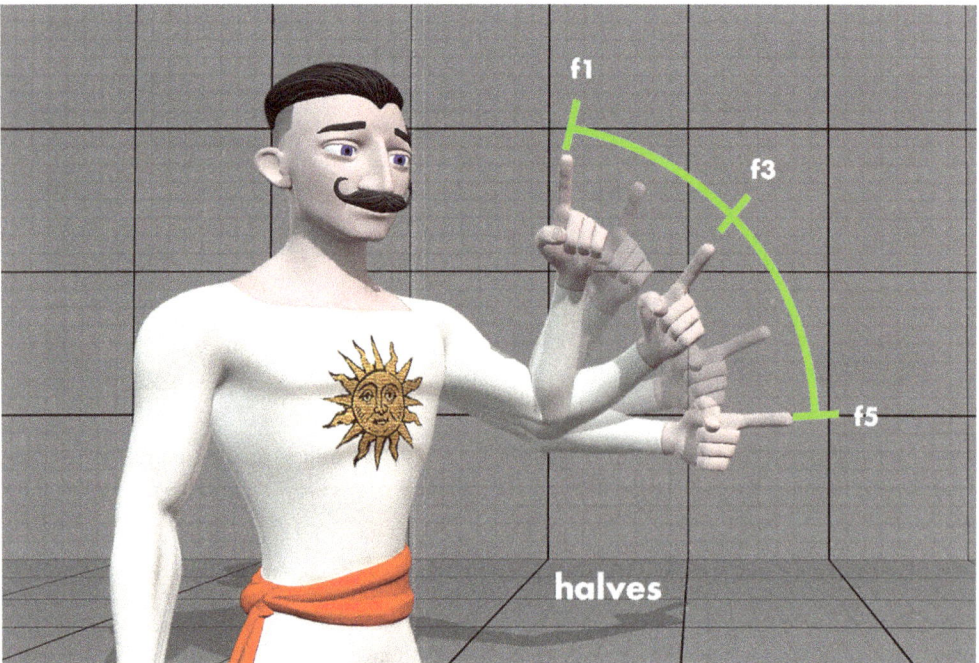

Figure 11.6

Thirds is when the breakdown is 1/3 of the way between two extremes. If you have an extreme on frames 1 and 5, frame 3 can favor either frame 3 or frame 5. This gives a quicker movement out of frame 1 or into frame 3.

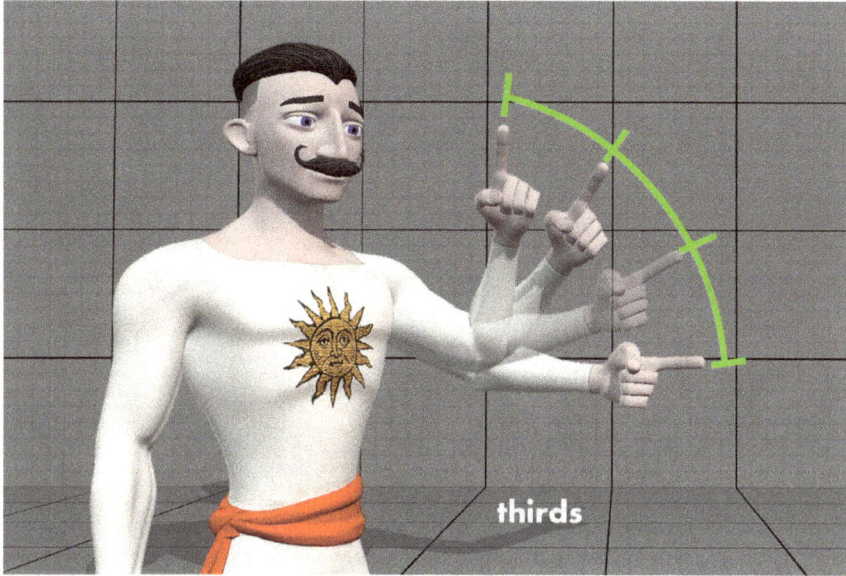

Figure 11.7

Favoring is exactly how it sounds — the breakdown "favors" one of the two extremes. Some animators will use a favoring breakdown at the start of a scene if they want their audience to take more notice of the first pose. Favoring breakdown is also great to use for snappy, darting actions — which we'll get to in a bit.

Figure 11.8

As we saw, when a character turns their head from their right to their left, the computer will make even inbetweens, and the timing will be floaty and boring — even with an arc and facial animation added.

Figure 11.9

In 2D animation it can be difficult to draw a "thirds" pose. Usually, the animator will draw their own breakdown third — unless they want to torture their inbetweener or clean-up artists. However, it's very easy to key on thirds in 3D.

Just do the same thing you did with halves, only for this example we'll keep it simpler.

A character turns their head from left on frame 1, to right on 3. If left to the computer, frame 2 would be a half.

Figure 11.10

To get a breakdown on thirds, slide frame 3 over to frame 4. This gives us two inbetweens.

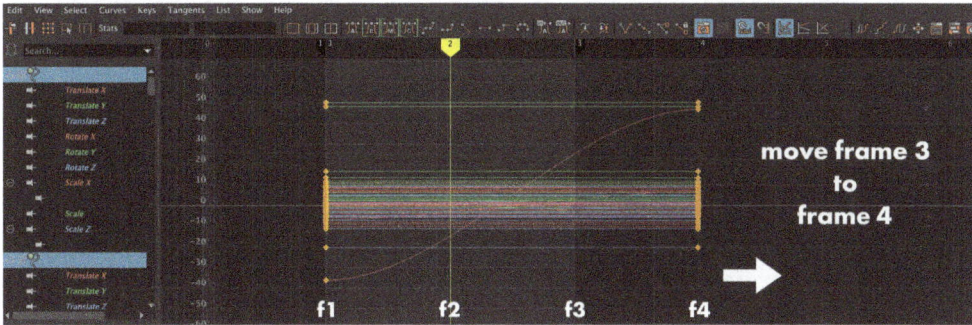

Figure 11.11

Key frame 2 — which is a third of the way between frame 1 and frame 4, favoring frame 1.

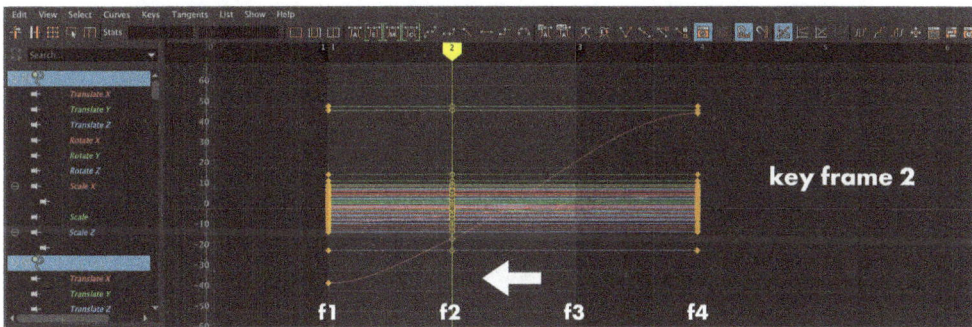

Figure 11.12

Now slide frame 4 back to frame 3. Frame 2 is now a third between frame 1 and 3, favoring frame 1.

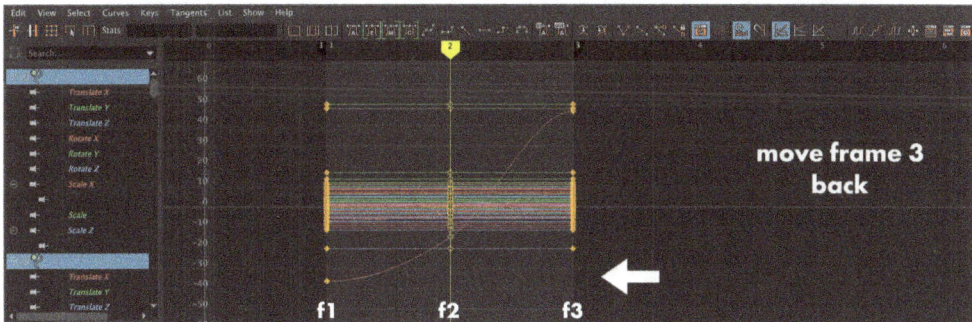

Figure 11.13

Easy enough! This may seem obvious, but you'll see how advantageous this is when you start to offset different body parts.

Create a favoring key the same way. If you want to have frame 2 favor frame 1, just extend frame 3 until you get the spacing on frame 2 that you want. Then key frame 2.

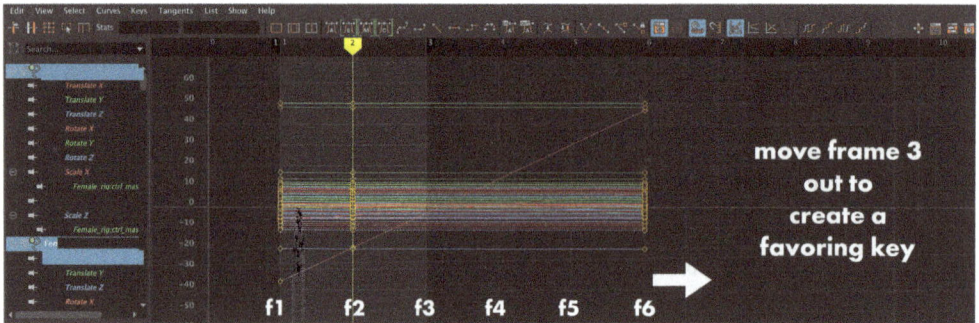

Figure 11.14

Now move frame 3 back to its original position. Frame 2 is a key favoring frame 1.

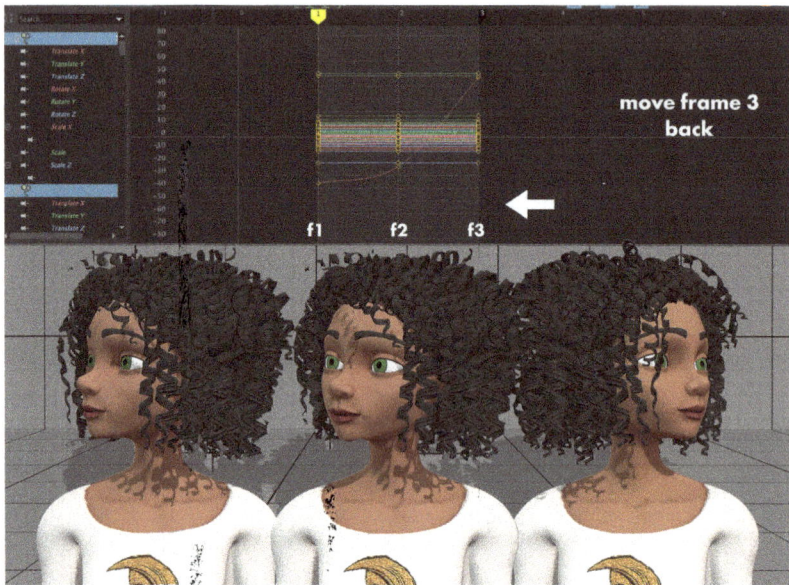

Figure 11.15

The animation isn't perfect, but it quickly puts you in the ball park. Now you can add all the bells and whistles such as head arcs, overlap, and face animation.

Figure 11.16

You can get some snappy actions using favoring keys. Lucifer the cat in **Cinderella** waves his arms comically when he thinks he knows what tea cup Gus the mouse is hiding under.

Ward Kimball uses favoring breakdowns to show a change of direction.

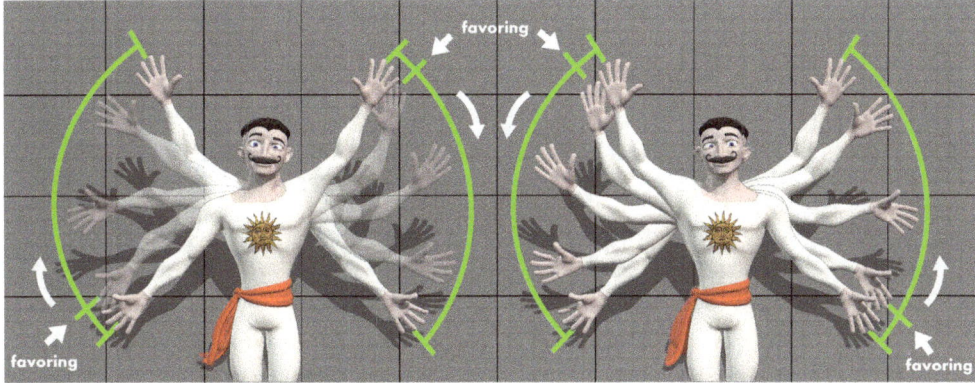

Figure 11.17

The pigeons in **Bolt** (2008) use favoring keys to snap their heads from pose to pose.

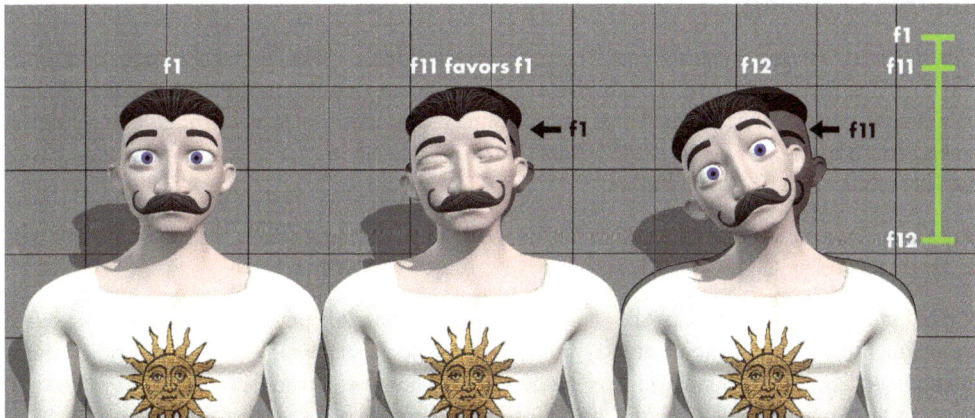

Figure 11.18

Thinking in charts it's easier to time each part of the body differently.

For instance, you can have three different timings on a character performing a silly action such as swaying their hips, waving their arms, and shaking their head.

The hips can sway on halves.

The head can shake on thirds, and the arms can swing with favoring timing.

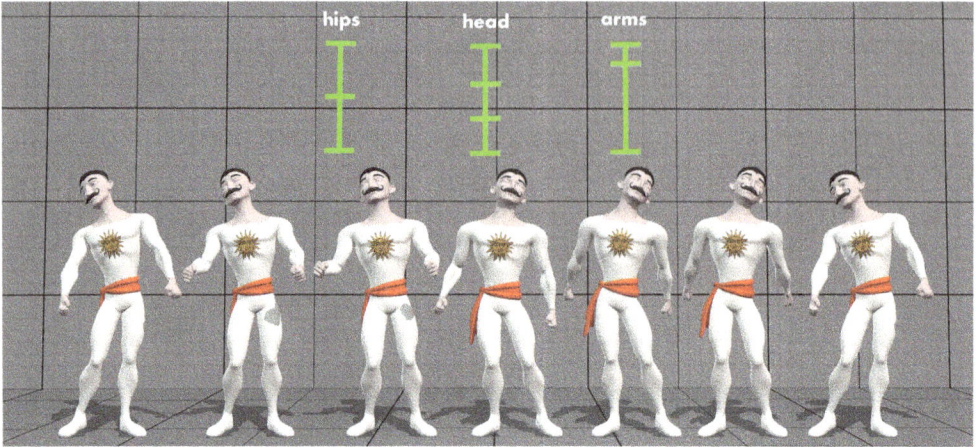

Figure 11.19

This is simplified a bit, but it shows how much easier it is to figure out timing when you think in charts.

Rhythm in Timing

"The rhythm and timing of animation is like a good musical score – it builds to crescendos and drops into quiet; it surges and it slows, it lifts and it falls," said Eric Larson. "An audience needs that change. It must have periods of excitement and periods of rest. Our action must have variety and vitality in timing lest it become monotonous and irritating. Action, like emotion, needs change to get and keep the viewer's interest. It has to be alive."[3]

Block your keys out in stepped mode to get the timing of your scene! Adjust the spacing of the keys to get an interesting tempo.

A blacksmith hammering a horseshoe needs to have a variety of speeds, or rhythms; otherwise it won't feel right. Lifting the hammer may start out slower to sell the weight. The speed increases as the hammer lifts, and then may slow as the head of the hammer flips over and changes direction. Bringing the hammer down to strike the horseshoe will have an even quicker speed.

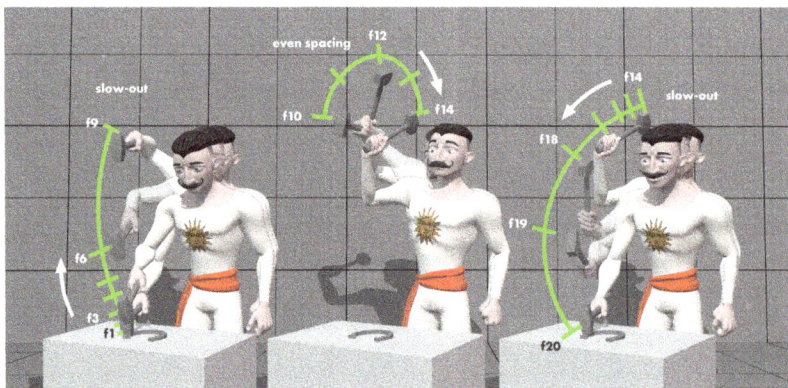

Figure 11.20

Even picking up a pencil needs a rhythm!

A character may reach for a pencil at a certain speed, but they don't just snatch it up at the same speed — their hand needs to slow down, like a docking spaceship, as the fingers contact the pencil.

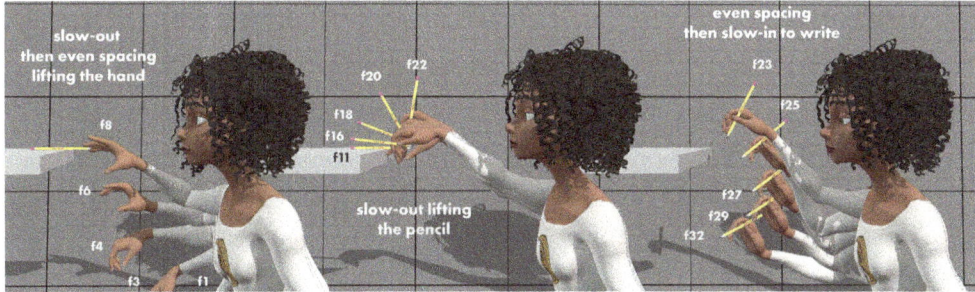

Figure 11.21

When they take hold of the pencil, we need to feel that it weighs something — around 0.2 ounces in case you were wondering. It may take two, three, or even four frames of the fingers actually on the pencil before your character picks up!

Lifting the pencil is a change of direction and takes time — not a whole lot of time, it's a pencil. The lift, however, needs to be at a different speed than it is when your character brings it down to write. Vary timing!

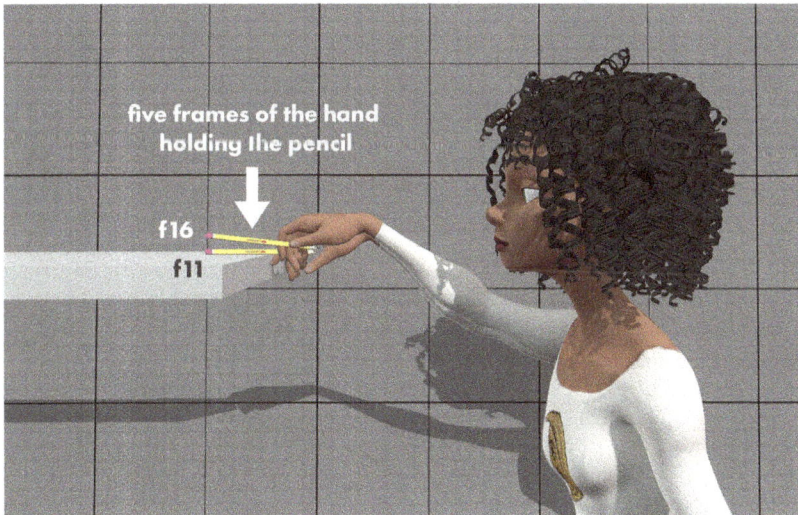

Figure 11.22

So many different speeds for just lifting a pencil! Vary the rhythm and spacing of your keys.

Animating to a Beat

"If you want to do good animation, you always have a sound track," said Tissa David, meaning a voice or music track. "I need either one or the other, otherwise I am in limbo."[4]

But what if you don't have a soundtrack?

If you don't have a soundtrack, add a metronome audio track to your scene. They have some great online metronomes. Create an audio file from the metronome beat and add it to your scene.

A character notices a ball has landed in their yard, so they throw it back over the fence.

Block out your key frames to a beat that matches the tempo you're picturing.

If you're unsure of the tempo, start with 120 beats. That's 12 frames per beat, or march time. Hit on the beat or between beats (every six frames).

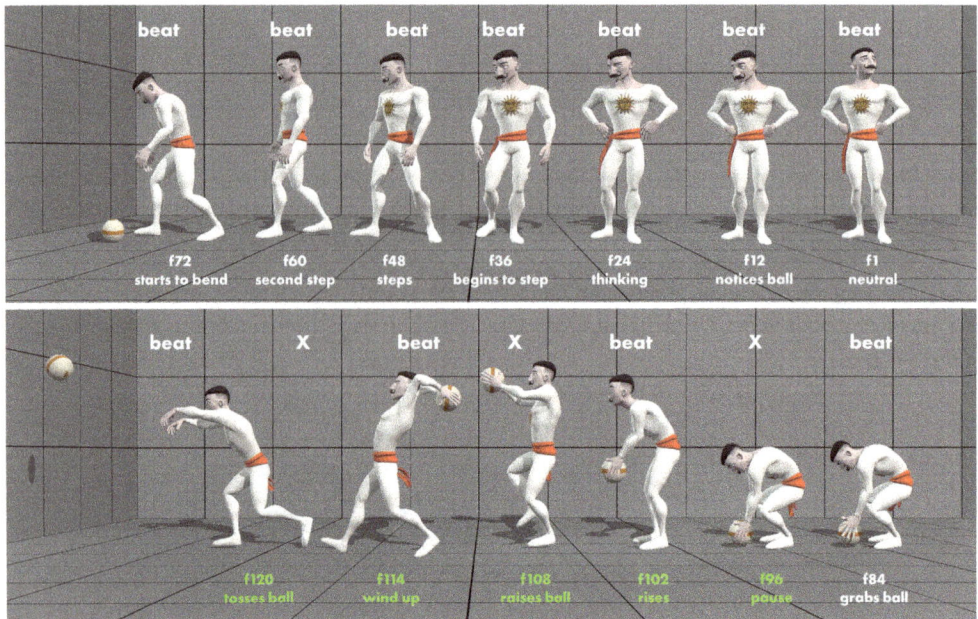

Figure 11.23

Use a metronome track. It will help you create a rhythm to your animation and help keep your animation from being boring. As Frank and Ollie wrote, a metronome will help you "pack more entertainment into small amounts of footage."[5]

24, 30 or 60 Frames Per Second

Many video games are animated at 30 or 60 frames per second (fps). How does this affect thinking in charts?

A half is still a half, a third is still a third, and favoring is still favoring. It's all relative.

How you handle breakdowns and inbetweens at either 30 fps or 60 fps is the same as it is at 24 fps.

This chart shows the timing formulas animators came up with for some types of locomotion.

Type of Locomotion	BPM	24 fps	30 fps	60 fps
Really fast run Tom in *Tennis Chumps*	480	3	3.75	7.5
Fast run Nick Wilde in *Zootopia*	360	4	5	10
March time walk Pink Panther	120	12	15	30
Relaxed walk Sheriff of Nottingham in *Robin Hood*	90	16	45	90
Slow walk Briar Rose walking in woods *Sleeping Beauty*	72	20	36	72

Figure 11.24

Animating a walk cycle at 60 fps takes some getting used to after animating at 24 fps.

A 3-frame 24 fps cartoony run, as Tom and Butch do throughout **Tennis Chumps**, is 3 frames. At 60 fps, the same 3-frame cartoony run is a 7.5 frame run. How do you key a fraction?

You don't. Choose to either make it a 7 or 8 frame run cycle. It might look snappier in 7 frames than it does at 8 frames — try them both and decide for yourself which feels better.

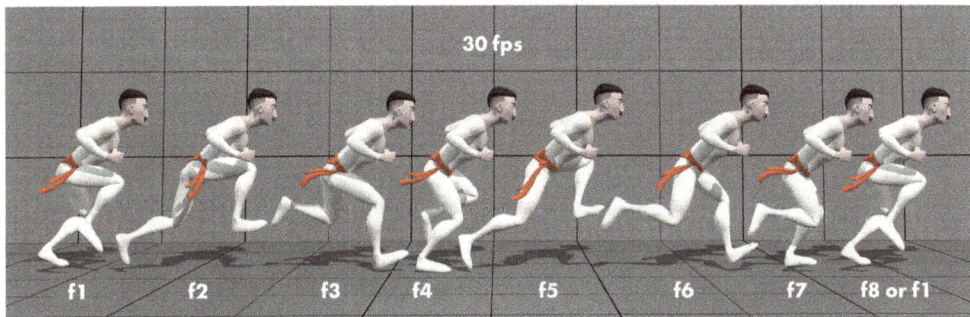

Figure 11.25

A walk cycle of less than 16-frames will give you less time for acting to read — great if you want to add more secondary action to your cycle (see Ch. 19).

Milt Kahl used a 16-frame cycle for the Sheriff of Nottingham in **Robin Hood**. "I wanted a guy who was really pleased with himself and feeling really good, and pompous," said Kahl. "Sixteens would just slow it down because he was going a little higher up and down. I decided I would get a little bit more feeling into it by getting the knees and elbows higher. I even led with the elbow. He came up high with it."[6]

A 12-frame formula march time walk or an 8-frame standard run cycle may need to be held steadier so that dialogue or secondary actions read.

A 20-frame walk is a character in no real hurry. Hal Ambro animated a 20-frame walk cycle for Briar Rose as she strolled through the woods swinging her basket in **Sleeping Beauty**.

Animating Dance

When animating a dance, especially a dance loop where the end leads back into the start, ignore the vocals and the melody and just listen to the beat. Find the tempo using a metronome, then pose out your keys to hit on, or a few frames ahead of, the beat (More on this in Ch. 21).

To find out on which frame the beats fall, multiply the frames per second (fps) times 60 (seconds), then divide by the beats per minute (bpm).

$$fps \times 60 \div bpm = frames\ per\ beat$$

To prove this, let's use the march walk.

$$24\ fps \times 60 \div 120\ bpm = 12$$

The beat hits every 12 frames. Ta-da!

Most dancers use what's called an "8 count". An 8 count is a group of eight beats — or two bars of music if you're musically inclined. It's simply counting to 8, then starting over again:

1, 2, 3, 4, 5, 6, 7, 8, 1, 2, 3, 4, 5, 6, 7, 8, etc.

An 8 count makes it easy to improvise on the beat. For instance, if you want your character to clap while dancing, it could look something like this:

1, 2, 3, 4, Clap, 6, 7, 8, Clap, 2, 3, 4, Clap, 6, 7, 8, etc.

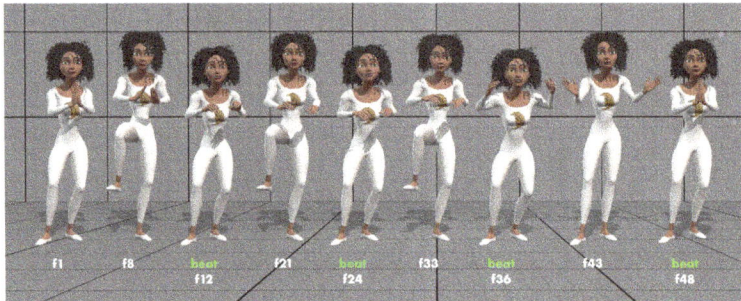

Figure 11.26

Knowing where the beat is makes it easier to offset the timing between the beats.

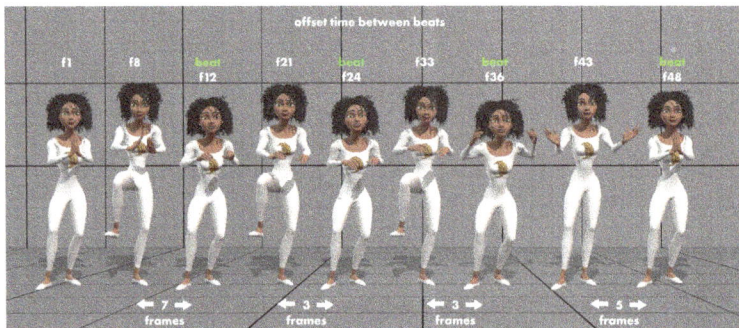

Figure 11.27

Frank Thomas animated the wonderfully timed scene of Pinocchio singing "I've Got No Strings" in *Pinocchio*.

It's 48 beats from when the spotlight turns on revealing Pinocchio to when the spotlight turns off. The song "I've Got No Strings" is 92 beats per minute. At 24 fps the beat hits every 15.65 frames.

How do you animate a dance when the beat is every 15.65 frames?

You don't!

To show Pinocchio's self-consciousness, Frank purposely offset the timing at the start of the song. Pinocchio sings, "to hold me down". Pinocchio sings the word "down" hitting on the 4th beat, but he points at the ground a beat behind, on the 5th beat — much to Milt Kahl's irritation!

To stay on the beat, Frank animates Pinocchio's dance steps hitting on both 15 and 16 frames.

The pointing gesture was easy to offset because Frank was aware of the beats. You don't have to wing it if you're aware of the beat!

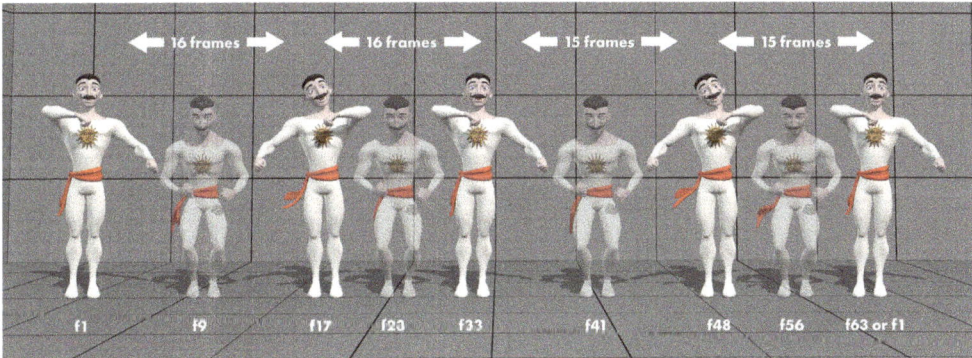

Figure 11.28

Direction Change Takes Time!

Any action with a change of direction, such as jumping, turning around, or lifting a pencil, takes time. When you rush an action, your animation will lose weight and be less believable.

If there isn't enough time to show proper weight, you're doing too much! Simplify your action!

Use charting to get your action to read.

If an action is too quick, use charting to adjust the spacing of the poses. Remember the bouncing ball!

If an action from a. to b. to c. is too quick, pull b. back a third. If it's still too quick, pull it back a half.

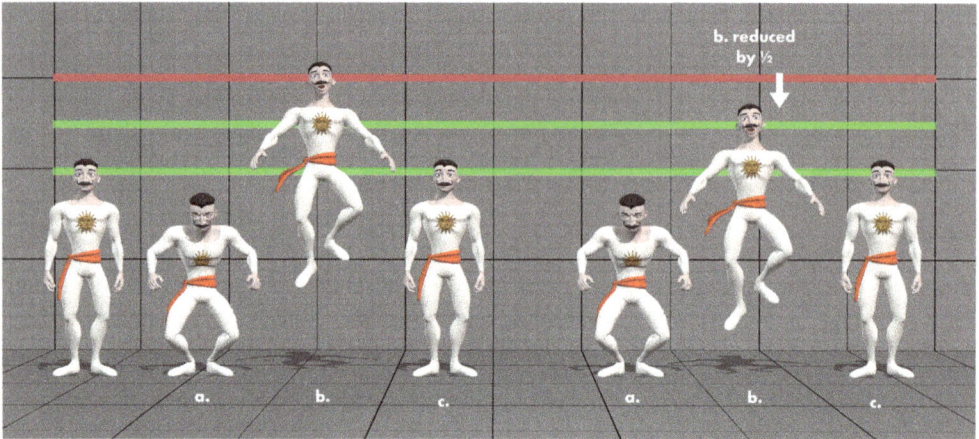

Figure 11.29

Animation Exercise — Try timing a ball or sphere while thinking in charts. Animate halves, thirds, and favoring. Animate poses close together and space them out. Then try animating head turns on halves, thirds, and favoring using the same method. Don't forget to add an arc! Then space them out to see how different the timing looks.

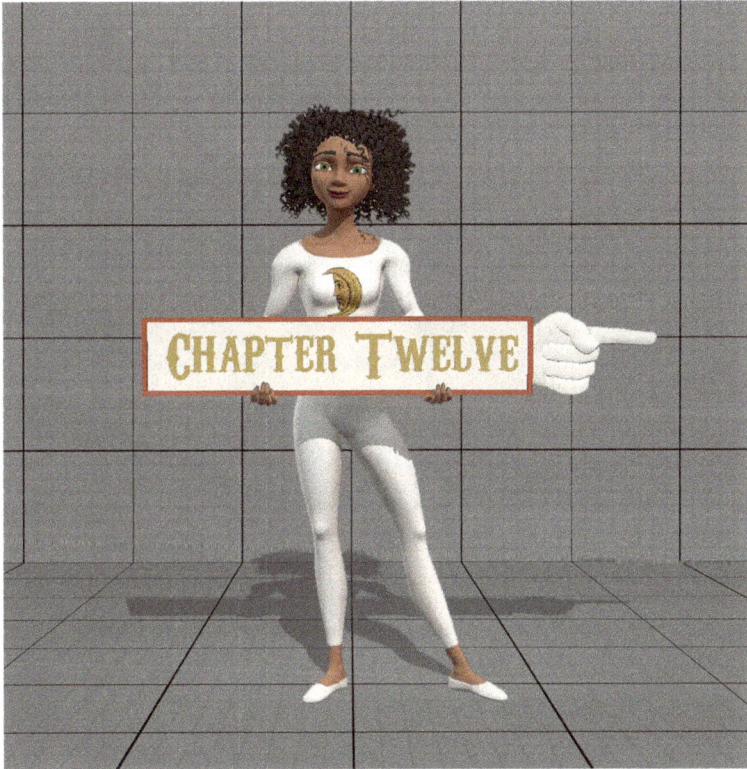

CHAPTER TWELVE

Chapter 12. Slow-In & Slow-Out

Introduction

Starting and stopping an action or changing direction takes time. When your animation looks too quick or doesn't read, many times it's because the animation isn't slowing in and out of poses properly. You can get wonderfully subtle results in 3D animation, but an improper slow-in or slow-out can make your animation look mushy. In this chapter we'll learn how to get snappy or subtle slow-ins and slow-outs and how to move through poses.

Spacing

As we know, spacing is how far apart your extremes, breakdowns and inbetweens are. The farther apart your spacing is, the quicker your action. The closer together your spacing is, the slower the action. Even spacing makes for constant speed.

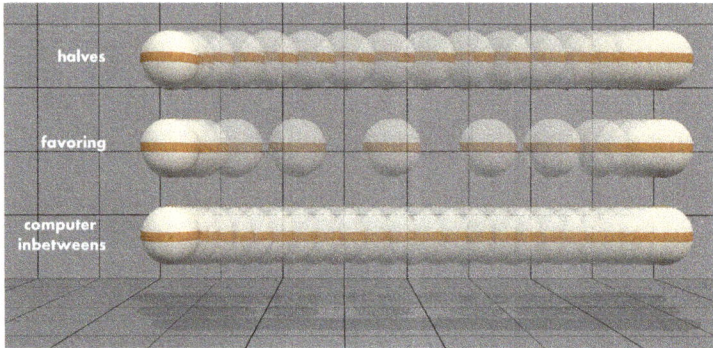

Figure 12.1

A finger point can be slow or quick, but there needs to be a progression to the spacing of the poses.

The hand slows out of the neutral pose, speeds up as the hand extends, and then slows into the point. The spacing gradually widens, then tightens.

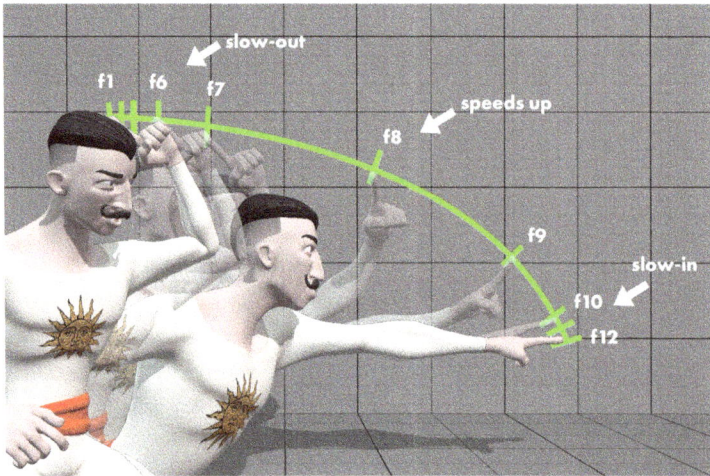

Figure 12.2

DOI: 10.1201/9781003361893-13

Poor spacing of keys, breakdowns, or inbetweens, at any speed, causes erratic action and can make your animation appear quicker. Delete any unnecessary keys, breakdowns or inbetweens. The better your spacing, the smoother and slower your scene will appear.

In this example (a) looks pretty good. But delete that key and the new position (b) follows a better arc.

These subtle changes will make your animation smoother!

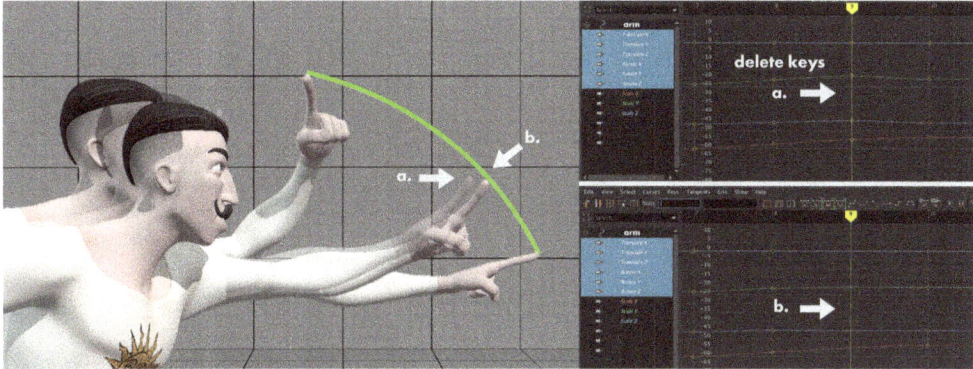

Figure 12.3

Slow-In & Slow-Out

Slow-in and slow-out, ease-in and ease-out, or cushion-in and cushion-out, call it what you like, they're all the same — they all refer to acceleration and deceleration. Things take time to start and stop moving.

We'll call it slowing-in and slowing-out.

If you raise your arm from your side, your arm takes time to begin moving up. Your arm slows-out of the resting position at the side of your body. Then moves quicker as it passes your waist. And slows-in as it stops overhead.

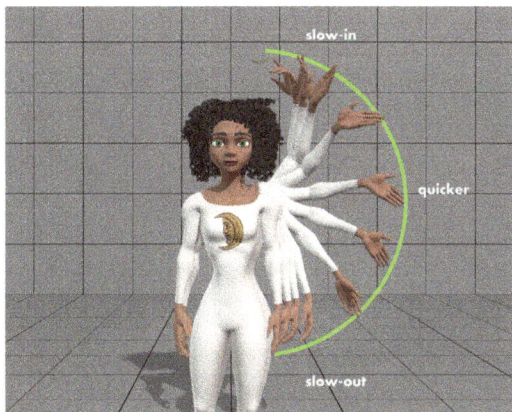

Figure 12.4

In traditional animation, a slow-in or slow-out is charted as half, half, half, half, half.

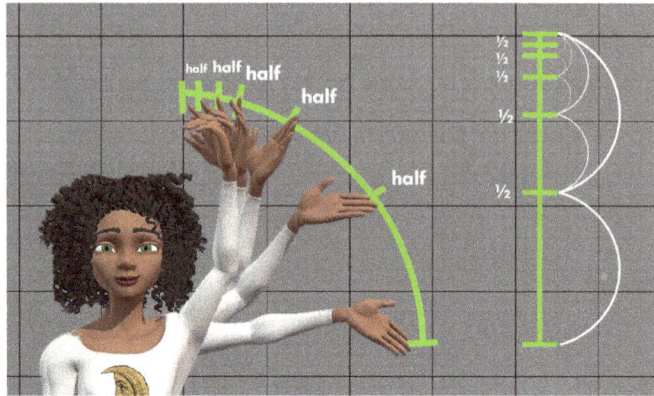

Figure 12.5

A character turns their head from their right to their left. The extremes are on frames 1 and 13. Frame 7 is a half.

Adding an arc to the head on frame 7 helps a little — however, because the computer adds the inbetweens, all the surrounding keys will be evenly spaced and you'll still have that boring, even computer timing.

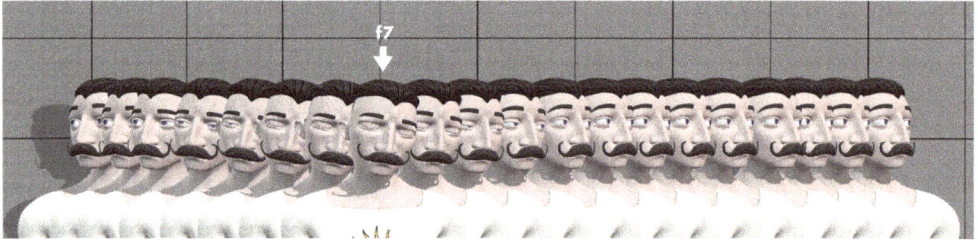

Figure 12.6

You can get traditional slow-ins and slow-outs through charting in the graph editor.

With the breakdown on frame 7, set a key on frame 4. Frame 4 is halfway between 1 and 7.

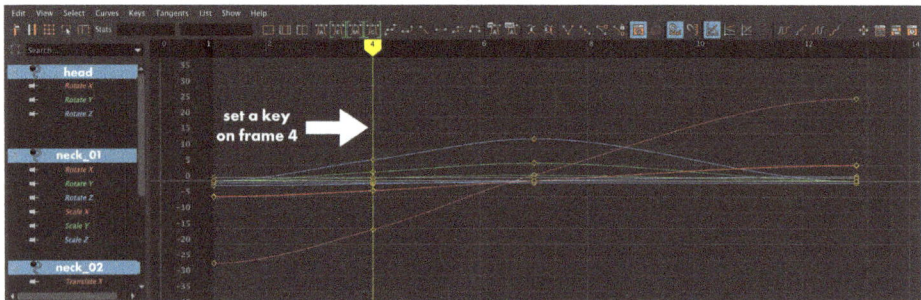

Figure 12.7

Now move frame 4 to frame 6.

Frame 6 is now halfway between frame 1 and frame 7.

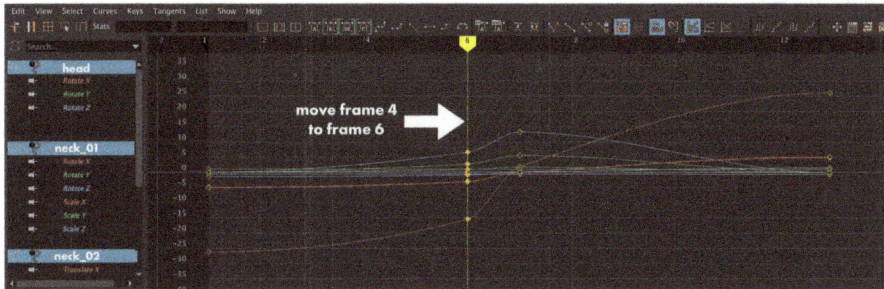
Figure 12.8

There are four inbetweens between frame 1 and frame 6. To make a half between frame 1 and 6 you'll have to slide frame 1 back to frame 0. Move frame 1 back to frame 0 and set a key on frame 3. Then move frame 3 to frame 5 and frame 0 back to frame 1.

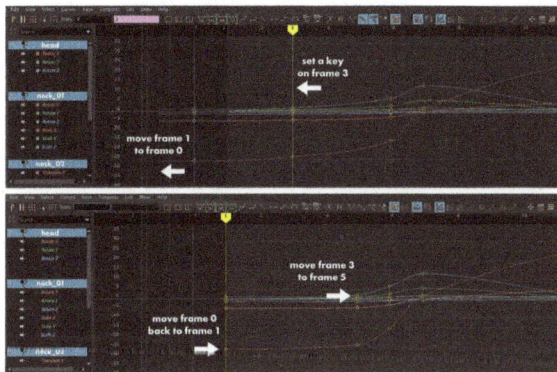
Figure 12.9

If you wanted, you could keep halving back to frame 1, but two keys are usually enough to control the slow-out.

The same would apply to the slow-in from frame 7 to 13. Set a key on frame 10, then move 10 back to frame 8. Frame 8 is now halfway between frame 7 and frame 13 etc.

You now have a snappier feel to the head turn because you're slowing-out of one pose and slowing-into another.

Of course, you'll want to tweak the arc of the head turn with a breakdown, but now the timing is better.

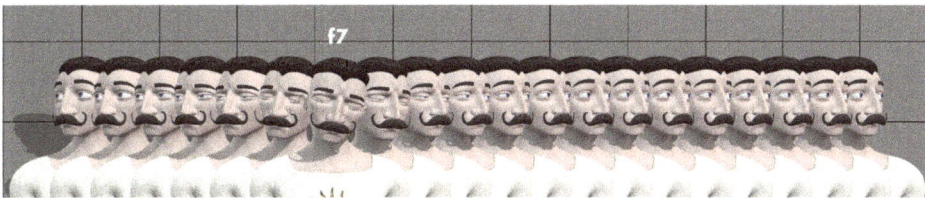
Figure 12.10

Can you create slow-ins and slow-outs using curves in the graph editor?

Of course, but understanding the traditional approach to slowing-in and out gets you used to thinking about spacing in charts!

A character falling forward in a cartoony way slows-out of a held pose. As with the bouncing ball, the spacing of the breakdown will determine the strength of the impact against the ground.

A breakdown farther from the ground (a) will give a hard hit. A breakdown closer to the ground (b) will give a softer hit.

A breakdown too far from the ground (c) may cause a pop.

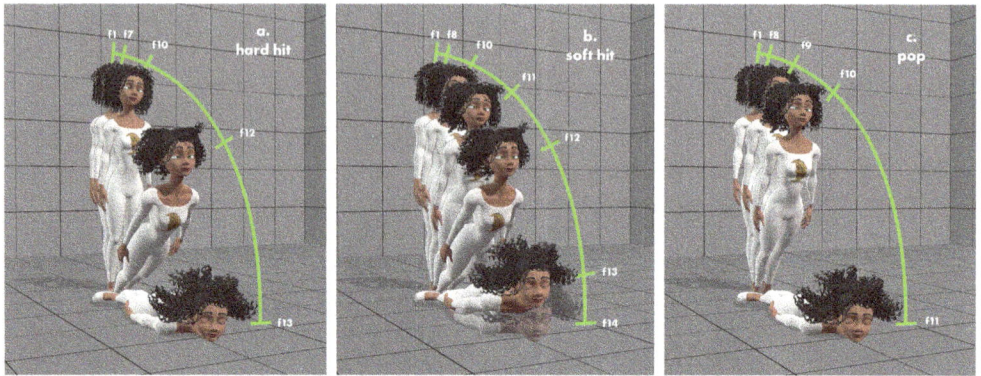

Figure 12.11

Speed

Use slow-outs and slow-ins when accelerating, decelerating, or changing direction. Use evenly spaced inbetweens when moving through an action.

A character swinging a baseball bat or a golf club may begin the action with a wind up. The bat is changing direction. This requires a slow-in to the anticipation pose and a slow-out of the anticipation pose.

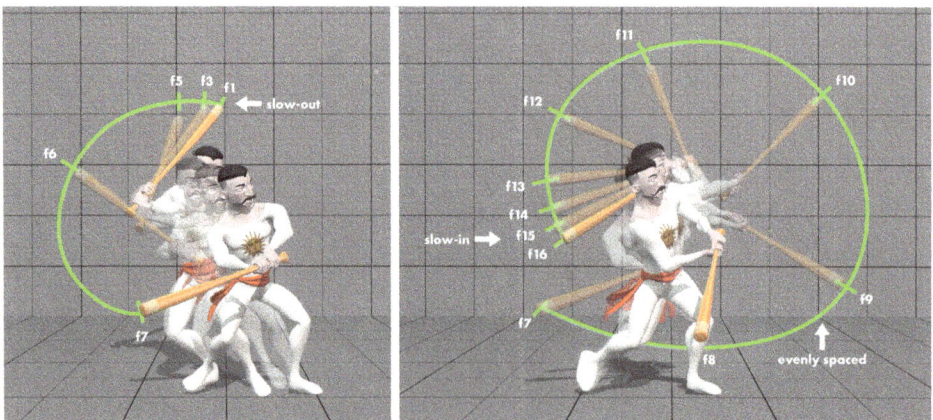

Figure 12.12

During the swing, the keys could be evenly spaced to show a constant speed. We're moving through the action.

Slow-out for acceleration and slow-in for deceleration. Even spacing for consistent speed.

Remembering this simple concept will help immensely with your timing!

Hit Poses

In animation there's more impact when you hit past the object you're hitting.

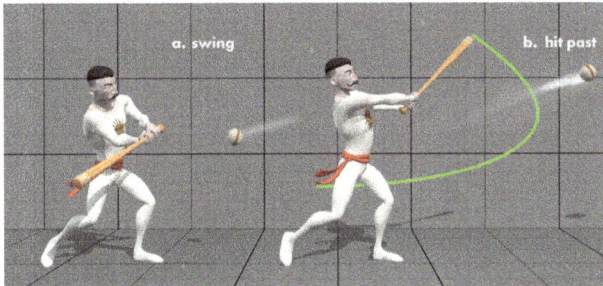

Figure 12.13

But sometimes, as in games, you'll need to actually hit an object at a specific point during the swing.

Key the hit pose as a storytelling pose.

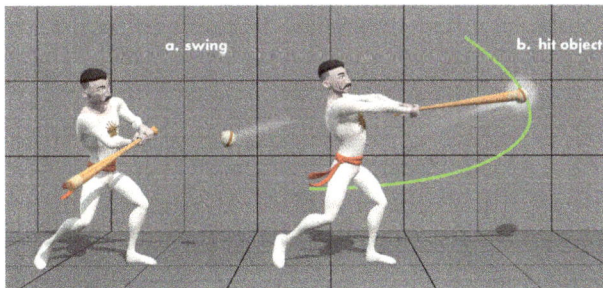

Figure 12.14

Moving Through Poses

If you want your audience to see certain poses, spend more time by them. Slow-in and slow-out of them.

A character is showing joy. Think of it as a ball reaching its peak in a bounce. There are more keys of the ball reaching its peak in a bounce so that you feel the moment of weightlessness.

Slow-in and slow-out of the 'showing joy' pose to emphasize it.

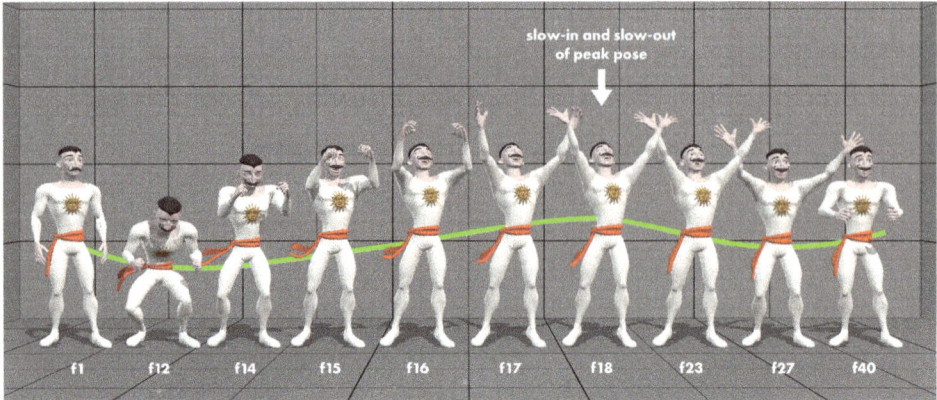

Figure 12.15

Moving too quickly through a pose can make your action look rushed — not to mention difficult for your audience to follow. The action will also lose weight and believability.

Moving Holds

"An animation drawing will go dead if it's held much more than a foot, or 24 frames, without something happening,"[1] said Ollie Johnston.

So, how do you keep held animation alive? Add a moving hold.

A moving hold is two extremes, one a little different than the other, which a character can drift between with a minimal amount of movement. Moving holds are meant to be subtle and are easy to do in 3D.

At least they're easier than drawing a lot of very close inbetweens!

One way to create a moving hold is to copy frame 1 to frame 21, then push frame 21 slightly. If you like the pose you're moving into, work in reverse and copy frame 21 to frame 1, and then change up that pose slightly.

Toggle back and forth making sure you have just the right amount of change in poses.

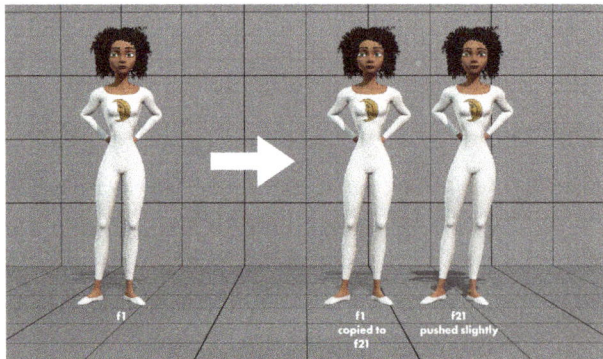

Figure 12.16

Slow-out of frame 1 and into frame 21 using charting! Halves, thirds, or favoring — whatever best suits the mood of the scene.

If the movement is too much, use charts to pull the scene back. Does pulling the frame back a third look better? If it's still too much, perhaps frame 10 or 11 looks better — around a half. Key frame 11 and copy it to frame 21. Then delete frame 11.

Think in charts!

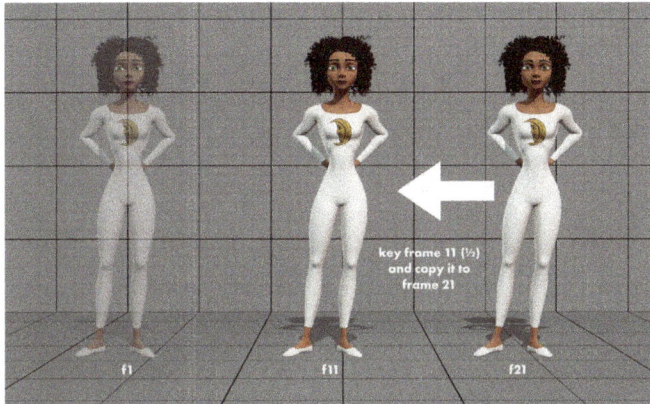

Figure 12.17

How does your animation play in reverse? Your animation played backward should look like live action played in reverse. It should have that stop and start, snappy feel to it.

If your scene played in reverse doesn't feel the same as live action in reverse, chances are your slow-ins and slow-outs are not good enough.

Remember — it always comes down to slowing-in or slowing-out, and even spacing for constant speed.

Animation Exercise – Animate a character raising their arm, pausing, and then lowering it again. Keep it simple! Try different speeds: thirds, halves, and favoring. How smooth and natural can you make the action?

Chapter 13. Overlap and Follow-Through

Introduction

Overlapping action and follow-through are often confused. What's the difference between the two?

Simply put, overlapping action is anything we can control, such as your head, torso, hips, legs, feet, arms, and hands. Follow-through is what you really can't control, such as hair, fabric, and loose flesh.

Does it matter what they're called?

Not really. Overlapping action can follow-through, and follow-through can overlap. You just need to understand the principles.

In this chapter we'll explore some easy-to-follow methods and formulas for achieving smooth, weighty, overlap and follow-through of the face, hair, and fabric.

What Moves First?

When we move, no two parts of our body move at the same time. When we stop, no two parts of the body stop at the same time. This is an overlapping action.

Many animators will tell you that motion starts from the hips, but what if your character is sitting on a chair or wheelchair or riding a bicycle? The torso may move first.

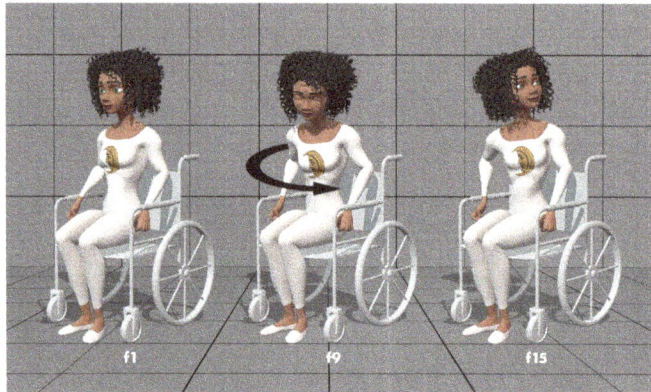

Figure 13.1

A character turning could start with the head moving first.

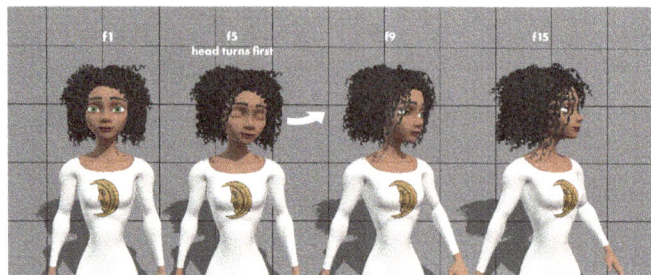

Figure 13.2

DOI: 10.1201/9781003361893-14

Or your character could turn but still be looking at something — the head stays steady while the hips or shoulders turn first.

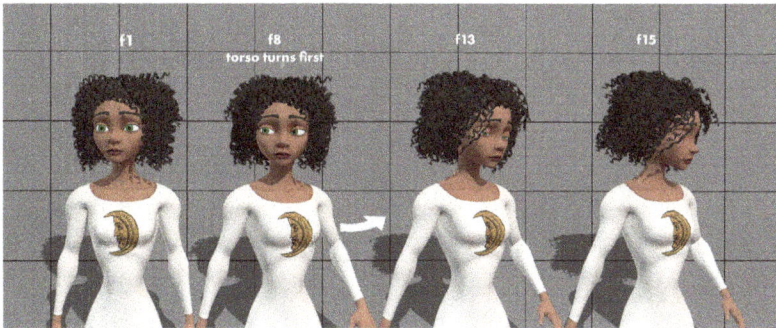

Figure 13.3

Different body parts can lead the action, just decide what makes sense for your scene.

Animating Overlap

A squishy bouncing ball is an example of basic overlap. After the ball squashes on the ground, the top half of the ball bounces up while the bottom half sticks to the ground.

Just as the ball is about to reach its peak, a favoring key, the bottom half catches up. Overlap.

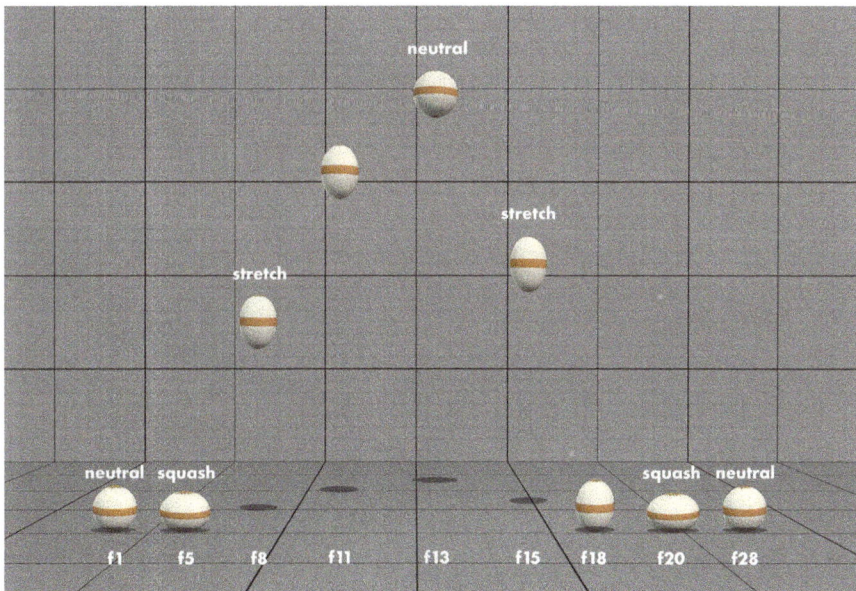

Figure 13.4

A character jumping up and down is similar to a squishy bouncing ball. From a neutral pose they squash down in anticipation. They leap up, their feet stick to the ground as they stretch. The arms drag behind the body.

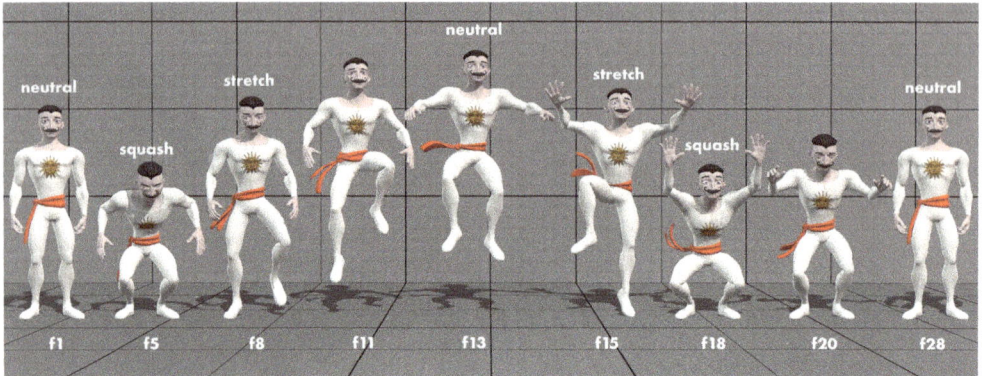

Figure 13.5

The hips slow-in to their peak translation. A few frames later the feet catch up.

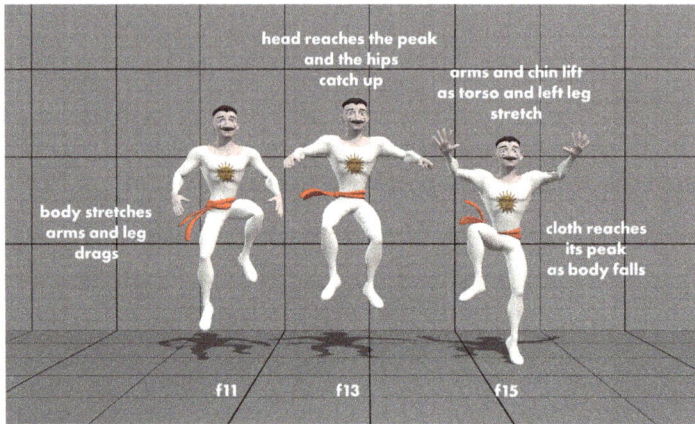

Figure 13.6

As they start to fall, their arms and chin raise as they stretch. The lower half squashes first as the upper half drags behind. As the hips rise, the arms fall and the chin drags.

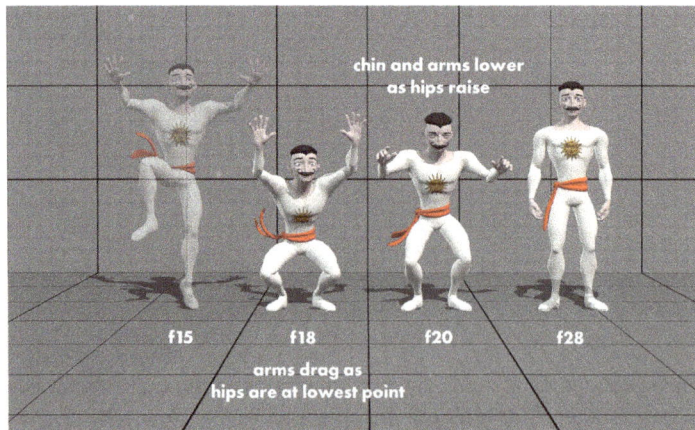

Figure 13.7

Layering

Overlap is layering actions. Use the graph editor to identify the extreme high and low or side-to-side translations and rotations, then space curves to layer the body. For instance, if a character starts to turn their head on frame 1, you could wait until frame 5 to start turning the body.

A character is in an idle and holding a baton, hears something, and turns. Their head first. A few frames later the body turns, dragging the upper arm. The hand could favor the idle pose. The baton catches up and your character is in another idle pose. One thing follows another.

Don't forget to follow the path of action!

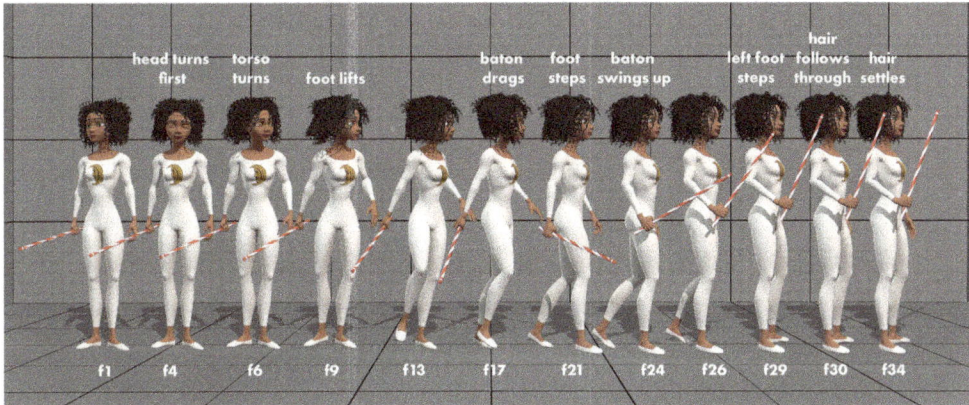

Figure 13.8

Sometimes you may not have time to separate overlap by more than a frame. If a frame is all you have — a frame is good enough!

Don't take overlap too literally. There's nothing wrong with all parts of the body hitting a pose at the same time on the same key frame for a more cartoony effect.

A character turns and points, hitting a dynamic pose.

Offset the timing of each body part on the way to the pointing pose. The body could turn on a half, while the hand pointing is on a third favoring the first extreme.

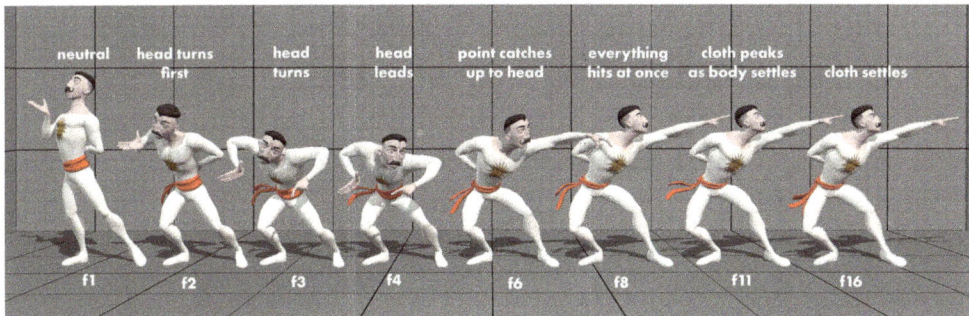

Figure 13.9

Contrasting Action

Always be on the lookout for opportunities to add contrasting actions, or different parts of the body moving in opposite directions. If the body lowers, raise the arms. If the body rises, lower the arms.

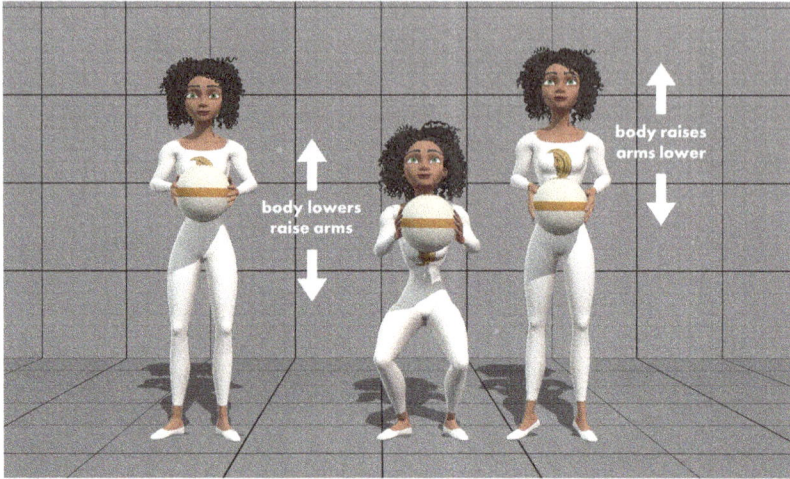

Figure 13.10

If the body turns to the right, move the arms to the left.

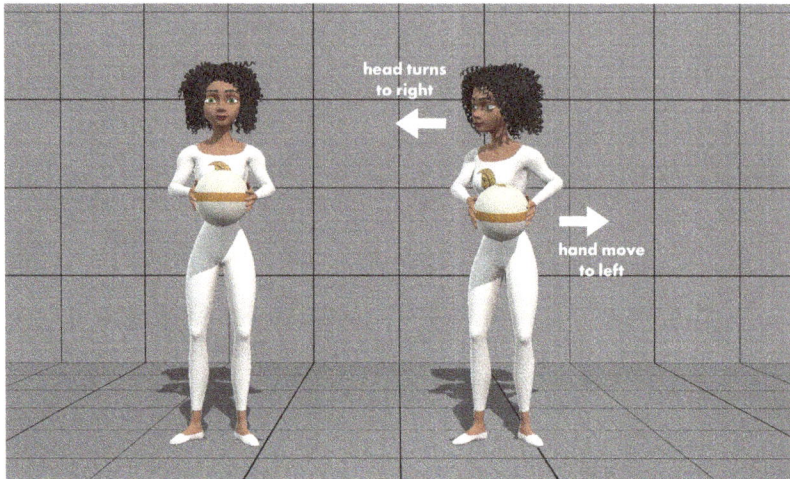

Figure 13.11

This doesn't mean you can't have a character raise their head to look at the sun while also raising their hand to cover their eyes.

Just don't move them together in the same direction at the same time.

Find a path for the hand that contrasts the movement of the head. For instance, the hand could move in first, then rise up before coming down to shield the eyes.

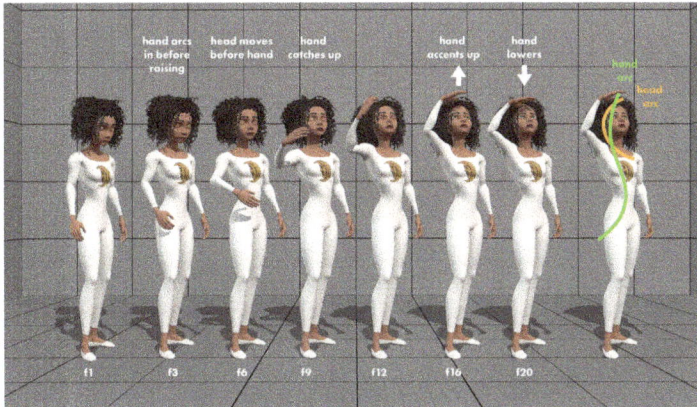

Figure 13.12

A character touches their toes. The body and hands move in the same direction, but there are any number of ways to offset them. As the body bends down, the hands could move up first. The body could anticipate up as the hands could drop, etc.

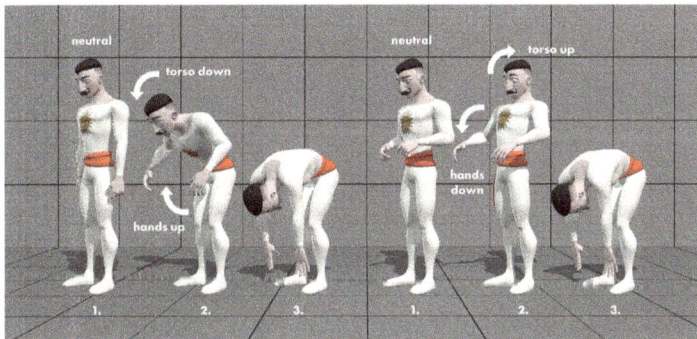

Figure 13.13

A very "Disney" thing to do is to raise the chin on the down pose in a walk cycle, then lower the chin moving into the up pose.

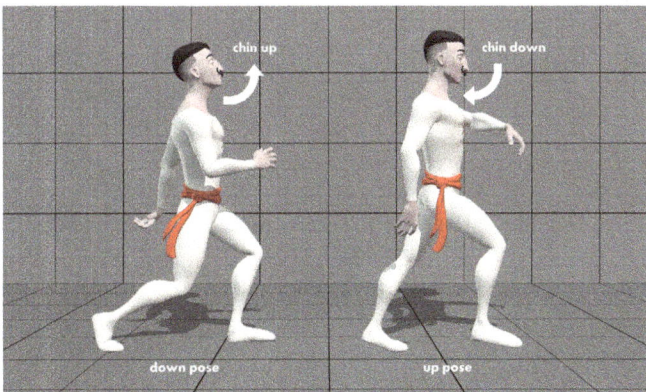

Figure 13.14

Double check your overlap. Scrub through your scene and look to see if any two things are moving together. If any two things are moving together — break them up!

A common issue with beginner animators is to have a character move their torso and head together as if they're one body part. Offset them.

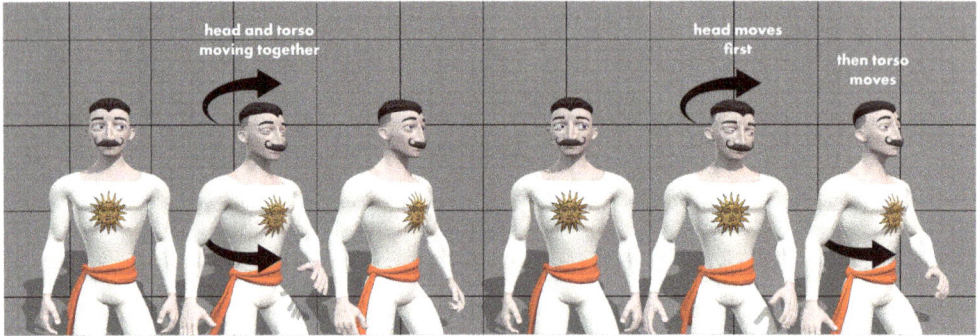

Figure 13.15

Response Time

Response time in video games is when you press the stick or bumper and there's a delay in your character's movement.

If there is a sudden loud noise behind a character, they won't move at the same moment they hear the noise. They'll wait a beat, and then react.

Figure 13. 16

This same response delay occurs with overlap. Even during a comedic action, a distracted character suddenly pulled by the arm won't move all at once, otherwise it will look as if one big shape is being pulled out of frame.

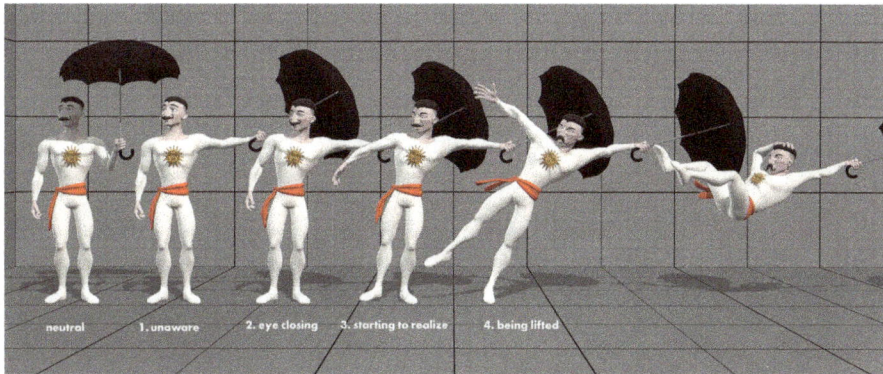

Figure 13.17

At first, your character may be unaware that their arm is being pulled.

Then, perhaps the eye on the side being pulled begins to close.

They are starting to realize they are being pulled.

One or both feet can lift next. See how long you can leave at least one foot planted for overlap!

"The more you understand about reality," said Richard Williams. "The funnier you can make your cartoon action."[1]

Follow-Through

As mentioned, follow-through is what you really can't control, such as hair, fabric, and loose flesh.

A head can show overlapping action when shaking back and forth. The features on the face and hair drag in the direction of the head movement. When the head stops or changes direction, things such as hair, cheeks, and jowls will still travel in the direction they were headed until they come to rest or are pulled in another direction.

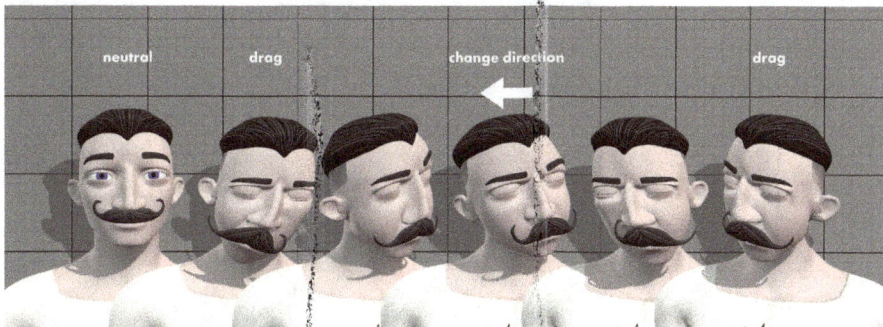

Figure 13.18

The timing of overlap depends upon the weight, thickness, and size of what's overlapping, but overlap should be at least a frame or two behind the controlling main action.

As a character walks, the hair or fabric joint closest to the main action will be pulled first. The successive joints will continue to move in the direction they were going until they too are pulled.

Separate the timing of each successive hair or fabric joint by at least a frame.

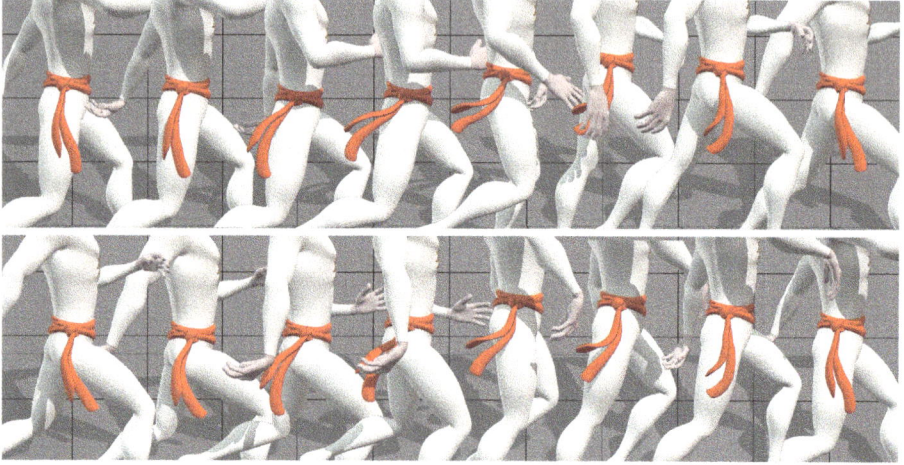

Figure 13.19

If a character stops suddenly, the hair or fabric will follow-through — continuing in the direction it was headed until it goes as far as it can go. It will then drop or swing to a rest.

S-Curves

Take equal sections out of the snaking sine wave, connect the ends together, and animate it, and you'll get a nice, overlapping wave action.

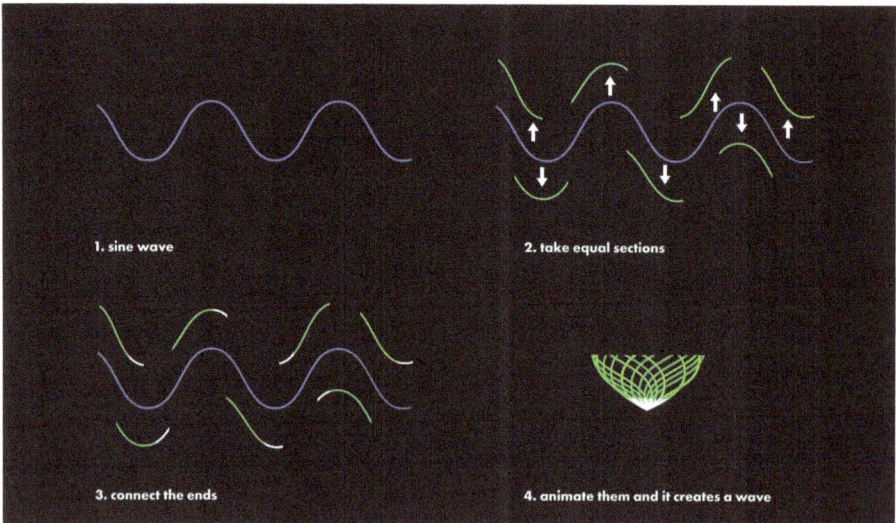

Figure 13.20

Anything that is flowing, such as hair or fabric, will move in an s-curve. Battle rope exercises in the gym, a bouncing pony tail, or Superman's waving cape move in a sinusoidal wave, sine wave, or s-curve.

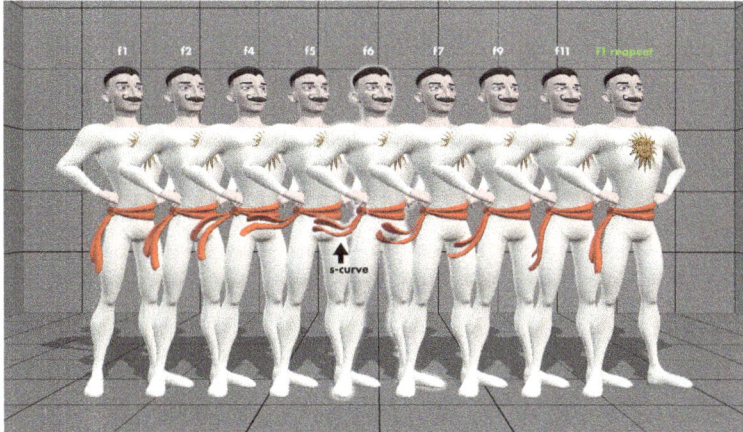

Figure 13.21

S-curves can be somewhat tricky.

The most basic way to block in an s-curve is by using four poses. Arcing over, arcing under, snapping over, and snapping under.

Arc over for when the curve reaches its peak height; snapping down for when it's being pulled down; arc under for the swing low; and snapping up for being pulled up.

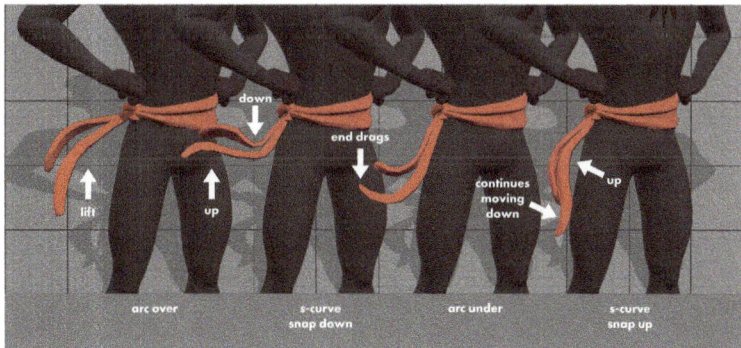

Figure 13.22

Like a snake tail, each segment of your s-curve should pretty much follow the same path as the segment before it.

Expansion and Contraction

A face stretches and squashes. This is expansion and contraction. Hair and fabric also expand and contract.

When animating hair, don't think of the individual strands, but the expanding and contracting mass.

At rest, hair is in a neutral pose. As the head turns, the hair contracts.

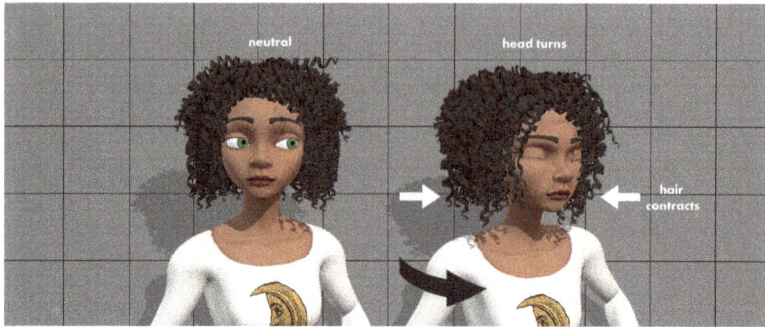

Figure 13.23

When the head stops moving, the hair expands. When the hair comes to a rest, it first contracts, then returns to a neutral pose.

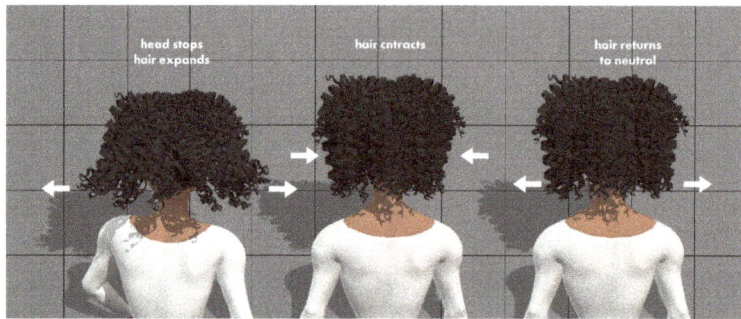

Figure 13.24

Don't get hung up perfecting hair or fabric too early! Until your main action is pretty much as good as you can get it — just rough in hair and fabric. When you're happy with your main action, then start polishing your hair or fabric.

A lot of time can be wasted reworking hair and fabric animation if your main action changes.

Animation Exercise – Animate a character turning and pointing. Delay parts of the body to show overlap in the head, arms, legs, hair, and fabric — if they have hair and fabric.

CHAPTER FOURTEEN

Chapter 14. Successive Breaking of Joints

Introduction

Successive Breaking of Joints is Art Babbitt's awkwardly named principle for using the skeleton to achieve fluid, overlapping action.

"All human action is controlled by this method of movement," wrote Michael Sporn. "A body can only bend at joints — knees, wrists, elbows etc. Any other break is artificial and verboten in trying to make your character seem real. Any animator of the human form would swear by it."[1]

In this chapter we'll learn about successive breaking of joints, and how to use it for more sophisticated animation.

Keep Your Character Believable

When Les Clark animated the "Goddess" in *The Goddess of Spring* (1934), she was intended to be a more lifelike character, a step closer to Snow White. Though Les animated her figure and features realistically, her arms were noodly rubber hoses, and the results embarrassed him. He apologized to Walt and Walt told him, "I guess we could do better next time."[2]

Les had two styles of animation for the Goddess: realistic and rubber-hose, and they didn't quite gel.

It's fine to add a curve to something that wouldn't curve in real life, such as a forearm, to show speed. But don't push it too much if it doesn't fit the character. The longer you show the arm curved, the less solid your animation will feel and the closer you're heading into rubber-hose territory.

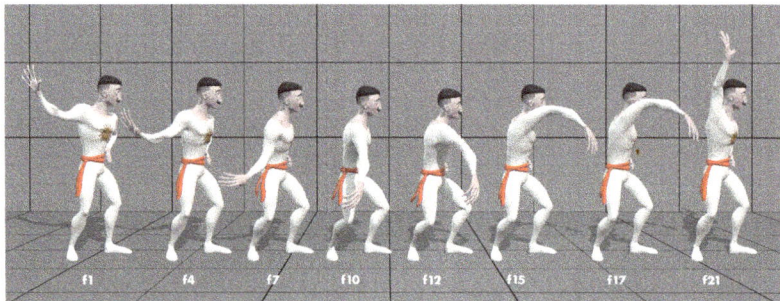

Figure 14.1

Tone it down!

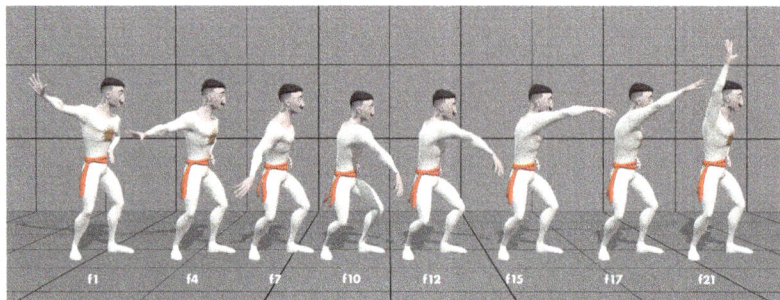

Figure 14.2

DOI: 10.1201/9781003361893-15

Smears and wipes are closer to rubber-hose animation in that they also cheat anatomy.

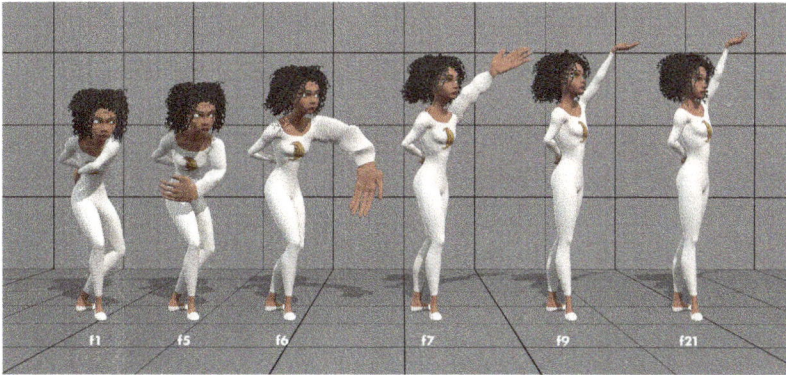

Figure 14.3

The same action can be achieved without cheating by using the skeleton.

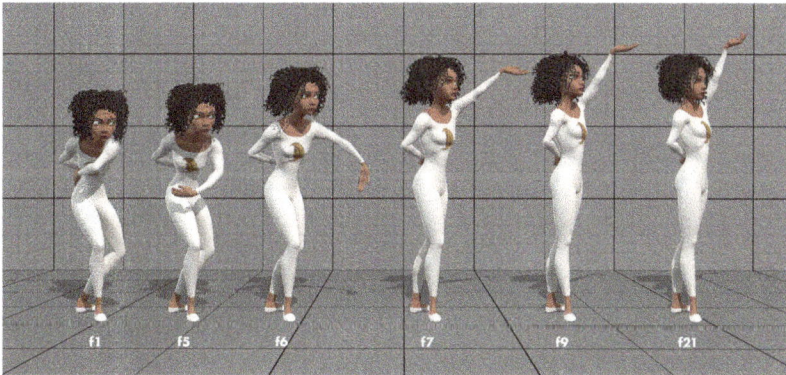

Figure 14.4

Curves with Straight Lines

Successive breaking of joints is getting arcs and curves using straight lines. If a character raises their arm and touches their head, they don't lift their arm straight and bend it at the last second.

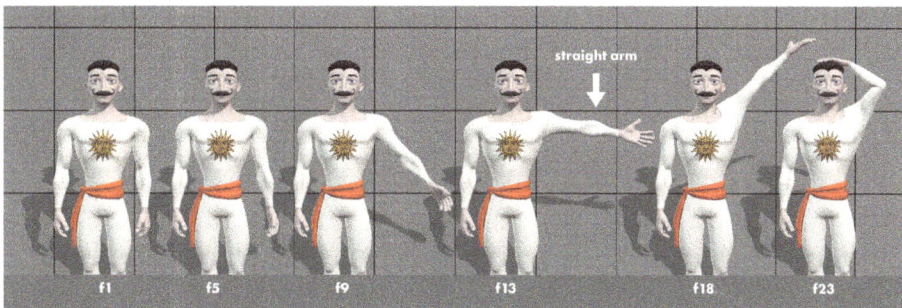

Figure 14.5

They break the joints gradually.

Their shoulder may rise. The elbow lifts and bends. The forearm moves. The wrist drags.

Each joint follows a clear path of action.

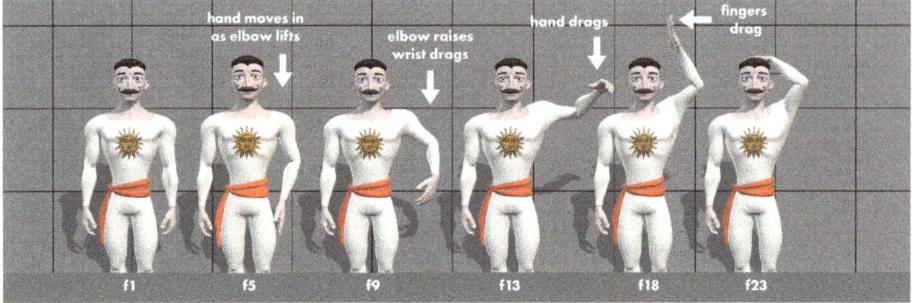

Figure 14.6

A character makes circular motions in front of their body with their hands; the left hand is moving clockwise — wax on, and the right hand is moving counter-clockwise — wax off.

Place a nurbs circle, torus, or flattened cylinder in front of your character to use as a guide.

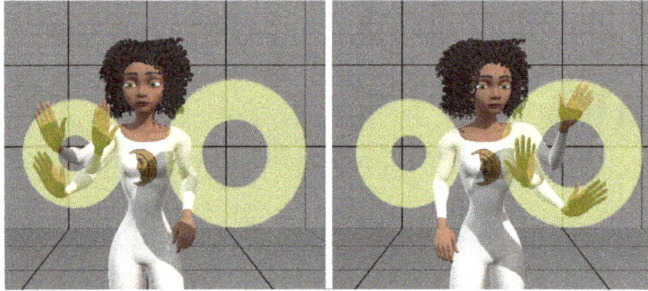

Figure 14.7

The shoulders need to move. How do you figure out where to put the high and low points of the shoulders? Put your own hand on your own shoulder and do the motion — wax-on.

The high point of the shoulder is perhaps when your character's hand is between the 1 o'clock and 11 o'clock position for each circle. The low points may be when your character's hand is at the 6 o'clock position.

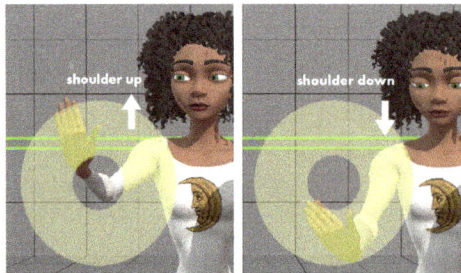

Figure 14.8

The elbow may lower when the hand is up and rise when the hand is down. Contrast.

Figure 14.9

Trouble Blocking in Arms?

If you have two key poses and are having trouble figuring out how to bend the arms to get the pose you want, position the hands where you'd like them to be! Place the hand along the path of action using charting!

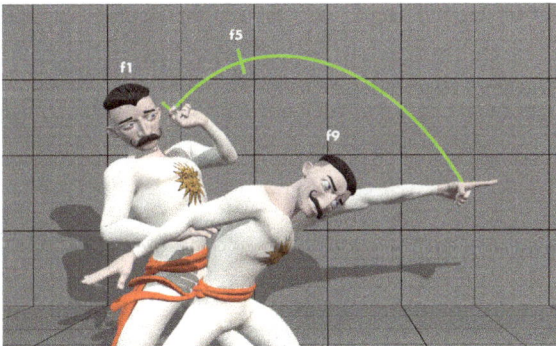

Figure 14.10

Once you put the hands in the spot you want, positioning the arms is easier. Look for balance.

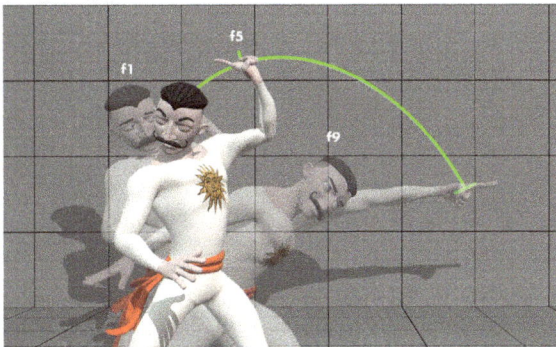

Figure 14.11

Believability

Successive breaking of joints is not limited to the arms — the whole body should follow this principle.

A character spikes a volleyball.

Figure 14.12

Starting with a neutral position on frame 1, they take a step forward. The hips shift over the supporting foot on frame 4 so they can lift their foot and take a step. As they step forward, their arms swing behind them and their back begins to arch. They lean back, off-balance on frame 12, as they step. The arms swing back in anticipation and reach their highest point. One thing happens after the other — successively!

Figure 14.13

Stepping into the jump on frame 14, the feet plant. On frame 16 the arms swing forward to help give power to the jump. The hands drag. They regain their balance on frame 18 for the jump.

The heels lift off the ground as they push up on frame 21. They're fully stretched now, rising off the ground. The arms are close together, anticipating moving outwards.

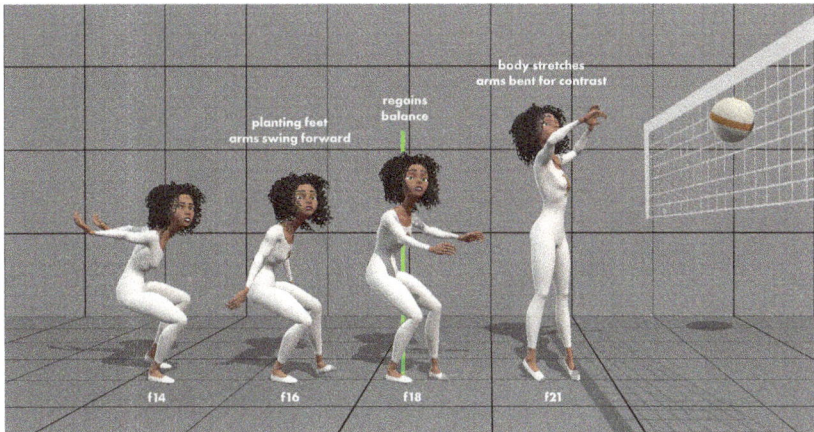

Figure 14.14

On frame 26, mid-air the back arches. The knees bend and the feet lift. The right arm rotates backward and bends at the elbow, ready to hit the ball. The left arm extends for balance.

For contrast the body stretches on frame 29 so that the hit has more power.

The right arm comes forward at the shoulder on frame 32, the elbow bent backward. The knees come forward for force and balance.

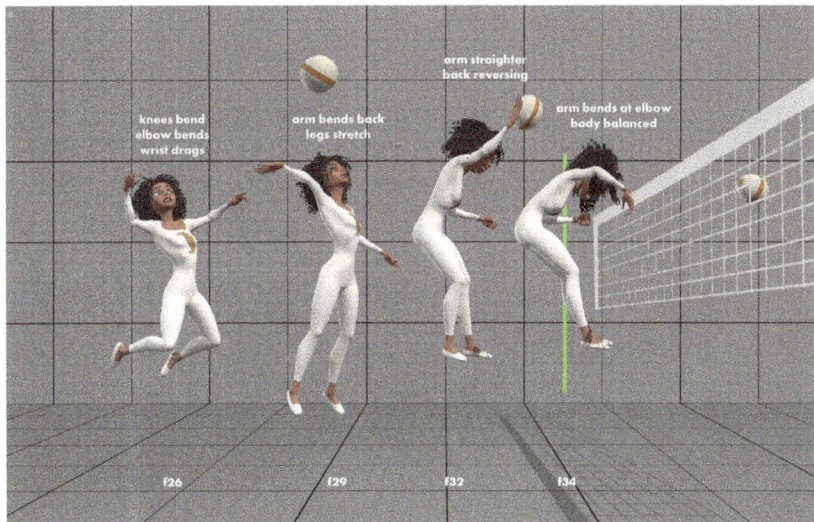

Figure 14.15

As they swing through the spike, the legs extend on frame 38 to prepare for the landing. The torso begins to unfold. The arms follow-through along the path of action on frame 41.

They land on the ground, squashing on frame 43. The arms swing forward to maintain balance on frame 45.

Finally, they rise into a neutral pose again.

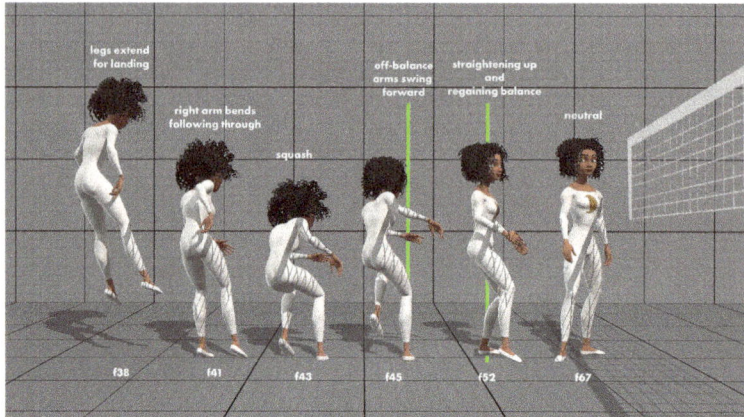

Figure 14.16

Bendy, curvy, and fluid motion throughout the body is achieved with a rigid skeleton. If your rig has flexy joints, push the curves in the body — but don't lose the skeletal landmarks such as elbows and knees!

Successive breaking of joints isn't just for realistic animation.

In the Tex Avery - Mike Lah cartoon **Deputy Droopy** (1955) a "mangy outlaw" slaps sidekick several times. For the slapping motion, the shoulder moves, and each arm "breaks" successively — even his hips move back and forth as his weight shifts!

The action is funnier because it's based on reality.

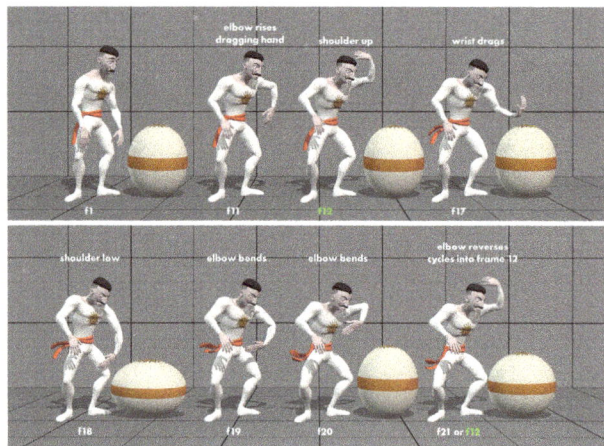

Figure 14.17

Overlap Successive Breaking of Joints

A common issue with successive breaking of joints is animation getting too robotic. This happens when you don't overlap actions. Don't move one joint, then the next joint, then the next joint, etc.

Overlap them!

A character steps and turns. Don't translate the hips, stop, and then rotate the torso.

Figure 14.18

Start rotating the head and torso while the hips translate. The timing could be however you'd like but overlap the action so that it feels natural.

Use the graph editor. If two body parts start and/or stop on the same frames, offset them!

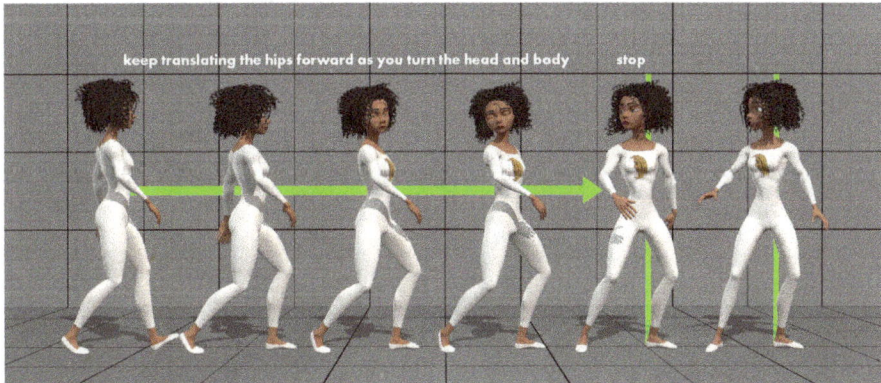

Figure 14.19

Animation Exercise — 1. With your character's arm at their side, lift the arm and put it on the top of their head. Break the joints successively as you raise the arm. Find an interesting path of action. Try to get it as smooth and weighty as possible.

2. Animate a character moving their hands in front of them, "Wax-on" and "Wax-off". Look at your animation from all angles. Keep the hand rotations an even distance from the body.

Chapter 15. Anticipation

Introduction

A common problem for beginner animators is leaving out an anticipation of an action. What happens is their animation may not read as well — one action blends into another without any set up. Or, their animation lacks oomph, because there's no contrast to the action.

In this chapter, we'll look at the importance of anticipations and how to adjust your animation so that you have enough time for anticipations.

Anticipations

Before you go one way, you must go the other way first.

"In the early days, Walt referred to anticipation as "aiming,"" [1] wrote Frank and Ollie. An anticipation alerts the audience to the action a character is about to do — like a misdirection by a magician, it says to your audience, "Look here!"

A character reaches into a hat. Before they reach into the hat, the character lifts their hand up so that the audience notices their hand. This makes it easier for the audience to follow the action. This is anticipation.

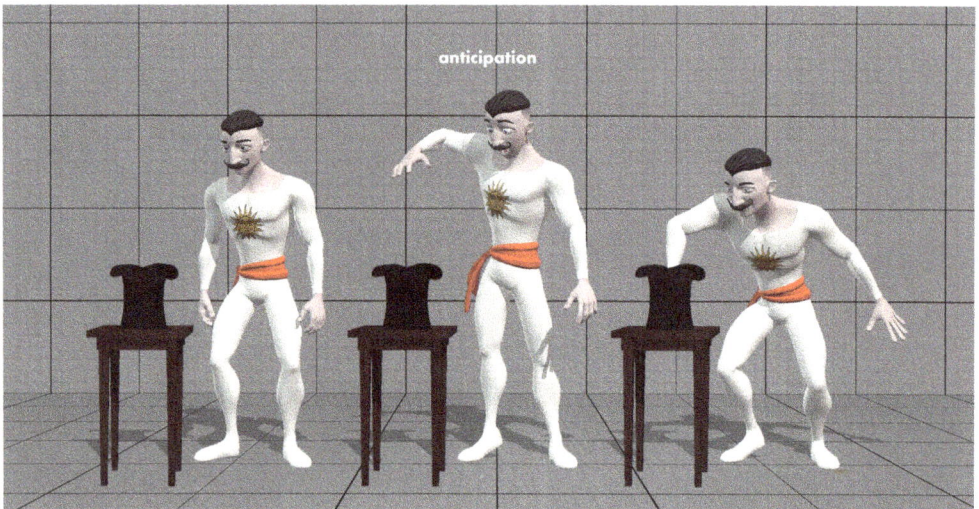

Figure 15.1

"Anticipation might be strong and violent, or it might be gentle and subtle, it can be anything in-between," wrote Eric Larson. "But it must be positive! It must be part of the mood and the action, and it must set the stage for the action which follows." [2]

A "take" is probably the most obvious example of an anticipation. For a take, a character reacts to something, squashes down in a big anticipation, then stretches in a "take".

DOI: 10.1201/9781003361893-16

Figure 15.2

Another classic example is an anticipation signaling that a character is about to run.

A character starts in an idle, does a big "Exit stage left" or "And away we go!" windup, then starts running. This type of anticipation is a running gag, no pun intended, seen often in Mickey Mouse, Tom and Jerry, and Snagglepuss shorts.

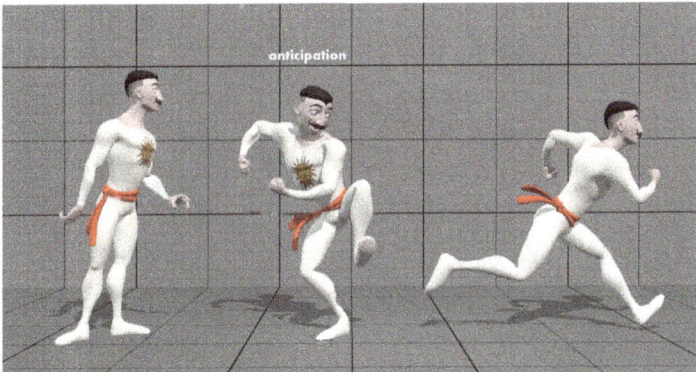

Figure 15.3

A jump without an anticipation looks as if your character is being pulled into the air by strings.

Figure 15.4

Add an anticipation and the jump has weight.

Figure 15.5

A character yelling could have two anticipations. Start with the idle pose, an inhaling anticipation, and a yell. The inhale is an anticipation to the yell.

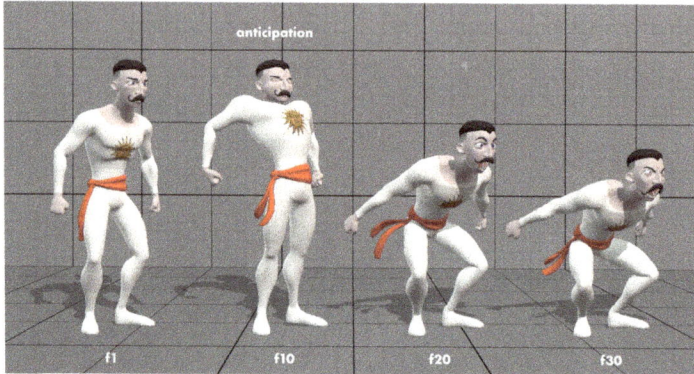

Figure 15.6

Now add an anticipation to the inhale. An anticipation to the anticipation!

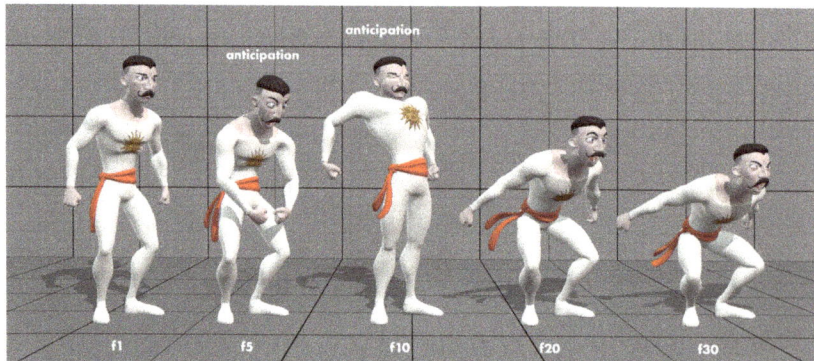

Figure 15.7

Anticipations add contrast. Actions always look better with contrast.

Subtle Anticipations

Even subtle actions read better with an anticipation added.

A character in an idle pose begins to walk. They don't just start walking; they first shift their weight over their supporting foot. This is an anticipation.

Try it! Stand in a neutral position, then lift your foot to start walking. You can't help but shift backward over the supporting foot before stepping forward.

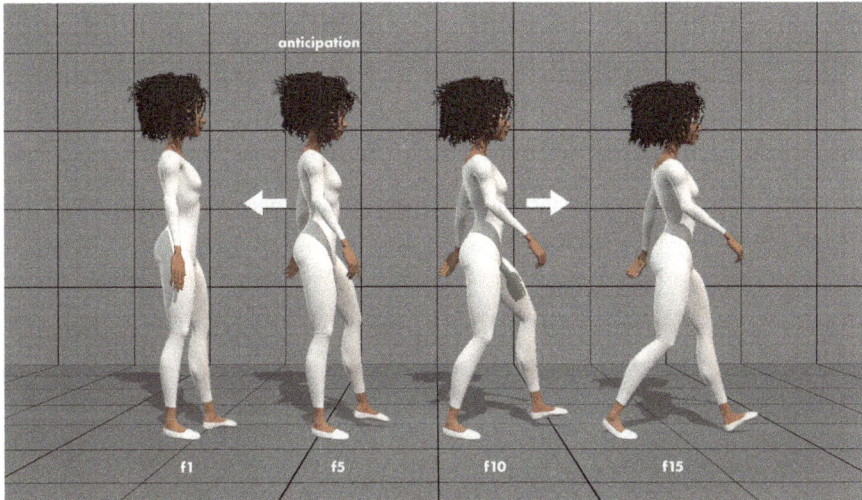

Figure 15.8

A character tosses a ball in the air. The character lowers the ball before tossing it up. The lowering is the anticipation to the toss.

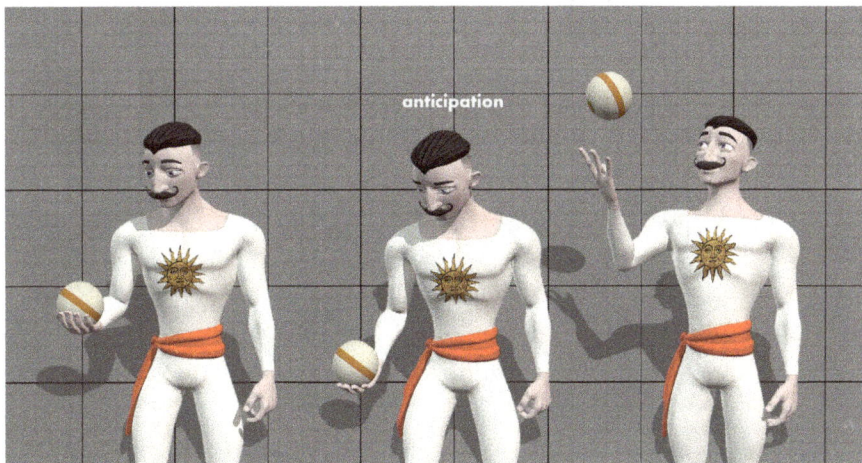

Figure 15.9

A character snaps their fingers. The arm bends at the elbow anticipating the snap before extending the arm for the snap.

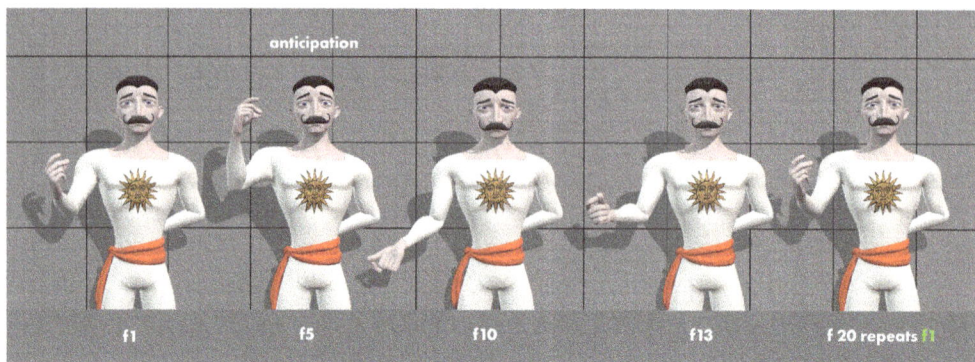

Figure 15.10

Anticipations help characters "get out of one thought and into another,"[3] wrote Eric Goldberg.

Changing facial expressions using anticipation can be similar to animating a take — with a neutral pose, or look, an anticipation, and a stretch.

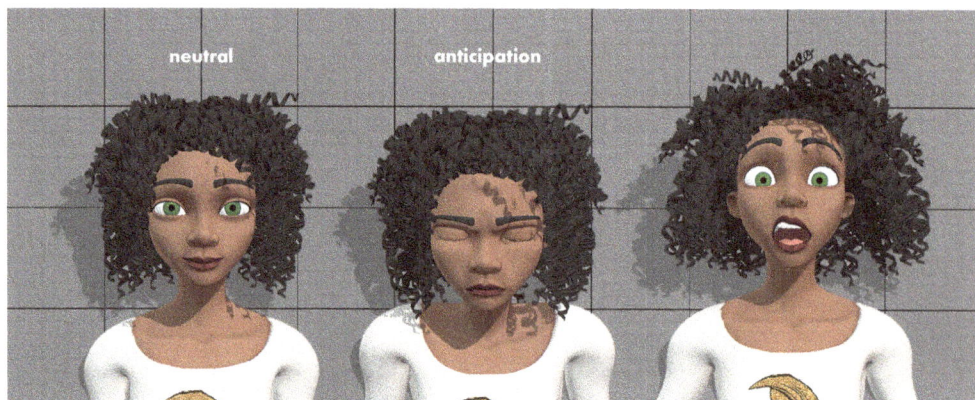

Figure 15.11

Does simply turning your head need an anticipation? Not always. But if you want to show a character thinking, adding a slight anticipation will help. Anticipations help transition from one thought to another.

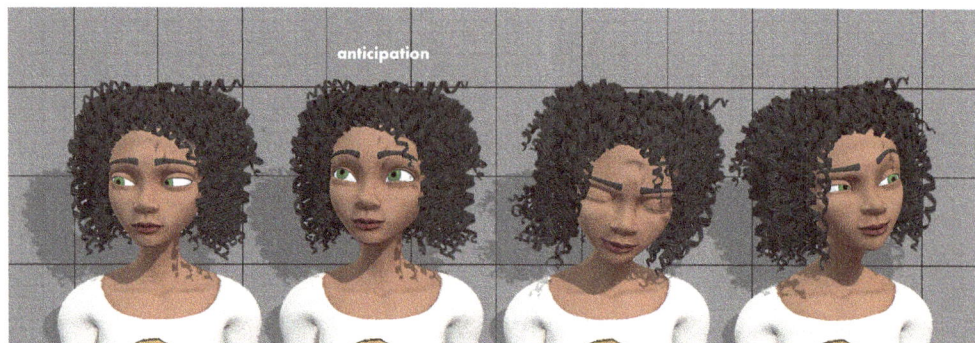

Figure 15.12

The Anticipation Must Never Be Bigger Than the Action!

In **Baseball Bugs** (1946) Bugs Bunny does a wild over-the-top anticipation to a pitch, only to lob the ball in slow motion. "Eh, I think I'll perplex him with my slowball."

Unless you're going for a comedic effect, the anticipation must never be bigger than the action!

Think of tossing a ball in the air; you wouldn't want an anticipation that is bigger than the actual toss.

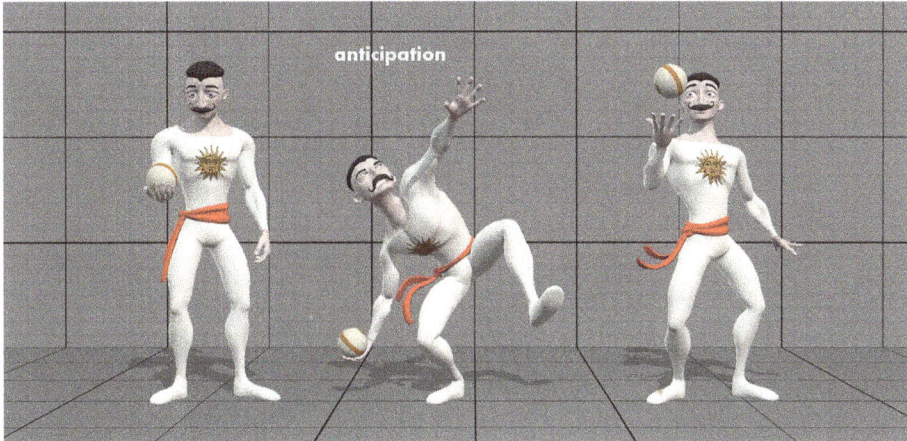

Figure 15.13

Adding Anticipations

Sometimes an anticipation should be one of your initial storytelling poses.

A character slamming their hand on a table needs the anticipation blocked out initially because, in this case, the anticipation is a storytelling pose. Without the anticipation, the scene could go in any number of directions.

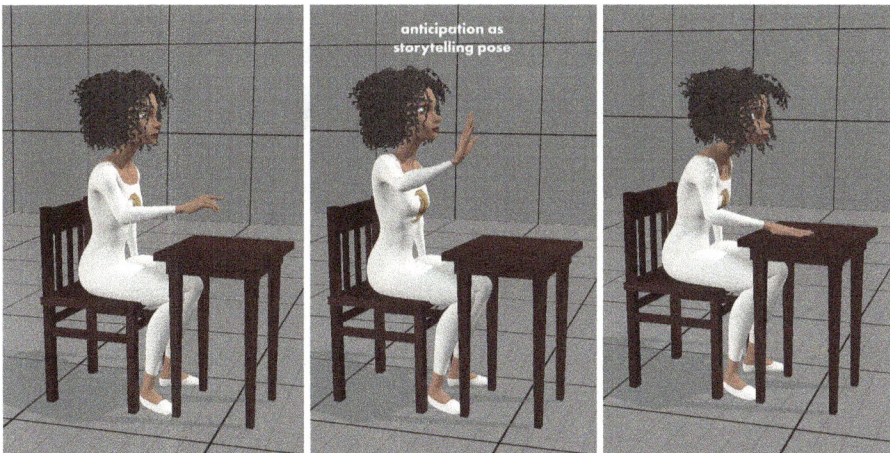

Figure 15.14

A character gets up from a chair. How much effort they put into the anticipation push off will tell a lot about your character.

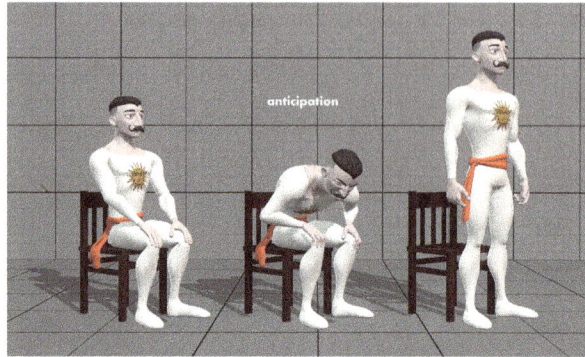

Figure 15.15

A character has their hands at their side, then turns their hands out in a gesture that seems to say "well?". Does this action need an anticipation?

Figure 15.16

Adding just a slight anticipation to the hands before the "well?" gesture gives it a little more "oomph!" because it shows contrast.

Figure 15.17

Look any place in your scene where your character is about to do an action. Ask yourself if the action would benefit from an anticipation.

Timing an Anticipation

How much time do you need for an anticipation? An anticipation is a change of direction — so think of them the same as a slow-in and slow-out.

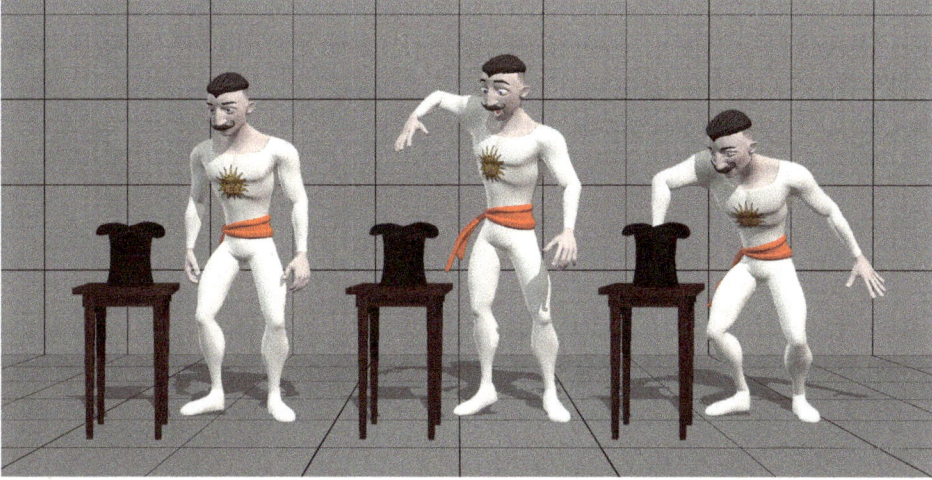

Figure 15.18

Start with a three frame slow-in with the body in the anticipation pose.

The timing can be however you'd like. You just want to slow-in and slow-out of the anticipation. It's just like the bouncing ball reaching its peak on a bounce.

For this example, we can slow-in to the anticipation on halves, then slow out on thirds to be a little zippier!

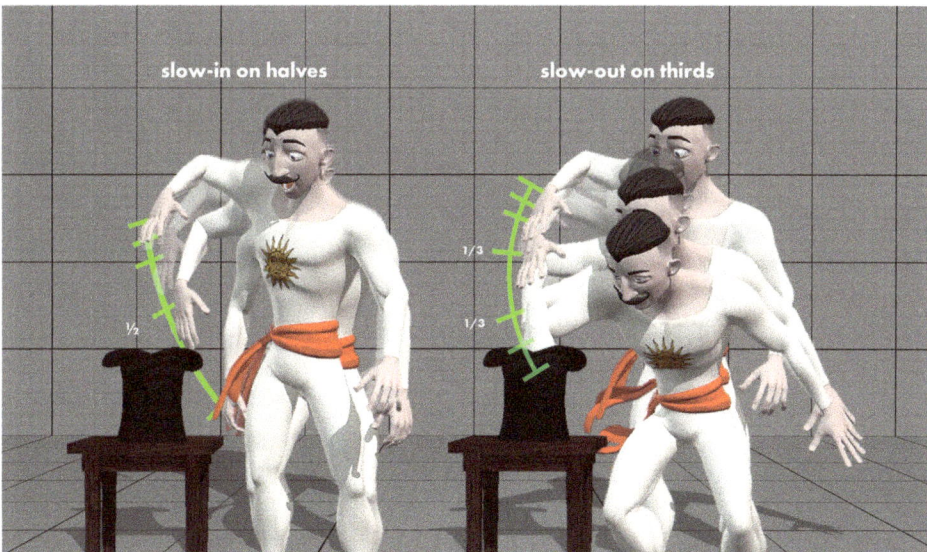

Figure 15.19

Anticipations as Character

Anticipation can be part of your character too! Laurel and Hardy often began actions with an anticipation. The Academy Award nominated short *Tit for Tat* (1935) is a great animation reference. Just about every gesture Laurel and Hardy make is preceded by an anticipation.

Maui in *Moana* (2016) often punctuates dialogue by lifting his shoulders and raising his head in anticipation.

Stan, Ollie, and Maui use anticipation as character!

Animation Exercise – Pose out an anticipation to a walk or run. Remember to watch your balance and step into the contact pose. Or animate a character getting up from a chair. Try adding an anticipation to the anticipation!

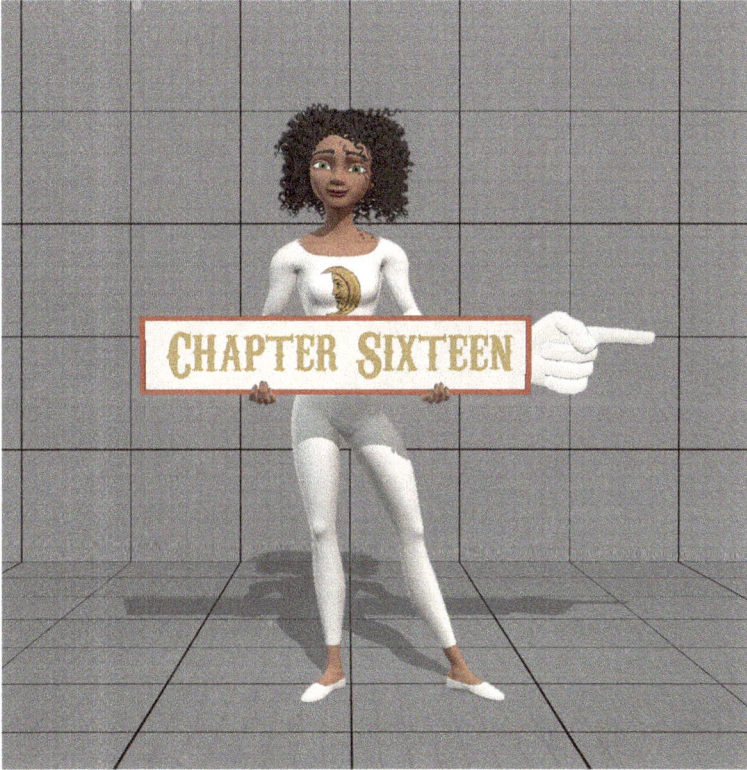

Chapter 16. Breakdowns and Inbetweens

Introduction

Your blocked in key poses look great, but after adding inbetweens your animation looks floaty or, perhaps, doesn't read because the action is too quick. So, how do you begin to inbetween your key poses?

With breakdowns!

A blocked-in scene can look fluid with just extremes and a few, well placed breakdown poses.

In this chapter we'll learn how to make breakdown poses. Then we'll discuss adding inbetweens and how to control their use.

Extremes, Breakdowns and Inbetweens

As we learned, keys, or extremes, are the storytelling poses. They are the poses that tell what the scene is all about.

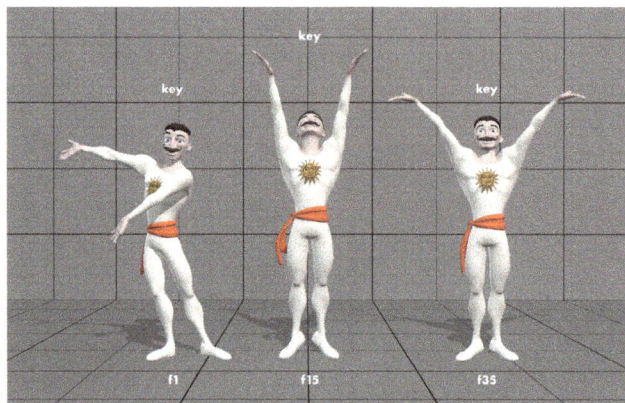

Figure 16.1

Breakdowns are the main keys you make between extremes. Breakdowns explain how you transition from one extreme key to the next.

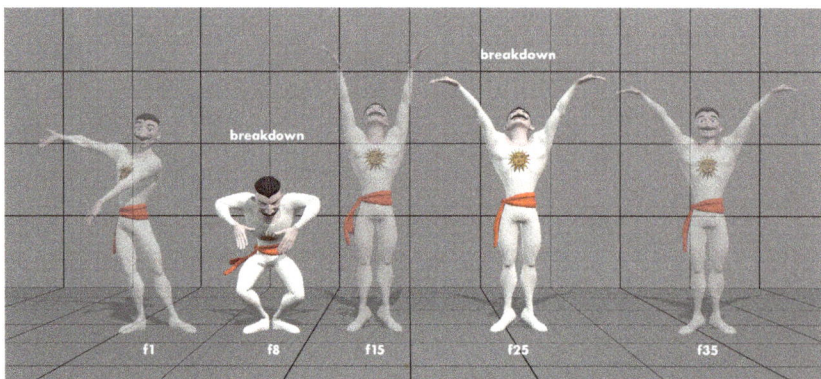

Figure 16.2

DOI: 10.1201/9781003361893-17

Inbetweens fill out the animation between the breakdowns and extremes.

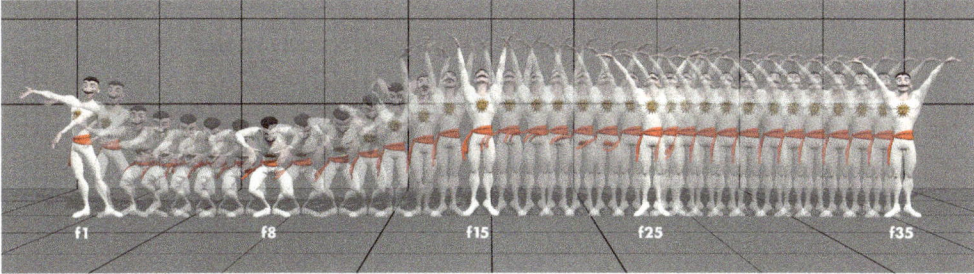

Figure 16.3

Breakdowns

If we have two extreme poses of a hand: one making a fist on frame 1, and the other an open hand on frame 10...

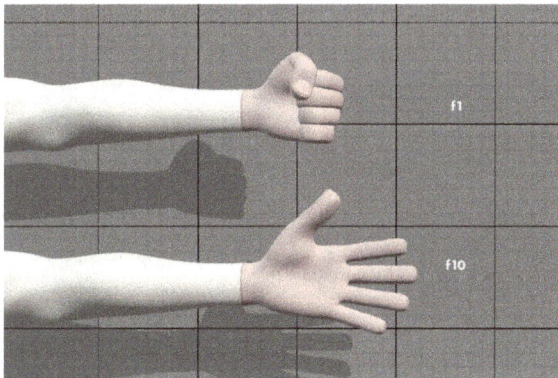

Figure 16.4

...a direct inbetween of the hand opening would be boring and make your animation floaty.

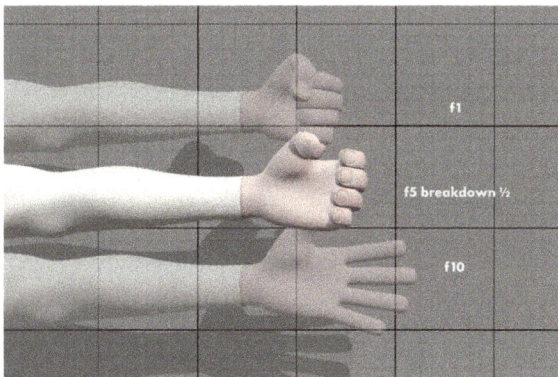

Figure 16.5

Let's have the hand open slowly at first, then quickly. Add a breakdown pose with the fingers favoring frame 1.

The fingers open slower from the fist pose, then quicker into the open hand pose.

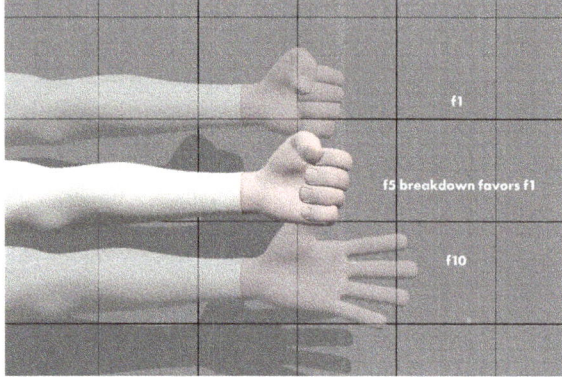

f1

f5 breakdown favors f1

f10

Figure 16.6

Add a second breakdown favoring frame 10 so that you move quickly through the middle and then slow-in.

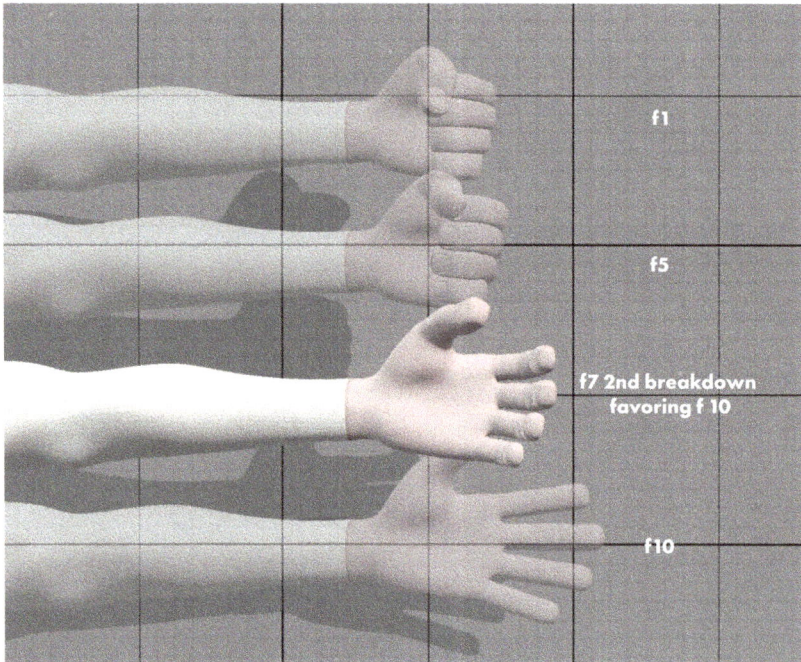

f1

f5

f7 2nd breakdown favoring f 10

f10

Figure 16.7

Breakdowns are similar to the Kuleshov effect in editing.

The Kuleshov effect was introduced by filmmaker, Lev Kuleshov, in 1918 and shows that a single shot spliced between two other shots can change the meaning of the scene.

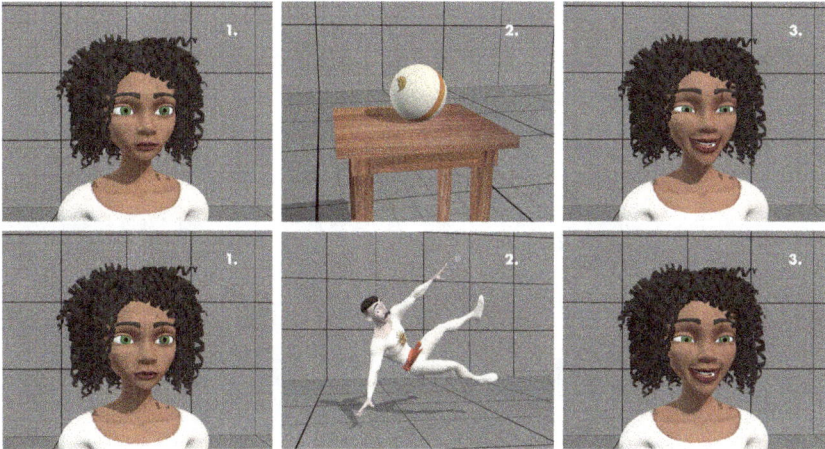

Figure 16.8

This is one of the things that makes adding breakdowns so much fun! You can be really creative changing the meaning of your scene with a breakdown.

Start with two poses: one pose is neutral and the next pose is angry.

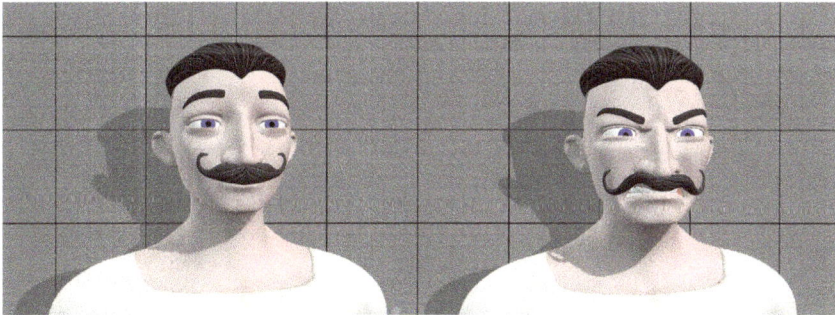

Figure 16.9

The breakdown helps explain how the character transitions from neutral to angry.

Add a breakdown that emphasizes the anger.

Figure 16.10

How Many Breakdowns?

Breakdowns describe transitions between poses, so one breakdown between two extremes will usually do. However, sometimes you'll need more than one breakdown for quicker actions or to clarify a transition. In this case you could have a breakdown next to a breakdown next to a breakdown!

For example, you may need several breakdowns to better describe an arc.

Figure 16.11

Or you may need a couple of breakdowns for an eccentric action, such as a quirky head movement using favoring keys.

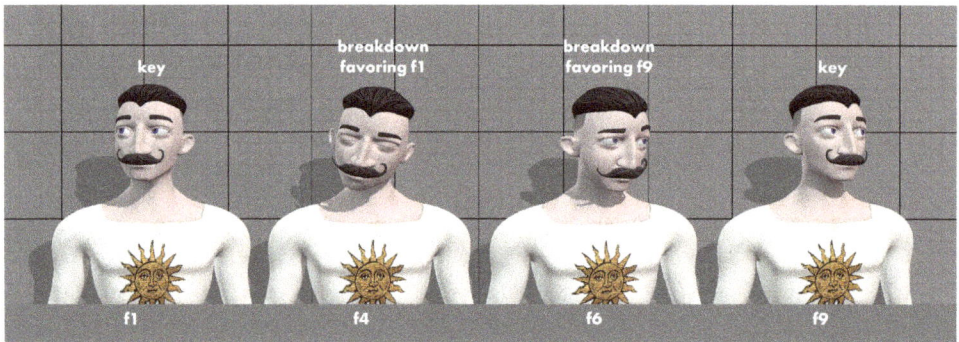

Figure 16.12

The passing or up pose in a walk cycle could be considered a breakdown. How you pose out the passing position will affect the attitude of your characters' walk, as in the Popeye-type shuffle.

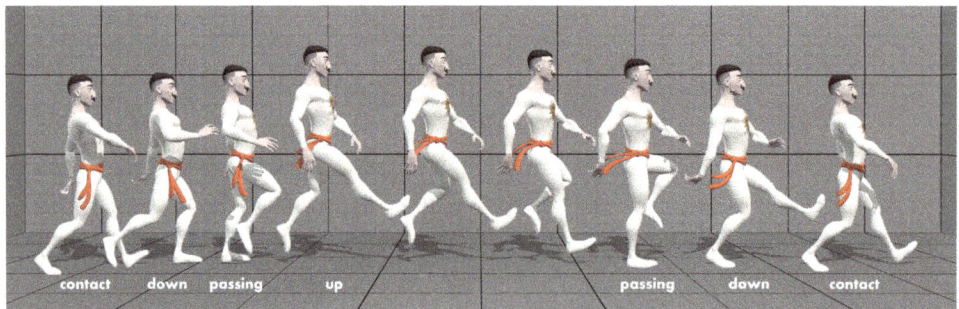

Figure 16.13

Overlap in a Breakdown

Adding overlap to a breakdown is fun. Instead of putting overlap on multiple inbetweens, just make a breakdown pose that contains the overlap you want.

It may take a while to get good at this, but once you do — it's a pretty neat thing to see in action!

A breakdown is key when adding overlap to the head. Think of the cranium as a ball when "leading with the cranium". The cranium "ball" is positioned along the path of action on thirds. Rotate the "ball" up or down on the breakdown. Then raise the chin when the head moves down.

It's old school and can approach cliché if used too much, but close the eyes on the breakdown pose!

Figure 16.14

Adding overlap to the hands in breakdown saves a lot of time and brain fatigue.

A character pats an object on their hip. Start with two extremes of the hand: one out to the side on frame 1, and the other against the hip on frame 6. Frame 15 is the same as frame 1 in a cycle.

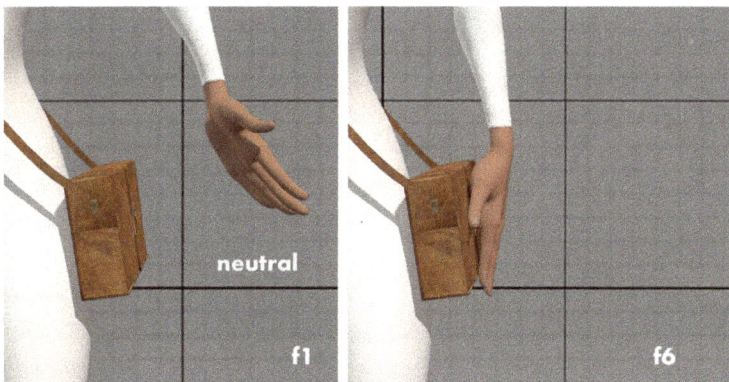

Figure 16.15

The first breakdown on frame 4 is the hand coming down to pat the bag. Tilt the angle of the wrist and fingers to favor frame 1. This adds automatic overlap to your breakdown by showing drag.

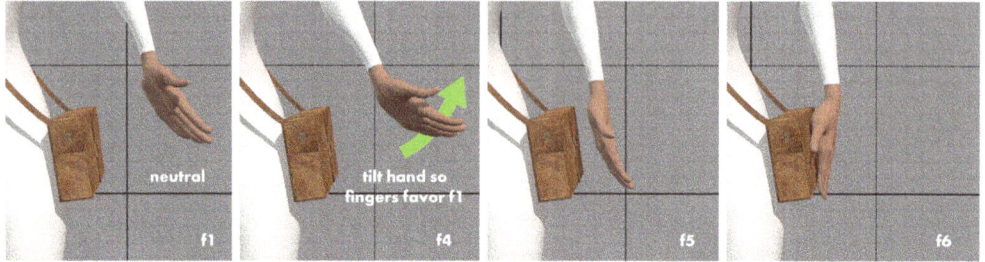

Figure 16.16

There's a change of direction after the pat, so, as the hand lifts off the bag, frame 11 can be a third favoring frame 6. Again, instead of making the breakdown pose straight and boring — add overlap to the breakdown by dragging the hand. Slow-in to frame 15.

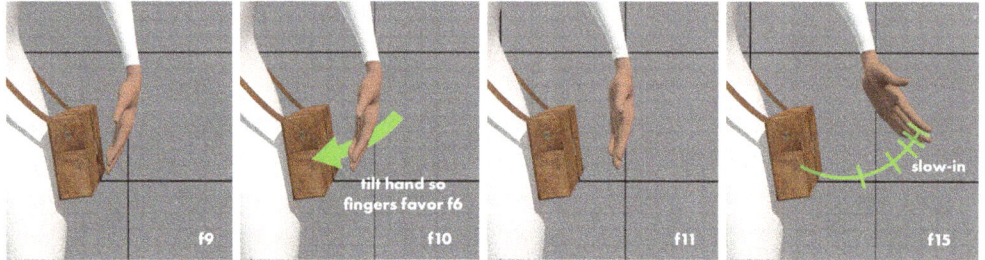

Figure 16.17

Be Fluid

Don't ruin an action with a poorly posed breakdown.

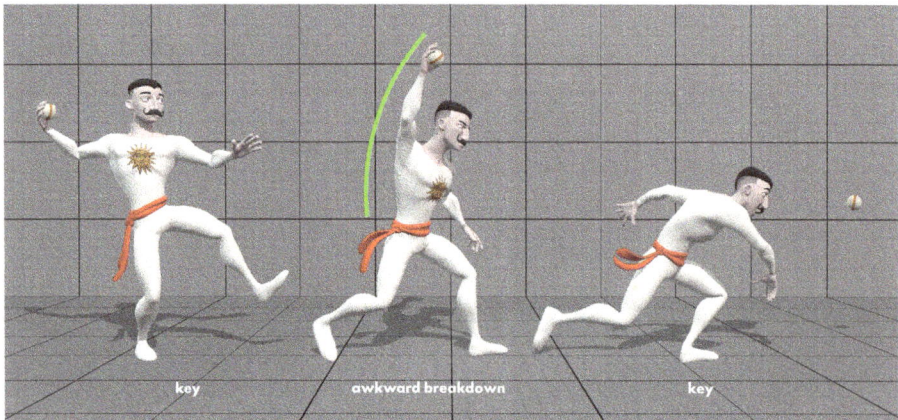

Figure 16.18

Breakdowns are meant to connect two extremes in the simplest, most fluid way possible!

Follow both a path of action and a line of action. As with a gesture, pose out your breakdown so that the anatomy follows the line of action.

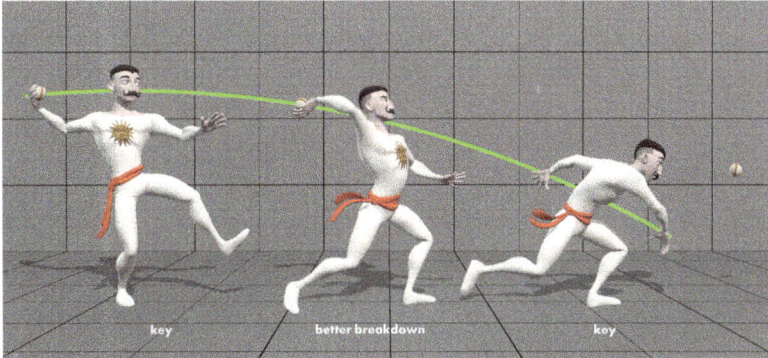

Figure 16.19

Keep refining your breakdowns until you get the smoothest action possible with the least number of frames.

The closer your extremes and breakdowns follow the path of action, the slower your animation will look!

Spacing Breakdowns

Space breakdowns to add more time to your storytelling poses or to move through them more quickly. Favoring, on thirds, halves, or someplace in-between — use whatever gives you the most snap!

As your character anticipates jumping, maybe the breakdown has the body on halves while the head and arms favor the neutral pose. Perhaps the body favors the in-air pose so that you feel the leap.

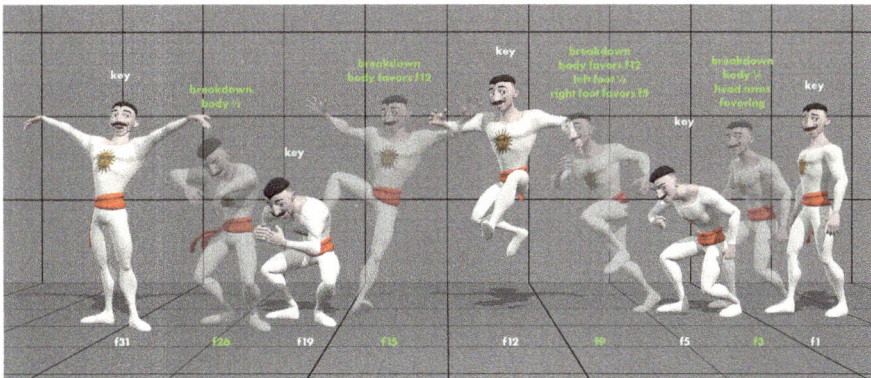

Figure 16.20

Toggle back and forth to refine breakdowns. Check your timing by playing your scene or shooting playblasts. Get used to looking at the graph editor to determine if you have enough time for an action. Compare the spacing in the graph editor with the timing of your scene in the viewport.

Train your eye!

If you're not getting the timing you like — move the breakdown.

Inbetweening

Inbetweens will be either slowing-in, slowing-out, or evenly spaced for when moving at a constant speed.

Don't make it any more complicated than that!

A character gestures, "All this will be yours!"

We can have two extremes starting with the anticipation pose on frame 1 and ending with the hand extended out over the kingdom on frame 25.

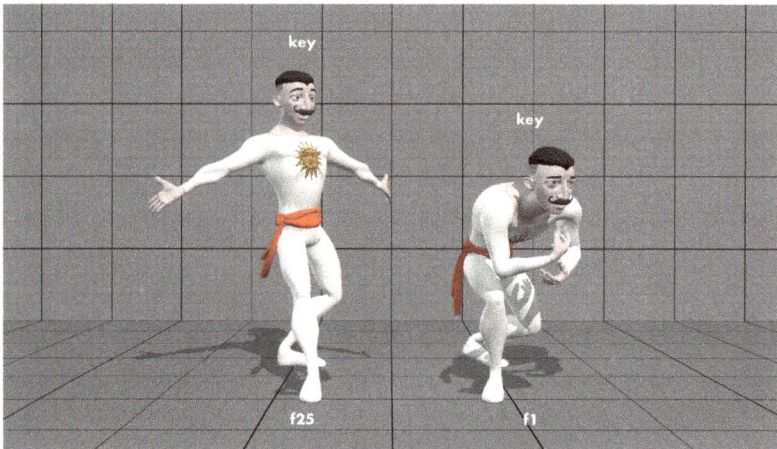

Figure 16.21

Next, we can add two breakdowns because we want to control the timing of the slow-out at the start, and the timing of the slow-in at the end.

The first breakdown will be at frame 9 and the second will be at frame 17.

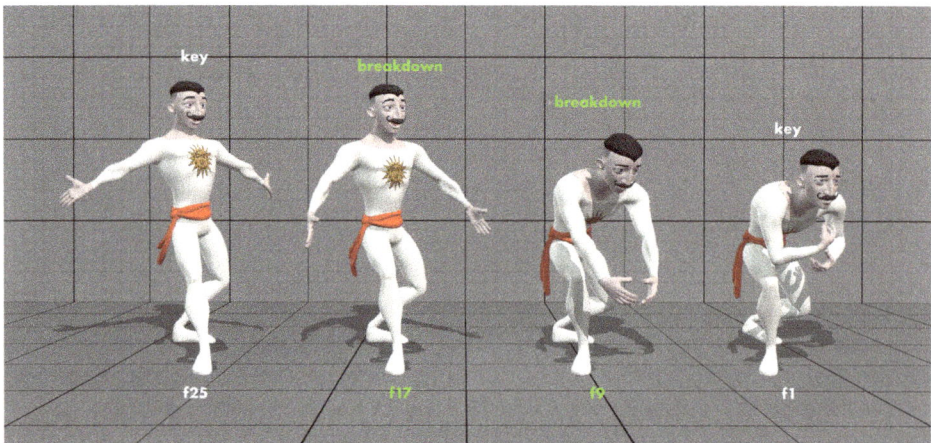

Figure 16.22

For the inbetweens, slow-out from frame 1 to frame 9, then slow-in from 17 to 25.

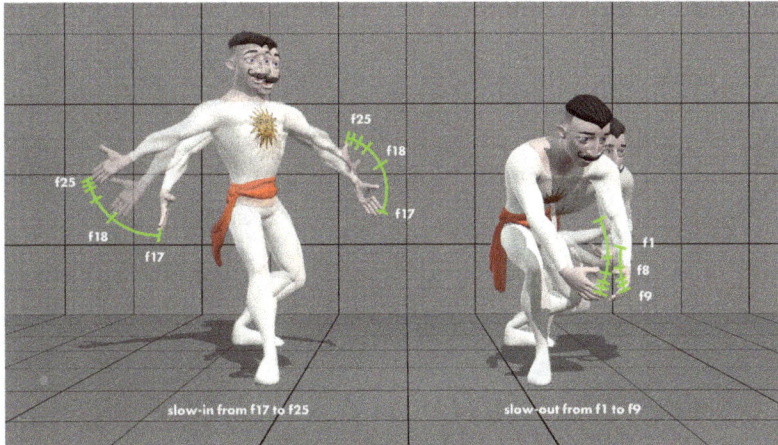

Figure 16.23

You may want a constant speed as the hand passes across the body, so keep the inbetweens even between the breakdowns.

If you want the hands to be snappier from the breakdown on frame 17 to the key on frame 25, let the arms on frame 19 be a third favoring frame 25.

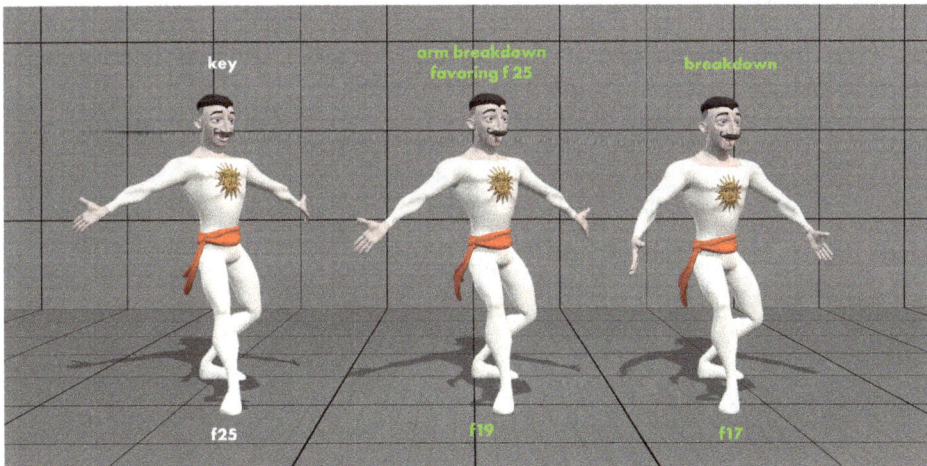

Figure 16.24

What Direction?

Should the breakdown arc left, right, up, or down?

Follow the path of action!

The position of the breakdown follows whatever arc your path of action follows.

Plan your breakdowns so that they lead from key to key in the most economical, interesting, and pleasing way. Create a pleasing pattern — without sacrificing the intent of the scene.

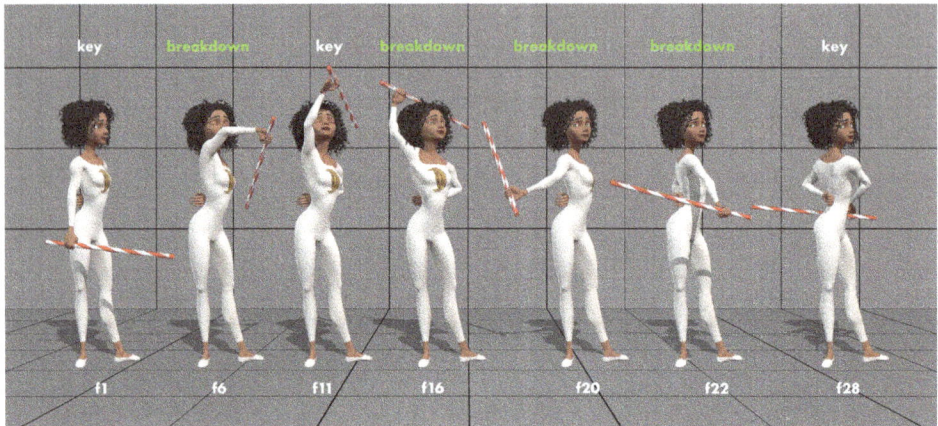

Figure 16.25

Moving Through Keys

Breakdowns are transitions between extremes, so don't feel that you can only use them to control slow-in's or slow-out's. Use breakdowns to control an action moving at a constant speed.

If you want a specific pose during a movement at a constant speed, such as a character swinging their foot around, use breakdowns to space the motion evenly.

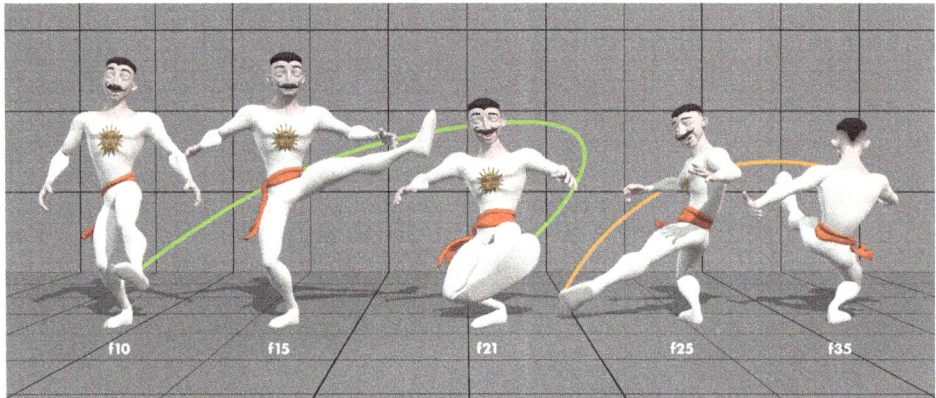

Figure 16.26

Popping Between Breakdowns

As we saw with the pigeons in *Bolt* using favoring keys to dart their heads from pose to pose, and Giovanni Jones stepping from the up pose right into a flat-footed pose in *Long Haired-Hare*, it's possible to pop into a pose that is dramatically different from the previous pose.

The key is to cushion the pop.

Just as with popping between extremes, to pop from one breakdown to another, you need several poses favoring the second extreme to soften the broad change in shape and spacing.

A character kicks a ball. Pop from the anticipation to the kick by cushioning the kick with several similar poses.

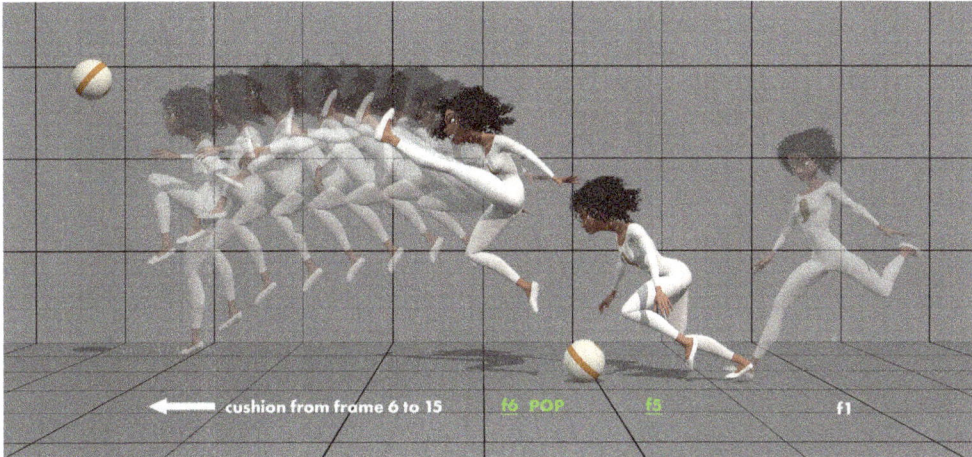

cushion from frame 6 to 15   f6 POP   f5   f1

Figure 16.27

A character gestures "ta-da!". Pop from the anticipation pose to the extreme "ta-da!" pose by cushioning the extreme.

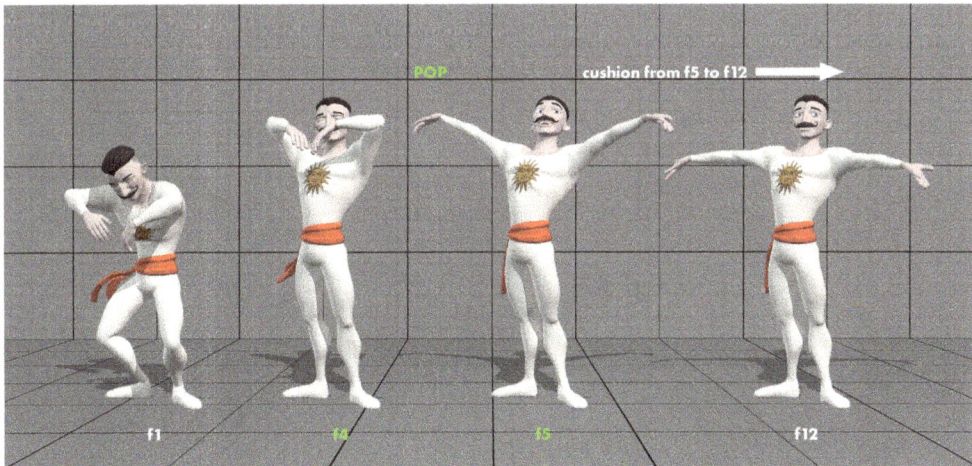

POP   cushion from f5 to f12

f1   f4   f5   f12

Figure 16.28

If the action moves too quickly, you can either tone down the reverse or add an inbetween.

Don't add a direct inbetween — that will only defeat the purpose of the pop! Instead, add an inbetween that favors one of the breakdowns.

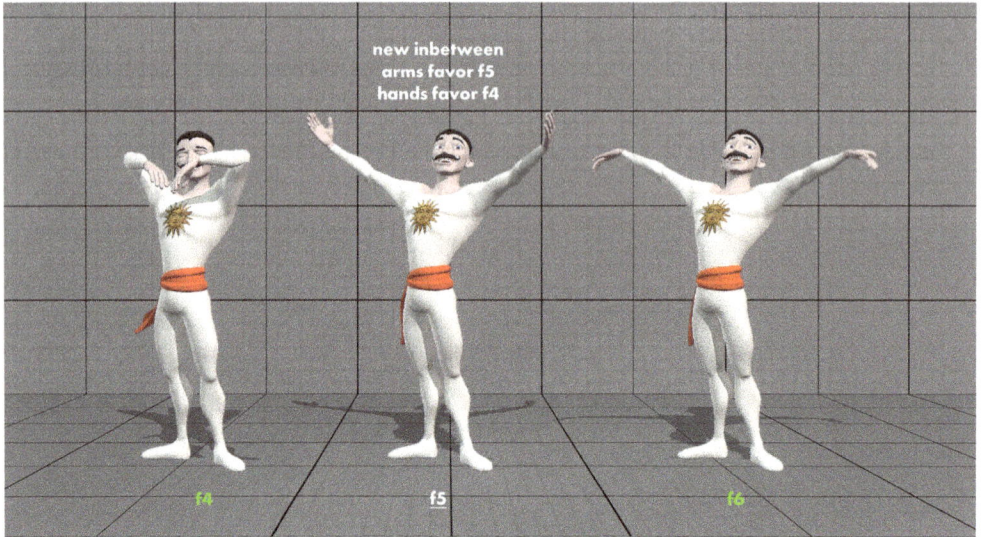

Figure 16.29

Animation Exercise – Keep it simple and pose out two extreme poses that show contrast. Then add a breakdown to show the transition between the two extremes. Playblast it in stepped mode and check your timing! When it looks the way you intended, add inbetweens. Remember to slow-in and slow-out of poses you want your audience to see — or use even spacing for constant speeds.

CHAPTER SEVENTEEN

Chapter 17. Accents

Introduction

Accents in animation have been referred to as punctuation marks for an action. Without accents, animation can become stiff. Improper use of accents can make animation mushy. In this chapter we'll look at hard and soft accents.

Hard Accents

There are two basic kinds of accents for animation; dialogue accents, which are used to emphasize words in a piece of dialogue, and body accents, which emphasize action.

They're similar, but for now, let's look at body accents. Body accents, which we'll just call an "accent," can be hard or soft.

A hard accent is when an action overshoots and comes back. The opening credits to **101 Dalmatians** are an easy way to picture a hard accent. The letters start out as small abstract shapes, overshoot into large letters, then settle back to their final size.

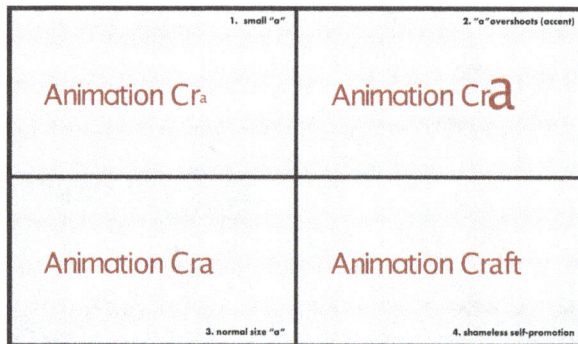

Figure 17.1

Mickey Mouse conducting "the stars and planets"[1] in The Sorcerer's Apprentice segment of **Fantasia** is a classic example of a hard accent. As Mickey points, his hand and finger stretch — then snap back.

We can animate a similar accented point — but not as over the top. First, block in the storytelling poses: the neutral start pose, the anticipation, and the point.

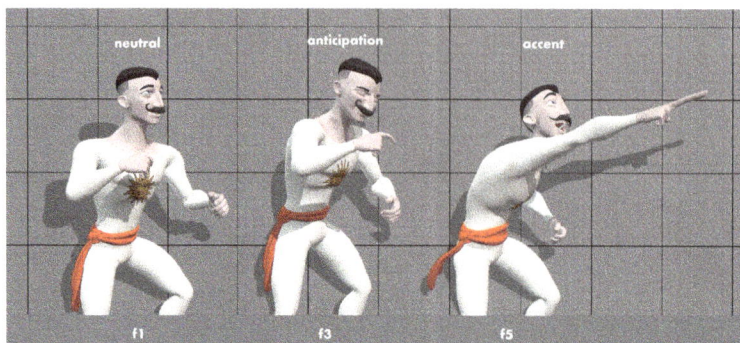

Figure 17.2

DOI: 10.1201/9781003361893-18

Next add a pose the accent can settle back into after the point.

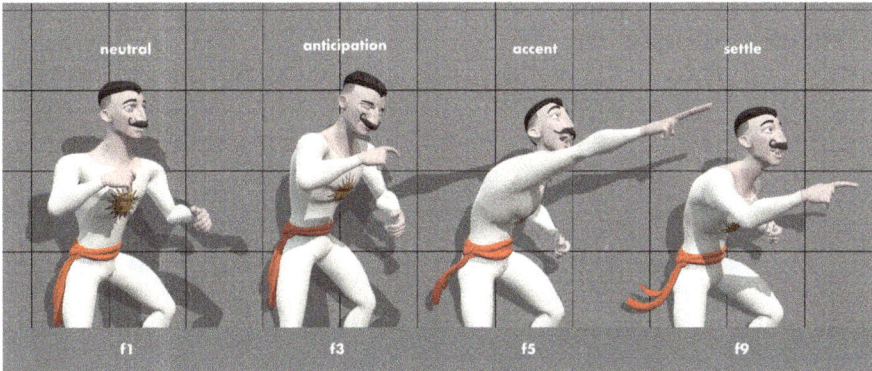

Figure 17.3

Slow-out of the anticipation into the pointing pose. The accent is a change of direction, which takes time, so you'll need to slow-out of the point extreme, the accent, into the settle pose.

Remember to arc the accent. Never come back along the same path.

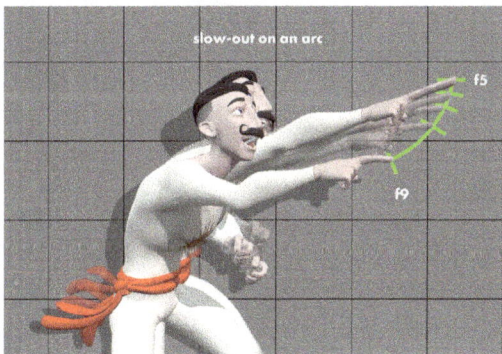

Figure 17.4

Don't place keys or breakdowns at the same height. This would be the same as placing the keys before and after a bouncing ball squash at the same height. Look for someplace different!

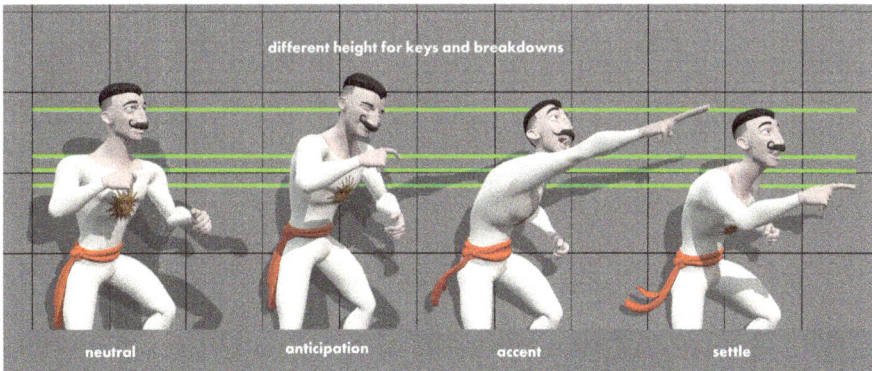

Figure 17.5

How many frames to slow-out of an accent? Three frames is a good start. Adjust the speed if it doesn't work for you. Sometimes you may want quicker recoil; sometimes you may want slower recoil. Do what works best for your scene.

A character performs a Jerome Robbins dance move, launching their leg in the air.

Even a professional dancer can't defy gravity and freeze their leg mid-air — so, we need to add a hard accent.

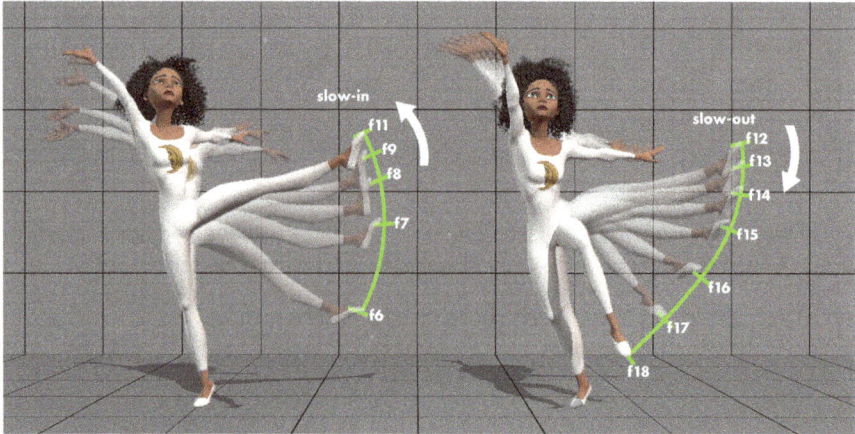

Figure 17.6

A character sitting up quickly wouldn't just sit up and freeze — their body would get to a certain point, and then recoil because of inertia. How much they recoil depends upon their size and speed.

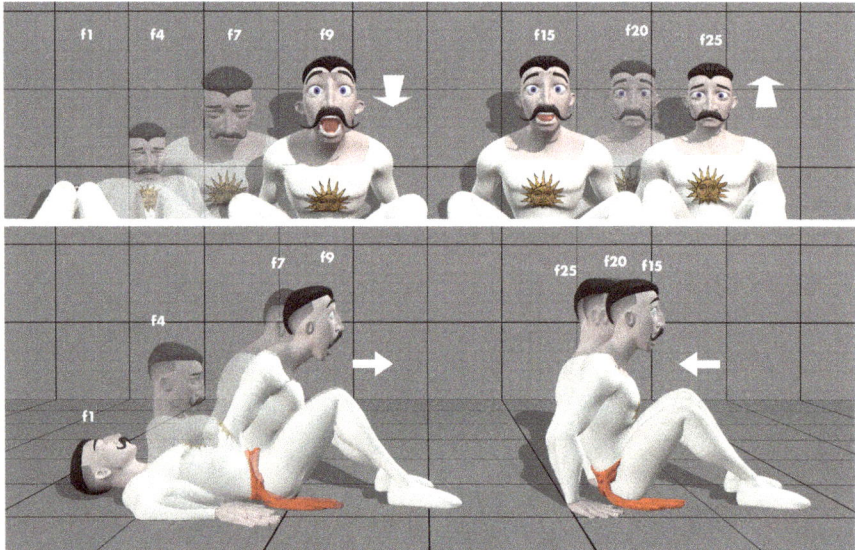

Figure 17.7

Use a hard accent for any kind of action that needs emphasis, shows a change of momentum, or a change of direction. Hard accents are also good for getting a nice snap to an action.

Add another extreme to the scene of the hand opening from the previous chapter with the open hand pose pushed a little farther. This adds a snap to the action of hand opening that you may not necessarily see but will feel.

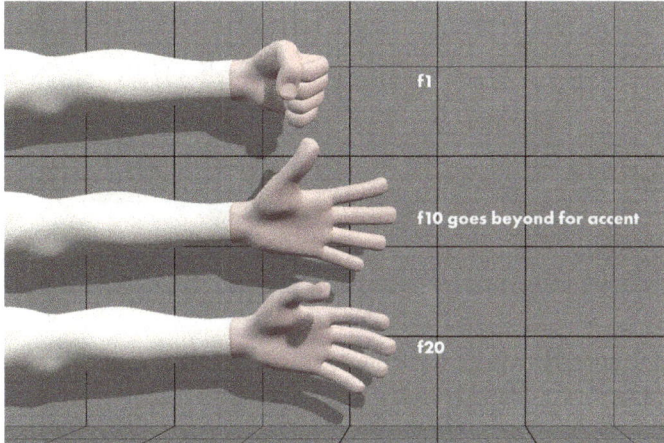

Figure 17.8

Soft Accents

Soft accents are basically slow-ins. Instead of bouncing back as in a hard accent, a soft accent hits a pose and continues to drift, or slows down to a stop.

A character points to themselves as if to say, "Me?" This gesture may not need a dramatic bounce back, so a soft accent would work.

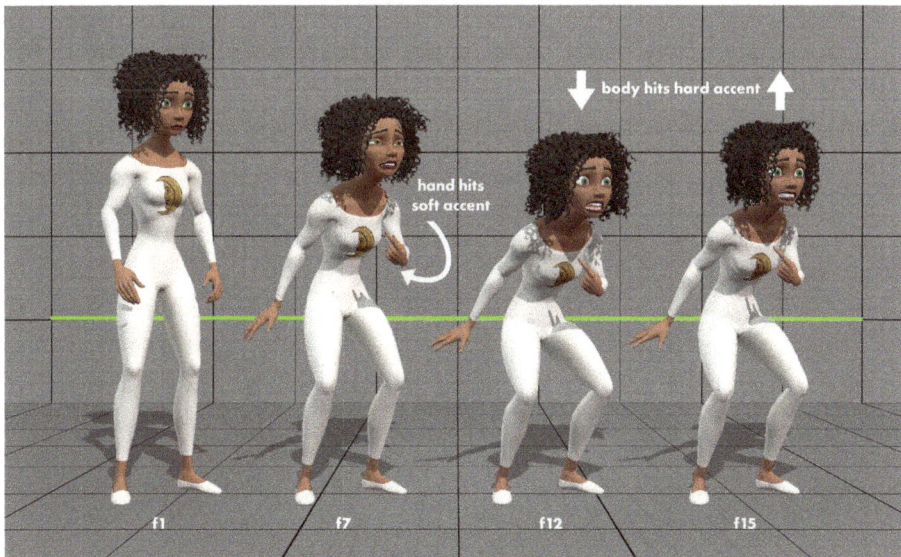

Figure 17.9

A soft accent could be someone leaning in to listen. This could be thought of like a moving hold.

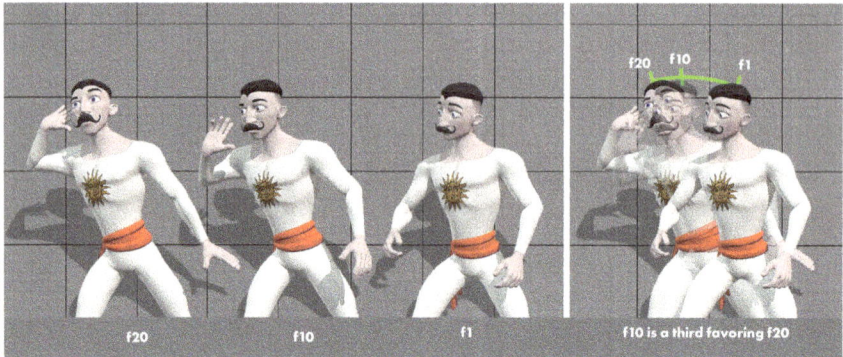

Figure 17.10

A character lifts their arms as if raising the dead. A hard accent might suggest a more hurried raising of the dead, going beyond the final pose and bouncing back.

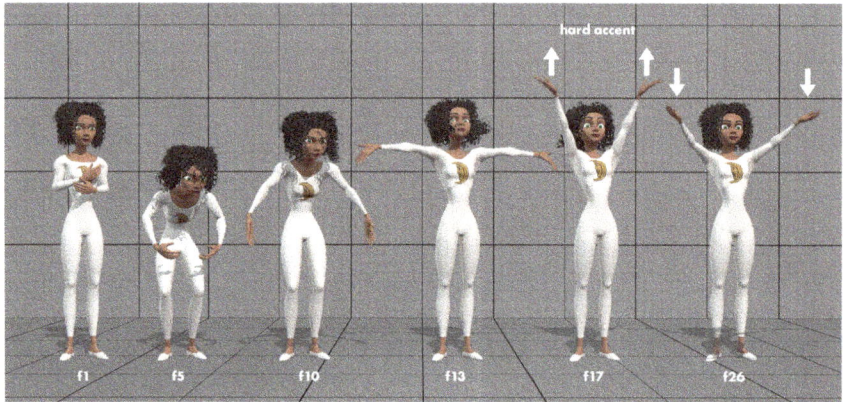

Figure 17.11

A soft accent slows into the final pose, suggesting a more controlled raising of the dead.

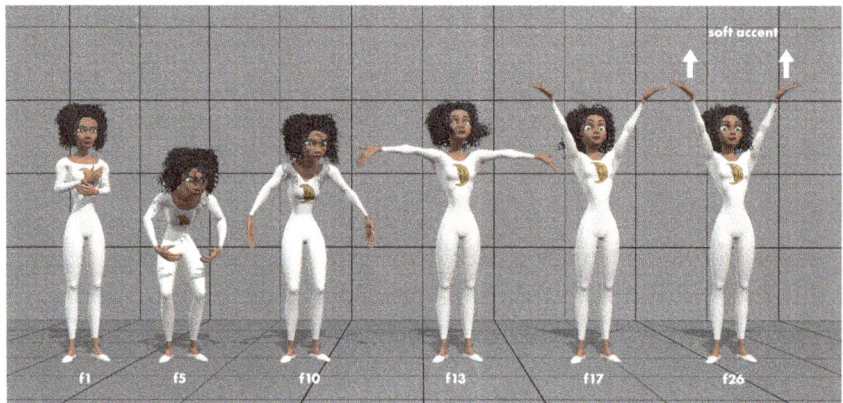

Figure 17.12

Coming to a Stop

How a character comes to a stop is up to you — it just needs to be believable.

One of the first things to think about is your accent; do you want to stop using a hard or a soft accent?

If your character has a lot of momentum, you may want a hard accent.

Appendages, fabric, and hair will continue to move after the body stops. And each of those will have either a hard or a soft accent!

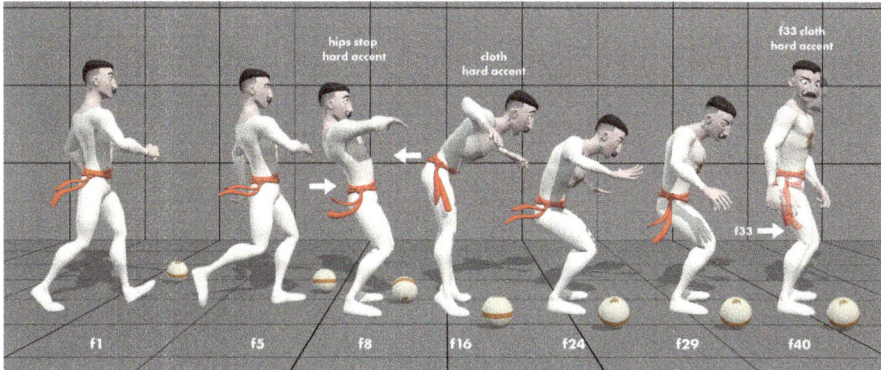

Figure 17.13

Daffy Duck sliding in on a soft accent to confront Bugs Bunny in Chuck Jones' *Rabbit Seasoning* (1952) — "Oh no you don't. Not again!" The animation is highly stylized, but Daffy still shows overlap in his arm.

Add an eye-blink after a character stops moving. "Blinking is a key part of keeping something alive,"[2] said the animator and Imagineering great, Blaine Gibson.

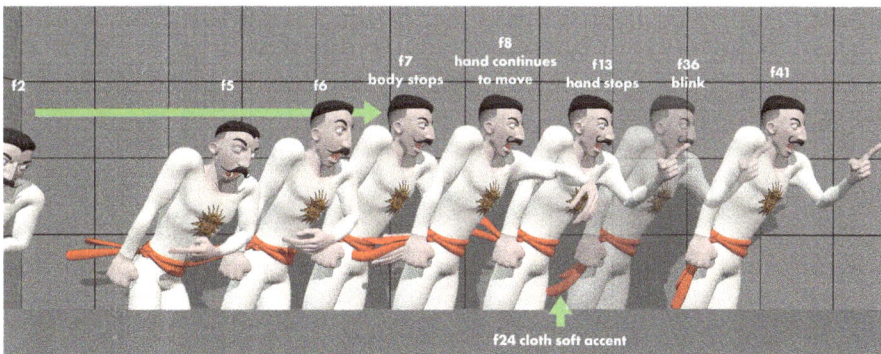

Figure 17.14

Takes

Takes are basically accents, and they can have both a hard accent and a soft accent.

A Tex Avery type take with a hard accent overshoots and comes back.

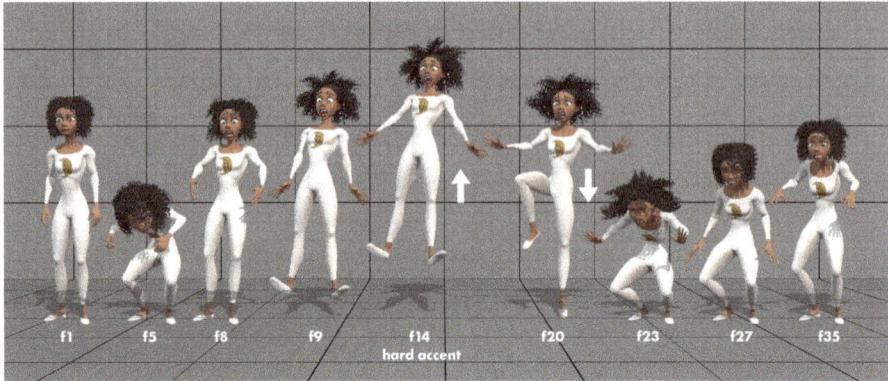

Figure 17.15

A take with a soft accent could hit a peak pose and freeze, or transition into a moving hold, or it could transition to something else altogether — such as a run cycle.

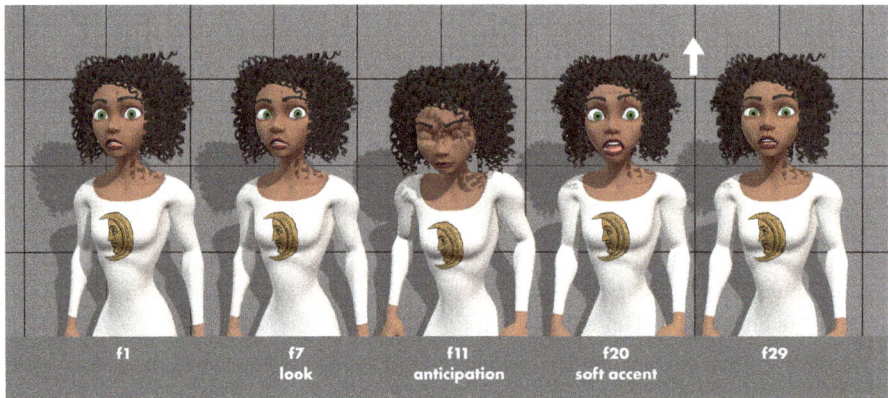

Figure 17.16

Animation Exercise — Animate a character pointing with both a hard and a soft accent. It doesn't need to be anything extravagant, just animate an arm pointing. Start with a neutral pose; go into an anticipation and then a point with a hard accent and a soft accent.

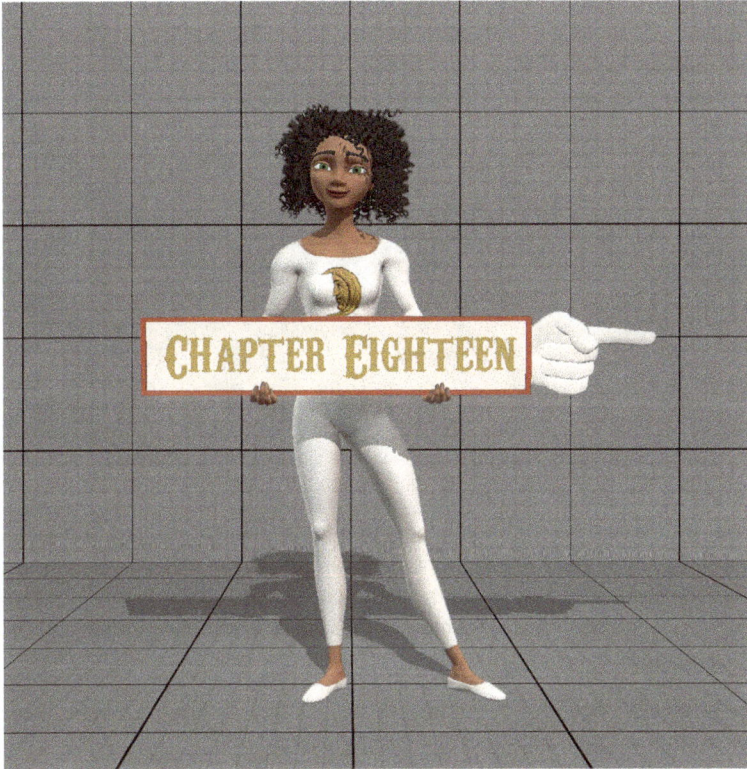

CHAPTER EIGHTEEN

Chapter 18. Secondary Action

Introduction

What gestures or actions are unique to your character? What gestures does your character make that add interest and individuality? In this chapter we'll look at secondary actions, actions that are layered over the main action to add personality and uniqueness.

Secondary Action

Donald Graham and Chuck Jones thought of secondary action as more like follow-through or overlapping action. "Donald Graham gave lectures to future animators at Disney's,"[1]said Jones about a lecture Graham gave on secondary action in 1937.[2] "Secondary action is any action that has no motive power of its own. Like — long hair sweeping round when you turn your head."[3]

Figure 18.1

Frank and Ollie, who would have certainly attended the same lecture, have a different definition of secondary action. Frank and Ollie thought of secondary action as gestures on top of the main action. "Secondary actions add excitement without conflicting with the basic movement,"[4] wrote Frank and Ollie. "If it conflicts or becomes more interesting or dominating in any way, it is either the wrong choice or is staged improperly."[5]

Your character has a main action — the statement made with storytelling extremes. Your character is happy, your character is sad, your character is angry, etc.

Figure 18.2

DOI: 10.1201/9781003361893-19

Secondary action is a gesture, or gestures, laid over the main action that adds specific detail and personality to your character.

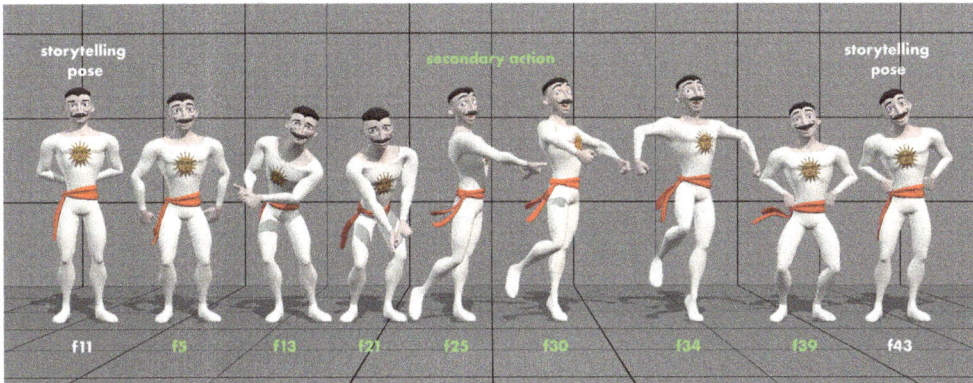

Figure 18.3

In *Rabbit Transit* (1947) Bugs Bunny is livid when he reads that the tortoise beat the hare. He spits out his carrot, gestures at the book, punches the air, claws at his face, points at the book accusingly, then holds his hands out in disbelief, "Who'd ever believe such a zany story?!"

These are all secondary actions animator Virgil Ross came up with to emphasize Bugs' anger and play upon his Brooklyn upbringing.

A character is nervous. What gesture could you think of to support the main action?

It could be something you've seen somewhere or invented yourself.

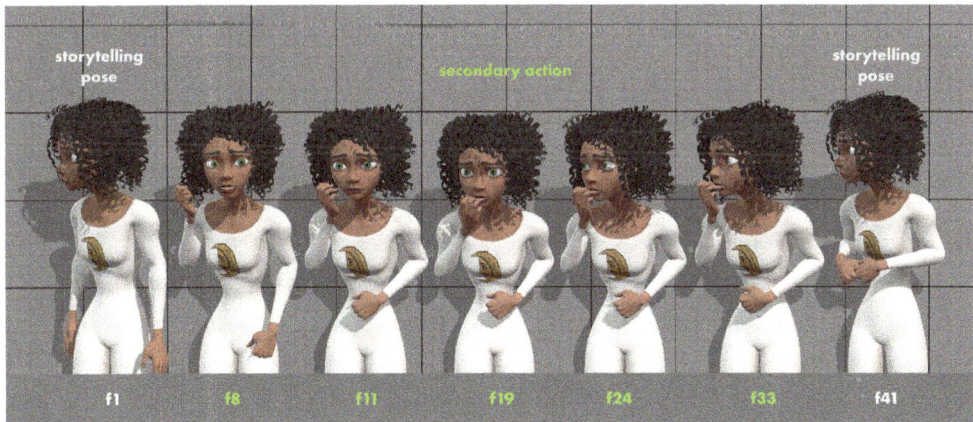

Figure 18.4

Always look for secondary actions that support your character's emotions.

Secondary action doesn't mean just broad gestures. In the same scene from *Rabbit Transit,* Bugs Bunny, lying on his stomach reading, switches the way his feet are crossed. Who would think to animate that? Virgil Ross!

Secondary action could be any piece of extra business that supports or adds to the main action.

A main action could be a character deep in thought.

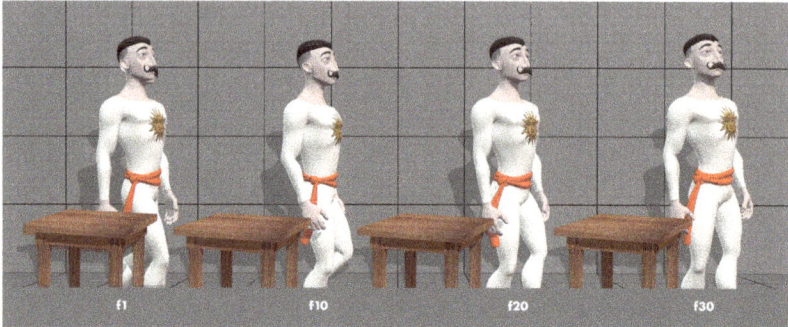

Figure 18.5

A secondary action could be your character touching something such as a table or their chin — or both. Touching something can add emotion.

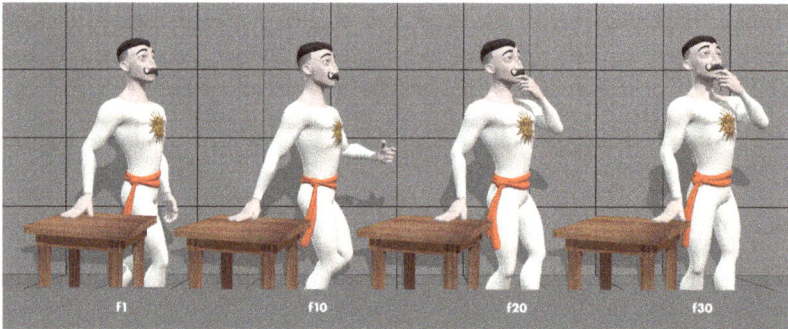

Figure 18.6

Handling props can have the same effect. Tissa David said that animation was always more interesting with a prop. Props add a familiar reality to an action. "They make it easier for you to do your job,"[6] said Stella Adler.

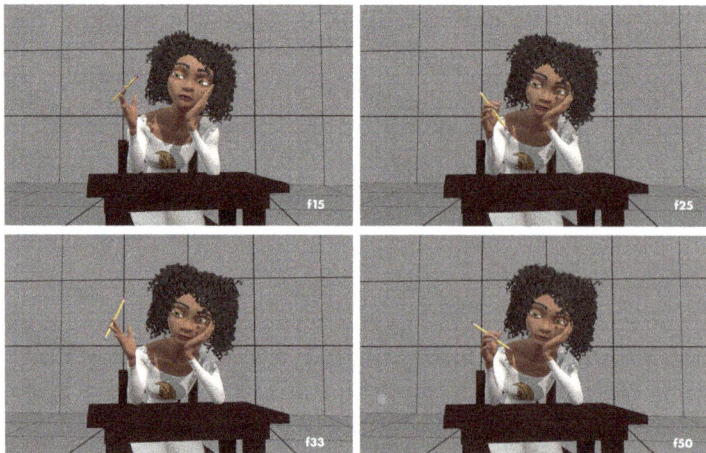

Figure 18..7

The main action of a character collapsing in disappointment.

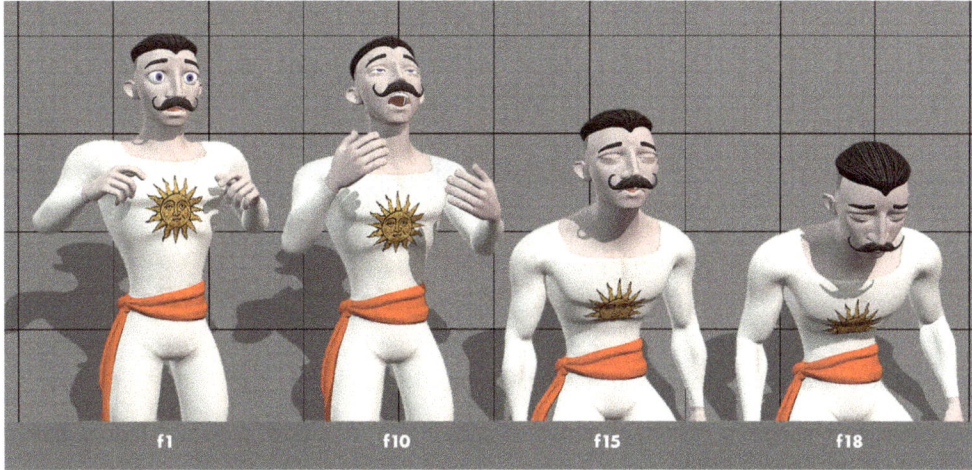

Figure 18.8

The secondary action could be their shaking their head. The shaking of the head could enhance the action or take away from it. Too much movement and your audience will only see the head shake.

A headshake is a change of direction, so pose out a head shake using favoring keys or thirds.

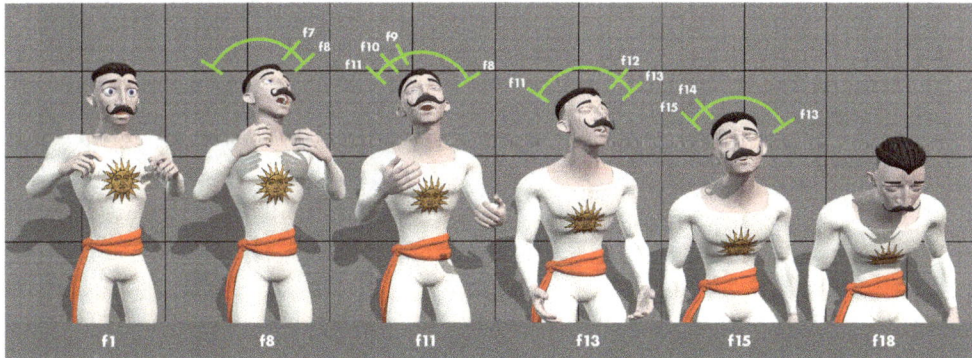

Figure 18.9

Animating Secondary Actions

In most cases secondary action will be posed out in your extremes and breakdowns. Sometimes, however, more organic secondary actions — such as nervous fidgets or circular hand gestures, may require more keys to explain the action.

In cases like this, it's best to get the main body action working right — while roughly blocking in the gesture. Don't fine tune a gesture only to have the body stiff as a board.

If we have a character with a look as if to say, "Seriously?!"

Figure 18.10

What gestures can you come up with to plus the expression?

This is where thumbnailing your ideas comes in handy. If you can't draw, draw stick figures, gather reference or act it out yourself.

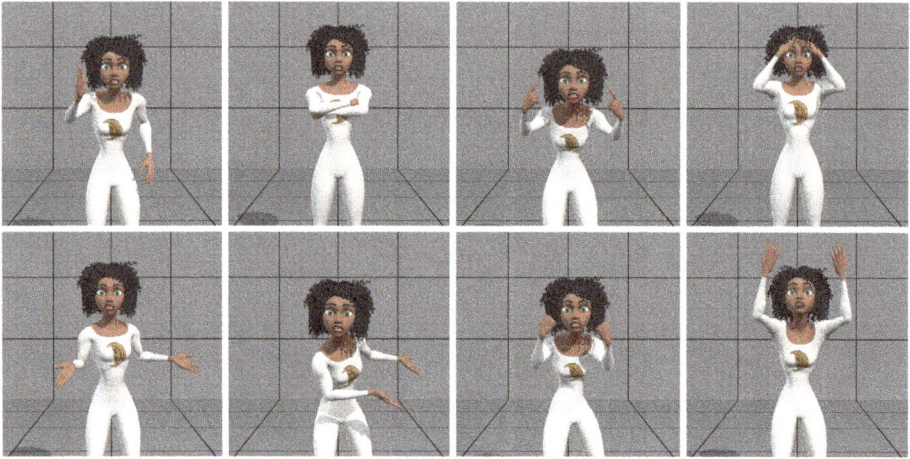

Figure 18.11

A character points their finger as if impressed. First, block in your storytelling poses: a neutral pose, an initial getting ready pose, and a point. Time it out in stepped mode to get the feeling you want.

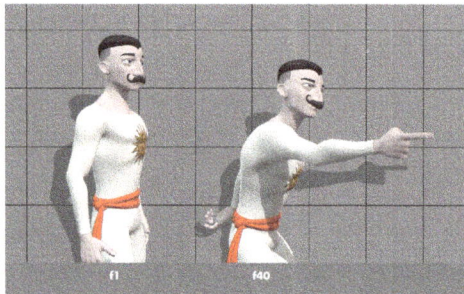

Figure 18.12

Add an anticipation breakdown for the arm. The body can already be moving forward as the arm bends back in anticipation.

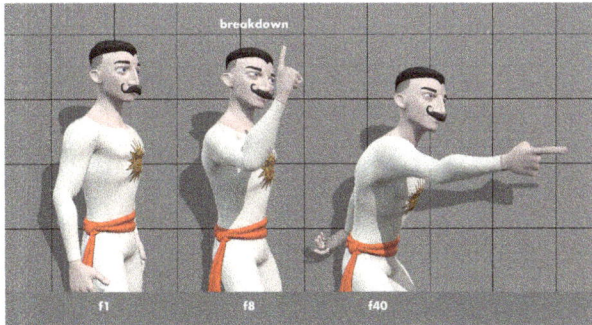

Figure 18.13

That looks good, but maybe you want more secondary action, such as a Milt Kahl finger waggle!

Just as when planning out how many bounces you want for a bouncing ball, decide how many waggles you want.

In this case four.

How much time do you have between the anticipation and the point? Start by blocking in four forearm down pointing poses. Try to time them so that you can add forearm up poses evenly between them.

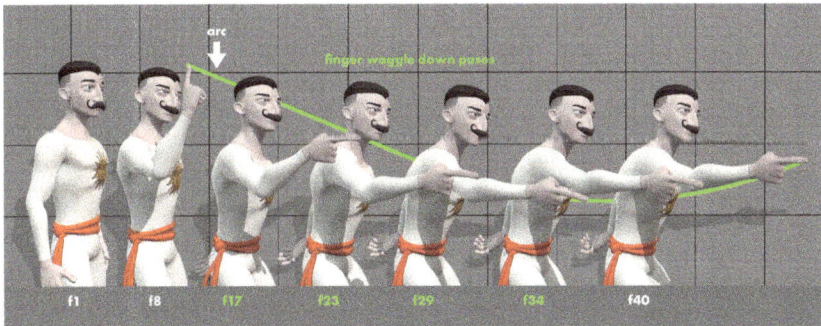

Figure 18.14

Now add the forearm up poses.

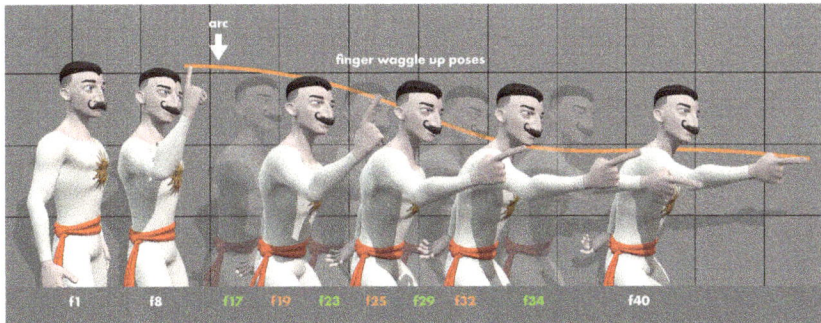

Figure 18.15

Where can you push the overlap?

Add breakdowns for the wrist and finger as it changes direction. Changing direction takes time, so slow-out favoring the previous extreme.

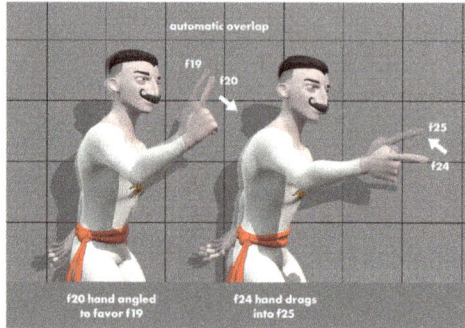

Figure 18.16

Common Problems

I once showed Tissa David a dialogue test and she said, "Oh dear, it's terribly over-animated." I had so many gestures that the point of the scene was lost.

Don't have too many actions going on in one scene.

Figure 18.17

Keep it simple.

Figure 18.18

Try not to block the face with secondary action.

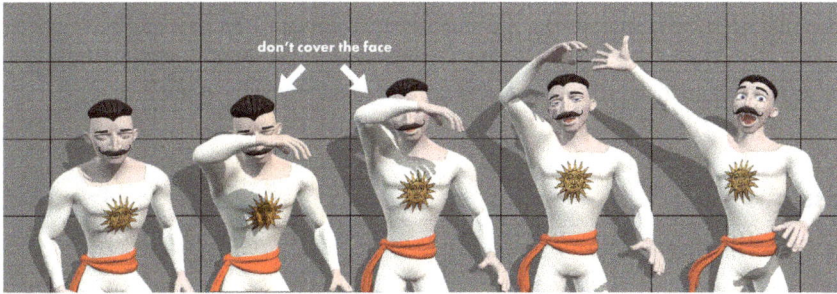

Figure 18.19

Plan action so that an arm or hand passes either before or after the face or eye. You wouldn't want to watch an actor with their hand always covering their face.

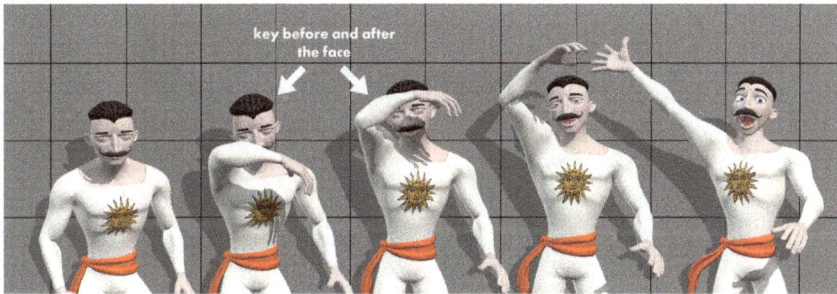

Figure 18.20

Secondary action is fun to animate because it's where you can add personality to your character.

Even if you're using reference, it's your personality that shows through because it's reference you've chosen or made your own!

"Keep it simple," said Charlie Chaplin. "Gestures are not to be seen. And I'm a gesture man. It's hard for me to keep them down."[7]

Animation Exercise — Think of an emotion that can be expressed in a simple movement with two storytelling poses — neutral and surprise or shock, confusion, anger, proud, or sad, etc. It could be a one-word sentence such as, "No!" or "What?" or "Alas!". Then add a secondary action gesture that supports, but doesn't overpower that emotion. Use a metronome to get your timing right!

Chapter 19. Expressions

Introduction

Expressions need to clearly illustrate the intended emotion and transition naturally from one expression to the next. In this chapter, we'll show how to achieve strong, expressive emotions; how to transition from one expression to the next; and some tricks to use when animating the face.

Expressions

The face can be divided into three sections:

- The top — the eyebrows and forehead

- The middle — the eyes and the root of the nose

- The bottom — the cheeks, mouth, nose, and chin

Figure 19.1

Each part of the face can move independently, but they all relate. When one part moves even slightly, it affects the other parts of the face.

Start with a neutral pose and squash the face dramatically. What happens? The brows lower, the chin raises, and everything in between is affected; the eyes squeeze, the cheeks puff out, and the lips tighten. Even the nostrils flare.

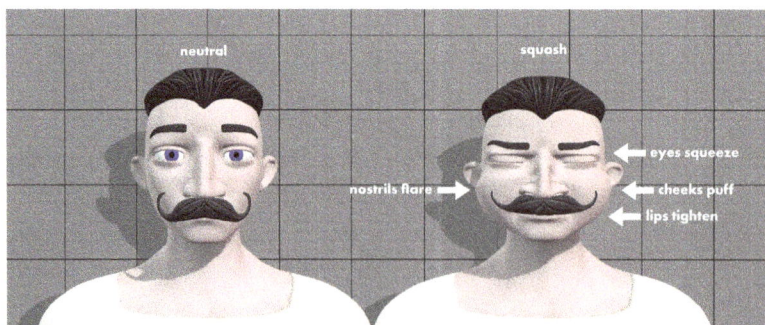

Figure 19.2

DOI: 10.1201/9781003361893-20

In a subtle squash, just the lips may tighten. The cheeks would puff out just a bit more from the neutral pose. Perhaps the lower part of the nose and lower eyelids raise a little.

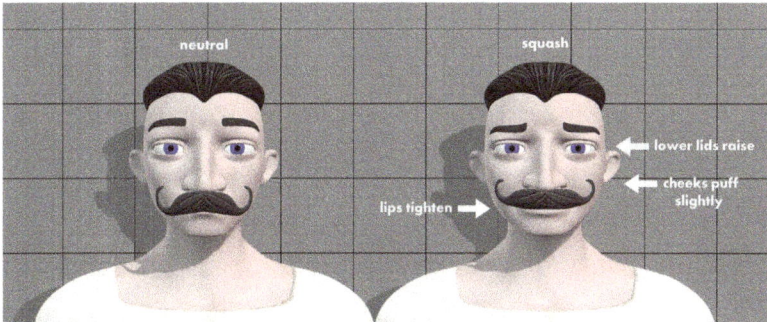

Figure 19.3

In a shocked "take" expression, the face may stretch dramatically. The brows raise, the eyes open wide, the jaw drops — pulling the cheeks in and the nose down. If your rig allows it, even the ears could be pulled down.

Figure 19.4

If your character subtly raises a brow in suspicion, the brow will pull the eyelid open — even if just a bit.

Figure 19.5

If your character raises their brows but squints, the cheeks can't help but raise a little.

Figure 19.6

One part of the face affects the other.

The 7 Basic Expressions

There are 43 facial muscles which can produce "more than ten thousand expressions".[1] Of the ten thousand expressions, "there are seven that have very clear facial signals — anger, sadness, fear, surprise, disgust, contempt and happiness,"[2] said Dr. Paul Ekman, a pioneer in the study of emotions and facial expressions, and consultant on *Inside Out* (2015).

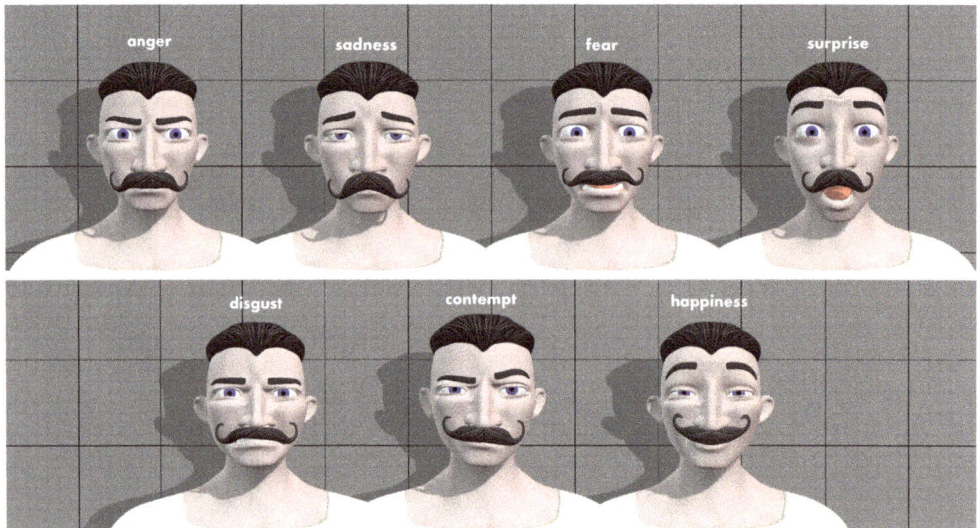

Figure 19.7

These seven expressions are universal and have distinctive clues, such as a lowered brow or a raised lip, that make them mean the same thing to just about everyone around the world.

Theoretically, expressions can only be held for up to four seconds. An expression held longer than four seconds becomes an emblem. An emblem is a substitute for dialogue, such as a thumbs up hand gesture.

A facial emblem could be an eye wink as if to say, "gotcha," a "whoops" expression after breaking something, or raising your eyebrows as if to say, "really?".

Figure 19.8

Do you need to know what an emblem is as an animator?

Not really.

But it's good to know that the longer you hold an expression without dialogue or gesturing, the less sincere your expression will be!

Keep it simple when posing out an expression. Begin with the simplest idea for an emotion. Start with snowmen!

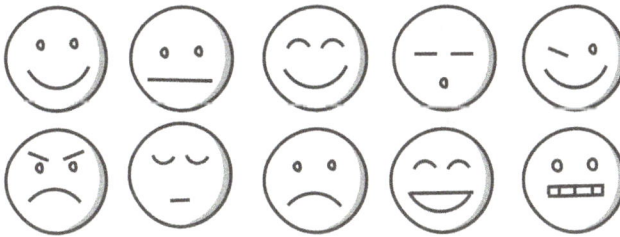

Figure 19.9

Don't get overly complicated trying to block in a smile. Start with a snowman.

Figure 19.10

Even if you're going to eventually change the expression, blocking in even a temporary expression will help push your pose!

Posing out a character yelling in anger without an expression may look fine. "I'm SO angry!"

But if you block-in an expression, you'll feel the pose more!

"Aargh! I'm SO angry!" Adding an expression makes the pose even angrier! "Aargh!"

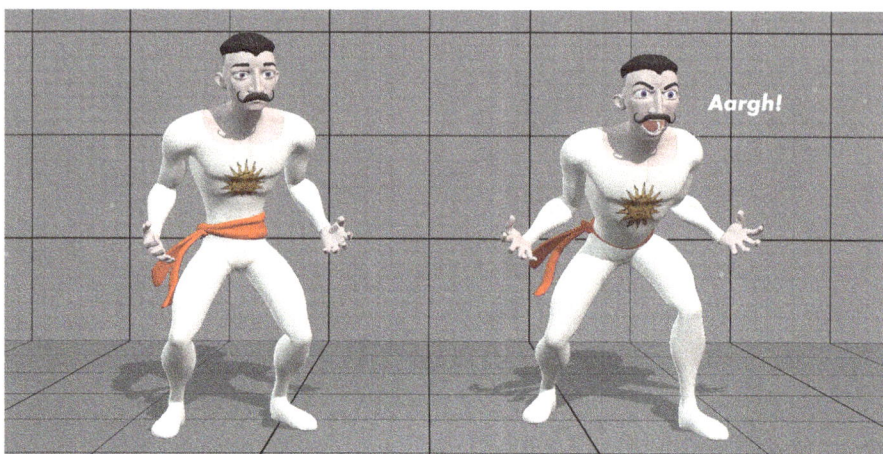

Figure 19.11

Surprise

"Surprise is the briefest emotion."[3] Surprise is a neutral emotion that doesn't say fear or shock, anger, or happiness — but can lead to any of those emotions.

Surprise can be subtle, "gasp" or broad, "GASP!".

Eyebrows are raised, the eyes are wide open — the white shows above the iris, and the jaw looks as if it dropped or fell open. The brows are not together.

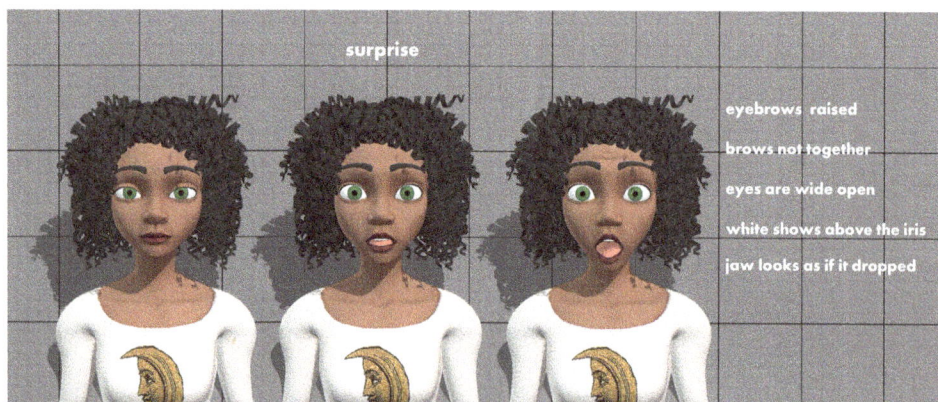

Figure 19.12

Fear

Fear can range from subtle apprehension to extreme, horrifying Edgar Allen Poe-like terror.

- Eyebrows are raised and drawn together; the eyes are open, the lower lid tense; the lips are stretched out or down.

- The fear mouth differs from surprise in that the lips are drawn back or down instead of dropping open.

- The eyebrows are closer together than in surprise.

Figure 19.13

Increase the level of fear by showing more white above the iris; raising and tightening (flattening) the lower eyelid; and opening the mouth by either pulling the lips tighter or drawing the teeth back more, as in a scream. "Aah!"

Figure 19.14

Disgust

Disgust is a strong dislike for something — something tastes or smells really awful, or your character finds something repulsive.

- Eyebrows are lowered, and the upper lip is raised.

- The lower lip may be raised or lowered; and, if your rig allows it, the nose is wrinkled.

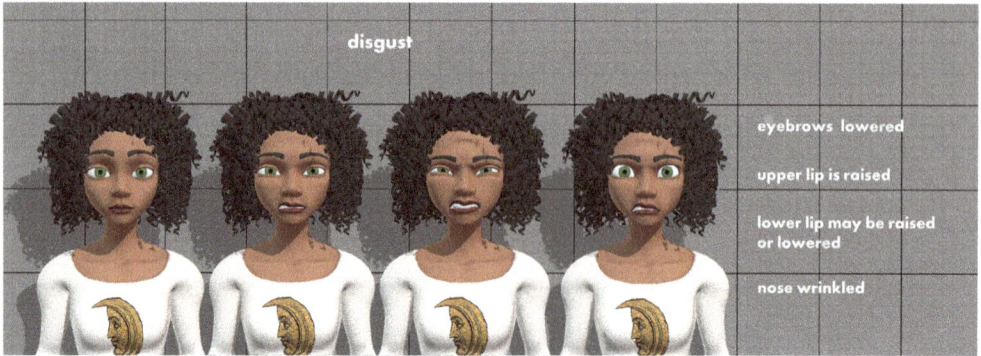

Figure 19.15

Disgust is limited in the number of variations you can make — it's either lips raised or lips together.

Remember that sections of the face relate! The more you raise your character's upper lip in disgust, the more the nose will push up and widen, and the more the cheeks will raise and push the lower eyelid up.

Figure 19.16

Raising the eyebrows during the disgust expression looks more like disbelief.

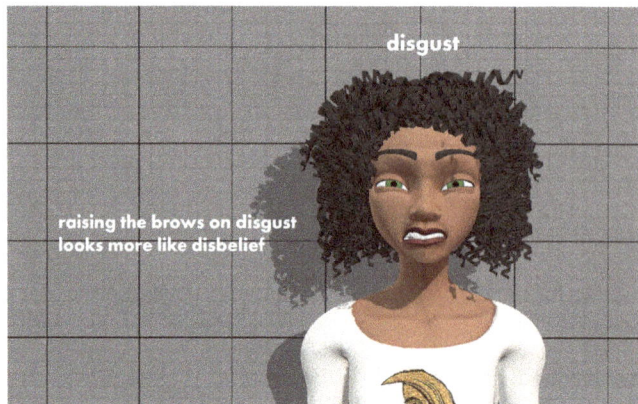

Figure 19.17

Contempt

Contempt is sort of like the sometimes "Y" vowel rule of expressions. It's similar to disgust but is only used when a character is judging someone or showing scorn. Contempt is shown by tightening and raising one side of the mouth.

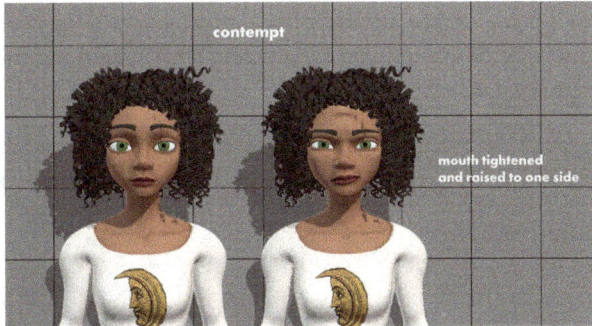

Figure 19.18

The more your character snarls on one side, the less contemptuous they look, and the more they look as if they find something disgusting.

Figure 19.19

Raising the eyebrows on contempt suggests disbelief.

Figure 19.20

Anger

Anger uses all three sections of the face. If all three sections of the face are not used, it won't be clear whether your character is truly angry. Anger can range from an irritated glare to full-on screaming rage.

- Brows are pulled down and brought together, either straight or angled; the eyelids are raised or lowered; the lips are tight and squared off — closed or drawn back. The mouth can be closed or open.

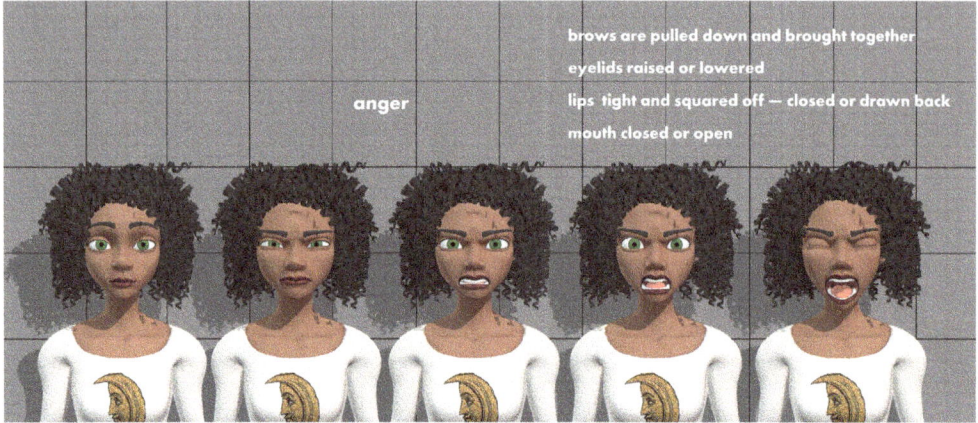

Figure 19.21

Anger is more successful if the eyes are focused on the object of anger. The eyebrows push down on the eyes, so you won't see the white above the iris.

Angy eyebrows and eyes with a surprised mouth show less anger and more "How dare you!".

Figure 19.22

Happiness

Happiness is shown mainly in the lower section of the face and the lower eyelids. Happiness can range from a slight grin to eyes closed rolling on the floor laughing.

With happiness there needs to be at least a hint of a smile. This means the corners of the mouth need to be raised — even if slightly.

The eyes narrow mostly from the lower lids pushing up.

The cheeks are raised, and the brows could be up.

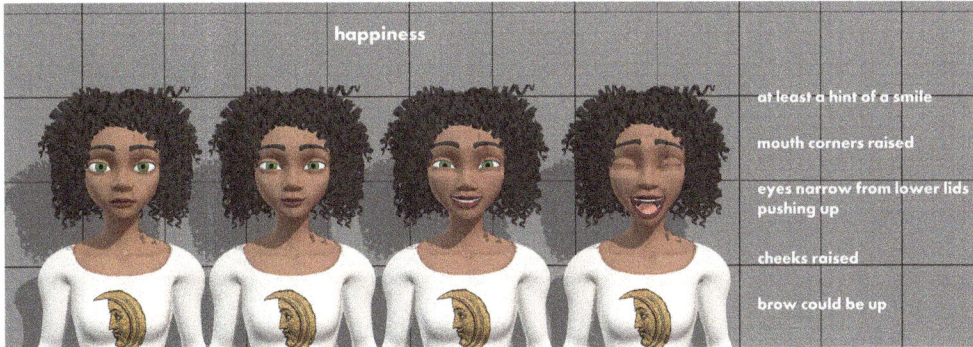

Figure 19.23

You can smile and not be happy. As when trying to hide how you truly feel.

Figure 19.24

Happiness with anger brows can be anything from a "gotcha" look to pure evil.

Figure 19.25

Happiness mixed with surprise is an expression that would only be shown for a moment.

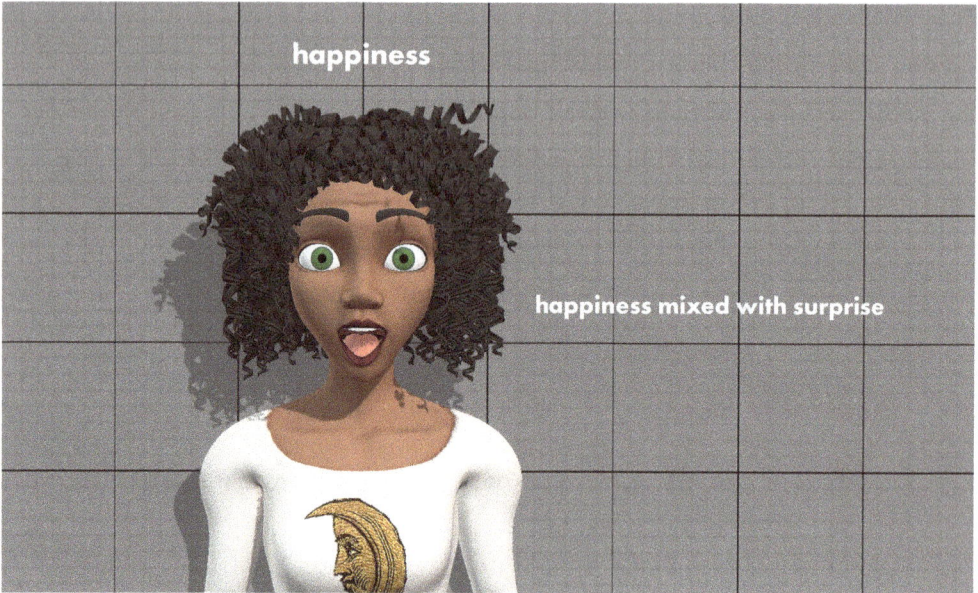

Figure 19.26

Sadness

For sadness, think of every part of the face dropping.

Eyelids turn down or droop. The corners of the mouth could be down. If the mouth is pulled down enough, the nostrils may also pull down.

Unlike fear where the whole brow is raised, for sadness, just the inner eyebrows are raised and could be drawn together. The lower the outer brows and the higher the lower eyelids, the sadder your character will appear. Sadness is not crying.

Figure 19.27

A nice trick is to pull the lips down slightly below the tooth line of your rig. It gives a little more exaggeration to the expression.

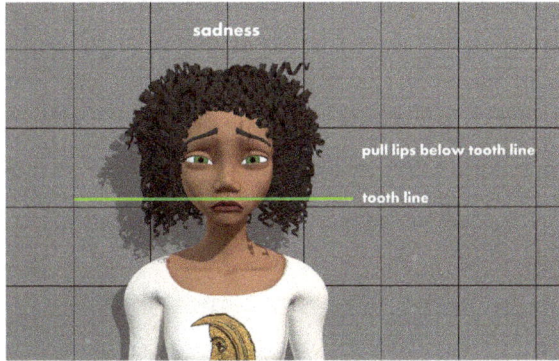

Figure 19.28

Sadness shown only in the mouth might be confused with a pout.

Figure 19.29

Sadness eyebrows and eyes with a smile could make your character look like a crying on the inside clown.

Figure 19.30

Don't feel limited to these examples! From the 7 basic expressions, you can make ten-thousand expressions. Good luck!

Breakdowns

How do you animate a character changing from a happy expression to an angry expression?

Add a breakdown!

Breakdowns between expressions can be used in the same manner as breakdowns between extremes.

An expression breakdown could be an anticipation either up or down or in a straight path.

An expression changing from happy and angry could have a breakdown squashing before going into the angry expression.

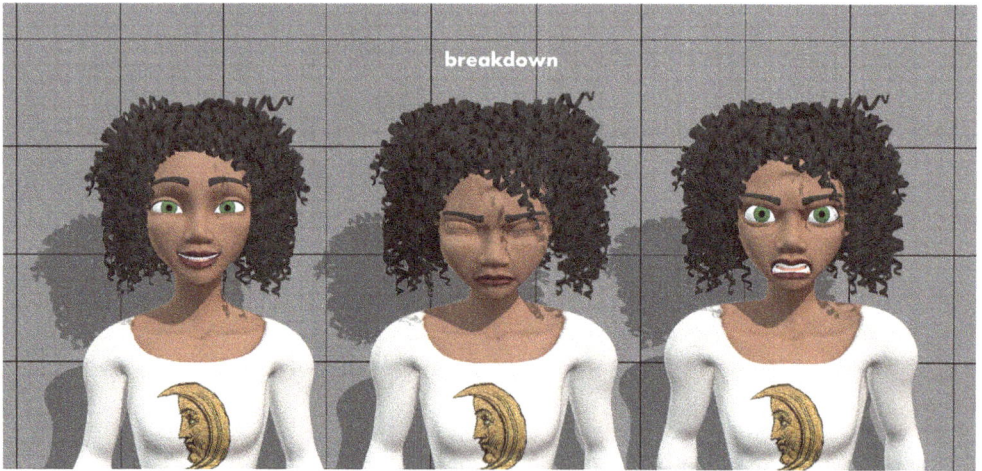

Figure 19.31

Or it could anticipate up, as with a surprised expression.

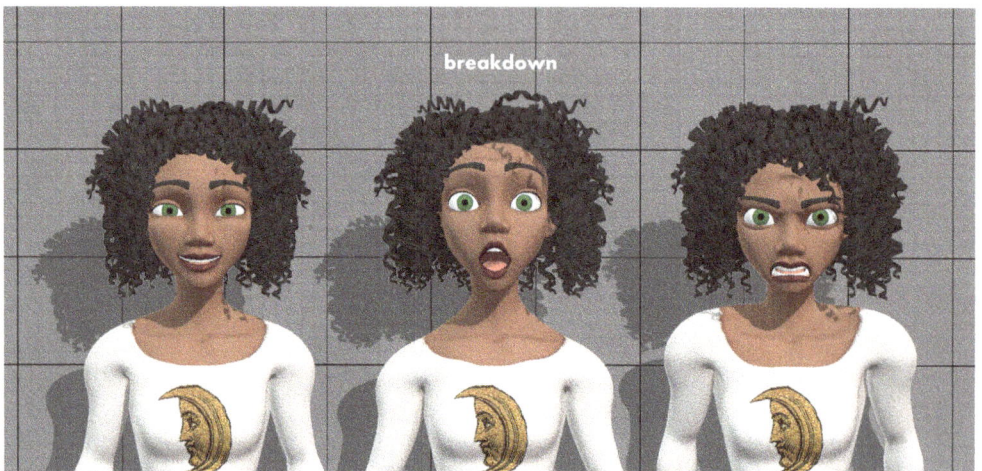

Figure 19.32

If the breakdown is too drastic, use parts of each expression. For instance, the upper half of the face could favor the surprised expression breakdown, while the lower half favors the angry expression.

Figure 19.33

Sometimes you may want to go straight from one expression to the next without an anticipation. Position the breakdown to favor either extreme to get a different timing and feeling.

Figure 19.34

The choice of breakdown from one expression to the next is endless. Choose the one that works best for your scene.

Overlap Expressions

Just as you overlap the body, one part of the face will move before another part.

Even if the expression change is quick, try to add overlap! A character with their eyes shut opens them. The brows could move first — leading the action. Then the eyes open.

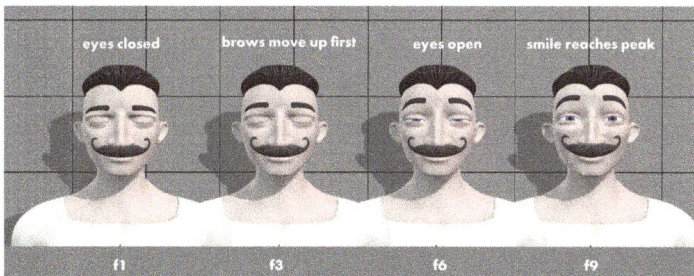

Figure 19.35

A character yells.

The brows could start to lower as the lips part; the nostrils raise; the ears anticipate up; the eyes squint; the jaw opens, pulling the ears back; perhaps the ears move back; the brows furrow, and the mustache overlaps.

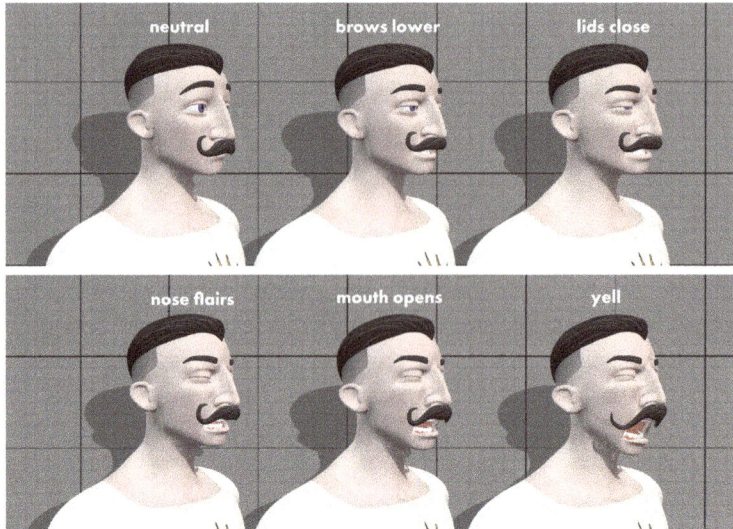

Figure 19.36

A character sighs.

Starting with a neutral pose: the brows lower as the mouth closes; then the eyes close; the brows then raise; the eyes open; the mouth opens; the eyes close and sigh.

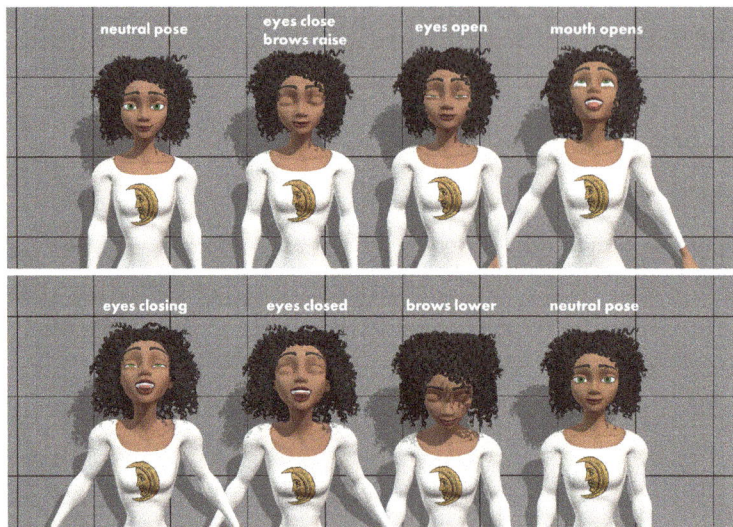

Figure 19.37

Overlapping expressions give a more organic, natural feel!

Blinks

"Blinking is a key part of keeping something alive,"[4] said animator and sculptor Blaine Gibson.

Slow-out and slow-in of a blink. Even an eyelid needs time to change direction!

The formula for a blink is open; 1/3 closed; closed for two frames; 1/3 open; open.

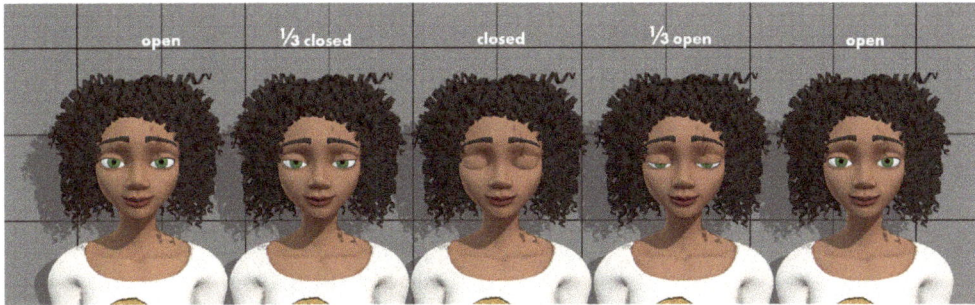

Figure 19.38

Unless your character's eyes are darting around, use a blink to emphasize the change of direction of a head turn or change in direction of a gaze.

Figure 19.39

You could even add overlap to the iris in a blink!

As a character blinks, have the iris move first, leading the blink. As the eyelid opens, the iris could be moving in the direction of the look.

Figure 19.40

In a real human blink, there is movement in both "the upper and lower eyelids,"[5] so why not add this detail to your animation? Instead of bringing the upper lid all the way down on a blink, bring the lower lid up a bit to meet the upper lid on the closed frame.

Avoid Clichés

"It is all too easy to jump the track and come up with mere stock-in-trade, histrionics and playacting,"[6] said the creator of method acting, Konstantin Stanislavski.

Avoid clichés! Try not to do something that was done a million times before. Come up with something original!

How many times have you seen this pose?

Figure 19.41

Body Attitude First

Animate the expression no matter how small, how far away, or how dark your scene is. You may not always see it, but you'll feel it!

"The body should always reflect the attitude that you're trying to do," said Ollie Johnston. "It shouldn't just be in the expression – it should be in the body, too."[7]

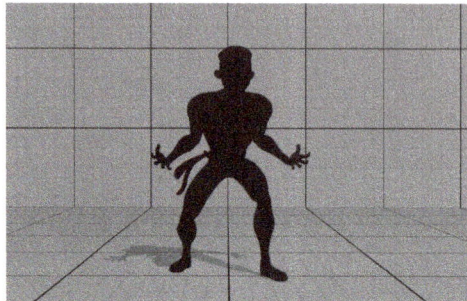

Figure 19.42

Animation Exercise — Pose out as many of the seven basic poses as you can (in other words, all seven, or at least three of them!) using the distinctive clues and see if someone can identify them.

CHAPTER TWENTY

Chapter 20. Dialogue

Introduction

Animating dialogue is more than just applying the formula phonemes. What if your character has no teeth? What do you do if your character talks really fast? What mouth shapes do you show and what do you leave out? Listening to your soundtrack and animating what you hear is key to animating successful dialogue scenes. In this chapter we'll look at animating dialogue that looks as it sounds!

Forget (Don't Forget) Formulas

Here's the classic dialogue mouth shape formula for vowels and consonants.

Figure 20.1

You saw it, now forget it!

It's a handy start, but some shapes are missing, like digraphs such as "sh" and "ch". And some of the formula letters don't fit certain words, such as the "y" in "you". Who looks like this when they say "you"?

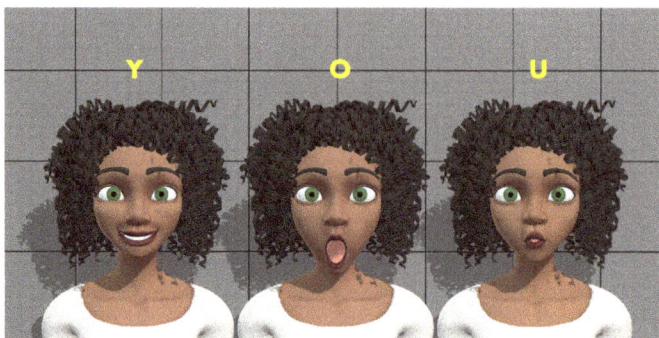

Figure 20.2

DOI: 10.1201/9781003361893-21

Using the formula to say "you" correctly, we might spell it as "u-w".

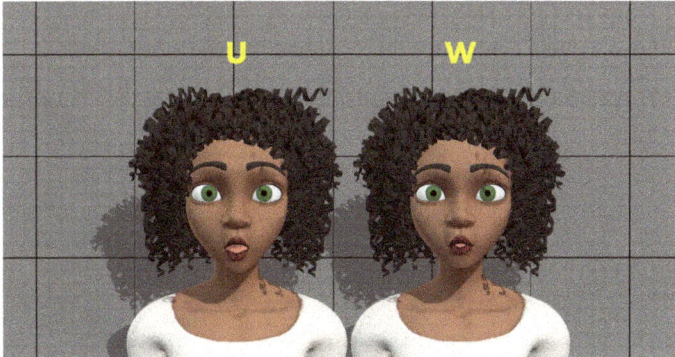

Figure 20.3

Don't animate how a word is spelled, animate how it sounds. "Chocolate" is not necessarily "Choc-o-la-te," it may sound more like, "Chock-o-lot," or just two syllables, as in "Chock-lit".

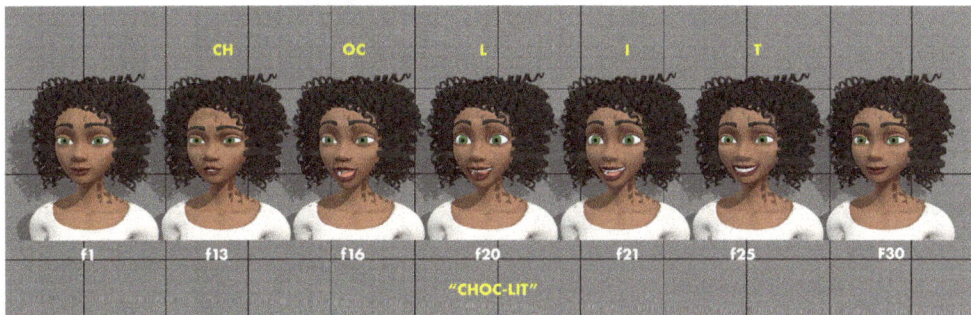

Figure 20.4

What do you do if you're animating a character speaking a language you don't know?

Use the formula as a guide to get your mouth shapes, phonemes, in the ballpark — but listen to your soundtrack. Animate the sound you hear and form mouth shapes unique to your character.

Animate the Sounds You Hear

Everyone has a unique way of speaking — not just the voice, but the way the mouth forms a word. People talk with their upper teeth showing, their lower teeth showing, or both upper and lower teeth. Others talk with a small mouth, an overbite, or a jutting jaw.

In *Little Red Riding Rabbit* (1944) Bugs Bunny mimics the Big Bad Wolf by repeating what the wolf says — same gestures, same expressions, and same sharp tooth mouth shapes.

"Hey now!" "Hey now!"

"Cut that out!" "Cut that out!"

"Say, wise guy!" "Say, wise guy!"

Manny Perez animated an animated character doing an impression of another animated character and it's brilliant!

This would never have worked if Bugs and the Wolf had formula mouth shapes.

Each person has a distinctive way of forming mouth shapes for not only the same word, but the same letter.

Figure 20.5

Accents

Accents are the section of a soundtrack where the most emphasis is placed. It could be a word, a syllable, or a musical beat that is louder or has more emotion.

A character says, "Get to the chopper!"

Don't animate the spelling of the words, "G-e-t t-o t-h-e c-h-o-p-p-e-r-!" Animate the way your actor pronounces it phonetically. "g**EHT** t**OO** d**A** ch**AH**-p**AH**!".

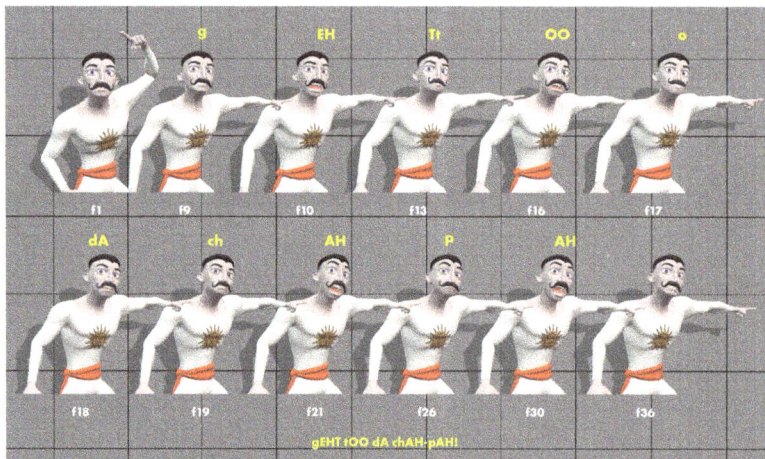

Figure 20.6

The **bold**, CAPITALIZED letters show where the emphasis, or accents, are in the soundtrack. Accents are enhanced with a stronger mouth shape, or a head or body gesture — any movement that gives your dialogue or action more punch.

Listen to your track. Where are the accents in the dialogue? Dialogue accents almost always move on vowels.

The early *Flintstones* are great to watch for head accents. Though the animation was limited, the animators were pros and knew how to get the most bang for the buck. They raised, turned, and lowered Fred's head to accent the dialogue heavy cartoons.

"Come on you, guys!" or "c**UH** m**O**n y**OO** g**UY**z!".

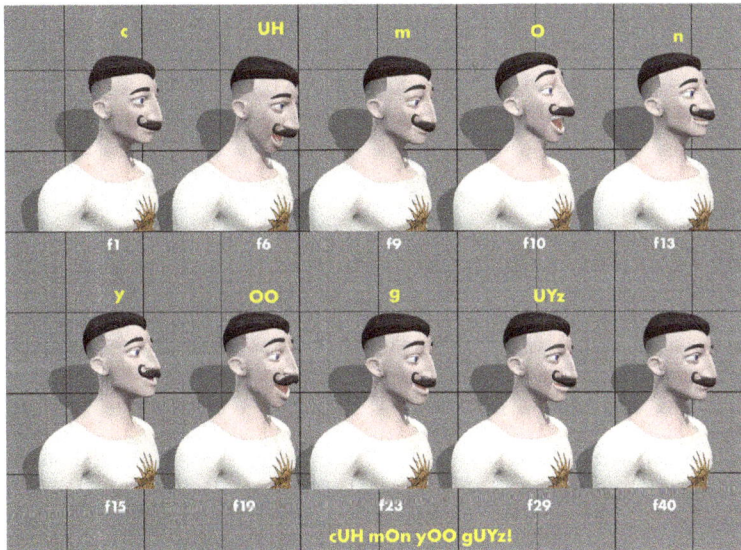

Figure 20.7

A character yells, "st**O**p!" with the accent on the "**O**". The head can move on the "**O**" in "st**O**p!".

The "st" in "st**O**p!" could be an anticipation.

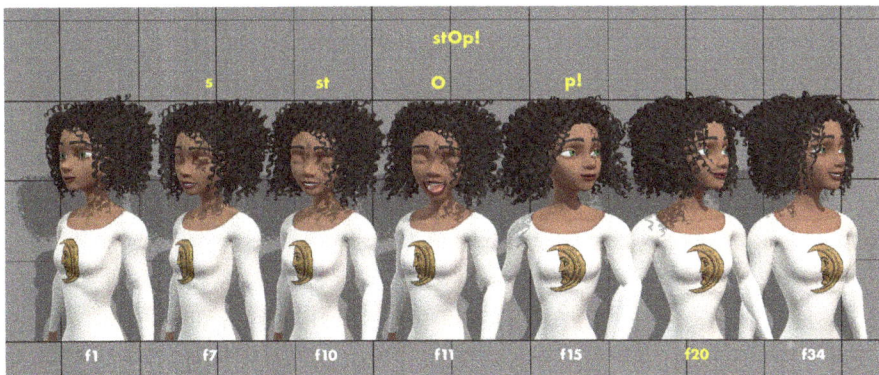

Figure 20.8

If the line "st**O**p!" is drawn out, as in "sss**STOOOO**pp!," you'll have more time for secondary action.

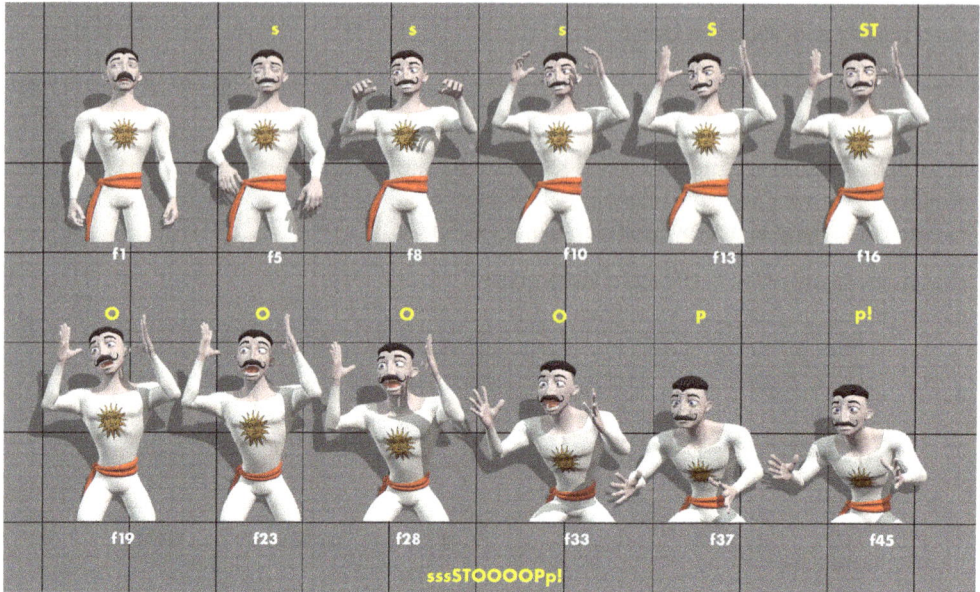

Figure 20.9

"Too often a novice hopes to accent a beat with exaggerated mouth action," said Grim Natwick. "Mouths can be funny, but they do little to help an accent — even with funny dialogue. A body accent, a dramatic posture, is the *Thing* — always."[1]

Don't animate a talking head with just the mouth moving. Emphasize words with both pushed mouth shapes and head and body gestures.

The X-sheet

In a perfect world, every animator would use an exposure sheet.

Exposure sheets, also called X-sheets, are used to "plan the animation production timing of an individual scene," wrote Preston Blair. "Each music beat, action accent, word sound, and timing detail has a number."[2]

Each line on an X-sheet is one frame. Every eight frames is marked with a dark black line. Two black lines are one foot of film, three black lines are one second. The black lines make it easier for animators working with an X-sheet to plan their timing.

A character says, "Use exposure sheet, please!". Write it out phonetically at the top of your X-sheet. "y**OOZ** exp**OZ**ure sh**EET**, pl**EE**ze!".

Import your audio into your scene, then scrub back and forth on the timeline "reading" your soundtrack. Write it out on an X-sheet or even a scrap of paper.

The "**O**" in "exp**OZ**ure" may last several frames. Indicate its length, and where it's the loudest, with a diminishing squiggly line or an inverted triangle.

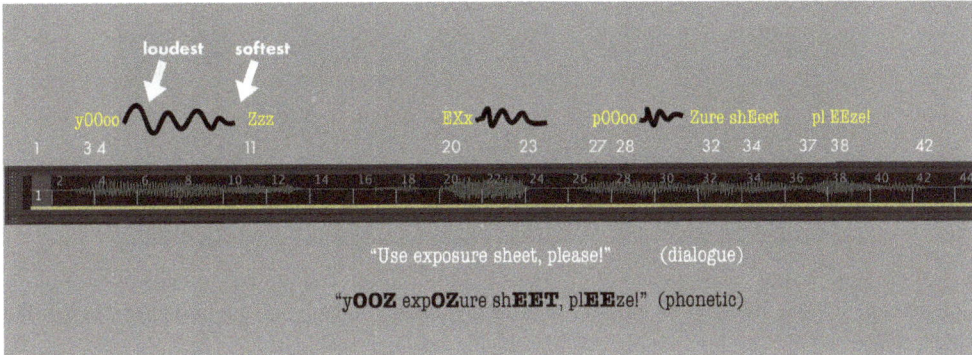

Figure 20.10

"Timing and animation are interconnected," said Tissa David. "You will get a sense of timing just by using exposure sheet... Use exposure sheet, *please!*"[3]

Don't wing it!

Inbetweening Dialogue

Having blocked in your dialogue, scrubbed through your timeline and written your dialogue out on an X-sheet, a notepad, or something else, you're ready to inbetween your mouth shapes.

A character says, "Frank" or Fra**A**nk". Straight inbetweens can make dialogue look mushy.

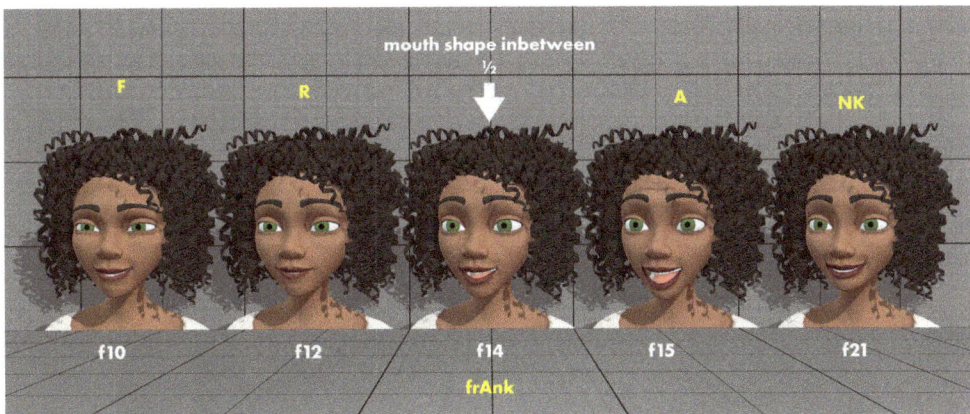

Figure 20.11

Most often you'll want to use favoring inbetweens to move from one shape to the next – such as the "r" in "Frank".

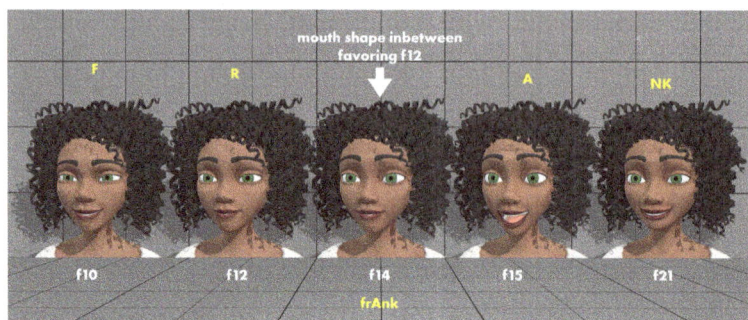

Figure 20.12

Consonants, by rule, need to be held for at least 2 frames — otherwise, you won't see or feel the mouth shape.

A character says, "Milt". "m**MIL**t". The "**M**" is held for several frames so that you feel it.

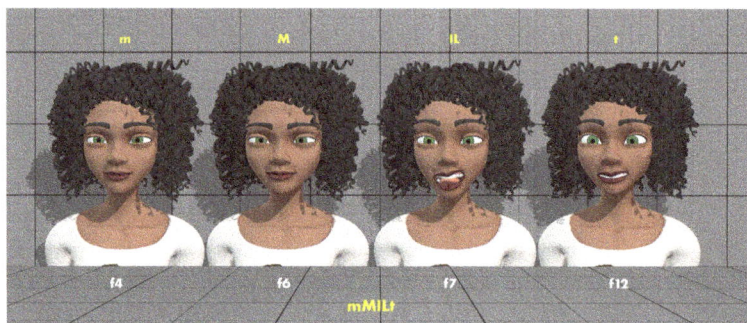

Figure 20.13

There is an exception to this rule — if you have a consonant, vowel, consonant, vowel,[4] word, or phrase, the consonant can be on a single frame. If your character says, "Muumuu," phonetically it could be, "m**OO**m**OO**."

The middle "m" can be held for just a single frame.

Vary the size of "**OO**" mouth shapes! Think of it like the bouncing ball. If the poses before and after the squash are at the same height, you'll see them more than the squash itself. Too big a movement may cause the mouth to flash.

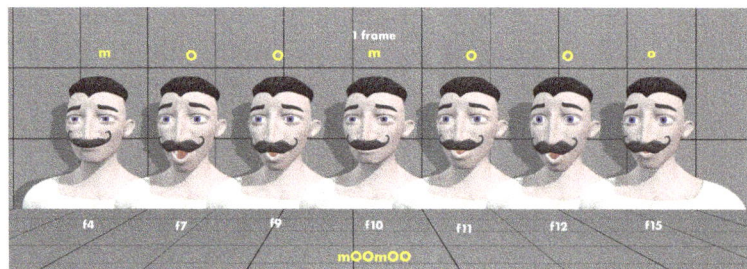

Figure 20.14

Popping into Vowels

Popping from a closed consonant to a big open vowel adds a lot of snap to dialogue. A character says, "Milt!" or "mILt!". Pop from the "m" in "mILt!" to the open "I".

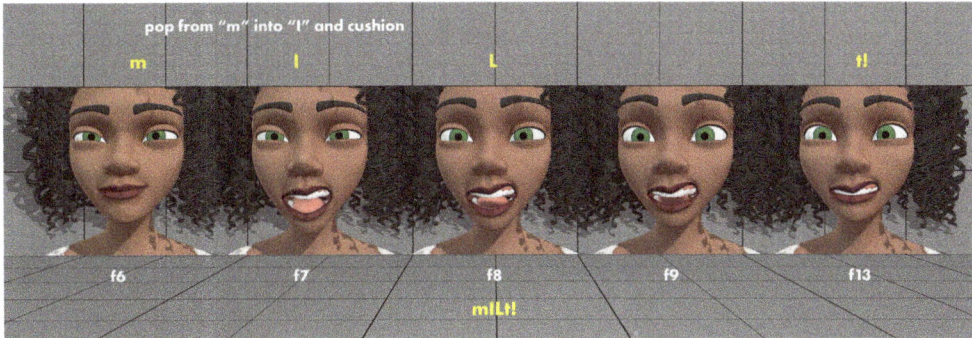

Figure 20.15

Squash and Stretch

The face is flexible! Compress and fill the cheeks on consonants when appropriate. Deflate the cheeks on the vowel.

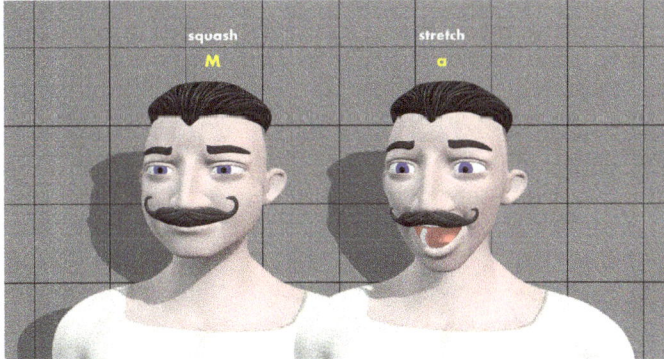

Figure 20.16

Swallow Syllables

There's no need to articulate every letter or syllable. Besides being over-animated, it can look a little silly.

Instead, swallow syllables when you can. That is, open the mouth for one syllable and then close it for the next.

If a character says "radish" or "rA-dISH," there's no need to animate every letter: R-a-d-i-s-h.

It can be just "r," open "**A**" and closed "d**ISH**". The "d-**ISH**" is swallowed, so to speak!

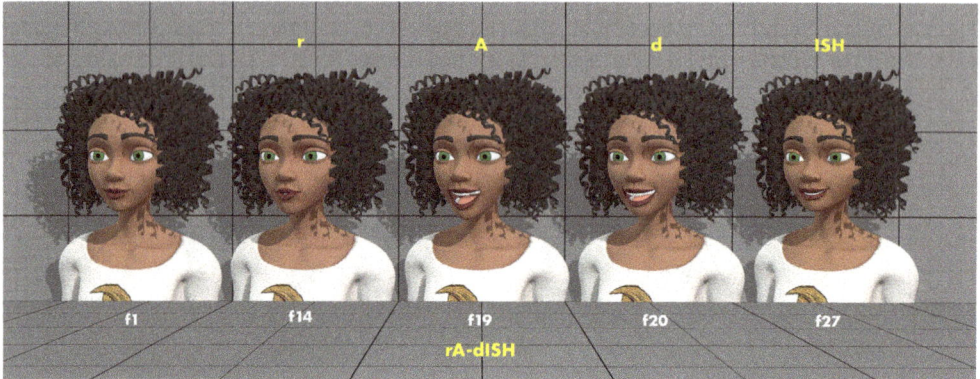

Figure 20.17

The Tongue

Don't place the tongue surfboard straight, halfway in the mouth. It's either up or down. Tongues move quickly when you speak, so placing the tongue in the middle of the mouth looks awkward. It's like having an eyelid halfway during a blink. It's kind of a no-no.

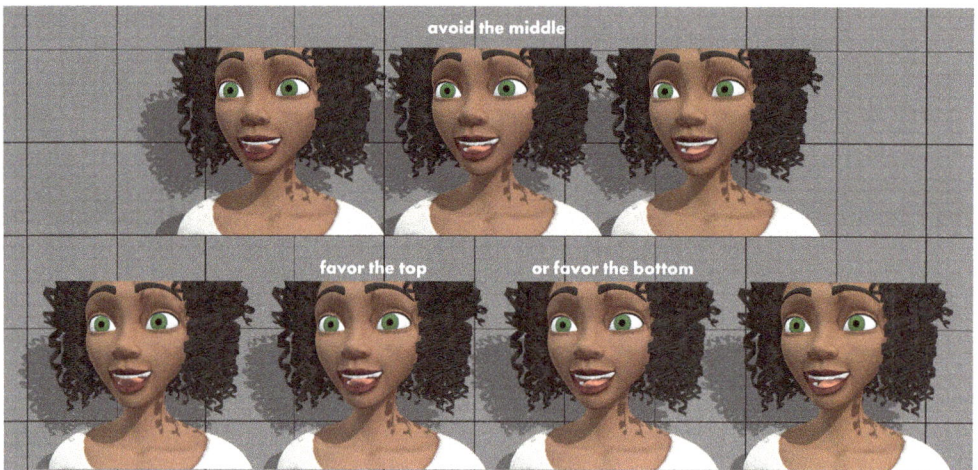

Figure 20.18

Progress the Action

Richard Williams made the concept "Progressing the Action" an animation term. "Go somewhere, anywhere as you speak,"[5] wrote Williams.

Progressing the action can be a moving hold or a quick movement. It could be forward, backward, or to the side. It could be a slow drift. Don't be a frozen talking mouth. Progress the action! Move!

Think of progressing the action as an accent!

A character says "What?" Move the head or body, progressing the action.

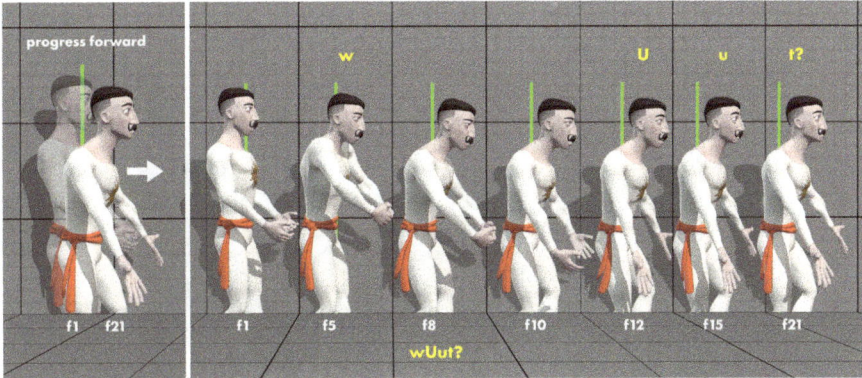

Figure 20.19

Frank Thomas' long-time assistant, Dale Oliver, said that on **101 Dalmatians** one of the directors, Clyde Geronimi, approved a scene of Pongo before the lip sync had been done. "Frank's phrasing was done so well that when Geronimi saw it he thought he actually saw that mouth working," said Oliver. "The phrasing with his head moving through the action [was so good that] Geronimi thought the dialogue was all done."[6]

Syncing Secondary Actions

A really bizarre thing that even Frank and Ollie can't explain, is syncing gestures to sound.

For some reason, the gesture needs to be three frames ahead of the dialogue. The Disney animators discovered this through trial and error. "No one knew why it should work," wrote Frank and Ollie. "But somehow it did."[7]

A character points and says, "What is that?". "whUt Is thAT?". The point needs to hit its extreme position three frames ahead of the "thAT" in "thAT?" — otherwise it will look as if it's late.

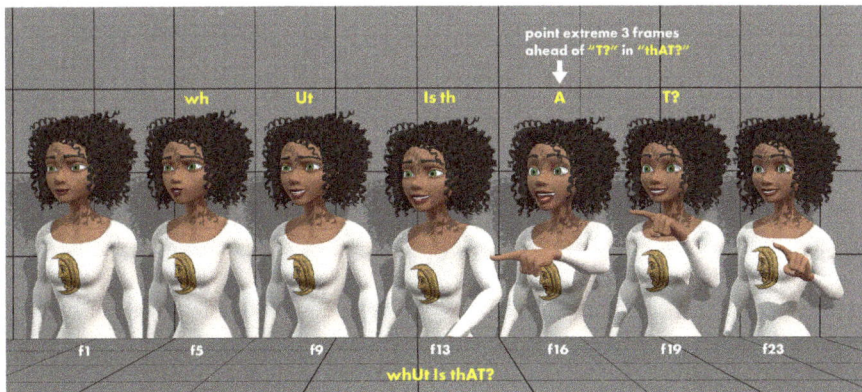

Figure 20.20

By the way, "whUt Is" is an example of swallowing syllables.

The "wh" mouth shape in "whUt" is closed. The mouth opens for "Ut". Then closes for "Is".

Closed. Open. Closed.

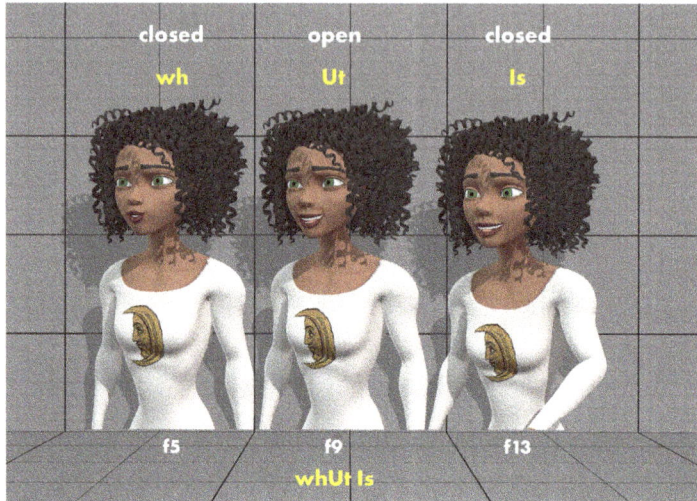

Figure 20.21

Plan your secondary action to be three frames earlier than the soundtrack. You have been warned!

Hold the Pose!

End your scene with the mouth shape of the last word spoken, or the expression that defines the last thought of your character. Don't change the mouth shape or expression without a reason. It makes the scene stronger. Hold the pose!

A character says, "**Why?**"

If that's the last pose of your scene, end with the "**y**?" mouth shape. Closing the mouth or changing the expression will only weaken the scene!

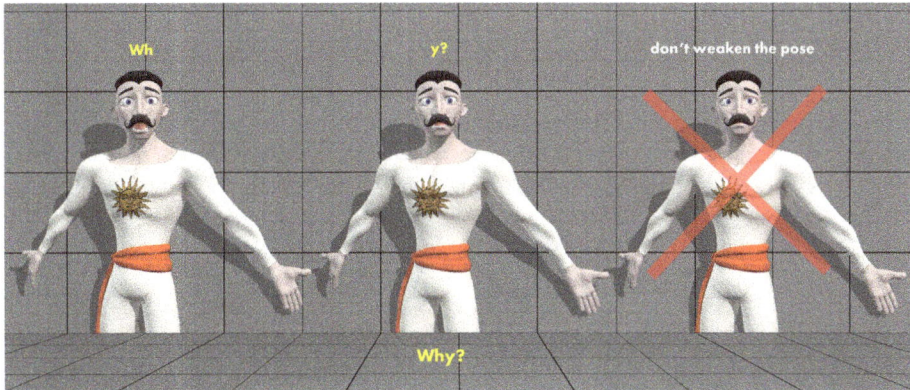

Figure 20.22

Gesture

Finally, remember that you should be able to get the gist of what your character is saying with the sound off!

"Dialogue is best expressed by the movement of the body," said Eric Larson. "If the whole body is not giving you the complete feeling of the dialogue, your lip movement isn't going to save it."[8]

Animation Exercise — Animate a short line of dialogue. Make sure the idea of the scene is expressed through the storytelling poses first. Block-in dialogue as you pose out your scene, even if it will eventually change.

Try adding a secondary action that syncs with the dialogue.

Chapter 21. Staging

Introduction

Poor placement of characters or objects in a scene, distracting camera work, or lack of continuity, can make a well animated scene difficult to follow. "Is there a grammar in filmmaking, the same way there is a grammar in literature? Well, sure there is," wrote director Martin Scorsese. "Even today, people are still struggling with new ways of telling stories through film, and they're still using the same tools."[1] Just as there are basic principles in animation, there is a grammar to film. In this chapter we'll show what you need to know to effectively set up a scene and connect a series of shots.

Film Grammar

Learning the tools of film can seem overwhelming. Orson Welles was so overwhelmed when he started filming *Citizen Kane* (1941) that he shut down the picture and went home. "God, there's a lot of stuff here I don't know," he told cinematographer Gregg Toland. "There's nothing I can't teach you in three hours,"[2] replied Toland.

So, give yourself three hours to study just the basics of film grammar and you too can be an Orson Welles!

Aspect Ratio

Up until 1953, movies were basically 1.33:1. This means that the frame width is 1.33 times the size of the height — which is always 1.

Figure 21.1

The higher the first number, the wider the screen. A standard letterboxed movie is 1.77:1 or 16:9.

DOI: 10.1201/9781003361893-22

Standard widescreen movies are 1.85:1. 2.35:1 is ultra-widescreen. It was originally called Panavision or CinemaScope.

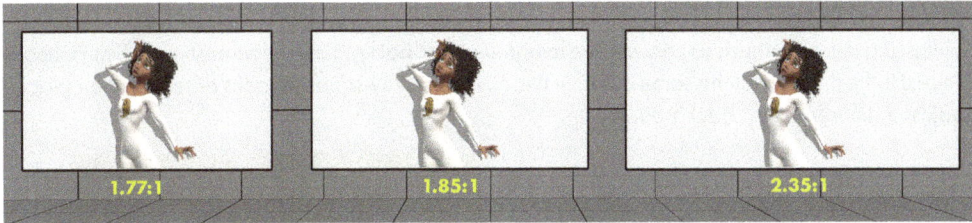

Figure 21.2

So, what aspect ratio will your scene, film, or game be and why does it matter?

Widescreen movies can be impressive cinematically, but it could be tricky fitting characters of vastly different heights in the same frame.

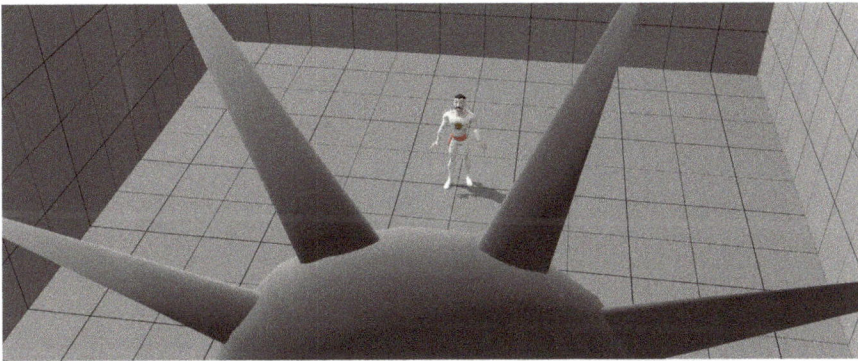

Figure 21.3

You can also get creative with the aspect ratio.

For *Samurai Jack* (2001), Genndy Tartakovsky frequently changes the aspect ratio and adds split screen effects to fit the mood of a scene — much like John Frankenheimer's *Grand Prix* (1966).

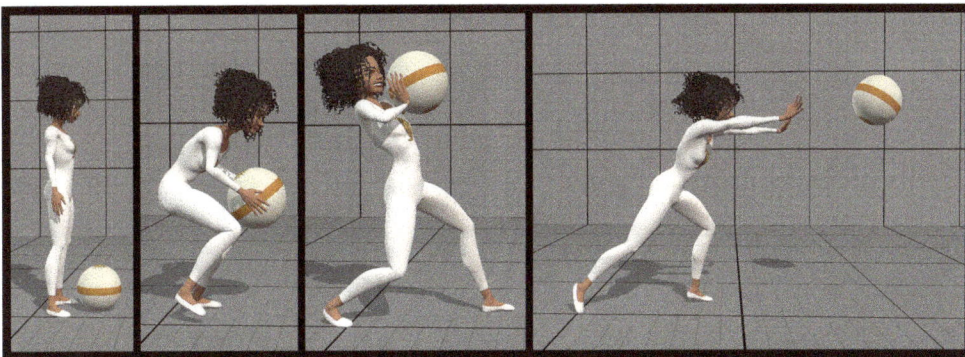

Figure 21.4

Aspect ratios are the frame and canvas for your scene. It's the first thing to think about for setting the mood of your scene.

Simultaneous Contrast and Contrast of Extension

Simultaneous contrast and contrast of extension have to do with color and contrast.

Contrast is a difference such as between the foreground and background colors or shades. Simultaneous contrast is the theory that the same color, in this case two grey squares, looks different when placed against a different color background.

Figure 21.5

Contrast of extension is the theory that warm colors come forward, while cool colors recede.

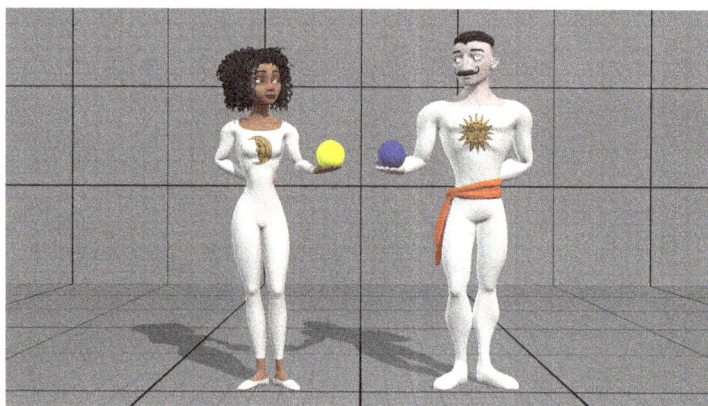

Figure 21.6

Unless you're doing it for a reason, you don't want your characters to get lost in the background because of poor color or tonal choices. Your characters need separation.

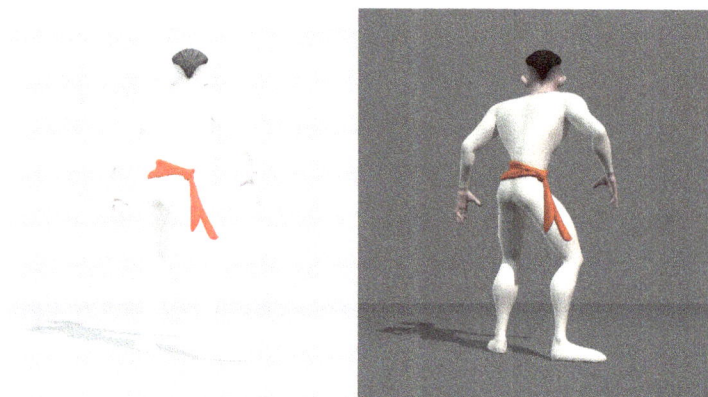

Figure 21.7

Filmmakers use simultaneous contrast and contrast of extension to lead the eye. In **North by Northwest** (1959) Hitchcock uses a yellow hatbox, a porter's red cap, and other warm colors to track a fleeing Cary Grant around the cool grays and blues of Grand Central Station.

Even if you forget the terms, simultaneous contrast and contrast of extension, think about color and contrast when you compose a scene.

Adding Interest to the Frame

Which of these three dots is the most pleasing?

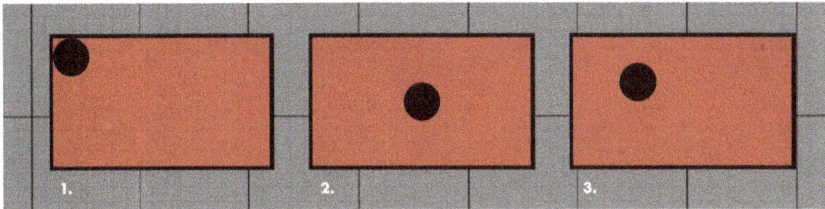

Figure 21.8

Dot 1 is close to the edge and leaves a lot of empty negative space. On a huge screen, or with less contrasting color, you would almost have to search for the dot.

Dot 2 feels cold and intimidating — like Luca Brasi in **The Godfather** (1972), because everything is centered and even.

Dot 3 feels better. It seems comfortable where it is, with just the right amount of negative space surrounding it.

Rule of Thirds

Draw two vertical lines and two horizontal lines over your frame, creating nine equal sections. The intersections of the lines are the points of interest — where important objects are often placed.

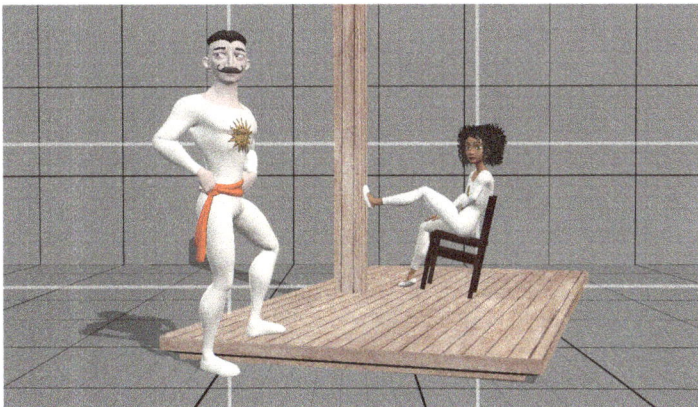

Figure 21.9

If you don't know where to place a character in a scene, place them along a vertical or horizontal rule of thirds line with their head at an intersection. Placing a character's eyes along the horizontal lines helps frame the head nicely.

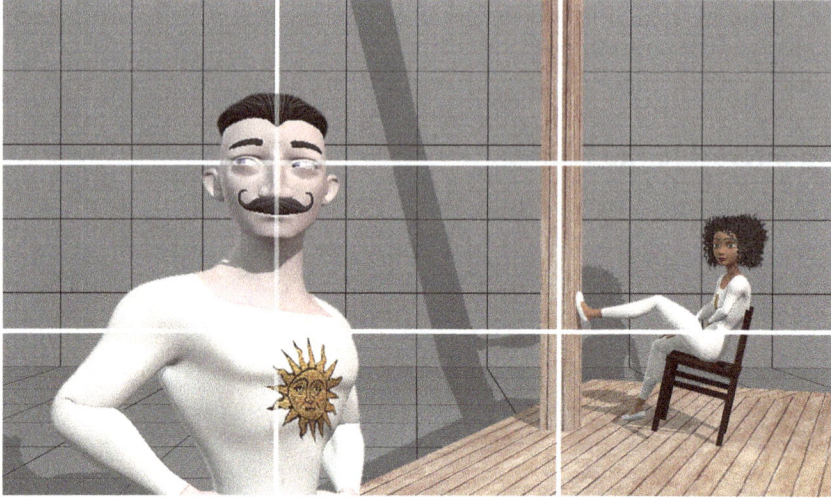

Figure 21.10

Golden Spiral

The Golden Spiral can be overkill for what we're doing, but it's used by painters and filmmakers to create a more harmonious image.

Very simply put, keep laying the side of a perfect rectangle, 1:1.618, on its side to make smaller and smaller rectangles. Then draw a spiral along the edges of the rectangles to find your point of interest. The horizontal line at .618 is arguably more pleasing than the rule of thirds for closeup and medium shots.

Figure 21.11

Perspective

Perspective in film or games gives the illusion of a three-dimension in a two dimensional medium.

One-Point

In one-point perspective the horizon line can be high or low, but all parallel lines lead to one vanishing point. One-point perspective can be a little less warm and fuzzy because of the unnatural symmetry. Stanley Kubrick used it to create a creepy, uneasiness. Wes Anderson uses it to create a fun shoebox diorama feeling.

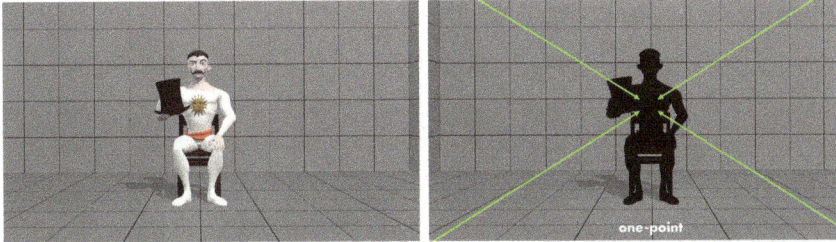

Figure 21.12

Two-Point

There are two-vanishing points with two-point perspective. Because you're showing an object at a 90° angle, two-point perspective is the easiest way to add depth and interest to a scene.

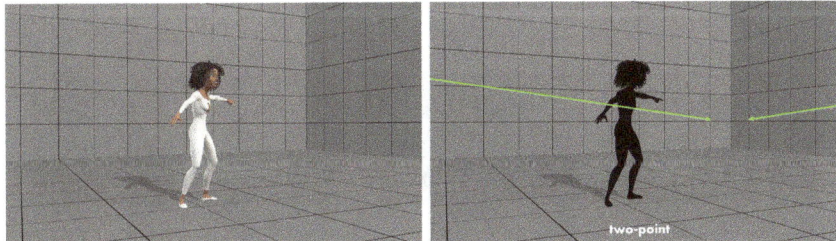

Figure 21.13

Three-Point

In three-point perspective the vanishing points are higher or lower than the horizon line. This means the camera is at a lower angle looking up, or a higher angle looking down — giving a more video game or Marvel movie feel.

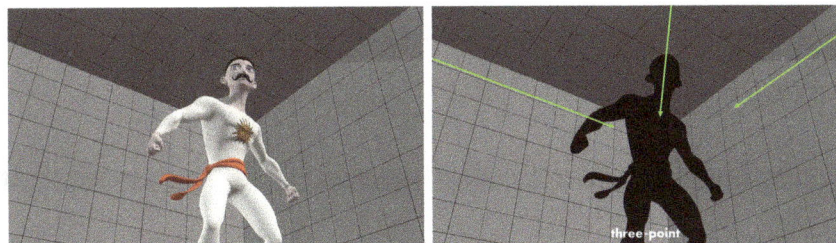

Figure 21.14

Lead Lines

A well animated scene won't read if it's placed against a cluttered or haphazard background. Lead lines guide the viewer in the direction you want them to look.

"When shapes are too busy, poorly arranged or designed they result in scarcely readable images," wrote Disney production designer Hans Bacher. "Simplifying and clarifying can improve these creating the quick readability for film."[3]

Arrange objects and characters so they lead to where you want the audience to look.

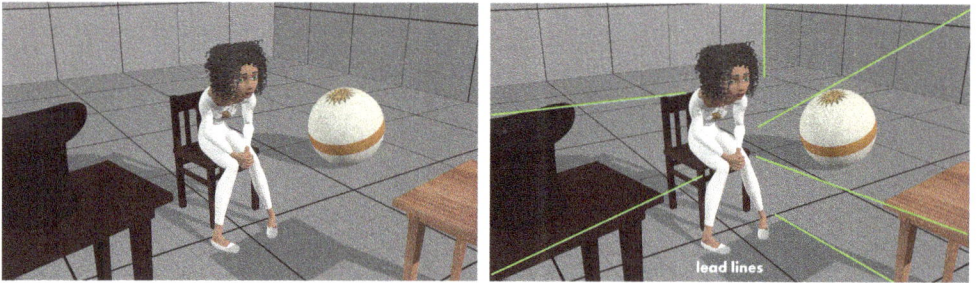

Figure 21.15

How does your scene look in thumbnail size? If it's too difficult to make out what's going on — simplify!

Figure 21.16

The Camera

Extreme long shot, long shot, medium shot, close-up, or extreme close-up deal with distance — how close the camera is to your character.

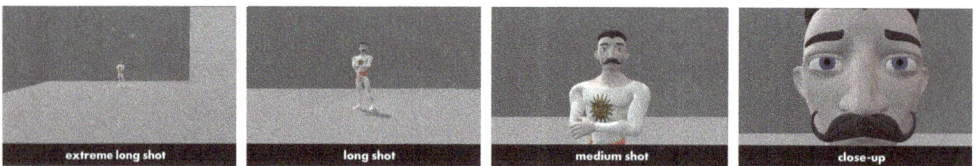

Figure 21.17

Level, high angle, low angle, and Dutch tilt deal with the angle of the camera itself.

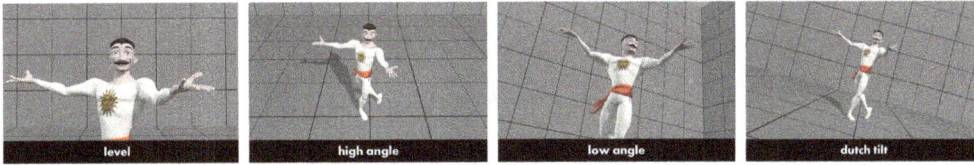

Figure 21.18

Pan, truck, dolly, and crane, deal with camera movement. Pan is keeping the camera stationary but swiveling left and right. Truck is physically moving the camera left and right. Dolly is moving the camera forward and backward. A crane shot is up and down.

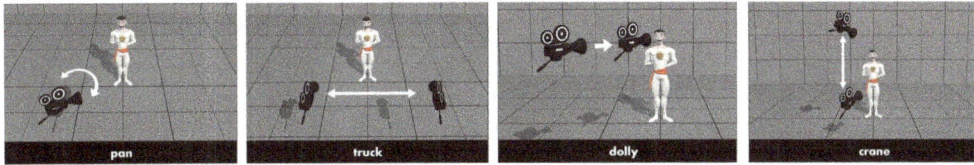

Figure 21.19

Lead Room and Head Room

If your character is on the left third of the frame looking right, the open space in front of them is the "lead room".

Placing your character on the right third of the frame looking right reduces the amount of lead room. It also creates tension.

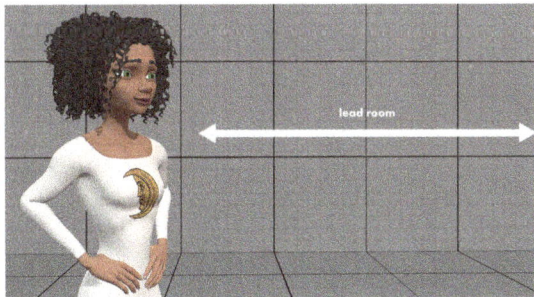

Figure 21.20

Figure 21.21

Head room is the space between the top of a character's head and the top of the frame. Use the rule of thirds or the golden ratio to determine proper head room!

Figure 21.22

Frame your character so that they have a comfortable amount of head room. Choose the amount of lead room to express the feeling you want in your scene.

The 180° and 30° Rule

The 180° rule in film is the theory that when you cut between two characters in a scene, the camera should stay on one side of the line of action.

Cameras (a), (b), and (c) adhere to the 180° rule.

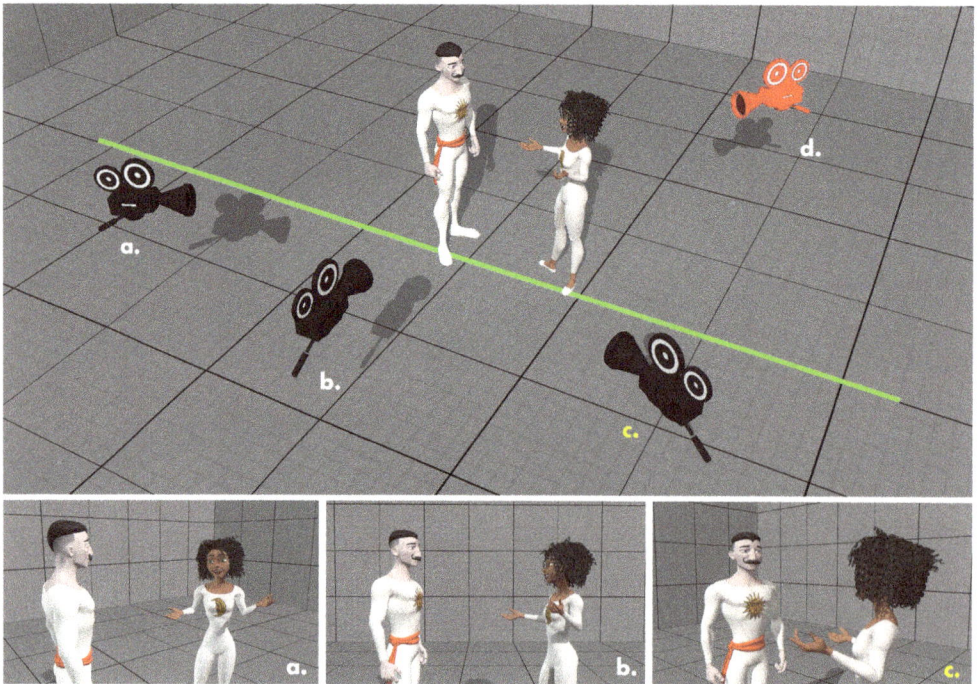

Figure 21.23

Filming across the line of action (d) will make it look as if the characters have switched places. This will take the viewer out of the scene.

Figure 21.24

The 30° rule is the theory that the camera must move at least 30° after a camera cut.

Otherwise, you'll get a jump cut — a cut that makes it look as if you've suddenly leapt forward in time.

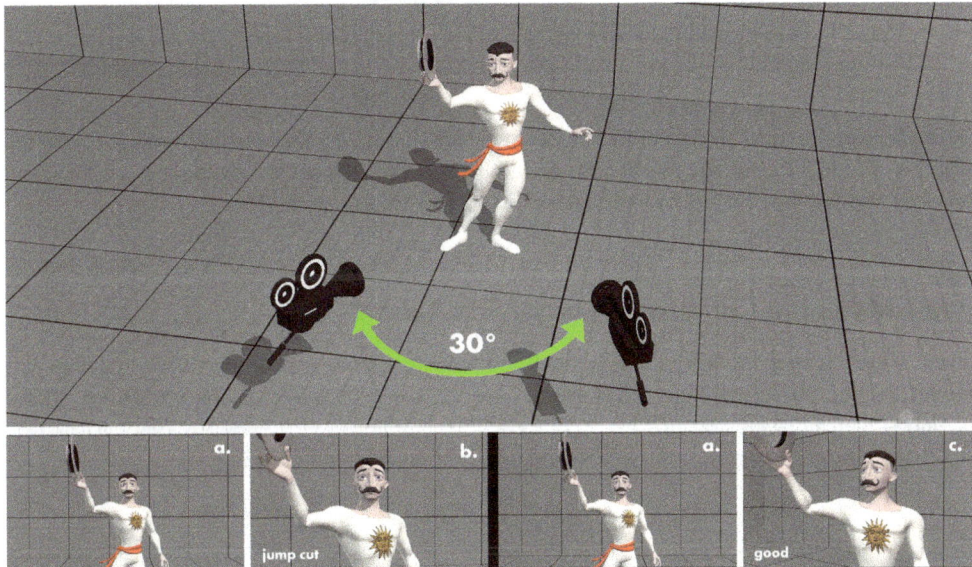

Figure 21.25

Continuum of Movement

"The eye is always attracted by movement. The audience's point of attention will always follow a moving object,"[4] wrote Bruce Block. With continuum of movement, "the picture-maker has control over what area of the screen the audience is watching."[5]

Match the point of interest from one shot to the next shot — otherwise, the audience will become disoriented and need time to catch up with the action.

A character moves from position (a) to position (b) in shot 1. In shot 2, the focus of the scene should be in the same area of the screen as the character was at the end of shot 1. The focus of shot 3 should be in the same area of the screen as the character was at the end of shot 2.

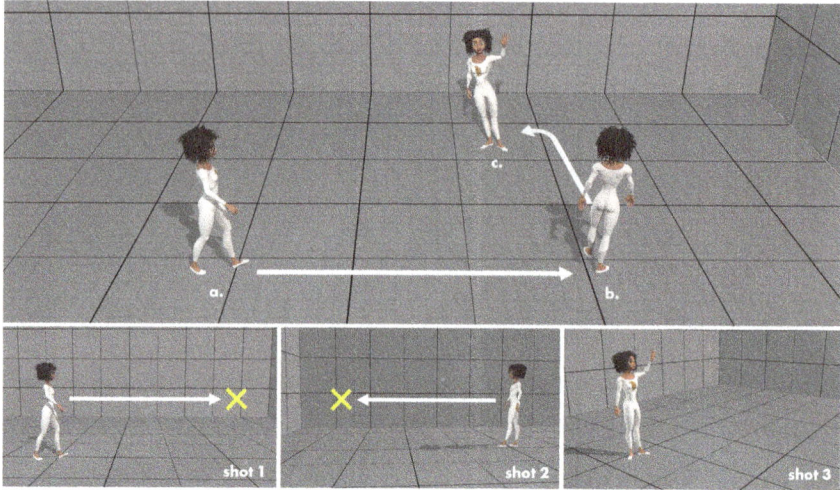

Figure 21.26

Steven Spielberg is a master of continuum of movement. This is why it's incredibly easy to follow the action in any of his films. Another master of continuum of movement is Brad Bird. The fight scene between Elastigirl and Screenslaver in *Incredibles 2* (2018) is — incredible!

Don't Move the Camera Ahead of The Action

Unless there's a specific reason, don't move the camera before a character starts moving. This telegraphs what the character is about to do. Instead, wait a beat after the character has started moving — then move the camera.

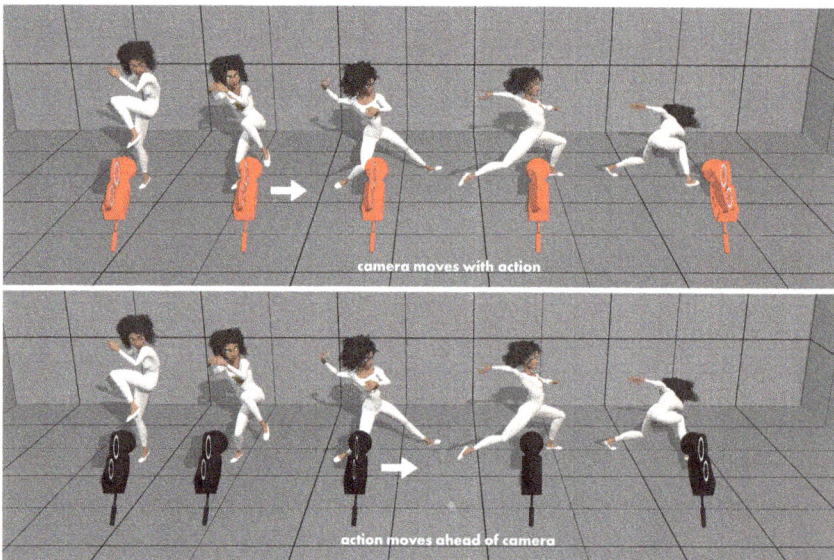

Figure 21.27   *Character Animation by Ryan Fisher*

Blocking

Blocking your scene, for film at least, means determining where your characters will be in a scene and how they'll move to best play to the camera.

What hand do you hold the object in that plays best to the camera? It sounds simple, but sometimes it's a tough choice.

Hold the object up in the hand closer to the camera and you may be covering the body. Hold the object in the hand further away from the camera and your character may take up more space.

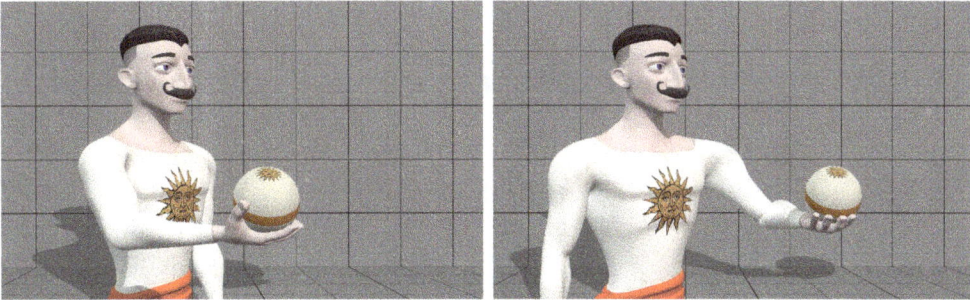

Figure 21.28

Introduce a second character and the blocking becomes more complicated. Which character is more important?

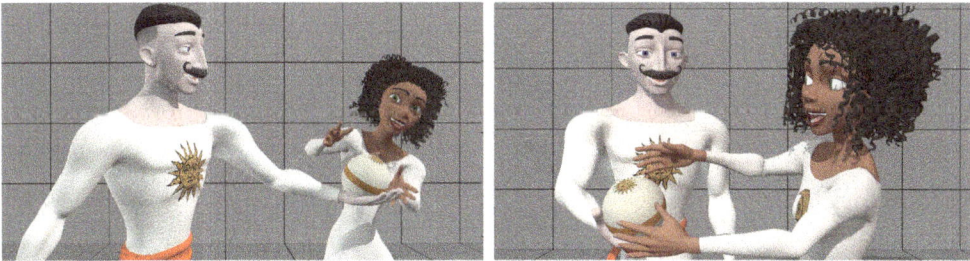

Figure 21.29

Arrange characters so that they relate to each other — even if they're not interacting. Create a rhythm and a unified shape. Hit F7 to see what the blocking looks like in silhouette.

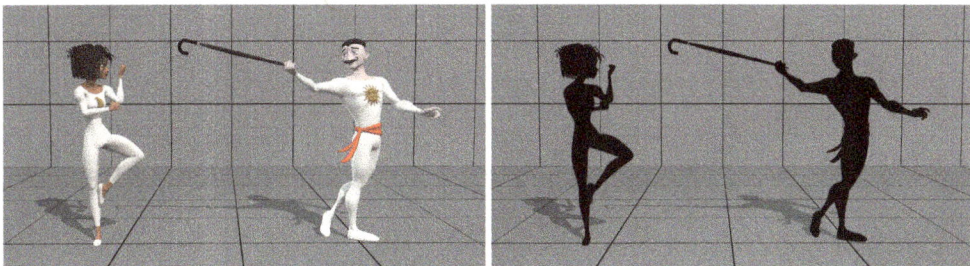

Figure 21.30

"The hardest thing to do in animation is nothing,"[6] said Milt Kahl. Keep the focus on what you want the audience to see at each moment.

Figure 21.31

Don't move a secondary character unnecessarily.

Figure 21.32

For arguably one of the best scenes in movie history, the flower girl sequence in **City Lights** (1931), Charlie Chaplin shot "342 takes for what ended up being just a three-minute sequence in the finished film."[7]

The scene is pure animation — the gestures and actions bigger than life. The staging is meticulously refined to be as simple and clear as possible. It's also wonderfully touching.

"Simplicity is a difficult thing to achieve,"[8] said Chaplin.

Chaplin, as the Little Tramp, avoids a policeman by ducking through a parked limousine. A blind girl selling flowers, Virginia Cherrill, hears the limo door close and mistakes Chaplin for a millionaire.

a. Cherrill calls to him, and Chaplin turns to his left, creating a nice line of action with his right arm and cane.

b. Cherrill holds a flower out, and Chaplin points to it with his right hand. He's switched the cane to his left hand — the top of his right hand pointing at the flower looking better against the Cherrill's palm.

c. When she accidentally drops the flower, Chaplin, not realizing she's blind, gives her a look. With his left hand on his hip, his elbow frames Cherrill. He's also tucked the cane under his right arm and holds the flower in his right hand. Cane, flower, and left hand create a direct line to Cherrill.

d. Chaplin holds the flower out with his left hand. He's bent forward, the cane angled down. A change of shape!

e. He switches the flower to his right-hand so he can tip his hat to her with his left hand. We can see his face and the flower this way.

f. He moves the cane to his left-hand so that he can look for a coin, his last, in his right pocket. Cherrill is in profile and Chaplin is looking at the camera, but they still relate to one another!

g. Chaplin helps her sit, holding her right hand with his left. This opens their bodies so that they both face the camera. He's switched the cane to his right hand again.

h. The real millionaire gets in the limousine. Cherrill thinks Chaplin has left. Chaplin sneaks off around the corner. His posture contrasts with the pose when he first turned to meet her.

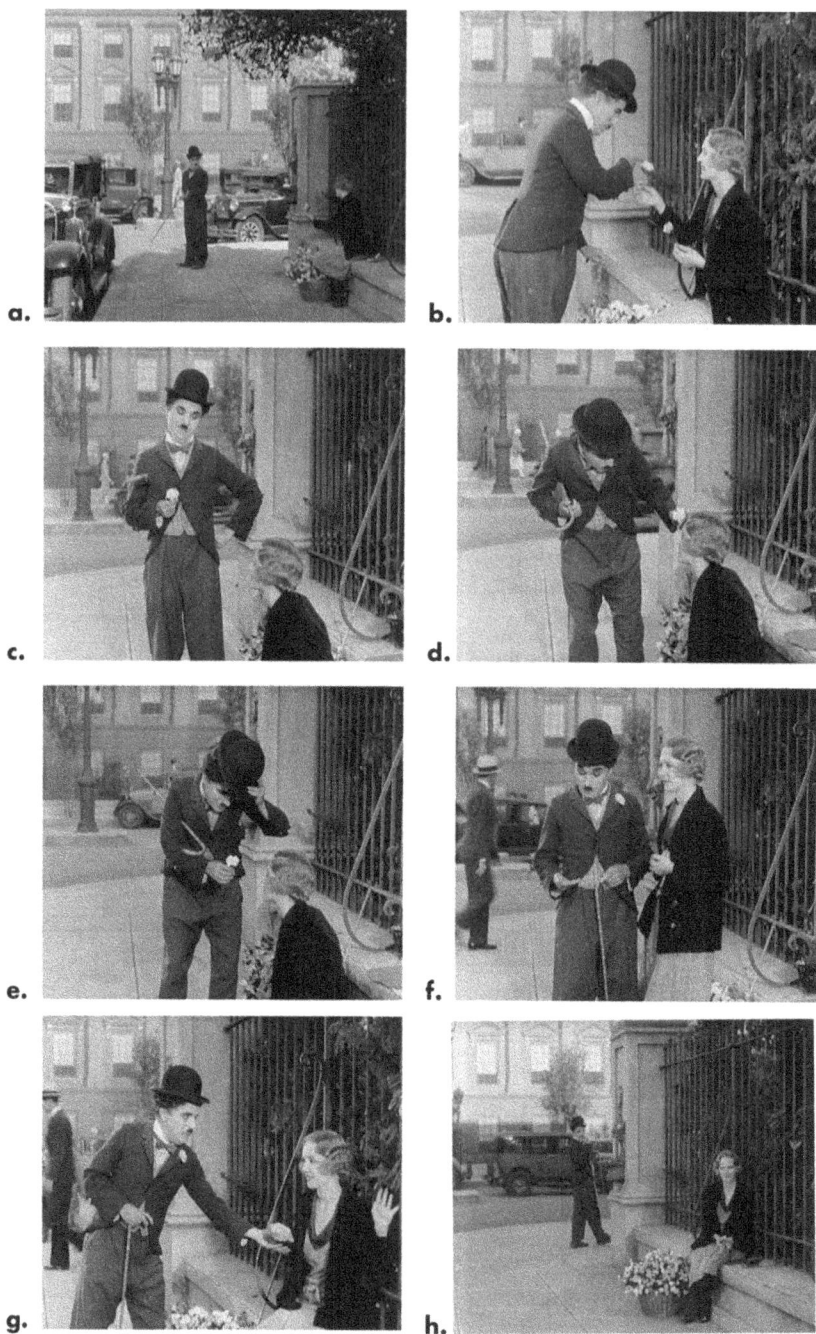

Figure 21.33

Rules Can Be Broken

Of course, rules are meant to be broken. If you want to place a character's head in the lower corner of the frame facing the edge of the screen — then do it!

Degas painted in widescreen, cut off figures, and placed characters in the lower corner of the canvas facing the edge long before Yasujirō Ozu's *Tokyo Story* (1953) or *Mr. Robot* (2015).

Why does a composition like this still work? Because the rules of composition work innately.

Learn the rules to make life easier, and then break them!

Figure 21.34

Animation Exercise – Animate a two character dialogue scene. Show them relating to each other. Apply the rule of thirds or the golden ratio. Watch your head and, if you have cuts, your lead room. Move the camera if you'd like. Place background objects to frame your character and not distract from the scene.

Chapter 22. Putting It All Together

Introduction

The Nine Old Men were masters of sophisticated movement, but how was it done? How did Milt Kahl animate Pongo in *101 Dalmatians* waking up, yawning, scratching an itch, and stretching in one movement?

Complicated actions are easier to achieve than a beginner animator would think if they relied less on intuition and more on building upon basic principles. In this chapter we'll break down animating a seemingly complicated action.

Reference and Soundtrack

A character says, "I bid you, adieu!" while bowing with a theatrical hand flourish.

The first thing to do is to listen to the soundtrack and write out your dialogue phonetically on an X-sheet, establishing the timing of your scene. Write it out any way you'd like — but write it out!

(Inhale) "**EYE** bBld y**OO**, **UH** d**OO**!"

frame 1	(inhale)		frame 28	
2			29	
3			30	oo
4			31	
5			32	
6			33	
7			34	
8			35	
9			36	
10	I		37	
11			38	
12			39	
13	b		40	Eh
14	B		41	
15	i		42	
16	i		43	D
17	I		44	
18	D		45	o o
19	d		46	
20			47	
21			48	
22	Y		49	
23			50	
24			51	
25			74	
26			75	(end)
27	o o		76	

Figure 22.1

Study your reference — you do have reference!

DOI: 10.1201/9781003361893-23

From the reference, pick out the storytelling poses. Do not copy every frame of the live action! Select just the extreme poses and breakdowns.

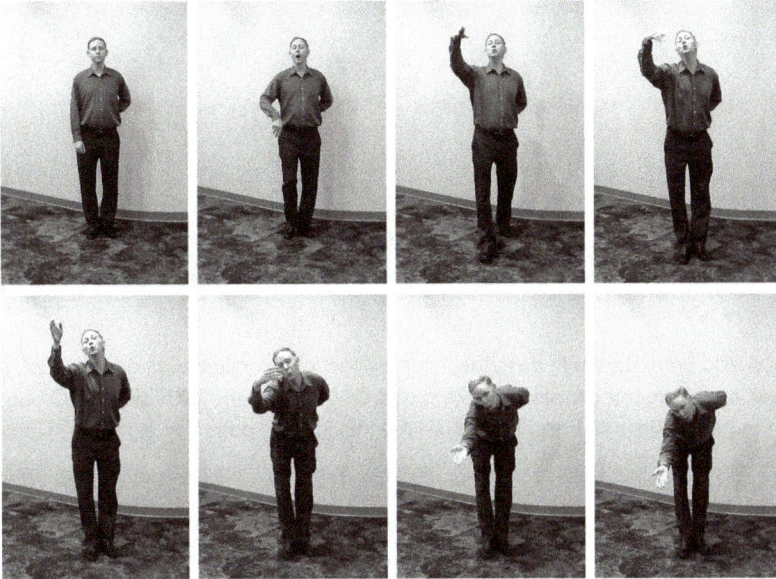

Figure 22.2

Storytelling Poses

Once you have all your reference images picked out, start blocking out your storytelling poses. The start pose and the bow pose tell the basic story. The dialogue ends around frame 58, so that's a good place to key bow pose.

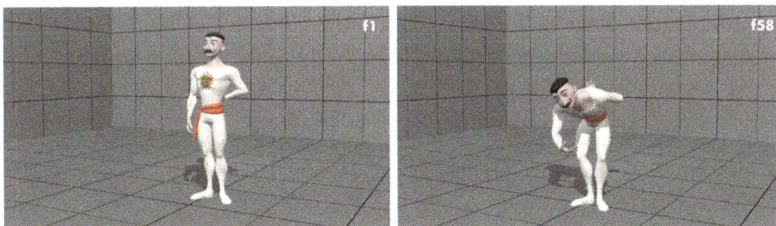

Figure 22.3

Breakdowns

Next add breakdowns. Work in stepped mode as you add breakdowns so that you focus on poses!

Which breakdown do we add first?

Our reference takes a step and raises their hand. This is an anticipation to the bow. It's also a good place to hit the "**OO**" in "**EYE** bBld y**OO**". The "**OO**" hits on frame 27 of the X-sheet. So, it makes sense to add the first breakdown on frame 27. Block in the expression and "**OO**" mouth shape, even if they change – it helps push the pose!

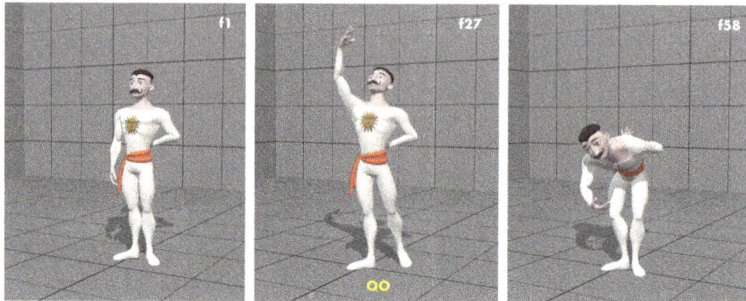

Figure 22.4

Next, we can add breakdowns to describe the transition to the anticipation on frame 27. If we move on the vowel, our character can start to take a step on the "**EYE**" in "**EYE** bBld y**OO**" on frame 10. Frame 10 can be a squash anticipation before the raised anticipation on frame 27. Contrast!

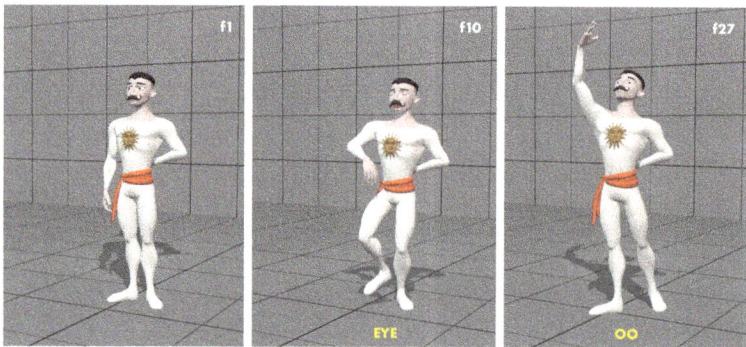

Figure 22.5

We can put the right foot down on frame 19. That's where the "d" in "bBld" hits. It's also about a third of the way between frame 14 and frame 27. The body could then drift through the "y**OO**" into frame 27.

The raised hand gesture should hit about three frames before the "y**OO**" or it will look off sync. If this doesn't have the snap you want, you can always move it. I made the right arm on frame 19 a breakdown favoring the up pose.

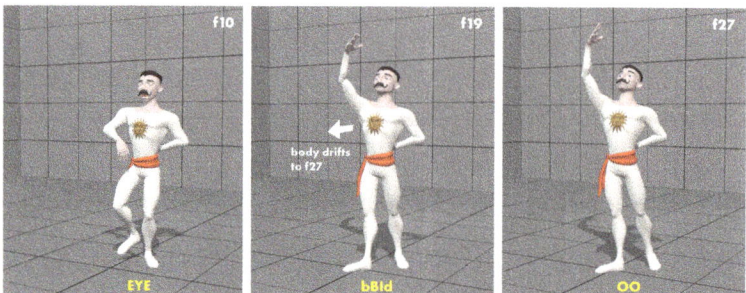

Figure 22.6

Our character can step forward with their left foot to bow. We can add another pose on frame 38 just before the "**UH**" in "**UH** d**OO**!" with the foot in position. If we want our character to take a quicker step, just move the foot flat key down until the timing feels right. For this example, I moved the foot flat key to frame 33.

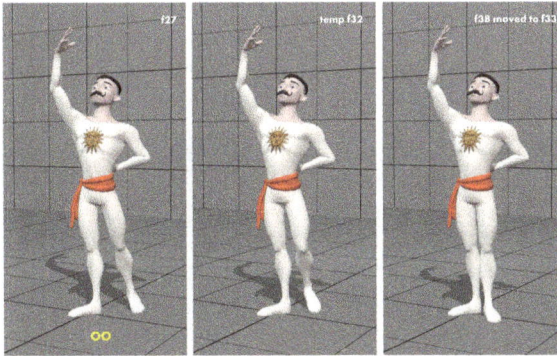

Figure 22.7

The "**OO**" in "**UH** d**OO**!" trails off at around frame 58. Again, you'll want the bow to hit at least three frames to be in sync with the dialogue. Do you want the body to hit the bow pose with a hard or soft accent? For this example we can add a hard accent at frame 51.

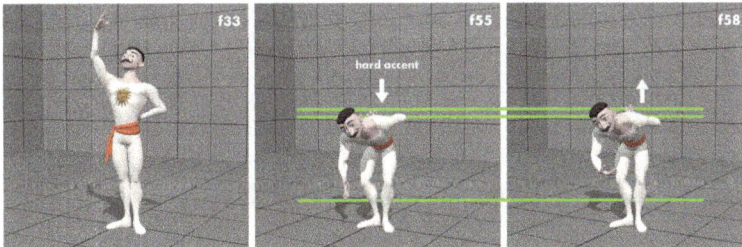

Figure 22.8

Did you notice that we haven't been worrying about inbetweens or the hand flourish yet?

Get the body working first while keeping secondary action in mind!

Your scene should be working now with just keys and breakdowns. If you film your scene, you may have to move the last few keys (frames 55 and 58) back temporarily to account for timing.

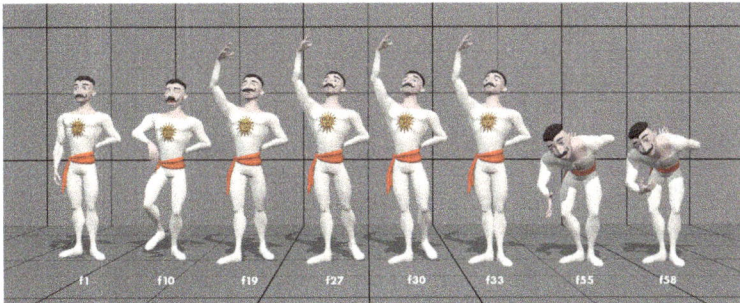

Figure 22.9

Secondary Action

Now we can add the secondary action of the hand flourish. We have at least twenty frames for the gesture - from around frame 38 to frame 58. For this example, we can have three circular motions as the character says, "adieu!!"

Block in one cycle of the hand flourish and get it looking nice. Use a translucent disc as a guide for the gesture. Then copy and paste the gesture two more times varying the size and speed of each cycle. There's nothing wrong with polishing the secondary action at this point.

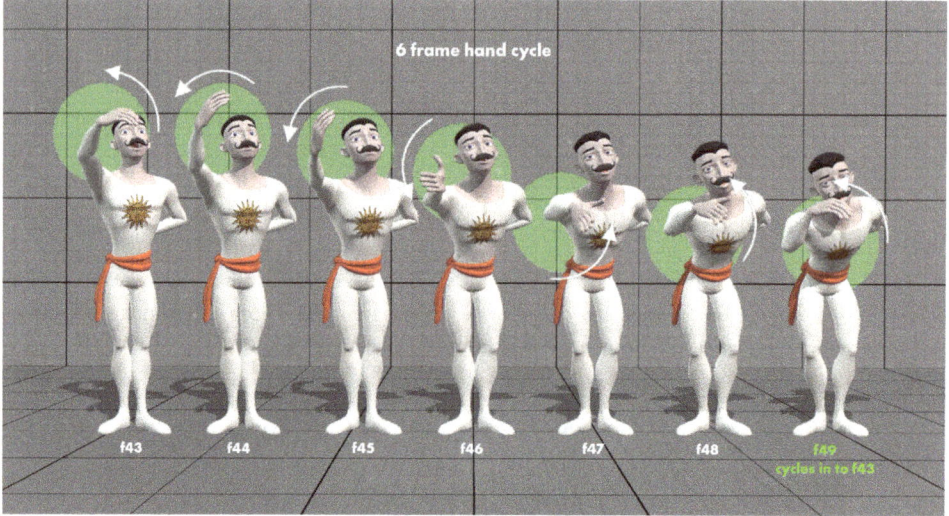

Figure 22.10

This is also a good point to flesh out the rest of the mouth shapes.

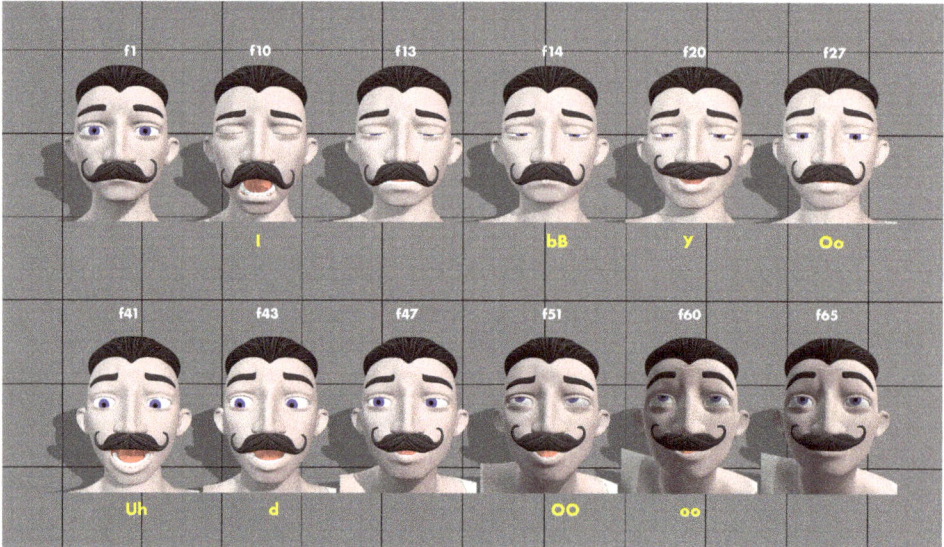

Figure 22.11

Inbetweening

Now you can begin to inbetween the scene. It may be good to work in sections, setting the tangents in the graph editor to spline.

For instance, frames 1-33, where the character takes the first step saying, "**EYE** bBld y**OO**," could be a section.

Keep it simple when inbetweening. Don't add unnecessary keys. Retain the timing in your block-in by slowing-in and slowing-out of poses and even spacing for constant speed.

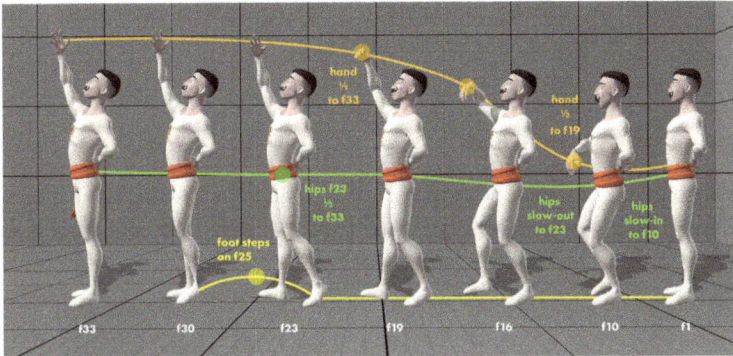

Figure 22.12

As you refine your animation, work from extreme to extreme, one tangent at a time.

For example, the character shifts their weight to take a step. The hips (X translation) are over the left foot on frame 10, then shift to the right foot on frame 30.

Delete all the in-betweens on the hips (X translation) from frame 10 to frame 30. Do this for every part of the body!

Simplify!

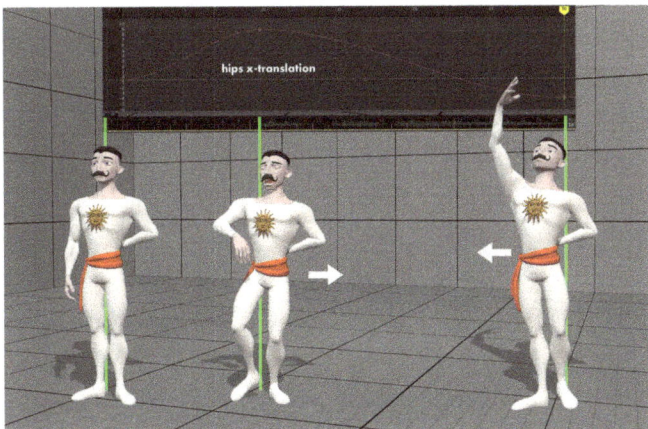

Figure 22.13

Add additional breakdowns when necessary.

For instance, the right arm may need another breakdown on frame 15 to define the path of action as it lifts.

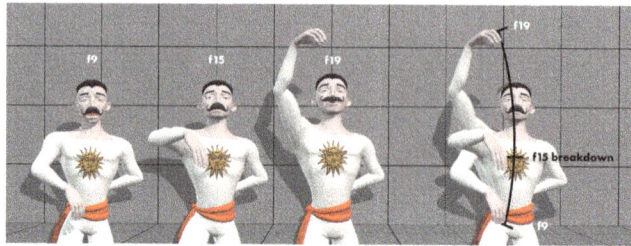

Figure 22.14

Overlap and Follow-through

Once you have your inbetweening done, see if your overlap can be pushed. The body hits a hard accent on frame 55. The head and left arm would react to that sudden change of direction. Add a bounce to the elbow a few frames after the body hits its lowest point.

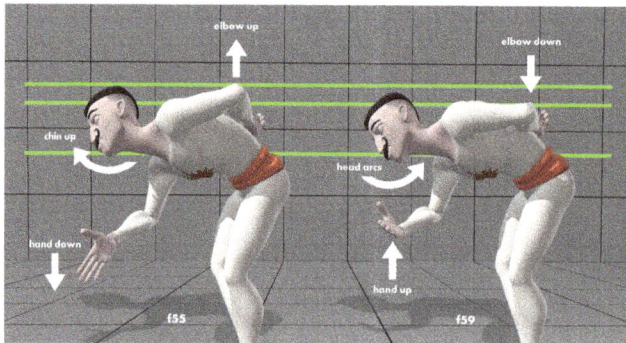

Figure 22.15

Animate any overlapping cloth or hair...

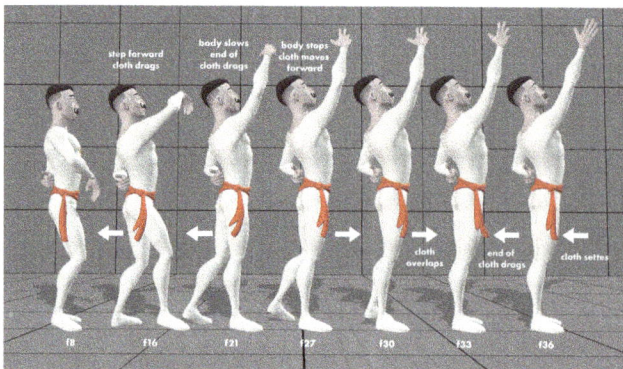

Figure 22.16

...and details such as secondary finger movement. Animate action not seen by the camera! You'll feel the action and the camera may change.

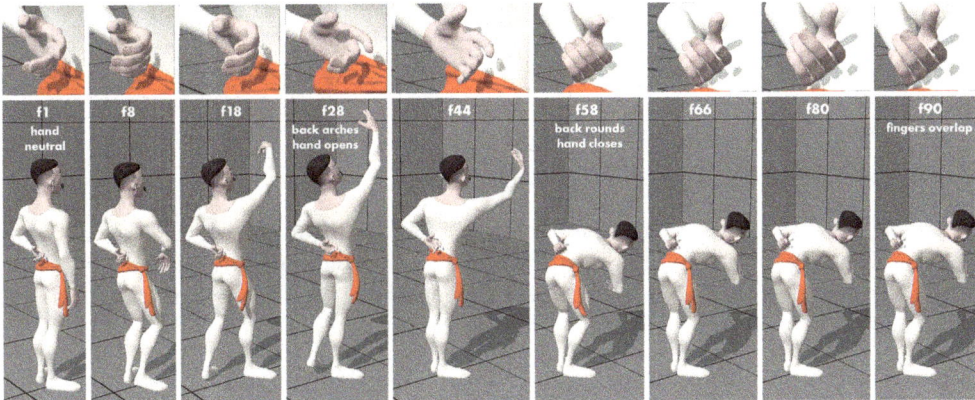

Figure 22.17

Add a blink to the end to keep the scene alive.

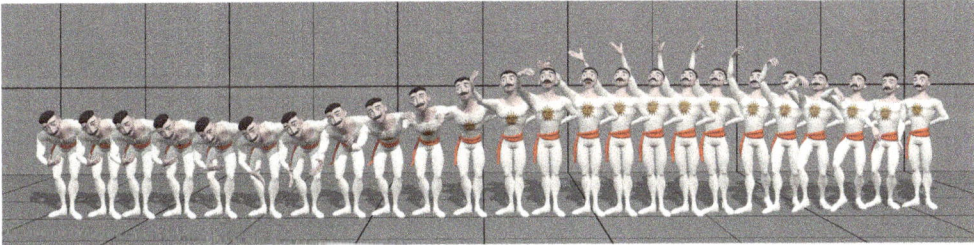

Figure 22.18

Obviously, there are many ways to animate a scene. To paraphrase Klaatu from **The Day the Earth Stood Still** [1951], "I don't pretend to have achieved perfection, but I have a system, and it works." For me, at least!

If this works for you or you can use this as a springboard — terrific!

Remember to keep it simple: your scene should work with just storytelling poses and breakdowns. Don't get bogged down with inbetweens trying to impress your audience!

Chapter 23. Critiquing a Scene

Introduction

How does your scene look? Did it turn out the way you wanted? Are you critiquing someone else's scene?

In this chapter we'll look at critiquing your scene, or someone else's — objectively.

Subjective versus Objective Criticism

"Some of your producers and directors may have worked their way up from the very bottom so that they understand animation," said Don Bluth. "They understand what the inbetweens are. They understand what story is. They understand all that. But sometimes out there, what you will run into is they don't really know, but they really want to be in charge."[1]

Subjective criticism is when someone gives a personal opinion rather than advice on how to fix your scene.

You animated a dragon walk cycle and they say, "I would have turned the feet in like a monitor lizard."

Figure 23.1

Well, maybe your dragon is not based on a monitor lizard.

Simon Otto, the head of character animation on **How to Train Your Dragon** (2010), said Toothless the Dragon, "was a mixture of a salamander and a black panther and a bird of prey."[2]

The audience may not have known that Toothless was based on a salamander, a black panther, and a bird of prey — but they accepted Toothless as a living character because his motion is believable.

"Make the audience forget that they're watching a drawing, or a line, or computer geometry,"[3] said Otto.

Unless you're animating someone else's character, animate *your* character *your* way.

Just make it believable.

Be mindful when you critique animation. Let it be their scene and not yours!

DOI: 10.1201/9781003361893-24

"I think it's terribly dangerous for an artist to fulfill other people's expectations," said David Bowie. "I think they generally produce their worst work when they do that."[4]

Objective criticism tells you what's wrong with your scene — why it's not working, why it's not believable. Poor acting choices may have to do with unconvincing animation, but most of the time it's something technical that takes you out of the scene.

Objective criticism is what we'll spend the rest of this chapter talking about.

Does the Scene Work?

If the scene is entertaining, easy to follow, and believable — move on! Do another scene.

Figure 23.2

Is the Scene Easy to Follow?

You shouldn't need to figure out what's going on in a scene. If a motion is too complicated or awkward, find a simpler and clearer path. Clear silhouette and staging! Fix anything that's confusing.

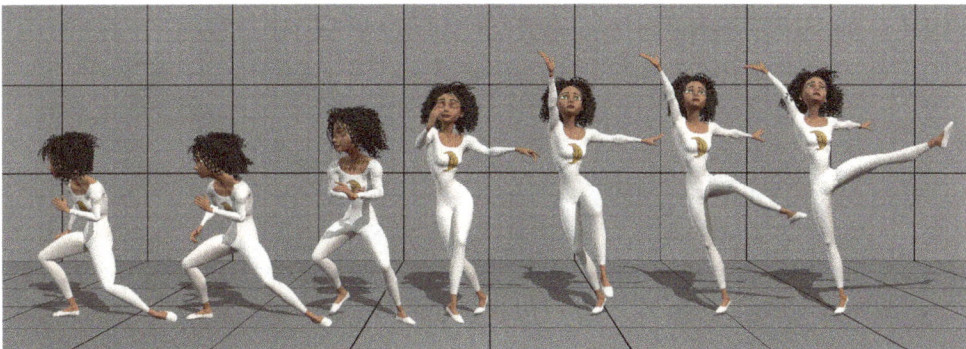

Figure 23.3

Do Poses Read Clearly?

If your poses aren't reading as intended, they're probably not strong enough. Even if your character is shy or meek, their poses need to be strong and interesting. Push your poses.

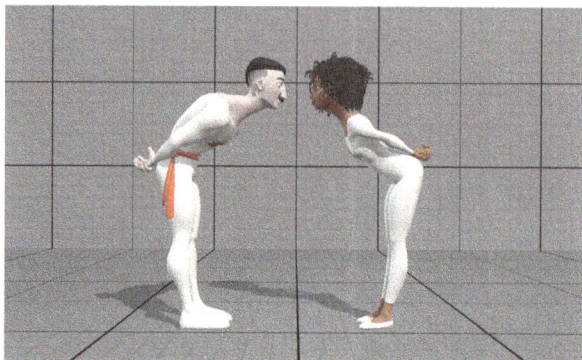

Figure 23.4

Do Emotions Read Clearly?

Do the facial expressions show the intended emotion? Do you have too many expressions? Clarify and simplify facial expressions.

Figure 23.5

Is the dialogue mushy? Favor mouth shapes so that dialogue looks crisp.

Figure 23.6

Is Your Character Too Stiff?

If your character is stiff, it's most likely because you're not getting a change of shape between poses.

Even for subtle actions, look for every opportunity for squash and stretch or a reversal in the body.

Animation is change!

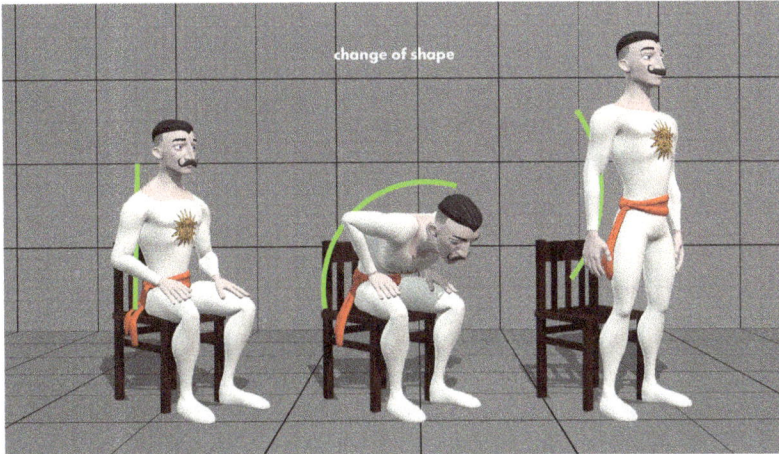

Figure 23.7

Check your Balance!

Is your character balanced throughout the scene from every angle? Weight shift is the key to believable animation!

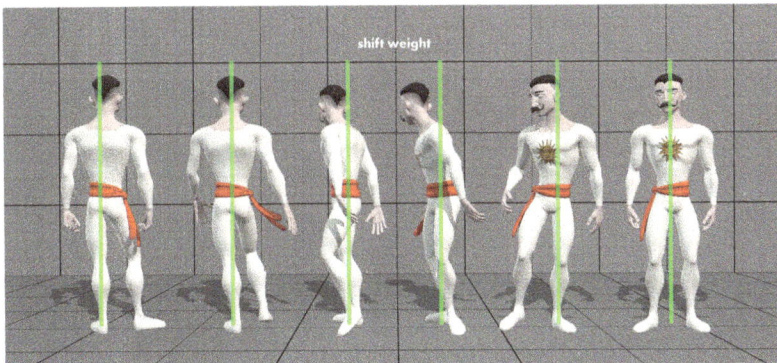

Figure 23.8

Compare the Upper and Lower Half of the Body

Cover the upper half of your character and look at the lower half. Are the hips moving and the weight shifting?

Don't move your character from just the waist up! Animate the lower half even if you won't see it because you'll feel it.

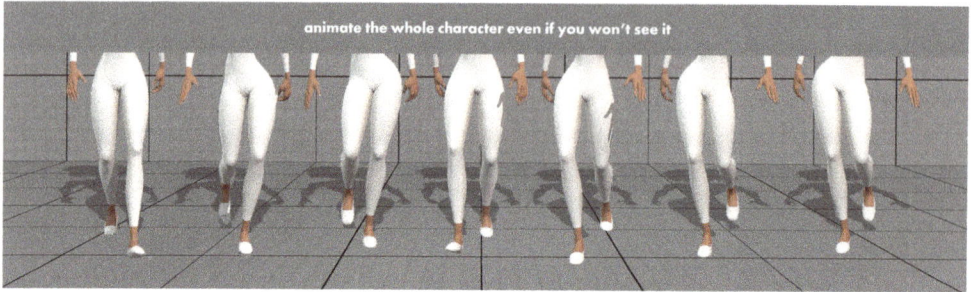

Figure 23.9

How's the Rhythm of the Scene?

Toggle back and forth. Do the key poses flow from one pose to the next? Adjust any part of a pose that breaks up the flow of the scene. Everything should follow an interesting path of action.

Figure 23.10

Is Anything Distracting?

Don't let any one thing draw attention away from the main action. If the main action of a scene is a kick, but an arm flying out draws your attention away from the foot — tone down the arm.

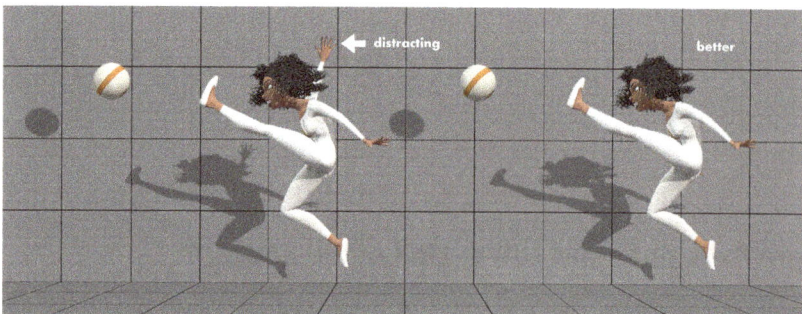

Figure 23.11

Is Your Scene Too Quick?

Actions moving too quickly may be difficult to follow. If you can, add time to actions that are too fast.

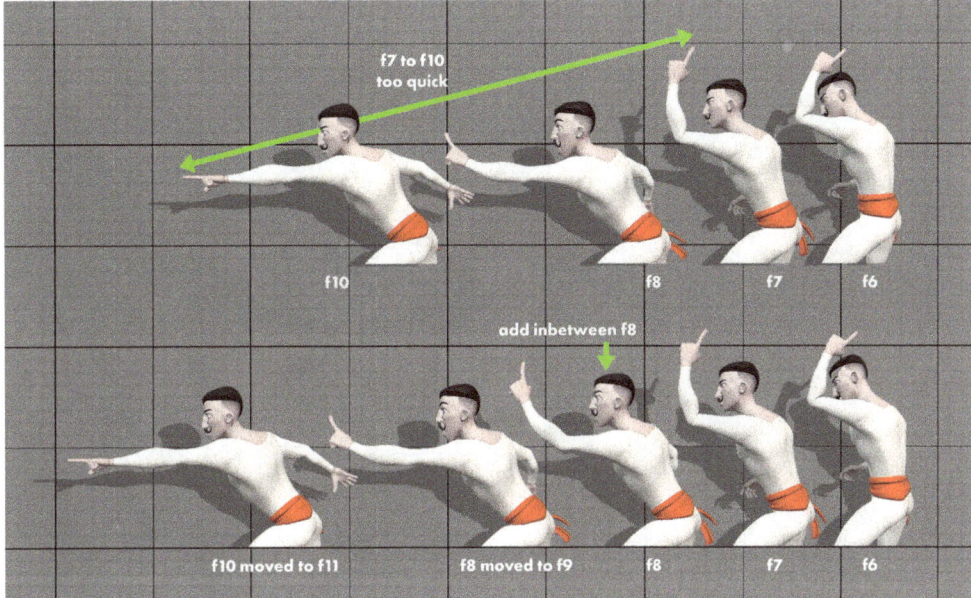

Figure 23.12

Are You Trying to Do Too Much?

If your scene isn't reading or seems too quick, you may also have too many actions in your scene.

It's painful, but cut any unnecessary actions. Don't over-animate!

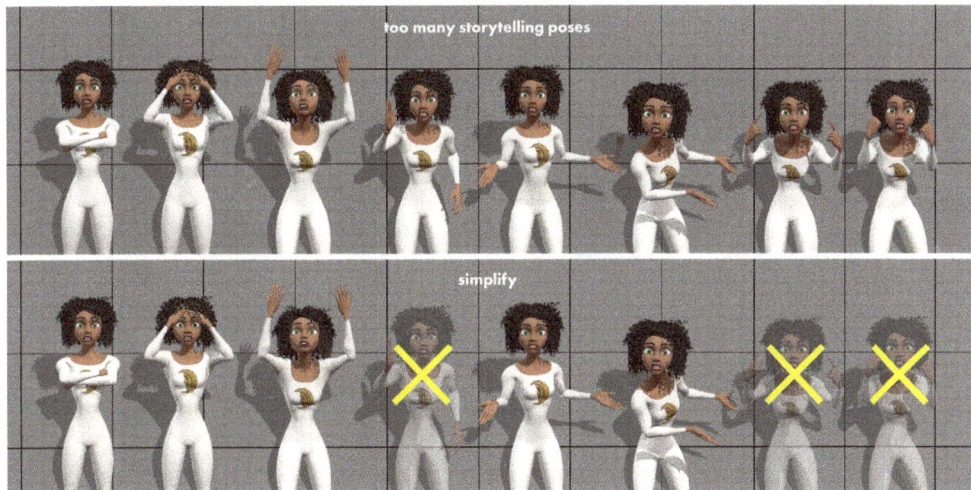

Figure 23.13

Is Your Scene Watery or Sluggish?

Watery or sluggish animation usually means your inbetweens are too evenly spaced. Slow-in and slow-out of poses you want the audience to see. Use even spacing for constant speed. Space inbetweens for snap!

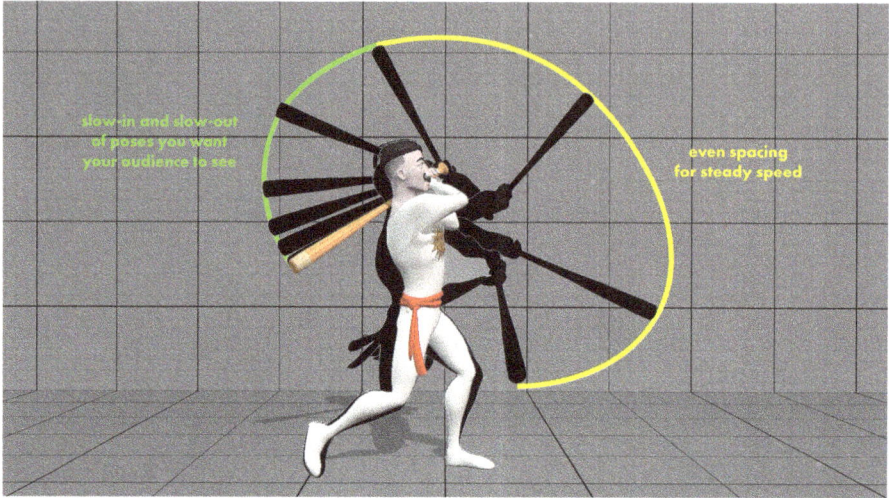

Figure 23.14

How Are Your Breakdowns?

Your key poses are working nicely, but are the breakdowns interesting and fluid? Breakdowns should augment the transition from one extreme to the next. Move the breakdown if the timing between extremes doesn't feel right.

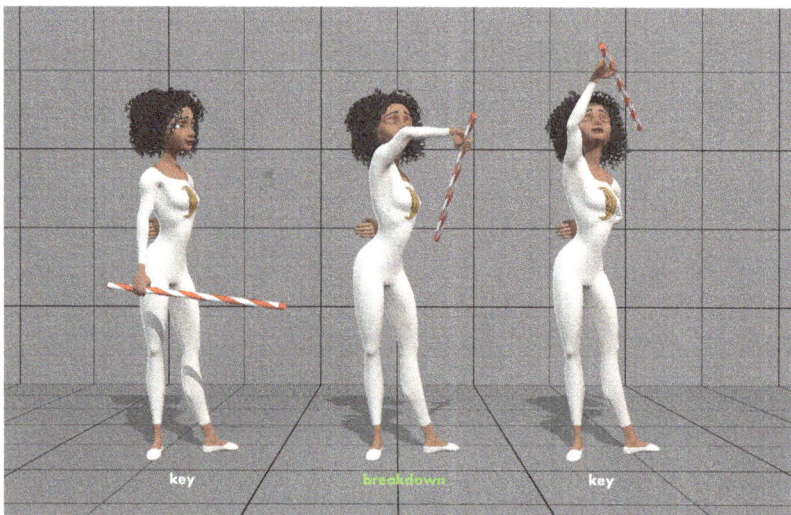

Figure 23.15

How Are Your Arcs?

Make arcs as smooth as possible. Check arcs in the graph editor. Simplify the curves for each tangent.

Is there a nice pattern to your arcs? Don't move out and back in the same direction.

Unless you're animating a machine, everything gets an arc — no matter how small!

Figure 23.16

Does Anything Move Together?

Offset anything moving together. For example, don't move the hips and the torso together, or the torso with the head — unless there's a reason. Show overlap!

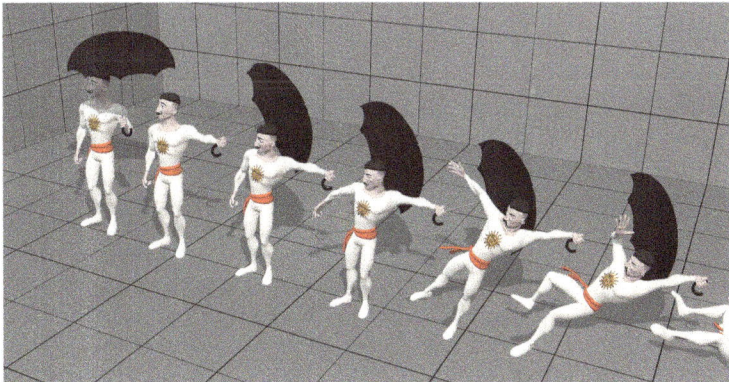

Figure 23.17

How's the Staging?

Is the animation shown off in the best possible way? Does the layout lead your eye to the main action or interfere with it? Check the head and lead room and watch out for tangents!

Figure 23.18

Check the Graph Editor

Even if your scene looks good, it's always good to look through your graph editor for glitches. Anything strange in the curve most likely will mean something strange is going on in your animation.

Figure 23.19

Did You Stick to Your Plan?

Did you stick to your plan, or did you start changing your scene around as you animated? Not having a clear plan is an easy way to get into trouble.

Plan your scene well and stick to it!

Show your scene to someone during the planning stage — before you start animating!

Frank and Ollie would drive to work together, talk about their scenes, and later show each other what they had come up with. "Weren't you going to do something here?" Ollie recalled telling Frank. And Frank may "point out what he liked about my drawings — which I didn't see," he said. "I couldn't have done it by myself."[5]

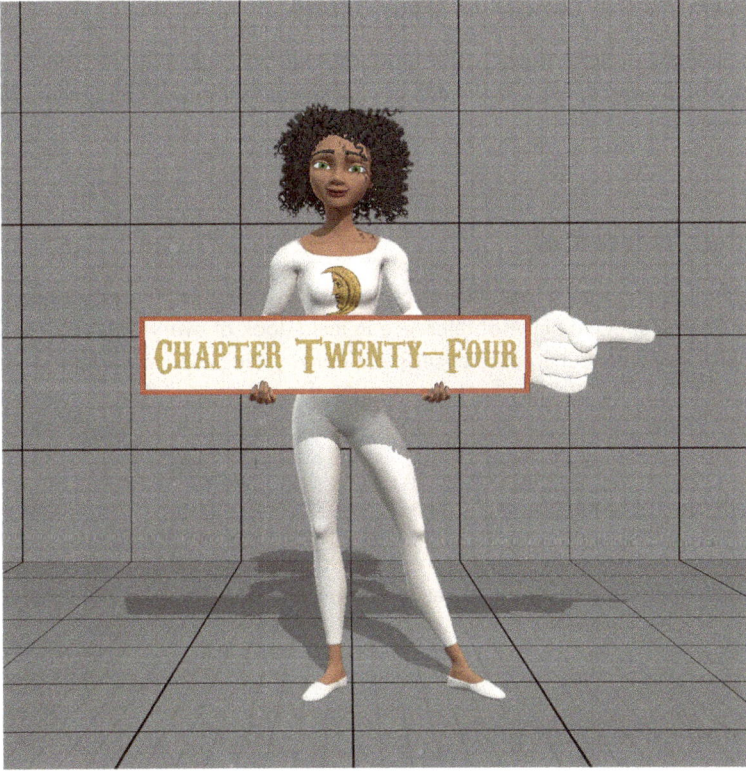
CHAPTER TWENTY-FOUR

Chapter 24. Scene Checklist

1. Where to Begin?

If you're working on a film, game, or any other type of project — get all the information you can up front: characters, length of scene, action, dialogue, layout, props, any reference they may have, etc.

If it's a personal test, do what you want to do. Otherwise, unless you're working for yourself or on a side project, you'll be animating someone else's idea.

2. Determine the Length of your Scene

If you have a dialogue or music track, you'll know how long your scene will be. Without a dialogue or music track, you'll need to know the length of your scene so that you can gather reference and plan your action.

3. Gather Reference!

It doesn't matter if your scene is for a film or game, or a personal test — gather reference. If you don't already have a specific piece of reference in mind, look at everything you can before you start. Thumbnail if you want but use reference! There's always an action, a posture, a weight shift, a gesture, etc. you'll find that you may not have thought of.

4. Analyze Reference

When analyzing video reference, don't copy every frame — pick out just the keys. Use the head or hips to find the highs and lows, the extreme forward and backward, or side to side movement as markers.

5. Do you have Dialogue?

 If you have dialogue, add your dialogue track to your time slider and then read your track. Scrub through the time slider and write down (on an X-sheet, notepad, or what have you) your dialogue phonetically noting the corresponding frame. This will save you a lot of time when you start keying your poses!

6. Click tracks

If you don't have a dialogue track, try using a click track. Add a sound file of a metronome beat to your scene. Pick a tempo, then animate your storytelling poses to the beat.

DOI: 10.1201/9781003361893-25

7. Set Your Staging

Plan where your character will start and end in the scene so that any background objects frame your character and don't interfere. Add an initial camera so that you can block in your animation to best show the action. Don't be preoccupied with the camera, camera cuts, camera moves, or effects. Animate!

8. Key Your Storytelling Poses

Using your reference extremes as a guide, pose out your storytelling extremes and push them beyond the reference!

Everyone works differently, but try posing your extremes in stepped mode! Don't worry about inbetweens — focus on getting strong poses and rhythm. Block in timing, even if it may change.

9. Block In Facial Expressions or Dialogue

As you pose out your storytelling poses, block in your facial expressions or dialogue mouth poses. Even if mouth shapes change, block them in to help push your poses!

10. Get a Change of Shape!

Get a change of shape in your poses! Animation is change! Toggle back and forth checking the change from one extreme to the next. Make sure they flow.

11. Watch Your Weight!

Keep the weight over the supporting limb unless your character is falling over. Check your scene from every angle to get proper weight shift. Shifting the weight adds believability!

12. Add Breakdowns

Once you have your extremes blocked in, start adding breakdowns to transition from one extreme to the next. Be creative with breakdowns. Look for something different! If your extremes and breakdowns are posed out nicely, your scene will work in stepped mode without inbetweens.

13. Rhythm

Vary timing. Spend time in the poses you want your audience to see. Shift extremes or breakdowns to get a nice rhythm.

14. Overlap

Check your overlap as you add breakdowns. Unless there's a reason, make sure nothing moves at the same speed.

15. Add Inbetweens

The last thing you should do is to add inbetweens. Do not start adding inbetweens before your extremes and breakdowns are perfect!

Slow-in and slow-out of poses you want your audience to see; use evenly spaced inbetweens for constant speed.

16. Polish Pass(es)

As good as your scene may have come out, you'll probably have to go through it at least once or twice (or 342 times if you're Charlie Chaplin!) to touch it up and adjust anything that may need adjusting. Maybe it's an arc that can be improved or a pose that can be pushed. Maybe it's polishing overlap on hair or clothing or adjusting your final camera. Whatever it is — don't settle!

"I feel very strongly that anything that you do, anything you do for an audience, is the best you can do," said Chuck Jones. "I think Somerset Maugham said that he stopped doing a short story when he could say to himself, "This is not the best I can do, it's the best I can do now."[1]

Footnotes

Introduction

1. Stella Adler, The Art of Acting, p. 260-261

Chapter 1

1. Richard Hubler, Interview with Milt Kahl, Walt's People Vol. 7, p. 176

2. Michael Barrier, Interview with Frank Thomas and Ollie Johnston, Walt's People Vol. 17, p. 64

3. Frank Thomas and Ollie Johnston, The Illusion of Life, p. 47

4. John Canemaker, Grim Natwick, Film Comment Magazine: Jan-Feb 1975, p. 61

Chapter 2

1. Donald Crafton, Before Mickey, the Animated Film 1898-1928, p. 7

2. Donald Crafton, Before Mickey, the Animated Film 1898-1928, p. 80

3. Donald Crafton, Before Mickey, the Animated Film 1898-1928, p. 60

4. John Canemaker, Winsor McCay His Life and Art, p. 184

5. John Canemaker, Winsor McCay His Life and Art, p. 177

6. John Canemaker, Winsor McCay His Life and Art, p. 177

7. John Canemaker, Winsor McCay His Life and Art, p. 179

8. Eleanor Keaton and Jeffrey Vance, Buster Keaton Remembered, p. 114

9. Frank Thomas and Ollie Johnston, The Illusion of Life, p. 22

10. Donald Crafton, Before Mickey, the Animated Film 1898-1928, p. 137

11. http://brayanimation.weebly.com/studio-history.html

12. Charles Solomon, Enchanted Drawings, The History of Animation, p. 28

13. Reg Hartt Presents Grim Natwick interviewed by Michael Gowling Toronto 1982 https://www.youtube.com/watch?v=4CEYYLr9tRU

14. John Canemaker, Felix: The Twisted Tale of the World's Most Famous Cat, p. 72-73

15. Donald Crafton, Shadow of a Mouse, p. 23

16. Frank Thomas and Ollie Johnston, The Illusion of Life, p. 43

17. Frank Thomas and Ollie Johnston, The Illusion of Life, p. 42

18. John Canemaker, Felix: The Twisted Tale of the World's Most Famous Cat, p. 69

19. John Canemaker, Felix: The Twisted Tale of the World's Most Famous Cat, p. 18

20. Michael Barrier, Hollywood Cartoons: American Animation in Its Golden Age, p. 193

21. Leonard Maltin, Of Mice and Magic: A History of American Animated Cartoons, p. 100

22. Leonard Maltin, Of Mice and Magic: A History of American Animated Cartoons, p. 189

23. Chuck Jones Interview, The Hand Behind the Mouse: The Ub Iwerks Story. 1999

24. Miriam Leslie Clark, Glimpses into the Golden Age of Disney Animation, p. 116

25. Leonard Maltin, Of Mice and Magic: A History of American Animated Cartoons, p. 193

26. Don Iwerks, Walt Disney's Ultimate Inventor: The Genius of Ub Iwerks, p. 54

27. Maureen Furness, Chuck Jones Conversations, Unpublished Interview with Ron Barbagallo 1999, p. 203

28. Frank Thomas and Ollie Johnston, The Illusion of Life, p. 35

29. Neal Gabler, Walt Disney: The Triumph of the American Imagination, p. 127

30. Don Hahn and Tracey Miller-Zarneke, Before Ever After: The Lost Lectures of Walt Disney's Animation Studio, p. 192

31. Les Clark Interviewed by Frank Thomas and Ollie Johnston September 18, 1978, Walt's People Vol. 8, p. 53

32. John Canemaker, Walt Disney's Nine Old Men & the Art of Animation, p. 16

33. John Canemaker, Walt Disney's Nine Old Men & the Art of Animation, p. 17

34. Miriam Leslie Clark, Glimpses into the Golden Age of Disney Animation, p. 116 -117

35. Don Hahn and Tracey Miller-Zarneke, Before Ever After: The Lost Lectures of Walt Disney's Animation Studio — Inter-Office Communication from Walt Disney to Donald Graham Dec 23, 1935, p. 66

36. John Canemaker, Walt Disney's Nine Old Men & the Art of Animation, p. 21

37. Don Peri, Working with Disney, p. 39

38. Don Hahn and Tracey Miller-Zarneke, Before Ever After: The Lost Lectures of Walt Disney's Animation Studio — Inter-Office Communication from Walt Disney to Donald Graham Dec 23, 1935, p. 64

39. Walt Disney, Growing Pains, American Cinematographer, March 1941, p. 107

40. Robert Perine, Chouinard: An Art Vision Betrayed, p. 25

41. Walt Disney, Growing Pains, American Cinematographer, March 1941, p. 107

42. Don Peri, Working with Disney, p. 6

43. Martin Krause and Linda Witkowski, Walt Disney's Snow White and the Seven Dwarfs: An Art in Its Making, p. 44

44. Don Peri, Working with Disney, p. 38

45. Leonard Maltin, Of Mice and Magic: A History of American Animated Cartoons, p. 53

46. Aljean Harmetz, The New York Times, Disney's "Old Men" Savor the Vintage Years, Sunday, July 4, 1993

47. Robert Perine, Chouinard: An Art Vision Betrayed, p. 28

48. Martin Krause and Linda Witkowski, Walt Disney's Snow White and the Seven Dwarfs: An Art in Its Making, p. 46

49. Barbara Kaplan Lane, The New York Times, Belated Salute for a Pioneer Animator, Sunday, Jan 31, 1993

50. Richard Fleischer, Out of the Inkwell: Max Fleischer and the Animation Revolution, p. 13

51. Richard Fleischer, Out of the Inkwell: Max Fleischer and the Animation Revolution, p. 14

52. Richard Fleischer, Out of the Inkwell: Max Fleischer and the Animation Revolution, p. 15

53. Mike Higgs, Bill Blackbeard Introduction to Popeye, 1995, p. 6

54. Chris Chaplin, Michael Crawford, Constantine Nasr, Mark Nassief, Out of the Inkwell: The Fleischer Story Harvey Deneroff Interview, 2008

55. Shamus Culhane, Talking Animals and Other People, p. 40

56. Michael Barrier, Hollywood Cartoons: American Animation in Its Golden Age, p. 179

57. Shamus Culhane, Talking Animals and Other People, p. 41

58. Shamus Culhane, Talking Animals and Other People, p. 41

59. Michael Barrier, Hollywood Cartoons: American Animation in Its Golden Age, p. 179

60. Shamus Culhane, Animation from Script to Screen, p. 207

61. Shamus Culhane, Talking Animals and Other People, p. 61

62. Shamus Culhane, Talking Animals and Other People, p. 62

63. Neil Gabler, Walt Disney, p. 179

64. Michael Barrier, Hollywood Cartoons: American Animation in Its Golden Age, p. 293

65. Richard Fleischer, Out of the Inkwell: Max Fleischer and the Animation Revolution, p. 96

66. Ray Pointer, The Art and Inventions of Max Fleischer: American Animation Pioneer, p. 186

67. Michael Barrier, Hollywood Cartoons: American Animation in Its Golden Age, p. 296

68. Michael Barrier, Interview with Frank Tashlin, May 29, 1971

69. Janet Maslin, Film: Animation Art of the Fleischers, NY Times, March 20, 1980

70. Jerry Beck, "Fleischer Becomes Famous Studios." Cartoon Research. June 21, 2007

71. Constantine Nasr, Mark Nasr, I Yam What I Yam: The Story of Popeye the Sailor, (2007) interview with Eric Goldberg

72. Mark Langer, Max and Dave Fleischer, Film Comment Magazine: Jan-Feb 1975, p. 54

73. Shamus Culhane, Talking Animals and Other People, p. 400

74. Jake S. Friedman, The Disney Revolt, p. 50

75. Imogen Sutton, Animating Art 1988 (Documentary)

76. Tom Sito - https://d23.com/walt-disney-legend/art-babbitt/

77. Milton Zolotow and Lawrence Weschler interview of Jules Engel, Walt's People Vol. 13, p. 164

78. Imogen Sutton, Animating Art, 1988 (Documentary) interview with Richard Williams

79. Sophie Determan, The Many Merry Eras of Disney, https://www.bfi.org.uk/features/many-merry-eras-disney

80. Jake S. Friedman, The Disney Revolt, p. 245

81. Jake S. Friedman, The Disney Revolt, p. 245

82. Jake S. Friedman, The Disney Revolt, p. 246

83. Milt Kahl Interview with Michael Barrier and Milton Gray, Nov. 4, 1976

84. John Canemaker, The American Animated Cartoon: A Critical Anthology - Vlad Tytla: Animation's Michelangelo, p. 94

85. Frank Thomas and Ollie Johnston, The Illusion of Life, p. 133

86. Richard Boleslavsky, Acting: The Frist Six Lessons, p. 77

87. Don Hahn and Tracey Miller-Zarneke, Before Ever After: The Lost Lectures of Walt Disney's Animation Studio, p. 148

88. John Canemaker, Vladimir Tytla: Master Animator, p. 19

89. John Culhane, Walt Disney's Fantasia, p. 185

90. John Culhane, Walt Disney's Fantasia, p. 194

91. Richard Boleslavsky, Acting: The Frist Six Lessons, p. 75

92. Richard Boleslavsky, Acting: The Frist Six Lessons, p. 78-79

93. Don Hahn and Tracey Miller-Zarneke, Before Ever After: The Lost Lectures of Walt Disney's Animation Studio, p. 141

94. Michael Sporn, Stanislavsky, Boleslavsky and Tytla's Smears & Distortions, http://www.michaelspornanimation.com/splog/?p=5803

95. Time Magazine, Cinema: Mammal of the Year, Dec 29, 1941

96. Frank Thomas and Ollie Johnston, The Illusion of Life, p. 133

97. Shamus Culhane, Animation from Script to Screen, p. 209

98. John Culhane, Walt Disney's Fantasia, p. 104

99. Mark Mayerson, Dumbo Part 8, June 13, 2010, http://mayersononanimation.blogspot.com/2010/06/dumbo-part-8.html

100. Shamus Culhane, Animation from Script to Screen, p. 172

101. John Canemaker, Vladimir Tytla: Master Animator, Katonah Museum of Art, p. 23

102. John Canemaker, Vladimir Tytla: Animation's Michelangelo, Cinefantastique Winter, 1976, p. 16

103. John Canemaker, Vladimir Tytla: Animation's Michelangelo, Cinefantastique Winter, 1976, p. 16

104. John Canemaker, Vladimir Tytla: Animation's Michelangelo, Cinefantastique Winter, 1976, p. 18

105. John Culhane, Walt Disney's Fantasia, p. 188

106. Christopher Finch and Linda Rosenkranz, Interview with Frank Thomas, Walt's People Vol. 6, p. 105

107. Don Peri, Working with Disney, p. 22

108. Frank Thomas and Ollie Johnston, The Illusion of Life, p. 120

109. John Canemaker, Walt Disney's Nine Old Men & the Art of Animation, p. 16

110. Neal Gabler, Walt Disney: The Triumph of the American Imagination, p. 182

111. Steve Hulett interview with Ward Kimball, Walt's People Vol. 6, p. 70

112. Charles Solomon, The History of Animation: Enchanted Drawings, p. 50

113. Frank Thomas and Ollie Johnston, The Illusion of Life, p. 120

114. John Canemaker, Walt Disney's Nine Old Men & the Art of Animation, p. 175

115. Christopher Finch and Linda Rosenkranz interview with Eric Larson, Walt's People Vol. 11, p. 68

116. Miriam Leslie Clark, Glimpses into the Golden Age of Disney Animation, p. 27

117. Steve Hulett Interview with Mark Kirkland, Walt's People Vol. 8, p. 123

118. Miriam Leslie Clark, Glimpses into the Golden Age of Disney Animation, p. 2

119. Christopher Finch and Linda Rosenkranz Interview with Ollie Johnston, Walt's People Vol. 6, p. 120

120. Los Angeles Times, Disney Artist's Funeral Set, November 25th, 1952

121. John Culhane Interview with Bill Justice, Walt's People Vol. 14, p. 228

122. Christopher Finch and Linda Rosenkranz Interview with Eric Larson, Walt's People Vol. 11, p. 74

123. Neal Gabler, Walt Disney: The Triumph of the American Imagination, p. 419

124. John Canemaker, Walt Disney's Nine Old Men & the Art of Animation, vii

125. Pete Docter, John Sibley – The Tenth Old Man, Walt's People Vol. 13, p. 277

126. John Canemaker, Interview with Glen Keane, Walt's People Vol. 11, p. 512

127. Jim Korkis, Interview with Marc Davis, Walt's People Vol. 7, p. 274

128. Armand Eisen, Interview with Marc Davis, Walt's People Vol. 7, p. 130

129. John Canemaker, Interview with Richard Williams, Walt's People Vol. 11, p. 335

130. Andreas Deja, The Nine Old Men: Lessons, Techniques, and Inspirations from Disney's Great Animators, p. 248

131. Theodore Thomas, Interview with Frank Thomas, Frank and Ollie (1995)

132. Michael Barrier interview with Frank Thomas and Ollie Johnston, Walt's People Vol. 17, p. 74

133. John Canemaker, Walt Disney's Nine Old Men & the Art of Animation, p. 53

134. Christopher Finch and Linda Rosenkranz, Interview with Milt Kahl, Walt's People Vol. 6, p. 125

135 Bob Thomas, Interview with John Lounsbery, Walt's People Vol. 10, p. 61

136. Christian Renaut Interview with Burny Mattinson, Walt's People Vol. 3, p. 227

137. Didier Getz, Interview with John Ewing, Walt's People Vol. 7, p. 313

138. John Canemaker, Interview with Ward Kimball, Walt's People Vol. 11, p. 203

139. Frank Thomas and Ollie Johnston, The Illusion of Life, p. 169

140. Andreas Deja, Deja View Blogspot, Jan 30, 2016, http://andreasdeja.blogspot.com/2016/01/lady-tramp-art.html

141. Frank Thomas and Ollie Johnston, The Illusion of Life, p. 174

142. Frank Thomas and Ollie Johnston, The Illusion of Life, p. 169

143. Eric Larson, 50 Years in the Mouse House, p. 53

144. Wes Sullivan, Interview with Dale Oliver, Walt's People Vol. 2, p. 222-223

145. John Canemaker, Walt Disney's Nine Old Men & the Art of Animation, p. 55

146. John Canemaker, Walt Disney's Nine Old Men & the Art of Animation, p. 77

147. John Canemaker, Interview with Richard Williams, Walt's People Vol. 11, p. 327

148. Rick Shale, Interview with Ward Kimball, Walt's People Vol. 5, p. 40

149. John Canemaker, Interview with Ward Kimball, Walt's People Vol. 11, p. 201

150. Todd James Pierce, The Life and Times of Ward Kimball: Maverick of Disney Animation, p. 45

151. Todd James Pierce, The Life and Times of Ward Kimball: Maverick of Disney Animation, p. 46

152. Thorkil B. Rasmussen, Interview with Ward Kimball, Walt's People Vol. 3, p. 33

153. Thorkil B. Rasmussen, Interview with Ward Kimball, Walt's People Vol. 3, p. 33

154. John Canemaker, Walt Disney's Nine Old Men & the Art of Animation, p. 192

155. John Canemaker, Interview with Ward Kimball, Walt's People Vol. 11, p. 204

156. Time Magazine, Cinema: Disney Strikes Back, Dec 07, 1953

157. Thorkil B. Rasmussen interview with Ward Kimball, Walt's People Vol. 3, p. 42

158. Michael Barrier, Interview with Ward Kimball, Walt's People Vol. 2, p. 110

159. Celbi Vagner Pegoraro, Interview with Floyd Norman, Walt's People Vol. 3, p. 205

160. Frank Thomas and Ollie Johnston, Interview with Les Clark, Walt's People Vol. 8, p. 66

161. John Canemaker, Walt Disney's Nine Old Men & the Art of Animation, p. 27

162. Pete Docter, John Sibley – The Tenth Old Man, Walt's People Vol. 13, p. 277-278

163. Robert Allen, interview with Bob Jones, Walt's People Vol. 9, p. 161

164. Didier Ghez, interview with Blaine Gibson, Walt's People Vol. 13, p. 449

165. John Canemaker, Interview with Richard Williams, Walt's People Vol. 11, p. 335

166. John Canemaker, Walt Disney's Nine Old Men & the Art of Animation, p. 167

167. Christian Renaut interview with Frank Thomas, Walt's People Vol. 2, p. 209

168. Christopher Finch and Linda Rosenkranz, Interview with Frank Thomas, Walt's People Vol. 6, p. 103

169. Pete Docter, Interview with Art Stevens, Walt's People Vol. 7, p. 333

170. Disney Family Album | Milt Kahl | Disney Animator | Director | Pinocchio | Cinderella | Disneyland - YouTube

171. Robin Allan and Dr. William Moritz, Interview with Milt Kahl, Walt's People Vol. 1, p. 220-221

172. Andreas Deja, Correspondence with Ted Thomas, https://andreasdeja.blogspot.com/2017/10/golden-poses.html

173. Charles Solomon, An Afternoon with Ollie Johnston, Frank Thomas & Pinocchio, ANIMATIONWorld, July 1998 https://www.awn.com/animationworld/afternoon-ollie-johnston-frank-thomas-and-pinocchio

174. Göran Broling, Correspondence with Frank Thomas, Walt's People Vol. 8, p. 368

175. John Province Interview with Marc Davis, Walt's People Vol. 1, p. 195

176. John Canemaker, Interview with Richard Williams, Walt's People Vol. 11, p. 323

177. Jack Hannah, Milt Kahl lecture at CalArts, April 2, 1976, Walt's People Vol. 7, p. 164

178. John Canemaker, Interview with Dale Oliver, Walt's People Vol. 11, p. 316

179. Iwao Takamoto, My Life with a Thousand Characters, p. 61

180. Christopher Finch and Linda Rosenkranz, Interview with Frank Thomas, Walt's People Vol. 6, p. 125

181. Amid Amidi, Inside UPA, p. 2

182. Michael Barrier, Interview with John Hubley, November 1976

183. Adam Abraham, When Magoo Flew: The Rise and Fall of Animation Studio UPA, p. 50

184. Adam Abraham, When Magoo Flew: The Rise and Fall of Animation Studio UPA, p. 50

185. Leonard Maltin Interview with Zack Schwartz, Walt's People Vol. 14, p. 23

186. Amid Amidi, Cartoon Modern, p. 115

187. John Culhane Interview with John Hubley, Walt's People Vol. 11, p. 88

188. Amid Amidi, Cartoon Modern, p. 115

189. John Culhane Interview with John Hubley, Walt's People Vol. 11, p. 88

190. Amid Amidi, Cartoon Modern, p. 117

191. Gerald Perry & Danny Perry, John D. Ford Interview with John Hubley, The American Animated Cartoon, p. 182

192. Gerald Perry & Danny Perry, David Fisher, Two Premieres: Disney and UPA, The American Animated Cartoon, p. 178

193. Michael Barrier, Hollywood Cartoons: American Animation in Its Golden Age, p. 525

194. Television Academy, Interview with Bill Melendez https://interviews.televisionacademy.com/interviews/bill-melendez?clip=35764#interview-clips

195. Television Academy, Interview with Bill Melendez https://interviews.televisionacademy.com/interviews/bill-melendez?clip=35764#interview-clips

196. Mark Langer Interview with Bill Hurtz, Walt's People Vol. 24, p. 72

197. Gene Seymour, No Hands and No Feet, but "Powerpuff Girls" Have Plenty of Wit, LA Times July 3, 2002

198. Eric P. Nash, The Lives they Lived: William Hanna, B. 1910; Stone-Age Visionary, NY Times Dec 30, 2001

199. Maureen Furniss, Chuck Jones Conversations Michael Barrier & Bill Spicer: An Interview w/ Chuck Jones, p. 39

200. Bill Hanna with Tom Ito, A Cast of Friends, p. 20

201. Bill Hanna with Tom Ito, A Cast of Friends, p. 28

202. Leonard Maltin, Of Mice and Magic: A History of American Animated Cartoons, p. 283

203. Animation Resources, Biography: Carlo Vinci, https://animationresources.org/biography-carlo-vinci-2/

204. Cat and Mouse: The Tail of Tom and Jerry documentary (2007), Interview with Joe Barbera

205. How Bill and Joe Met documentary (2004), Interview with Joe Barbera

206. Leonard Maltin, Of Mice and Magic: A History of American Animated Cartoons, p. 288

207. Bill Hanna with Tom Ito, A Cast of Friends, p. 41

208. Joe Barbera, My Life in 'Toons: From Flatbush to Bedrock in Under a Century, p. 74

209. Bill Hanna with Tom Ito, A Cast of Friends, p. 72

210. Bill Hanna with Tom Ito, A Cast of Friends, p. 72

211. Bill Hanna with Tom Ito, A Cast of Friends, p. 60

212. Leonard Maltin, Of Mice and Magic: A History of American Animated Cartoons, p. 289

213. Cat and Mouse: The Tail of Tom and Jerry documentary (2007), Interview with Eric Goldberg

214. Leonard Maltin, Of Mice and Magic: A History of American Animated Cartoons, p. 298

215. T.R. Adams, Tom and Jerry: Fifty Years of Cat and Mouse, p. 28

216. Bill Hanna with Tom Ito, A Cast of Friends, p. 50

217. Mark Kausler, Tom & Jerry: The Cartoon Animator is an Artist Too, Film Comment, Jan-Feb 1975

218. Jerry Beck, The Hanna-Barbera Treasury, p. 29

219. Charles Solomon, Joseph Barbera, 95: Animation Giant Co-created 'Flintstones, 'Yogi Bear', LA Times, Dec 19, 2006

220. Darrell Van Critters, Interview with Mike Lah, Walt's People Vol. 11, p. 98

221. John Canemaker, Tex Avery: The MGM Years, p. 11

222. Joe Adamson, Tex Avery: King of Cartoons, p. 135

223. Joe Adamson, Tex Avery: King of Cartoons, p. 140

224. Michael Barrier, Hollywood Cartoons: American Animation in Its Golden Age, p. 328

225. Michael Barrier, Hollywood Cartoons: American Animation in Its Golden Age, p. 329

226. Maureen Furniss, Chuck Jones Conversations, p. 207

227. Maureen Furniss, Chuck Jones Conversations, p. 21

228. Cat and Mouse: The Tail of Tom and Jerry documentary (2007), Interview with Leonard Maltin

229. Constantine Nasr, Eric Goldberg Interview, King-Size Comedy: Tex Avery and the Looney Tunes Revolution

230. Darrell Van Critters, Interview with Mike Lah, Walt's People Vol. 11, p. 117

231. Darrell Van Critters, Interview with Mike Lah, Walt's People Vol. 11, p. 117

232. Maureen Furniss, Chuck Jones Conversations, p. 187

233. Joe Adamson interview with Tex Avery, Tex Avery: King of Cartoons, p. 188

234. Darrell Van Critters, Interview with Mike Lah, Walt's People Vol. 11, p. 117

235. John Canemaker, Tex Avery: The MGM Years, p. 159

236. Joe Adamson interview with Tex Avery, Tex Avery: King of Cartoons, p. 178

237. Joe Adamson, Interview with Tex Avery, Tex Avery: King of Cartoons, p. 187

238. Leonard Maltin, Of Mice and Magic: A History of American Animated Cartoons, p. 292

239. Constantine Nasr, Tex Avery interview, Drawn for Glory: Animation's Triumph at the Oscar, 2008

240. Maureen Furniss, Chuck Jones Conversations, p. 208

241. Michael Barrier and Milton Gray, An Interview with Bob Clampett, Funnyworld No. 12, p. 36

242. Peter Alvarado, Man from Wackyland - Art of Bob Clampett, 2004

243. Michael Barrier and Milton Gray, An Interview with Phil Monroe (1976) http://www.michaelbarrier.com/Interviews/Monroe/Monroe1976.html

244. Michael Barrier, Hollywood Cartoons: American Animation in the Golden Age, p. 452

245. Michael Barrier, Hollywood Cartoons: American Animation in the Golden Age, p. 452

246. Michael Barrier and Milton Gray, An Interview with Bob Clampett, Funnyworld No. 12, p. 30

247. Austin Kelly Interview with Mark Kausler, The Magic of **Freeze**-Framing: Episode 19, https://www.youtube.com/watch?v=56-ob96LanY

248. Michael Barrier, Interview with Phil Monroe, 1987, http://www.michaelbarrier.com/Interviews/Monroe/Monroe1987.html

249. Jerry Beck, Behind the Tune - Drawn to Life: The Art of Robert McKimson, 2007

250. Michael Barrier Interview, Behind the Tunes: Drawn to Life - The Art of Robert McKimson (2007)

251. Robert McKimson, Jr., I Say, I Say... Son!, p. 21

252. Michael Barrier, Interview with Robert McKimson, 1971, http://www.michaelbarrier.com/Interviews/McKimson/McKimson.html

253. Jerry Beck and Will Friedwald, Warner Bros. Animation Art, p. 31

254. Martha Sigall, Living Life Inside the Lines: Tales from the Golden Age of Animation, p. 74

255. Michael Barrier, Interview with Phil Monroe, 1987, http://www.michaelbarrier.com/Interviews/Monroe/Monroe1987.html

256. Michael Barrier, Interview with Phil Monroe, 1976, http://www.michaelbarrier.com/Interviews/Monroe/Monroe1976.html

257. Robert McKimson, Jr., Behind the Tune - Drawn to Life: The Art of Robert McKimson, 2007

258. Michael Barrier, Commentary for Baby Bottleneck

259. Margaret Selby, Chuck Jones: Extremes and In-Betweens - A Life in Animation (2000)

260. Greg Ford, Interview with Chuck Jones, Conrad the Sailor commentary

261. Stan Woodward, Chuck Jones Interview at Animation Lab at Capital Children's Museum, https://archive.org/details/ChuckJones_Anilab_Intv2_1989_U027

262. Margaret Selby, Chuck Jones: Extremes and In-Betweens - A Life in Animation (2000)

263. Michael Sporn, McGrew's Aristo-Cat, http://www.michaelspornanimation.com/splog/?p=1921

264. John Musilli, Chuck Jones interview in The Boys from Termite Terrace, 1975

265. Joe Adamson, Interview with Michael Maltese, Film Comment Magazine: Jan-Feb 1975

266. John Musilli, John Canemaker interview in The Boys from Termite Terrace, 1975

267. Television Academy Interviews, Phil Roman, https://interviews.televisionacademy.com/interviews/phil-roman?clip=121474#interview-clips

268. Michael Barrier, Interview with Phil Monroe, 1987, http://www.michaelbarrier.com/Interviews/Monroe/Monroe1987.html

269. Michael Barrier and Milton Gray, Interview with Phil Monroe, 1976 http://www.michaelbarrier.com/Interviews/Monroe/Monroe1976.html

270. Michael Barrier Commentary on A Bear for Punishment

271. Official Ken Harris website, http://www.masteranimator.com/bio.html

272. Chuck Jones, Chuck Jones: Extremes and InBetweens - A Life in Animation

273. Television Academy Interviews, Phil Roman, https://interviews.televisionacademy.com/interviews/phil-roman?clip=121474#interview-clips

274. Joe Adamson, Bugs Bunny: Fifty Years and Only One Grey Hare, p.83

275. Cassandra Siemon and Tom Sito, Biography: Ben Washam, https://animationresources.org/4528/

276. Michael Barrier, Interview with Ben Washam, Commentary on Duck Amuck

277. Chuck Jones, Chuck Amuck, p. 139

278. Michael Barrier, Hollywood Cartoons: American Animation in Its Golden Age, p. 444

279. Steven Hartley, Lloyd Vaughan Obituary and Info,

http://likelylooneymostlymerrie.blogspot.com/2012/01/lloyd-vaughan-obituary-and-info.html

280. Jim Lehrer, In Memoriam: Chuck Jones, Interview with John Canemaker

281. Constantine Nasr, David DePatie Interview, Friz on Film, 2006

282. Chris Walsh, Animation: The Art of Friz Freleng, Backstage with Friz and Co., p. 11-12

283. Constantine Nasr, Friz Freleng Interview, Friz on Film, 2006

284. Greg Ford, Commentary on Back Alley Oproar

285. Friz Freleng with David Weber, Animation: The Art of Friz Freleng, p. 126

286. Michael Barrier, Hollywood Cartoons: American Animation in Its Golden Age, p. 472

287. John Province, Interview with Virgil Ross, Animato! Number Nineteen, p. 18

288. Chris Walsh, Animation: The Art of Friz Freleng, Backstage with Friz and Co., p. 18

289. Barbara Richards, Warner Club News, What's Up, Doc? A Splice of Cartoon Life, Oct 1955

290. Jerry Beck, "I Tawt I Taw a Puddy Tat": Fifty Years of Sylvester and Tweety, p. 63

291. Don M. Yowp, Baseball Bugs Backgrounds, https://tralfaz.blogspot.com/2016/03/baseball-bugs-backgrounds.html

292. Michael Barrier, Interview with Phil Monroe, 1987, http://www.michaelbarrier.com/Interviews/Monroe/Monroe1987.html

293. John Province, Interview with Virgil Ross, Animato! Number Nineteen, p. 19

294. Mark Kausler, Friz on Film, 2006

295. Devon Baxter, Animator Profiles: Arthur Davis, https://cartoonresearch.com/index.php/animator-profiles-arthur-davis/

296. Chris Walsh, Animation: The Art of Friz Freleng, Backstage with Friz and Co., p. 11-12

297. Constantine Nasr, Friz Freleng Interview, Friz on Film, 2006

298. Constantine Nasr, Leonard Maltin Interview, Friz on Film, 2006

299. John Canemaker, The Animated Raggedy Ann and Andy, p. 94

300. John Canemaker, John Canemaker Interviews Richard Williams | MoMA LIVE

https://www.youtube.com/watch?v=Y1zED7aXuPI

301. John Canemaker, The Animated Raggedy Ann and Andy, p. 95

302. Jeff Lenburg, Who's Who in Animated Cartoons, p. 354

303. Mario Cavalli and Alex Amelines, Interview with Richard Williams, http://www.onehugeeye.com/richard-williams/

304. John Canemaker, The Animated Raggedy Ann and Andy, p. 91

305. Mike Dorner, Richard Williams: The Thief Who Never Gave Up, 1982

306. http://www.masteranimator.com/bio.html

307. Natasha Sutton Williams, A Tribute to My Father Richard Williams: The King of Animation, https://lwlies.com/articles/richard-williams-daughter-tribute-who-framed-roger-rabbit/

308. Natasha Sutton Williams, A Tribute to My Father Richard Williams: The King of Animation, https://lwlies.com/articles/richard-williams-daughter-tribute-who-framed-roger-rabbit/

309. John Canemaker, The Animated Raggedy Ann and Andy, p. 100

310. Imogen Sutton, Animating Art, 1988

311. Tom Sito, http://tomsito.com/blog.php?post=6191

312. Tom Gutteridge, Interview with Richard Williams, I Drew Roger Rabbit, 1988

313. Maureen Furniss, Chuck Jones Conversations, Joe Adamson Interview with Chuck Jones, p. 62

314. This Amazing Medium with Richard Williams, https://www.oscars.org/search/site/Richard%20williams

315. Michael Sporn, The Richard Williams Mystique, https://www.michaelspornanimation.com/splog/?p=4073

316. John Canemaker, John Canemaker Interviews Richard Williams | MoMA LIVE

317. Donald Heraldson, Creators of Life: A History of Animation, p. 274

318. Derek Malcolm, Williams's Magic Carpet, Arts Guardian, Feb 24, 1973

319. Michael Sporn, Cobbling, 08 Jan 2013, http://www.michaelspornanimation.com/splog/?p=3263

320. John Canemaker, John Canemaker Interviews Richard Williams | MoMA LIVE

321. Tom Gutteridge, Interview with Richard Williams, I Drew Roger Rabbit, 1988

322. Fraser MacLean, Setting the Scene: The Art and Evolution of Animation Layout, p. 160

323. John Canemaker, The Animated Raggedy Ann and Andy, p. 89

324. Tom Gutteridge, Interview with Richard Williams, I Drew Roger Rabbit, 1988

325. John Canemaker, The Animated Raggedy Ann and Andy, p. 193

326. John Canemaker, The Animated Raggedy Ann and Andy, p. 193

327. Michael Sporn, Gramps – Anew, 08 Oct 2012, http://www.michaelspornanimation.com/splog/?p=3169

328. Ross Anderson, The Making of Roger Rabbit: Pulling a Rabbit Out of a Hat, p.38

329. Making "Who Framed Roger Rabbit" with Richard Williams https://www.oscars.org/videos-photos/amazing-medium-richard-williams

330. Bernard Weinraub, An Animator Breaks Old Rules and New Ground in 'Roger Rabbit' https://www.nytimes.com/1988/08/01/movies/an-animator-breaks-old-rules-and-new-ground-in-roger-rabbit.html?searchResultPosition=9

331. John Province, Interview with Virgil Ross, Animato! Number Nineteen, p. 19

332. Box-Office Mojo, https://www.boxofficemojo.com/title/tt0096438/

333. James B. Stewart, Disney War, p. 89

334. Kevin Schreck, Interview with Michael Schlingmann, Persistence of Vision, 2012

335. Mark Mayerson, Persistence of Vision, https://mayersononanimation.blogspot.com/search?q=+Ken+Harris

336. Jerry Beck, The Animated Movie Guide, p. 23

337. Michael Sporn, Modern Animation, 06 Jun 2013, http://www.michaelspornanimation.com/splog/?p=8845

338. John Canemaker, John Canemaker Interviews Richard Williams | MoMA LIVE

339. Eric Goldberg talks about the benefits of pose to pose in CG animation at CTN - https://www.youtube.com/watch?v=l9Wy9x-msck

340. Tom Gutteridge, Interview with Richard Williams, I Drew Roger Rabbit, 1988

341. Chuck Jones, Chuck Jones: Extremes and InBetweens - A Life in Animation

Chapter 3

1. Eric Larson, 50 Years in the Mouse House, p. 162

2. Frank Thomas and Ollie Johnston, The Illusion of Life, p. 50

Chapter 4

1. Don Hahn and Tracey Miller-Zarneke, Before Ever After: The Lost Lectures of Walt Disney's Animation Studio, p. 73

2. Walt Stanchfield, Drawn to Life: 20 Golden Years of Disney Master Classes, p. 227

3. Michael Chekhov, To the Actor: On the Technique of Acting, p. 59

4. Steve Huston, Figure Drawing for Artists: Making Every Mark Count, p. 49

5. Carson Van Osten, Disney Comic Strip Artist's Kit, p. 3

6. Frank Thomas and Ollie Johnston, The Illusion of Life, p. 56

7. Tony Cipriano, as told to author

Chapter 5

1. Christopher Finch and Linda Rosenkranz interview with Eric Larson, Walt's People Vol. 11, p. 68-69

2. E.G. Lutz – Animated Cartoons: How They are Made Their Origin and Development, p. 58

3. Glen Keane, A System for Planning and Timing Animation, https://archive.org/details/Animation_Glen_Keane_Notes

4. John Culhane interview with Lese Clark, Walt's People Vol. 12, p. 37

5. James Baxter, Oscar Academy: Drawing on the Future: Mentorship in Animation, https://www.youtube.com/watch?v=nxSTrG9Ji-4

6. Charna Halpern, Dele Close and Kim "Howard" Johnson, Truth in Comedy: The Manual of Improvisation, p. 15

7. Glen Keane Interviewed by Didier Ghez, May 2, 1997, Walt's People Vol. 2, p. 342

Chapter 6

1. Walt Stanchfield and Don Hahn, Drawn to Life Volume 1: 20 Golden Years of Disney Master Classes - The Walt Stanchfield Lectures, P. 396

2. Al Hirschfeld, The Hirschfeld Century, P. 240

3. Al Hirschfeld, The Hirschfeld Century, P. 240

4. Frank Thomas and Ollie Johnston, The Illusion of Life, p. 65

5. Abigail Rockwell, Norman Rockwell: Artist or Illustrator? https://americanillustration.org/wpcontent/uploads/2016/05/15.08.25_AbigailRockwell.pdf

6. Francois Truffaut, Hitchcock, p. 81

7. Robin Allan and Dr. William Moritz, Interview with Milt Kahl, Walt's People Vol. 1, p. 221

8. Eric Larson, 50 Years in the Mouse House, p. 137

9. Eric Larson, 50 Years in the Mouse House, p. 138

10. Chuck Jones, Jones, Chuck Amuck: The Life and Times of an Animated Cartoonist, p. 101

11. Jack Hannah, Milt Kahl lecture at CalArts, April 2, 1976, Walt's People Vol. 7, p. 184

12. Wes Sullivan Interview with Iwao Takamoto, Walt's People Vol. 6 p. 290

13. Ron Merk Interview with Ken O'Connor, Walt's People Vol. 18 p. 97

Chapter 7

1. Richard Williams, The Animator's Survival Kit – Animated, 2001

2. Chris Kritley, http://www.clinicalgaitanalysis.com/teach-in/kinematics.html

3. Stella Adler, The Art of Acting, p. 59

4. Reg Hartt presents Grim Natwick interviewed by Michael Gowling Toronto 1982 https://www.youtube.com/watch?v=4CEYYLr9tRU

5. Leonard Maltin, Of Mice and Magic: A History of American Animated Cartoons, p. 53

6. Greg Ford and Richard Thompson interview with Chuck Jones. Film Comment Jan-Feb 1975, p. 24

Chapter 8

1. Chuck Jones Film Comment interview Jan – Feb 1975, p. 23

2. Michael Sporn, Moving Feet, 02 Feb 2010, http://www.michaelspornanimation.com/splog/?p=2131

Chapter 9

1. Frank Thomas and Ollie Johnston, The Illusion of Life, p. 62

Chapter 10

1. Frank Thomas and Ollie Johnston, The Illusion of Life, p. 290

2. John Canemaker Interviews Richard Williams | MoMA LIVE https://www.youtube.com/watch?v=Y1zED7aXuPI

3. Jack Hannah, Milt Kahl lecture at CalArts, April 2, 1976, Walt's People Vol. 7, p. 183

Chapter 11

1. Joe Adamson, Interview of Richard Huemer, https://static.library.ucla.edu/oralhistory/text/masters/21198-zz0008ztp4-3-master.html#session1a

2. Grim Natwick, Dick Huemer 1898-1979: Homage to a Star, http://www.huemer.com/animate2.htm

3. Eric Larson, 50 years in the Mouse House, p. 167-168

4. John Canemaker, Interview with Tissa David at NYU, April 24, 2006

5. Frank Thomas and Ollie Johnston, The Illusion of Life, p. 43

6. Richard Hubler, Interview with Milt Kahl, Walt's People Vol. 7, p. 183

Chapter 12

1. Ollie Johnston Lecture, Feb 1978, Walt's People Vol. 7, p. 201

Chapter 13

1. Tom Gutteridge, Interview with Richard Williams, I Drew Roger Rabbit, 1988

Chapter 14

1. Michael Sporn, Tyler Breaking Joints, 10 Jan, 2008, http://www.michaelspornanimation.com/splog/?p=1331

2. Didier Ghez, Walt's People Vol. 8, Les Clark interviewed by Frank Thomas & Ollie Johnston Sept. 18, 1978, page 60

Chapter 15

1. Frank Thomas and Ollie Johnston, The Illusion of Life, p. 52

2. Eric Larson, 50 Years in the Mouse House, p. 119

3. Eric Goldberg, Character Animation Crash Course, p. 31

Chapter 17

1. John Culhane, Walt Disney's Fantasia, p. 35

2. Blaine Gibson, Interviewed by Paul F. Anderson, Walt's People Vol. 8, p. 325

Chapter 18

1. Greg Ford and Richard Thompson, *Interview with Chuck Jones, Film Comment Magazine*: Jan-Feb 1975, p.30

2. Donald Graham, *Class on Action Analysis: Secondary Action – Phases of an Action*, Monday, March 1, 1937

3. Chuck Jones, *Chuck Reducks: Drawings from the Fun Side of Life*, p. 190

4. Frank Thomas and Ollie Johnston, *The Illusion of Life*, p. 63

5. Frank Thomas and Ollie Johnston, *The Illusion of Life*, p. 64

6. Stella Adler, *The Art of Acting*, p.50

7. David Robinson, *Chaplin: His Life and Art*, p. 749

Chapter 19

1. Greg Ford and Richard Thompson, Interview with Chuck Jones, Film Comment Magazine: Jan-Feb 1975, p. 30

2. Donald Graham, Class on Action Analysis: Secondary Action – Phases of an Action, Monday, March 1, 1937

3. Chuck Jones, Chuck Reducks: Drawings from the Fun Side of Life, p. 190

4. Frank Thomas and Ollie Johnston, The Illusion of Life, p. 63

5. Frank Thomas and Ollie Johnston, The Illusion of Life, p. 64

6. Stella Adler, The Art of Acting, p.50

7. David Robinson, Chaplin: His Life and Art, p. 749

Chapter 20

1. Grim Natwick, Reading a Soundtrack, Cartoonist Profiles, No. 35, Sept. 1977, p. 23

2. Preston Blair, Cartoon Animation, p. 198

3 John Canemaker, Interview with Tissa David at NYU, April 24, 2006

4. Eric Goldberg, Character Animation Crash Course, p. 157

5. Richard Williams, The Animators Survival Kit, p. 314

6. Wes Sullivan, Interview with Dale Oliver, Walt's People Vol. 2, p. 231

7. Frank Thomas and Ollie Johnston, The Illusion of Life, p. 461

8. Thorkil B. Rasmussen, Interview with Eric Larsen, Walt's People Vol. 2, p. 277

Chapter 21

1. Master Class with Martin Scorsese, https://cinephiliabeyond.org/master-class-with-martin-scorsese/

2. Peter Brunette, Orson Welles Interviews, p. 183

3. Hans Bacher and Sanatan Suryavanashi, Vision: Color and Composition for Film, p. 63

4. Bruce Block, The Visual Story – Seeing the Structure of Film, TV, and New Media, p. 140

5. Bruce Block, The Visual Story – Seeing the Structure of Film, TV, and New Media, p. 146

6. Milt Kahl interviewed by Robin Allan and Dr. William Moritz, 1985, Walt's People Vol. 1, p. 219

7. Hooman Mehran commentary, City Lights Criterion Collection

8. Richard Meryman, Interview with Charlie Chaplin 1966, https://www.charliechaplin.com/en/quotes

Chapter 23

1. Don Bluth, Learn to Animate: DVD Disc 3

2. Bill Desowitz, DreamWorks Unleashes the Dragons, https://www.awn.com/animationworld/dreamworks-unleashes-dragons

3. Simon Otto and Stuart Sumida, Dragon's Flight School, CTN, https://tv.creativetalentnetwork.com/dragons-flight-school

4. Michael Apted interview with David Bowie, Inspirations, 1997

5. Theodore Thomas, Interview with Ollie Johnston, Frank and Ollie, 1995

Chapter 24

1. Interview with Chuck Jones, Tom and Jerry... and Chuck, 2009

Selected Bibliography

Adamson, Joe. *Bugs Bunny: Fifty Years and Only One Grey Hare*, 1990.

Amidi, Amid. *Cartoon Modern*, 2006.

Bacher, Hans. *Dream Worlds: Production Design for Animation*, 2007.

Bacher, Hans and Sanatan Suryavanashi. *Vision: Color and Composition for Film*, 2018.

Barbera, Joseph. *My Life in 'Toons: From Flatbush to Bedrock in Under a Century*, 1994.

Barrier, Michael. *Hollywood Cartoons: American Animation in Its Golden Age*, 1999.

Beck, Jerry. *"I Tawt I Taw a Puddy Tat": Fifty Years of Sylvester and Tweety*, 1991.

Block, Bruce. *The Visual Story: Creating the Visual Structure of Film, TV, and Digital Media*, 2001

Canemaker, John. *Animated Raggedy Ann and Andy, The*, 1977.

_____. *Felix: The Twisted Tale of the World's Most Famous Cat*, 1991.

_____. *Walt Disney's Nine Old Men & the Art of Animation*, 2001.

_____. *Winsor McCay His Life and Art*, 1987.

Clark, Miriam Leslie. *Glimpses into the Golden Age of Disney Animation*, 2019.

Crafton, Donald. *Before Mickey, the Animated Film*, 1982.

_____. *Shadow of a Mouse*, 2013.

Culhane, John. *Walt Disney's Fantasia*, 1983.

Culhane, Shamus. *Animation from Script to Screen*, 1988.

Deja, Andreas. *The Nine Old Men: Lessons, Techniques, and Inspirations from Disney's Great Animators*, 2015.

_____. *Talking Animals and Other People*, 1986.

Fleischer, Richard. *Out of the Inkwell: Max Fleischer and the Animation Revolution*, 2005.

Friedman, Jake S. *The Disney Revolt*, 2022.

Furniss, Maureen. *Chuck Jones Conversations*, 2005.

Gabler, Neal. *Walt Disney: The Triumph of the American Imagination*, 2006.

Ghez, Didier. *Walt's People Volumes 1-27: Talking Disney with the Artists Who Knew Him*, 2005-2023.

Goldberg, Eric. *Character Animation Crash Course*, 2008.

Hahn, Don and Tracey Miller-Zarneke. *Before Ever After: The Lost Lectures of Walt Disney's Animation Studio*, 2015.

Hanna, Bill with Tom Ito. *A Cast of Friends*, 1996.

Iwerks, Don. *Walt Disney's Ultimate Inventor: The Genius of Ub Iwerks*, 2019.

Jones, Chuck. *Chuck Amuck: The Life and Times of an Animated Cartoonist*, 1989.

_____. *Chuck Jones: Extremes and InBetweens - A Life in Animation*, 2000.

_____. *Chuck Reducks: Drawings from the Fun Side of Life*, 1996.

Krause, Martin and Linda Witkowski. *Walt Disney's Snow White and the Seven Dwarfs: An Art in Its Making*, 1994.

Larson, Eric. *50 Years in the Mouse House*, 2015.

MacLean, Fraser. *Setting the Scene: The Art and Evolution of Animation Layout*, 2011.

Maltin, Leonard. *Of Mice and Magic: A History of American Animated Cartoon*, 1980.

McKimson, Jr., Robert. *I Say, I Say... Son!*, 2012.

Peri, Don. *Working with Disney: Interviews with Animators, Producers, and Artists*, 2021.

_____. *Working with Walt: Interviews with Disney Artists*, 2008.

Solomon, Charles. *Enchanted Drawings, The History of Animation*, 1989.

Stanchfield, Walt and Don Hahn. *Drawn to Life: 20 Golden Years of Disney Master Classes*, 2023.

Takamoto, Iwao. *My Life with a Thousand Characters*, 2009.

Thomas, Frank and Ollie Johnston. *Disney Animation: The Illusion of Life*, 1981.

Williams, Richard. *The Animator's Survival Kit*, 2012.

Index

A

A Bird in a Guilty Cage 42

A Christmas Carol 44

A Dream Walking 13

A Falling Hare 38

A Hare Grows 42

A Hare Grows in Manhattan 42

A Tale of Two Kitties 40

A Wild Hare 35, 38

Accents 9, 28, 51
    Dialogue Accents 213, 249–251, 255
    Hard Accent 90, 213, 215–219, 278, 281
    Soft Accent 216–219, 278

Acrobatty Bunny 38, 42

Action Analysis 15, 28, 96, 312

Actor 3, 14, 17, 22, 41, 68, 81, 228, 249

Actors 60, 81, 83, 84

Actress 29

Adler, Stella 1, 110, 223

Advanced Walk Cycles 139

Aladdin 46

Alice In Wonderland 21, 23–25, 28, 29

Ambro, Hal 25, 44, 45, 156

Anatomical 90, 96

Anatomy 20, 38, 62, 137, 182, 206

Anderson, Wes 264

Anger 202, 222, 228, 231, 233, 237, 238

Animating Dance 157

Animation
    Believability 22, 47, 48, 51, 90, 110, 167, 185, 294
    Believable 1, 11, 12, 18, 25, 31, 69, 85, 90, 93, 110, 111, 143, 158, 181, 218, 283, 284, 286
    Good Judgement 47, 48, 91

Animation Craft 1

Anthropomorphic 23, 25, 48

Anticipate 174, 241, 243

Anticipation 4, 33, 34, 49, 79, 89, 93, 112, 165, 170, 185, 189–197, 207, 210, 213, 214, 219, 226, 241, 242, 250, 276, 277

Appeal 4, 9, 10, 18, 19

Arc 74, 119–124, 126, 135, 137, 149, 159, 162–164, 178, 203, 208, 214, 290, 295

Arcing 124, 178

Arcs 4, 33, 51, 73, 83, 85, 88, 119, 123, 124, 126, 145, 151, 182, 290

Aristocats 28

Arm 24, 28, 60, 62, 68, 89, 124, 126, 129, 130, 136, 162, 168, 172, 175, 176, 181, 182, 186–188, 192, 218, 219, 226, 228, 272, 277, 281, 287

Arms 8, 28, 38, 67, 75, 83, 107, 108, 119, 126, 129, 130, 132, 135–137, 139, 152, 169–171, 173, 179, 181, 184–186, 206, 208, 217

Aspect Ratio 259, 260

Astaire, Fred 42

Aurelius 16

Automatic Overlap 205

Avery, Frederick Bean "Tex" 16, 30, 33–36, 187, 219

Axe Me Another 13

B

Babbitt, Art 15, 16, 25, 30, 31, 43, 45, 46

Baby Bottleneck 37, 48

Bacher, Hans 265

Back Alley Oproar 41

Bad Luck Blacky 35

Bad Ol' Putty Tat 42

Bakes 18

Bakes, George 18

Balloon Land 9

Bambi 23, 28

Band Concert, The 10, 11

Barbary-Coast Bunny 39

Barbera, Joe 16, 31–34, 43, 90

Barbera, Joseph 16, 32, 34, 43

Barge, Ed 33–34

Barré, Raoul 8

Barrier, Michael 9, 14, 35, 37–38, 40–41

Baseball Bugs 41, 42, 194

Battaglia, Aurelius 16

Beat 13, 29, 154, 155, 157, 158, 175, 222, 249, 251, 269, 293
    Animating to a Beat 154
    Animating Dance 157

Believability 22, 47, 48, 51, 90, 110, 167, 185, 294

Believable 1, 11, 12, 18, 25, 31, 69, 85, 90, 93, 110, 111, 143, 158, 181, 218, 283, 284, 286

Betty Boop 5, 8, 9, 13

Bird, Brad 269

Blackton, J. Stuart 7–8

Blair, Preston 16, 251, 313

Blinks 244

Block, Bruce 268

Blocking 62, 73, 87, 184, 224, 226, 233, 270, 276

Blocking In Arms 184

Bluth, Don 283

Bluto 13

Boleslavsky, Richard 17

Bone 33, 45

Bone Trouble 33

Bosustow, Stephen 16, 24, 29–31

Bouncing Ball 47, 51, 52, 55, 56, 58, 105, 145, 158, 165, 170, 196, 214, 226, 253

Bowie, David 284

Brasi, Luca 262

Bray, J.R. 8, 12, 13

Breakdowns 1, 8, 55, 57, 74, 81, 114, 124–125, 132–133, 145–150, 161–165, 199–211, 214, 224, 226–227, 241, 242, 276–278, 280–282, 289, 294, 295
    How Many Breakdowns 203

Buccaneer Bunny 41, 42

Bugs and Thugs 42

Bugs Bunny 35, 37–42, 48, 126, 139, 194, 218, 222, 248

Bullwinkle 31

Bully For Bugs 38, 40

C

Cactus Kid, The 10

Camera 7, 8, 12, 15, 34, 37–39, 43–45, 68, 69, 99, 259, 264–70, 272, 274, 282, 294, 295
   180° and 30° Rule 267
   Crane 266
   Dolly 266
   Dutch Tilt 265
   High Angle 265
   Low Angle 38, 265
   Movement 266
   Pan 266
   Truck 266

Can You Take It 13

Canemaker, John 7–9, 11, 17, 20, 24, 25, 39, 40

Cannon, Bobe 30, 40

Cannon, Robert "Bobe" 30

Captain Hook 22, 29

Captain Underpants: The First Epic Movie 22

Cat and the Mermouse, The 33

Cat Concerto, The 33

Champin, Ken 42

Change In Shape 210

Change Of Direction 152, 154, 158, 196, 205, 214, 215, 224, 244, 281

Change Of Shape 47, 272, 286, 294

Chaplin, Charlie 12, 68, 228, 272–273, 295

Character 7–9, 14, 15, 17, 18, 20, 21, 23,24, 28–31, 33, 38, 41, 47, 48, 51, 59–63, 65–71, 73, 74, 76, 77, 81, 83, 84, 86–91, 93, 94, 96–100, 103, 104, 106–108, 110–114, 116–124, 126, 128, 132, 136, 139, 141, 143, 149, 152, 154–157, 163, 165–170, 172–177, 179, 181–183, 185, 188–195, 197, 202, 204, 206, 207, 209, 210, 215–219, 221–225, 228, 230, 233, 234, 236, 237, 239–244, 247–254, 256– 258, 263, 265–271, 274, 275, 277–280, 283, 285–287, 294

Character Animation 7, 15, 38, 197, 283

Charting 23, 158, 163, 168, 184

Charts 23, 125, 145, 147, 152, 153, 155, 159, 165, 168

Chekhov 60

Chernobog 17

Cherrill, Virginia 272

Cheshire Cat 24

Chiniquy, Gerry 41, 45

Cipriano, Tony p.68

Clampett, Bob 9, 36, 37

Clark, Les 10, 12, 19, 20, 24, 25, 34, 76, 181

Cleworth 25

Clichés 245

Click Track 293

Cloth 281

Cohl, Emile 7–8

Cole, Corny 45

Çonrad The Sailor 39, 306

Contact Pose 127, 128, 130, 132–136, 138, 139, 142, 197

Contempt 231, 236

Contraction 178

Contrapposto 64, 65, 111, 114, 118

Contrast 28, 36, 47, 48, 51, 65, 73, 77, 79, 80, 85, 87, 89, 107, 114, 123, 131, 184, 186, 189, 191, 195, 211, 261, 262, 277

Contrasting Arcs 123, 124

Contrast Of Extension 261, 262

Contrasting Poses 77

Costello, Billy (aka Red Pepper Sam) 14

Count, Mark 309

Counterbalance 7, 97, 98, 106

Crafton, Donald 8

Crane 22, 266

Cross-Cutting 39

Culhane, Shamus 13–15, 18

Curve 71, 141, 178, 181, 291

Curves 140, 164, 172, 182, 187, 290

Curving 98

Cycles 7, 9, 31, 49, 85, 86, 127, 128, 130–132, 134–143, 156, 174, 203, 204, 219, 279, 283

D

Daffy Doodles 38

Daffy Duck 35, 37–40, 42, 48, 218

Dance 9, 22, 24, 34, 40–42, 157, 158, 215

Darling, George 22

David, Tissa 1, 9, 25, 44, 45, 110, 154, 223, 227, 252

Davis, Art 41, 42, 146

Davis, Marc 9, 11, 17–21, 25, 29

Day the Earth Stood Still, The 282

Degas, Edgar 274

Deneroff, Harvey 13

DePatie, David 41

Deputy Droopy 36, 187

Design 10, 16, 21, 30, 31, 38, 39

Dialogue 14, 18, 23, 28, 33, 34, 40, 156, 197, 213, 227, 231, 232, 247, 250–252, 254, 256, 258, 274–276, 278, 285, 293, 294
  Inbetweening Dialogue 252
  Popping 8, 34, 209, 210, 254
  Swallow Syllables 254
  Tongue 255

Dialogue Accents 213, 250

Dimension 30

Disgust 231, 234–236

Disney Animation 4, 19, 23, 45

Disney Concept 30

Disney Strike 16

Disney Studio 10, 12, 17–20, 38

Disney, Walt 9, 10, 73

Dixie Land Droopy 35

Dolly 266

Donald Duck 24

Down Pose 49, 131, 132, 134, 135, 139, 142, 143, 174

Dr. Seuss 31

Droopy Dog 35, 36, 187

Duck Amuck 40

Duck Dodgers in the 24½th Century 39

Dumbo 17, 18, 20, 24, 33

Dunning, George 43

Dutch Tilt 265

E

Ease-In 162

Ease-Out 162

Easter Yeggs 38

Eastman, P. D. 16

Eisenstein, Sergei 39

Ekman, Dr. Paul 231

El Gaucho Goofy 22

Ellis, Izzy 37

Elmer Fudd 35, 37, 40

Emotion 17, 18, 21, 25, 37, 39, 40, 59, 68, 71, 78, 153, 222, 223, 228, 229, 231, 232, 233, 249, 285

Engel, Jules 16, 30

Exaggeration 4, 22, 37, 83, 240
    Exaggerate 85–87, 90, 91, 108

Exposure Sheet 251, 252
    X-Sheet 251, 252, 275, 276, 293

Expression 7, 8, 14, 18, 20, 21, 33, 39, 59, 62, 78, 193, 225, 229–233, 235–237, 239–243, 245, 248, 257, 277, 285, 294

Extremes 33, 48, 73, 146–148, 161, 163, 167, 199, 200, 203–207, 209–211, 221, 224, 241, 289, 294, 295

Eyebrows 18, 40, 50, 229, 232–237, 239, 240

Eyelids 90, 230, 234–235, 237, 239, 244, 255

F

Fabric 169, 176–179, 218

Facial Animation 7, 8, 59, 78, 149, 193, 231, 232, 285, 294

Falling 28, 37–39, 96–98, 108, 109, 116, 117, 165, 294

Famous Studios 15

Fantasia 15, 17, 18, 22–24, 44, 213

Fantasmagorie 7

Fear 9, 39, 231, 233, 234, 239

Ferguson, Norm 25, 45

First Bad Man, The 35

Fisher, David 31, 84, 303

Fisher, Ryan 77, 84, 269

FK 69

Flat Hatting 30

Fleischer, Dave 13

Fleischer, Max 12, 298

Fleischer Studio, The 8, 12–15, 32

Flourish 275, 278, 279

Follow-Through 169, 176, 177, 186, 221, 281

Foot Plant 111, 117, 133

Ford, Greg 41

Formulas 8, 11, 155, 169, 247
    Dialogue 14, 18, 23, 28, 33, 34, 40, 156, 197, 213, 227, 231, 232, 247, 250–252, 254, 256, 258, 274–276, 278, 285, 293, 294
    Run Cycle 49, 85, 141–43, 156, 219
    Walk Cycle 86, 127, 128, 130–132, 134, 136–143, 156, 174, 203, 283

Fowl Play 13

Fractured Fairy Tales 31

Frame 7, 12, 25, 33, 36, 42, 44, 53–55, 58, 77, 84, 89, 114, 115, 125, 127, 128, 130–132, 134, 138, 143, 145, 147–151, 156, 157, 163, 164, 167, 168, 172, 175–177, 185, 186, 196, 200, 201, 204, 205, 207, 208, 244, 251, 253, 259, 260, 262, 263, 266, 267, 274, 276–281, 293, 294

Frame-by-frame 7, 42

Frankenheimer, John 260

Frankensteined 63

Frankensteining 3

Freleng, Isadore "Friz" 9, 36, 41, 42

G

Geppetto 15, 22

Gerald McBoing Boing 31

Geronimi, Clyde 256

Gertie The Dinosaur 7, 8, 10

Gesture 29, 37, 60–63, 77, 88, 137, 158, 195, 197, 206, 207, 210, 216, 221–222, 224–225, 227–228, 231, 248, 250–251, 256, 258, 272, 277, 279, 293

Goldberg, Eric 15, 33, 35, 38, 46, 193

Golden Poses 28, 73

Golden Ratio 267, 274

Golden Spiral 263

Gollub, Morris 20

Good Judgement 47, 48, 91

Goofy 15, 21, 22, 25

Gorilla My Dreams 38

Gould, Manny 37

Graham, Donald 10, 11, 15, 31, 38, 59, 96, 221

Grant, Cary 262

Graph Editor 55, 56, 119, 124–126, 140, 163–164, 172, 188, 206, 280, 290, 291

Great Poochini 36

Gribbroek, Robert 39

Grouping 63–64

Grumpy 18, 93

Gulliver 13–15

Gulliver's Travels 14

H

Hair 33, 169, 176–179, 218, 221, 281, 295

Hair-Raising Hare 40

Hanna, Bill 16, 31–35, 43, 90, 303, 304

Happiness 231, 233, 237–239

Hard Accent 90, 213, 215–219, 278, 281

Hare Ribbin 38

Harman-Ising 32, 34

Harris, Ken 30, 38–40, 43–44, 46, 76

Haunted Hotel, The 7

Haunted Mansion, The 21

Hawaiian Holiday 21

Head Room 266, 267

Headless Horseman 22

Hearst International 8

High Angle 265

Hilberman, David 29–30

Hirschfeld, Al 83

His Bitter Half 42

Hitchcock, Alfred 84, 262

Horner, Richard 44

How Many Breakdowns 203

How To Ride a Horse 22

Hubley, John 16, 29–31, 44

Huemer, Dick 42, 146

Hurtz, Bill 30–31

I

I Taw a Putty Tat 42

Ichabod Crane 22

IK 69, 71, 137, 139

IK And FK 69

Inbetweening Dialogue 252

Inbetweens 1, 3, 8, 36, 40, 69, 74–75, 81, 104, 113, 119, 124, 133–134, 139, 143, 145–147, 149–150, 155, 161–165, 167, 199–200, 204, 207–208, 211, 252, 278, 282–283, 289, 294–295

I Never Changes My Altitude 14

Inside Out 231

I-Ski Love-Ski You-Ski 14

It's a Mad, Mad, Mad, Mad World 31

I Yam What I Yam 14

Iwerks, Ub 9, 10, 15, 25, 34

J

Jackson, Wilfred 10

Jay Ward Productions 31

Johnston, Ollie 1, 4, 8, 17, 19–21, 37, 44, 167, 245

Jones, Bob 25

Jones, Chuck 8–10, 16, 29, 31, 32, 34–36, 38–41, 43–44, 46, 48, 89–90, 110–111, 218, 221, 295

Jones, Giovanni 139, 209

Julian, Paul 30

Jump 19, 24, 30, 37, 51, 58, 62, 77–79, 94, 104, 112, 116–117, 158, 170, 185, 190–191, 206, 245, 268

Jungle Book 23, 25, 29, 94

K

Kaempffert, Waldemar 12

Kahl, Milt 1, 3, 16, 19–23, 25, 43–44, 46, 76, 86, 90, 94, 127–128, 140–141, 156, 158, 226, 271, 275

Kausler, Mark 34, 37, 42

Keane, Glen 1, 20, 73, 81

Keaton, Buster 8–9, 42

Kimball, Ward 12, 19, 20, 22–25, 31, 152

Kinematics 96

King, Hal 25

King of the Mardi Gras 13

Kit For Cat 42

Klaatu 282

Klynn, Herb 30

Koko the Clown 12–13

Kubo and the Two Strings 48

Kubrick, Stanley 264

L

Lady and the Tramp 22–23, 28

Landing 34, 48, 62, 79, 104, 116–117, 142, 186

Langer, Mark 15

Lantz, Walter 9, 20

Larriva, Rudy 31

Larson, Eric 20, 23, 47, 60, 73, 86, 153, 189, 258

Laugh-O-Gram Studio 9

Laurel and Hardy 197

Layering 172

Lead Lines 265

Leatherbarrow, John 44

Levitow, Abe 44

Line of Action 60–63, 66, 70–71, 74, 88, 109, 121, 137, 141, 206, 267–268, 272

Lip Sync 14, 256

Lip-Syncing 33

Little Red Riding Rabbit 41, 248

Little Runaway 34

Littlejohn, Bill 33

Long Haired Hare 139, 209

Looney Tunes 13, 32

Lounsbery, John 20, 22, 25

Love, Ed 16

Low Angle 38, 265

Lucas, George 45

Lucky Ducky 35–36

Lutz, E.G. 73

M

Madam Mim 29

Mad Doctor, The 15

Magical Maestro 30, 36

Magoo's Canine Mutiny 3, 127

Maleficent 21

Maltese, Mike 34, 39, 45

Maltin, Leonard 9, 12, 35–37, 39, 42

Man and the Moon 24

Man in Space 24

Mary Poppins 45, 88

Marx Brothers 40

Mattinson, Burny 22

Maugham, Somerset 295

Maya 69, 75

Mayer, Jerry 32

Mayerson, Mark 18, 45

McCay, Winsor 7, 8, 10

McGrew, John 39

Mckimson, Bob 37–38

McKimson, Tom 37

Mechanics 7, 9, 12, 38, 79, 84

Medusa, Madam 3, 29, 90, 127, 140

Melendez, Bill 16, 31, 37

Méliès, Georges 7

Mercer, Jack 14

Merrie Melodies 13, 32

Messmer, Otto 8–9

Mickey Mouse 9–11, 20, 24, 67, 190, 213

Mickey's Fire Brigade 9

Mintz, Charles 9, 34

Miyazaki, Hayao 9, 46

Moana 197

Maui 197

Monroe, Phil 31, 37–40, 42, 139

Moore, Fred "Freddie" Freddy 3, 19–22, 24, 33, 73, 91

Morning, Noon and Night Club 13

Movement 1, 3, 7, 9–11, 13, 15, 19, 20, 28, 34–35, 41, 73, 77, 83, 85–86, 93, 96, 106, 111, 119, 124, 134, 140, 143, 145–146, 148, 167–168, 173, 175–176, 181, 203, 209, 221, 224, 228, 244, 250, 253, 255, 258, 266, 268–269, 275, 282, 293

Moving Holds 167

Mr. Duck Steps Out 24

Mr. Magoo 3, 16, 30–31, 127

Muse, Kenneth "Ken" 16, 33–34

Music 9–10, 13, 20, 23, 73, 127, 153–154, 157, 249, 251, 293

My Bunny Lies Over the Sea 39

My Favorite Duck 39

N

Naisbitt, Roy 44

Natwick, Grlm 5, 8–9, 31, 45, 146, 251

Negative Space 67, 262

Neutral Pose 47, 51, 73, 87, 112, 118, 126, 161, 170, 179, 186, 193, 206, 219, 225, 229–230, 243

Neutral Position 100, 103, 114, 117, 185, 192

Neutral Start 73, 213

Neutral Volume 47

Nicholas, George 44

Night On Bald Mountain 17

Noble, Maurice 16, 39

Nolan, Bill 8–9

Northwest Hounded Police 36

O

O'Connor, Ken 91

Objective Criticism 283–284

Oh What A Knight 9

Old Grey Hare, The 37–38

Olive Oyl 13, 15

One Froggy Evening 39–40

One Hundred and One Dalmatians 21–22, 25, 28
   101 Dalmatians 213, 256

One-Point Perspective 264

Otto, Simon 283

Overlap, 3, 7, 13, 36–37, 93, 115, 135–136, 151, 169–170, 172, 175–176, 179, 187–188, 204–205, 218, 227, 242–244, 281, 290, 295

Overlap Expressions 242

Overlapping Action 4, 169, 176, 181, 221

Ozu, Yasujirō 274

P

Partch, Virgil 16

Passing Pose 127, 130–132, 134, 136–142

Path Of Action 74–75, 79, 81, 116, 119–120, 123, 133, 137, 146, 172, 183–184, 186, 188, 204, 206, 208, 281, 287

Patterson, Don 16

Patterson, Ray 16, 33–34

Pecos Bill 24, 29

Pecos Pest 33

Peet, Bill 45

Perez, Manuel "Manny" 42, 249

Perspective 9, 16, 37, 39, 44, 263, 264
    One-Point Perspective 264
    Two-Point Perspective 264
    Three-Point Perspective 264

Peter and the Wolf 23

Peter Pan 21, 22, 29

Peterson, Ken 10

Pink Panther 41, 43

Pinocchio 4, 15, 18, 20, 22–24, 28, 29, 158

Pirates of the Caribbean 21

Pluto 25, 33

Popeye 8, 13–15, 31, 203, 298, 299
    Costello, Billy (aka Red Pepper Sam) 14
    Mercer, Jack 14

Popeye the Sailor Meets Sinbad the Sailor 13

Popping 8, 34, 165, 209, 210, 254

Porky 37, 39

Pose to Pose 4, 8, 9, 35, 36, 40, 52, 75, 80, 111, 113, 152, 209

Posing 33, 41, 59–71, 75, 76, 111, 117, 232–233, 294
    Contrapposto 64, 65, 111, 114, 118
    Gesture 29, 37, 60–63, 77, 88, 137, 158, 195, 197, 206, 216, 222, 224, 228, 231, 250, 256, 258, 277, 279, 293
    Grouping 63, 64
    Line Of Action 60–63, 66, 70, 71, 74, 88, 109, 121, 137, 141, 206, 267, 268, 272
    Negative Space 67, 262
    Silhouette 39, 67–69, 71, 270, 284

Postman Panic 31

Powerpuff Girls 31

Principles Of Animation 1, 4, 15, 36, 46

Progress the Action 255, 256

Putty Tat Trouble 41

Q

Quiet Please 33–34

Quimby, Fred 32

R

Rabbit Fire 40

Rabbit Of Seville 40

Rabbit Seasoning 48, 218

Rabbit Transit 222

Racketeer Rabbit 42

Raggedy Ann and Andy: A Musical Adventure 44–45

Reference 12, 15, 23, 28, 30, 60, 81, 84–88, 91, 197, 225, 228, 275–276, 293–294

Reitherman, Wolfgang "Woolie" 20–22

Reluctant Dragon, The 20

Rescuers, The

3, 21, 29, 90, 127, 140

Response Time 175

Rhapsody Rabbit 42

Roadrunner and Coyote Cartoons 43

Robin Hoodlum 30

Rock-a-Bye Bear 35

Rockwell, Norman 310

Rocky and Bullwinkle 31

Roger Rabbit 35, 45, 308, 309–310, 313

Roman, Phil 39–40

Ross, Virgil 41–42, 45, 222

Rotoscope 12, 14, 88

Rubber–hose 8–10, 13, 19, 31, 91, 181–182

Rubin, Edgar 67

Rule of Thirds 262–263, 267, 274

Run Cycle 49, 85, 127, 141–43, 156, 219

S

7 Basic Expressions 231, 240
    Anger 202, 222, 228, 231, 233, 237, 238
    Contempt 231, 236
    Disgust 59, 231, 234–236
    Fear 231, 233–234, 239
    Happiness 231, 233, 237–239
    Sadness 60, 231, 239–240
    Surprise 231, 233, 234, 237, 239

S-Curve 9, 177–178

Saludos Amigos 29

Saturday Evening Puss 33

Schlesinger, Leon 34–35, 38

Schlingmann, Michael 45

Schwartz, Zack 29, 30

Secondary Action 4, 21, 156, 221–228, 251, 256–258, 278–279

Segar, E.C. (Elzie Crisler) 13

Selzer, Eddie 38

Sharpsteen, Ben 15

Shere Kahn 29, 94

Silhouette 39, 67–69, 71, 270, 284

Slap Happy Lion 36

Sleeping Beauty 21–22, 28, 31, 156

Slick Hare 41–42

Slow-In and Slow-Out 4, 161–168

Slow-In 4, 56, 161–168, 171, 196, 201, 205, 207–209, 211, 216, 244, 289, 295

Slow-Out 4, 161–168, 196, 207–209, 211, 214–215, 227, 244, 289, 295

Slue-Foot Sue 29

Smith, Frank 31

Snow White and The Seven Dwarfs 5, 11–12, 15, 17, 33, 43

Snow White 9, 11–12, 14–18, 20, 24, 28, 33, 43, 44, 93, 110, 181

Soft Accent 216–219, 278

Solid Poses 4

Solid Serenade 33

Soundtrack 40, 155, 247–251, 257, 275, 313

Spacing 13, 51, 52, 104–106, 110, 114, 145–146, 150, 153–154, 158, 161–162, 165–166, 168, 206, 210–211, 280, 289

Spacing Breakdowns 206

Speed 7, 35, 90, 141, 153–154, 161–162, 165, 166, 168, 181, 207–209, 215, 279, 280, 289, 295

Spence, Irven "Irv" 33–34, 45

Spielberg, Steven 45, 269

Spike (Tom and Jerry) 33–36

Sporn, Michael 18, 39, 44–46, 113, 181

Squash and Stretch 4, 22, 23, 36, 47–51, 54, 55, 88, 110, 254, 286

Stanchfield, Walt 60, 83

Stanislavski, Konstantin 17, 245

Steamboat Willie 10

Steinberg, Saul 30

Stepped Tangents 75, 143, 153, 211, 225, 276, 294

Stevens, Art 28

Storytelling Poses 73–76, 81, 87, 166, 194, 199, 206, 213, 221, 225, 228, 258, 276, 282, 293–294

Straight Ahead Action 4, 42, 51

Stratos Fear 9

Stromboli 18

Stubbe, George 20

Subjective 283

Successive Breaking of Joints 7, 36, 48, 136, 181–182, 185, 187

Super Rabbit 48

Superman 13–15, 48, 178

Surprise 228, 231, 233–234, 237, 239, 241–242

Swallow Syllables 254, 256

Sword in the Stone, The 28–29

Symphony In Slang 30, 36

Sync 10, 14, 29, 33, 256, 258, 277–278

Syncing Secondary Actions 256

T

Tafuri, Nick 15

Takamoto, Iwao 29, 90

Takes 33, 36, 51, 218

Tartakovsky, Genndy 260

Tashlin, Frank 14

Tempo 41, 153, 155, 157, 293

Tendlar, Dave 13

Tennis Chumps 33, 156

Termite Terrace 36

Terry, Paul 8, 32

Terrytoons 15, 18

Texas Tom 33

Thief and the Cobbler, The 44–45

Thomas, Frank 1, 3–4, 8, 10–11, 17, 19–22, 25, 28–29, 44, 76, 88, 158, 256

Thomas, Ted 28

Three-Point Perspective 264

Thumper 28

Tigger 28

Timing 1, 4, 13, 22–23, 32–33, 35–36, 41–42, 47, 51–52, 73, 88, 96, 104, 106, 110, 124–125, 145–159, 163–164, 166, 172, 176–177, 188, 196, 206–207, 211, 228, 242, 251–252, 275, 278, 280, 289, 294

Toland, Gregg 259

Tom and Jerry 13, 16, 33–34, 88, 190

Tongue 255

Toot, Whistle, Plunk and Boom 24, 30

Toy Story 48

Translating your Walk Cycle 137

Triplet Trouble 33–34

Truck 266

Tweetle Dee and Tweetle Dum 23

Two-Point Perspective 264

Tytla, Vladimir (Bill) 8, 15, 17, 18, 45, 110

V

Van Beuren Animation Studio 32

Van Dyke, Dick 45, 88

Vaughan, Lloyd 40

Victory Thru Hare Power 38

Vinci, Carlo 32

W

Waldman, Myron 13

Walk Cycle 86, 127–143, 156, 174, 203, 283
  Advanced Walk Cycles 139
  Contact Pose 127–128, 130–136, 138–139, 142, 197
  Down Pose 105, 127, 131–132, 134–135, 139, 140,142–143, 174
  Passing Pose 127, 130–132, 134, 136, 140–142
  Translating Your Walk Cycle 137
  Up Pose 49, 127, 132, 136, 139, 140–143, 174, 203, 209, 277
  Walk Formula 3, 127, 139

Walky Talky Hawky 38

Washam, Ben 30, 38, 40

Weight 3, 4, 7, 11, 17, 22, 34, 51, 64–66, 69, 70, 84, 85, 88, 93–96, 98–112, 114, 118, 130–131, 134, 141, 143, 153, 158, 167, 176, 187–188, 191–92, 280, 286, 293–294

Weight And Balance 3–4, 93–110

Weightlessness 166

Welles, Orson 259

What's Opera Doc 39–40

Who Framed Roger Rabbit 45

Wile E. Coyote 40

Williams, Richard 16, 21, 25, 29, 43–46, 66, 94, 128, 176, 255

Wind Rises, The 46

Winnie The Pooh and The Blustery Day 28

Woody Woodpecker 20

World Space and Object Space 70

X

X-Sheet 251–252, 275–276, 293

Y

Yogi Bear 32

Yosemite Sam 42

Z

Zemeckis, Robert 45

Zipping Along 40

Zoot Cat, The 33–34

Zukor, Adolph 13

Credits

Layout and Design — Lenore Annand

Character Rigs — Ricardo Medina Fernández

Character Models — Daniel Driussi

Environment —Jeff S. Panek

Props — Matthew Young

Additional Animation and Rigging — Ryan Fisher

Lighting and Additional Rigging — Kellie Driscoll

Reference Actor — Ron Weaver

Featuring the Voice Talents of — Ron Weaver, Stephanie de Sousa and Jamie Robertson

Sound Recording — Rich Grula

Reference Photos and Video — Stephanie de Sousa

Index —David Annand

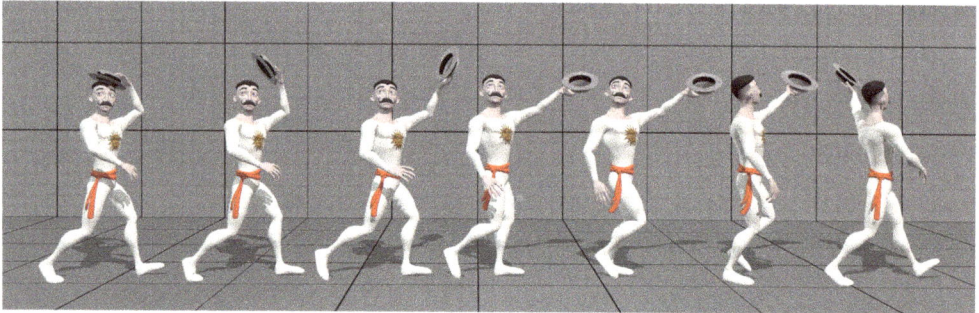

For Product Safety Concerns and Information please contact our EU
representative GPSR@taylorandfrancis.com
Taylor & Francis Verlag GmbH, Kaufingerstraße 24, 80331 München, Germany

9 781032 422398